Noël Coward
Plays: Four

Blithe Spirit, Present L~~aughter, Thi~~~~s Happy Br~~
To-night at 8.30 (W~~ays a~~nd A~~~~~~~~
~~Red~~ ~~Pepper~~

"He is simply a phe~~~~
occur ever again in th~~~~

"His triumph has been ~~to join t~~wo things ever dissociated
in the English mind: hard work and wit." Kenneth Tynan

This volume contains Coward's three best plays from the
1940s, as well as three shorter plays from the *To-night at 8.30*
sequence.

"This is riotously witty stuff . . ." said the *Daily Mail* of *Blithe Spirit*
in 1941. "I laughed and laughed and laughed at an impudent
yarn about a writer whose first wife was conjured from the grave
to squabble cattily with her successor . . ."

Of *Present Laughter* W. A. Darlington wrote in 1943: "His chief
characters are all members of a highly successful theatrical firm,
with Mr. Coward himself playing Garry Essendine, the romantic
actor who is the firm's chief asset . . . Let us be clear about it.
There is no edification in this play, but there is any amount of fun."

And of *This Happy Breed* the next day, Darlington wrote: "In shape
it is the simple chronicle of what happened to the Gibbons family
in the years 1919–39, when they lived at No. 17, Sycamore Road,
Clapham Common . . . Not a typical Coward play, you perceive . . .
Here, for the first time in his brilliant career, we have him writing
with sympathy, understanding, and admiration of the common
man."

Of the three shorter plays written in 1935 as acting, singing, and
dancing vehicles for Gertrude Lawrence and Coward himself, *Ways
and Means* is "a twentyish little farce", *The Astonished Heart* is a
serious piece about a psychiatrist's obsession with one of his
patients, and "*Red Peppers*" is the famous "vaudeville sketch
sandwiched in between two parodies of music-hall songs".

NOËL COWARD

Plays: Four

Blithe Spirit
Present Laughter
This Happy Breed
and
Ways and Means
The Astonished Heart
"Red Peppers"
from
To-night at 8.30

Introduced by Sheridan Morley

Methuen Drama

METHUEN'S WORLD DRAMATISTS

This collection first published in Great Britain in 1979 in simultaneous hardback and paperback editions by Eyre Methuen Ltd.
Reprinted, with revised introductory material, 1983, 1985, 1987 by Methuen London Ltd

Reprinted, with a new introduction, in 1990 by Methuen Drama, Michelin House, 81 Fulham Road, London SW3 6RB.

Blithe Spirit was first published in Great Britain in 1942 by Heinemann and republished in 1960 in Play Parade Vol. 5. It is reprinted here by arrangement with William Heinemann Ltd.

Present Laughter was first published in 1943 by Heinemann and republished in 1954 in Play Parade Vol. 4.

This Happy Breed was first published in 1943 by Heinemann and republished in 1954 in Play Parade Vol. 4.

To-night at 8.30 was first published in 1936 by Heinemann and republished in 1954 in Play Parade Vol. 4.

ISBN 0 413 46120 3

Printed and bound in Great Britain by
Cox & Wyman Ltd, Reading

Contents

Introduction

This fourth volume of the collected plays of Noël Coward opens with one he never intended to write at all, though it was to become the most commercially successful and long-running of all his comedies. At the outbreak of War in 1939, Noël had taken a curious vow not to write anything 'for the duration': twenty months later, although already exhausted from long and arduous concert tours for the troops, he began to realise the pointlessness of abandoning his craft as a dramatist and, in five days during a brief spring holiday on the beach at Portmeirion in North Wales, he constructed the 'improbable farce' that is *Blithe Spirit*.

Not by coincidence is this a play that mocks sudden death at precisely the moment when the bombs were bringing it to Britain: but a whole decade earlier, in Act II of *Private Lives*, Noël had unconsciously begun to map out the territory for *Blithe Spirit*:

AMANDA: What happens if one of us dies? Does the one that's left still laugh?

ELYOT: Yes, yes, with all his might.

AMANDA: That's serious enough, isn't it?

ELYOT: No, no it isn't. Death's very laughable, such a cunning little mystery. All done with mirrors.

AMANDA: Darling, I believe you're talking nonsense.

ELYOT: So is everyone else in the long run. Let's be superficial and pity the poor philosophers. Let's blow trumpets and squeakers and enjoy the party as much as we can, like very small, quite idiotic schoolchildren. Let's savour the delight of the moment. Come and kiss me darling, before your body rots and worms pop in and out of your eye sockets.

The final victory over death was, for Noël, to laugh at it, so what more natural than to write a comedy about a ghost: 'I shall ever be grateful', he noted later, 'for the almost psychic gift that enabled me to write *Blithe Spirit* in five days during one of the darkest years of the war. It was not meticulously constructed in advance, and only one day elapsed between its original conception and the moment I sat down to write it. It fell into my mind and onto the manuscript. Six weeks later it was produced, and it ran for four and a half years'.

For about thirty years, until it was eventually overtaken by *Boeing-Boeing*, *Blithe Spirit* remained the longest-running comedy in the history of the British theatre: in Noël's original draft, the character of the eccentric medium, Madame Arcati, was to have been a small role designed for his beloved friend and fellow-playwright Clemence Dane, who had expressed a fleeting desire to act. But in the actual writing, the character of Arcati developed to the point where she became central and crucial to the comedy: apart from that major change however, the play remained precisely as written, with only two lines ever cut in rehearsal.

Noël himself directed the first cast with Margaret

Rutherford as Arcati, Kay Hammond (who was also to go on to the David Lean film version) as Elvira, and Cecil Parker as the unfortunately twice-married Charles, both of whose wives end up attacking him from beyond the grave. On the first night, the only dissenting voice came from a lady in the Dress Circle who shouted out that it was rubbish and rude to spiritualism, and although Graham Greene for the *Spectator* found it 'a weary exhibition of bad taste', the rest of the reviews were exuberantly enthusiastic and the feeling generally was that here Coward had written an ideally escapist entertainment, flippant and careless about death and yet funny and sturdy enough to be a constant source of joy and hilarity to theatregoers for the rest of the war.

Not for the first time in his career, though arguably for the last, Noël at the beginning of his forties had written a play which was exactly what theatregoers wanted at precisely the moment they wanted it most. Judged purely at the box-office, Noël was right in thinking *Blithe Spirit* the most successful of all his plays, and even one of his sternest critics, Professor Allardyce Nicoll, accepted it as 'a minor comic masterpiece of the lighter sort'. But it lies well outside the mainstream of Noël's earlier hit comedies, if only because we are not here faced with a closed, self-perpetuating group of central characters coping with themselves but in isolation, cut off from an alien world outside them. The end of the Thirties, the coming of the war and the two years that Noël had spent away from the typewriter seemed to change both his dramatic style and his sense of development: there is more plot in *Blithe Spirit* than in any of his comedies of the Twenties or Thirties, and it marks the beginning of a new period in his work as a dramatist. From now on his plays were to have much less in common with each other: all the old recurrent themes, the immorality and ultimate futility of the Bright Young Things, the witty central characters battling almost incestuously with each other and fending off an unamused and disapproving outside world, all ended with the 1930s, and Coward's later comedies were now to exist, whether successfully or not, independently in their own right, without back-references to the society or accepted conventions of their time.

Coward himself was briefly to take over the central role in *Blithe Spirit* from Cecil Parker during its first long London run, and then to tour it extensively around the provinces in a triple-bill with two other plays in this volume (*This Happy Breed* and *Present Laughter*). Apart from the David Lean film of 1944 which Noël co-produced, *Blithe Spirit* also ran lengthily and triumphantly on stage in Paris, and in America on both Broadway and many tours. It has frequently been revived in Britain, most recently in a National Theatre production by Harold Pinter starring Maria Aitken and Richard Johnson, and then in a West End staging of 1985 with Joanna Lumley and Simon Cadell. It has also been frequently televised, and in 1964 became a Broadway stage musical called *High Spirits* for which Beatrice Lillie made her last stage appearance, as Madame Arcati, and Noël himself wrote some (uncredited) lyrics for a score by Hugh Martin and Timothy Gray.

'*Present Laughter*', wrote Noël, 'is a very light comedy and was written with the sensible object of providing me with a bravura part. It was an enormous success. I received excellent notices, and to my bewilderment and considerable dismay, the play was also reasonably acclaimed. This so unnerved me that I can say no more.'

In fact the play dates from 1939, a few months before the outbreak of war, when Noël had decided that in the interests of experiment and the Inland Revenue he would write two new and totally contrasting plays (the other was to be *This Happy Breed*, which follows it in this volume) with a view to staging them simultaneously with the same company of actors. In the early stages of rehearsal, however, Noël was summoned to Downing Street and asked to head up the British Information Service in Paris, since war was now thought to be imminent: a few weeks later it was declared, and the première of both plays was duly postponed until the autumn of 1942, when Coward took them out on a very long tour with *Blithe Spirit*.

Like *Hay Fever*, written twenty years earlier, *Present Laughter* is a comedy about the 'theatricals' that Noël best knew and loved and cherished in his public and private lives, but this time written as a star vehicle for himself. Over the years the play has nevertheless proved a well-oiled and perfectly satisfactory vehicle for a number of others, most recently Nigel Patrick and Peter O'Toole and Tom Conti and Albert Finney.

Its central character, Garry Essendine, is in many ways the world-weary, middle-aged projection of the dilettante, debonair persona first accorded to Coward by the media after the success of *The Vortex* back in 1924. He is a witty, tiresome, self-obsessed, dressing-gowned figure who struts through the play like an educated peacock. But at the end of the first act, there is a revealing moment when Essendine, through whom can be very loudly heard the voice of his creator and player, is called upon to give some advice to an importunate young playwright of the next generation:

> To begin with, your play is not a play at all. It's a meaningless jumble of adolescent, pseudo-intellectual poppycock. It bears no relation to the theatre or to life or to anything . . . If you wish to be a playwright, you just leave the theatre of tomorrow to take care of itself. Go and get yourself a job as a butler in a repertory company, if they'll have you. Learn from the ground up how plays are constructed, and what is actable and what isn't. Then sit down and write at least twenty plays one after the other, and if you can manage to get the twenty-first produced for a Sunday-night performance, you'll be damned lucky.

'A potent mixture of self-exposure and self-celebration', was Noël's own verdict on Garry and *Present Laughter* in 1972, and somewhere in there is a lot of the truth, not only about Coward in mid-career but also about the group of friends, secretaries, managers and lovers which formed itself around his star presence. In a sense no play he ever wrote was more autobiographical, but in another sense the conjuring trick is still intact: Garry is not really Noël, merely a reflection of him through a series of mirrors, and if the play is about anything very philosophical, it is surely about the price of fame and the cost of charm.

From the West End sophistication of *Present Laughter* to the South London suburbia of *This Happy Breed* (the other play he had written in 1939 for eventual production in 1942) was a very long jump indeed, but one that Coward made as playwright and as actor with consummate agility. *This Happy Breed* is a domestic *Cavalcade*, the saga of one lower-middle-class family and their various personal trials and tribulations through the twenty years that separated the Armistice from Munich.

From his early childhood, Noël had known Clapham Commoners like these ('I was born somewhere in the middle of the social scale, and so got a good view of both upper and lower reaches'), and a tendency in his writing to make them over-articulate was more or less offset by the accuracy with which he depicted the changing pattern of their family life through one generation. *This Happy Breed* is a microcosmic, if sometimes faintly patronising, impression of what England was like for one family at one special time in her history, in which the action comes second to the dialogue and the ultimate heroine is the mother country herself.

Noël himself was, as usual, the most perceptive of the play's critics:

It is a suburban, middle-class family comedy covering the period between the Armistice in 1918 to the humiliating year of 1938, when the late Neville Chamberlain spent so much time in the air. Many of the critics detected in this play an attitude on my part of amused patronage and condescension towards the habits and manners of suburban London. They implied that in setting the play in a milieu so far removed from the cocktail and caviare stratum to which I so obviously belonged, I was over-reaching myself and writing about people far removed from my superficial comprehension.

In this, as usual, they were quite wrong. Having been born in Teddington, and having lived respectively at Sutton, Battersea Park and Clapham Common during all my formative years, I can confidently assert that I know a great deal more about the hearts and minds of ordinary South Londoners than they gave me credit for. My metamorphosis into a 'Mayfair Playboy' many years later was entirely a journalistic conception. Since I achieved my first real theatrical success with *The Vortex* in 1924, I have moved observantly and eagerly through many different cliques and classes of society. Being a natural writer with a constant eye on human behaviour I have also moved, without undue imaginative strain, through Regency and Victorian society as well. I also have a sound working knowledge of the Navy, the Army and the Air Force. To ascribe preconceived social limitations to a creative writer is a common error of the critical mind; it is also a critical revelation of the common mind.

I wrote *This Happy Breed* in the spring of 1939. My personal criticism of it as a play is that the character of Frank Gibbons is a fraction more than life-size. His views are too clearly expressed to be quite true to life. I have no doubt whatever that he would hold such views, but to my mind his articulateness throughout the play concedes too much to theatrical effectiveness. Had he been a character in a novel, this error could have been eliminated; the author could have explained his feelings and reactions without imposing upon him the burden of speaking them aloud. However, *This Happy Breed* was a play written for the theatre, and must stand or fall within the theatre's necessary limitations. The other characters are well drawn, and I am particularly attached to Aunt Sylvia and Granny. They were none of them written with the faintest patronage or condescension but with sincerity, affection and the inherent understanding that is a result of personal experience.

This Happy Breed ran successfully in London through the spring of 1943 in repertory with *Present Laughter*, was subsequently filmed by David Lean with Robert Newton, Celia Johnson, John Mills and Stanley Holloway, and was televised in America a decade later by Coward himself.

The last three plays in this volume are a further selection from *Tonight at 8.30*, the collection of nine one-act dramas and musicals which Noël wrote for himself and Gertrude Lawrence to play in the West End and on Broadway in 1936. (Three more of the plays may be found in Volume Three of this series.)

Ways and Means was, wrote Noël, 'a Twentyish little farce set in the then fashionable South of France. I never cared for it much, but as an opener (to one of the triple-bills) it served its purpose'. It also serves as an oblique tribute to Frederick Lonsdale, the master of this genre of houseparty-comedy and one of Noël's acknowledged masters in the naturalist West End of the early 1920s.

The Astonished Heart was an altogether more serious and ambitious one-acter: 'I thought then', wrote

Noël, 'and I still think that its theme, the decay of a psychiatrist's mind through personal sexual obsession, was too esoteric to appeal to a large public. It gave us however, good opportunities for dramatic acting'.

Red Peppers, which closes the volume, was an infinitely more light-hearted affair, a lovingly cynical tribute to the lost music-halls of the First World War where both Noël and Gertie had served some sort of childhood apprenticeship. 'It is', wrote Noël, 'a vaudeville sketch sandwiched in between two parodies of music-hall songs. We always enjoyed playing it and the public always enjoyed watching us play it, which was of course highly satisfactory'.

Written as an alternating sequence of triple-bills to fend off the very real boredom that Noël and Gertie had found in playing the same script eight times a week, whereas here six different scripts could be played on matinée days alone, *Tonight at 8.30* ran triumphantly for limited seasons on both sides of the Atlantic in 1936, and was revived with rather less success in America just after the war with Noël directing Gertie and Graham Payn in the leading roles. Almost all the plays were to end up sooner or later on film, none more successfully than *Still Life* which in 1945 became the Celia Johnson/Trevor Howard classic *Brief Encounter*.

Of the three plays here, *The Astonished Heart* became a full-length feature film with Noël and Celia Johnson and Margaret Leighton in 1950, while *Ways and Means* and *Red Peppers* turned up in a 1950 anthology called *Meet Me Tonight*.

Since then, the sheer cost of staging nine plays simultaneously has forbidden any major stage revival of the full sequence, though the plays are frequently revived in sets of three, and are much used in my own *Noël and*

Gertie stage anthology which first opened in the West
End at the Comedy Theatre in December 1989, with
Simon Cadell and Patricia Hodge in the title roles.

SHERIDAN MORLEY
June, 1990

Noël Coward 1899-1973: A Chronology

A list of Dramatic Works, in order of writing, with years of first productions in Great Britain and America. (Individual songs contributed to Revues are omitted.)

	Written	Produced Britain	U.S.A.
The Last Chapter (Ida Collaborates) (One Act with Esmé Wynne: under the pseudonym of "Esnomel")	1916	1917 (tour)	—
Woman and Whisky (One Act with Esmé Wynne)	1918	1918 (tour)	—
The Last Trick (Unproduced)	1918		
The Impossible Wife (Unproduced)	1918		
(Unknown Title) (Unproduced)	1918		
The Rat Trap	1918	1926	—
Crissa (Unfinished Opera with Esmé Wynne and Max Darewski)	1919/20		
"I'll Leave it to You"	1919	1920	1923
Barriers Down (Unproduced)	1920		
The Young Idea	1921	1922 (tour) 1923 (London)	1932
Sirocco	1921	1927	—
The Better Half (One Act)	1921	1927	—
Bottles and Bones (One Act)	1922	1922	—
A Young Man's Fancy (Unproduced Adaptation from the French of Louis Verneuil's *Pour Avoir Adrienne*)	1922		
The Queen Was in the Parlour	1922	1926	1929
Mild Oats (Unproduced One Act)	1922		
London Calling! (Revue in collaboration with Ronald Jeans)	1922/3	1923	—
Weatherwise (One Act)	1923	1932	—
Fallen Angels	1923	1925	1927
The Vortex	1923	1924	1925
Hay Fever	1924	1925	1925
Easy Virtue	1924	1926	1925
On With The Dance (Revue)	1924/5	1925	—

	Written	Produced	
		Britain	U.S.A.
Semi-Monde	1926	1977 (Glasgow)	—
"*This was a Man*"	1926	—	1926
The Marquise	1926	1927	1927
Pretty Prattle (One Act)	1927	1927	—
Home Chat	1927	1927	1932
The Year of Grace! (Revue)	1927/8	1928	1928
Bitter Sweet (Operette)	1928/9	1929	1929
Private Lives	1929	1930	1931
Post Mortem (First produced: Germany: P.o.W. Camp 1944)	1930	1966 (amateur)	—
Some Other Private Lives (One Act)	1930	1930	—
Cavalcade	1930/1	1931	—
Words and Music (Revue)	1932	1932	—
Design for Living	1932	1937	1933
Conversation Piece (Romantic Comedy with Music)	1933	1934	1934
Point Valaine	1934	1944	1935
To-night at 8.30 (Ten One Act Plays)	1935/6	1935/6	1936
Operette (Operette)	1937	1938	—
Set to Music (Revue)	1932/8	—	1938
Present Laughter	1939	1942	1946
This Happy Breed	1939	1942	1949
Time Remembered (Unproduced)	1940	—	—
Blithe Spirit	1941	1941	1941
Sigh No More (Revue)	1945	1945	—
Pacific 1860 (Musical Romance)	1946	1946	—
Peace in our Time	1946	1947	—
Long Island Sound (Unproduced: Based on *What Mad Pursuit?*, one of his short stories in *To Step Aside*)	1947		
Island Fling (*South Sea Bubble*)	1949	1956	1951
Ace of Clubs (Musical Play)	1949	1950	—
Relative Values	1951	1951	1954
Quadrille	1951/2	1952	1954
After the Ball (Musical Play based on Oscar Wilde's *Lady Windermere's Fan*)	1953	1954	1955

	Written	Produced	
		Britain	U.S.A.
Nude with Violin	1954	1956	1957
Volcano (Unproduced)	1957		
Look After Lulu! (Based on	1958	1959	1959
Feydeau's *Occupe-toi d'Amélie*)			
Waiting in the Wings	1959/60	1960	—
Sail Away (Musical Comedy)\	1959/61	1962	1961
The Girl Who Came to Supper	1962	—	1963
(Musical Comedy based on Terence			
Rattigan's *The Sleeping Prince*. Music			
and lyrics only, book by Harry			
Kurnitz)			
Suite in Three Keys	1965	1965	1974
(a) *A Song at Twilight*			(a & c)
(b) *Shadows of the Evening*			
(c) *Come into the Garden Maud*			
Star Quality (Based on a	1966	1982	—
short story of the same title			
published in 1951)			

A selection of plays by Noël Coward was published under the title *Play Parade* by Heinemann (London) in September 1934, and by Doubleday Doran (New York) in December 1934, with a preface by Coward. The plays were: *Cavalcade, Bitter-Sweet, The Vortex, Hay Fever, Design for Living, Private Lives* and *Post Mortem*.

A second selection, *Collected Plays of Noël Coward – Play Parade Volume II* was published in 1939. It included: *This Year of Grace!, Words and Music, Operette,* and *Conversation Piece*. A second edition was revised and enlarged in 1950 to include *Easy Virtue* and *Fallen Angels*.

Volume III was published in 1950 and included: *The Queen Was In the Parlour, "I'll Leave It to You", The Young Idea, Sirocco, The Rat Trap, "This Was a Man", Home Chat* and *The Marquise*.

Volume IV appeared in 1954 with: *To-night at 8.30* (*We Were Dancing, The Astonished Heart, "Red Peppers", Hands Across the Sea, Fumed Oak, Shadow Play, Ways and Means, Still Life,* and *Family Album*), *Present Laughter* and *This Happy Breed*.

Volume V followed in 1958 and included: *Pacific 1860*, *Peace in Our Time*, *Relative Values*, *Quadrille* and *Blithe Spirit*.

Volume VI, published in 1962, contains: *Point Valaine*, *South Sea Bubble*, *Ace of Clubs*, *Nude with Violin* and *Waiting in the Wings*.

(Volumes II–VI were published in London only.)

There only remained uncollected *Look After Lulu!* (solo edition 1959) and *Suite in Three Keys* (solo edition 1966) which are now included in this anthology.

The only produced plays still unpublished are *Semi-Monde* (written 1926, produced 1977), *Star Chamber* (the tenth play from *To-night at 8.30*, written and produced 1936), *Sail Away* (1961) and *Star Quality* (adapted in 1966 from a short story, produced 1982).

BLITHE SPIRIT

An Improbable Farce in Three Acts

CHARACTERS:
EDITH, *a maid*
RUTH
CHARLES
DOCTOR BRADMAN
MRS. BRADMAN
MADAME ARCATI
ELVIRA

The action of the play passes in the living-room of CHARLES
CONDOMINE'S *house in Kent.*

ACT I

ACT II

ACT III

ACT 1

SCENE I

The scene is the living-room of the CONDOMINES' *house in Kent.*

The room is light, attractive and comfortably furnished. The arrangement of it may be left to the discretion of the producer. On the right there are french windows opening on to the garden. On the left there is an open fireplace. At the back, on the left, there are double doors leading into the dining-room. Up left, on an angle, there are double doors leading to the hall, the stairs, and the servants' quarters.

When the curtain rises it is about eight o'clock on a summer evening. There is a wood fire burning because it is an English summer evening.

EDITH *comes in from the hall carrying, rather uneasily, a large tray of cocktail things. Comes to centre table with tray of drinks. Sees there is not room so puts it on drinks table up stage right, with a sigh of relief.*

RUTH *comes in centre briskly. She is a smart-looking woman in the middle thirties. She is dressed for dinner but not elaborately.*

RUTH: That's right, Edith.
EDITH: Yes'm.
RUTH: Now you'd better fetch the ice-bucket.
EDITH: Yes'm.

3

RUTH (*arranges ornaments on piano*): Did you manage to get the ice out of those little tin trays?

EDITH: Yes'm—I 'ad a bit of a struggle though—but it's all right.

RUTH: And you filled the little trays up again with water?

EDITH: Yes'm.

RUTH (*crosses to window and arranges curtains*): Very good, Edith—you're making giant strides.

EDITH: Yes'm.

RUTH: Madame Arcati, Mrs. Bradman and I will have our coffee in here after dinner and Mr. Condomine and Dr. Bradman will have theirs in the dining-room—is that quite clear?

EDITH: Yes'm.

RUTH: And when you're serving dinner, Edith, try to remember to do it calmly and methodically.

EDITH: Yes'm.

RUTH: As you are not in the Navy it is unnecessary to do everything at the double.

EDITH: Very good, 'm.

RUTH: Now go and get the ice.

EDITH (*straining at the leash*): Yes'm.
> *She starts off at full speed.*

RUTH: *Not* at a run, Edith.

EDITH (*slowing down*): Yes'm.
> EDITH *goes.*
> RUTH *crosses to fireplace, gives a comprehensive glance round the room.*
> CHARLES *comes in centre to back of sofa. He is a nice-looking man of about forty wearing a loose-fitting velvet smoking-jacket.*

CHARLES: No sign of the advancing hordes?

4

RUTH: Not yet.

CHARLES (*going to the cocktail tray*): No ice.

RUTH: It's coming. I've been trying to discourage Edith from being quite so fleet of foot. You mustn't mind if everything is a little slow motion to-night.

CHARLES: I shall welcome it. The last few days have been extremely agitating. What do you suppose induced Agnes to leave us and go and get married?

RUTH: The reason was becoming increasingly obvious, dear.

CHARLES: Yes, but in these days nobody thinks anything of that sort of thing—she could have popped into the cottage hospital, had it, and popped out again.

RUTH: Her social life would have been seriously undermined.

CHARLES: We must keep Edith in the house more.

EDITH *comes in slowly with the ice-bucket.*

RUTH: That's right, Edith—put it down on the table.

EDITH (*puts ice-bucket on drinks table—up stage right*): Yes'm.

CHARLES: I left my cigarette-case on my dressing-table, Edith—would you get it for me?

EDITH: Yes, sir.

She runs out of the room.

CHARLES: There now!

RUTH: You took her by surprise.

CHARLES (*at the cocktail table*): A dry Martini, I think, don't you?

RUTH *takes a cigarette from box on mantelpiece and lights it, then crosses and sits in arm-chair.*

RUTH: Yes, darling—I expect Madame Arcati will want something sweeter.

CHARLES: We'll have this one for ourselves anyhow.

RUTH (*taking a cigarette and sitting down*): Oh, dear!

CHARLES: What's the matter?

RUTH: I have a feeling that this evening's going to be awful.

CHARLES: It'll probably be funny, but not awful.

RUTH: You must promise not to catch my eye—if I giggle—and I'm very likely to—it will ruin everything.

CHARLES: You mustn't—you must be dead serious and if possible a little intense. We can't hurt the old girl's feelings, however funny she is.

RUTH: But why the Bradmans, darling? He's as sceptical as we are—he'll probably say the most dreadful things.

CHARLES: I've warned him. There must be more than three people and we couldn't have the vicar and his wife because (a) they're dreary, and (b) they probably wouldn't have approved at all. It had to be the Bradmans.

> EDITH *rushes into the room with* CHARLES'S *cigarette-case.*

(*Taking it.*) Thank you, Edith—steady does it.

EDITH (*breathlessly*): Yes, sir.

> EDITH, *with an obvious effort, goes out slowly.*

CHARLES: We might make her walk about with a book on her head like they do in deportment lessons.

> CHARLES *comes to right of* RUTH *and gives her cocktail.*

CHARLES: Here, try this.

RUTH (*sipping it*): Lovely—dry as a bone.

CHARLES (*raising his glass to her*): To 'The Unseen'!

RUTH: I must say that's a wonderful title.

CHARLES: If this evening's a success I shall start on the first draft to-morrow.

RUTH: How extraordinary it is.

CHARLES: What?

RUTH: Oh, I don't know—being in right at the beginning of something—it gives one an odd feeling.

CHARLES: Do you remember how I got the idea for 'The Light Goes Out'?

RUTH (*suddenly seeing that haggard, raddled woman in the hotel at Biarritz*): Of course I remember—we sat up half the night talking about it. . . .

CHARLES: She certainly came in very handy—I wonder who she was.

RUTH: And if she ever knew, I mean ever recognised, that description of herself—poor thing . . . here's to her, anyhow. . . . (*She finishes her drink.*)

CHARLES: Have another.

RUTH: Darling—it's most awfully strong.

CHARLES (*pouring it*): Never mind.

RUTH: Used Elvira to be a help to you—when you were thinking something out, I mean?

CHARLES (*pouring out another cocktail for himself*): Every now and then—when she concentrated—but she didn't concentrate very often.

RUTH: I do wish I'd known her.

CHARLES: I wonder if you'd have liked her.

RUTH: I'm sure I should—as you talk of her she sounds enchanting—yes, I'm sure I should have liked her because you know I have never for an instant felt in the least jealous of her—that's a good sign.

CHARLES: Poor Elvira. (*Comes to left of* RUTH *and gives her cocktail.*)

RUTH: Does it still hurt—when you think of her?

CHARLES: No, not really—sometimes I almost wish it did—I feel rather guilty. . . .

7

RUTH: I wonder if I died before you'd grown tired of me if you'd forget me so soon?

CHARLES: What a horrible thing to say. . . .

RUTH: No—I think it's interesting.

CHARLES: Well, to begin with, I haven't forgotten Elvira—I remember her very distinctly indeed—I remember how fascinating she was, and how maddening —I remember how badly she played all games and how cross she got when she didn't win—I remember her gay charm when she had achieved her own way over something and her extreme acidity when she didn't—I remember her physical attractiveness, which was tremendous, and her spiritual integrity which was nil. . . .

RUTH: You can't remember something that was nil.

CHARLES: I remember how morally untidy she was. . . .

RUTH: Was she more physically attractive than I am?

CHARLES: That was a very tiresome question, dear, and fully deserves the wrong answer.

RUTH: You really are very sweet.

CHARLES: Thank you.

RUTH: And a little naïve, too.

CHARLES: Why?

RUTH: Because you imagine that I mind about Elvira being more physically attractive than I am.

CHARLES: I should have thought any woman would mind—if it were true. Or perhaps I'm old-fashioned in my view of female psychology. . . .

RUTH: Not exactly old-fashioned, darling, just a bit didactic.

CHARLES: How do you mean?

RUTH: It's didactic to attribute to one type the defects

of another type—for instance, because you know perfectly well that Elvira would mind terribly if you found another woman more attractive physically than she was, it doesn't necessarily follow that I should. Elvira was a more physical person than I—I'm certain of that—it's all a question of degree.

CHARLES (*smiling*): I love you, my love.

RUTH: I know you do—but not the wildest stretch of imagination could describe it as the first fine careless rapture.

CHARLES: Would you like it to be?

RUTH: Good God, no!

CHARLES: Wasn't that a shade too vehement?

RUTH: We're neither of us adolescent, Charles, we've neither of us led exactly prim lives, have we? And we've both been married before—careless rapture at this stage would be incongruous and embarrassing.

CHARLES: I hope I haven't been in any way a disappointment, dear.

RUTH: Don't be so idiotic.

CHARLES: After all your first husband was a great deal older than you, wasn't he? I shouldn't like you to think that you'd missed out all along the line.

RUTH: There are moments, Charles, when you go too far.

CHARLES: Sorry, darling.

RUTH: As far as waspish female psychology goes, there's a strong vein of it in you.

CHARLES: I've heard that said about Julius Cæsar.

RUTH: Julius Cæsar is neither here nor there.

CHARLES: He may be for all we know—we'll ask Madame Arcati.

RUTH: You're awfully irritating when you're

determined to be witty at all costs—almost supercilious.

CHARLES: That's exactly what Elvira used to say.

RUTH: I'm not at all surprised—I never imagined—physically triumphant as she was—that she was entirely lacking in perception.

CHARLES: Darling Ruth!

RUTH: There you go again. . . .

CHARLES (*kissing her lightly*): As I think I mentioned before I love you, my love.

RUTH: Poor Elvira.

CHARLES: Didn't that light, comradely kiss mollify you at all?

RUTH: You're very annoying, you know you are—when I said 'Poor Elvira' it came from the heart—you must have bewildered her so horribly.

CHARLES: Don't I ever bewilder you at all?

RUTH: Never for an instant—I know every trick.

CHARLES: Well, all I can say is that we'd better get a divorce immediately. . . .

RUTH: Put my glass down, there's a darling.

CHARLES (*taking it*): She certainly had a great talent for living—it was a pity that she died so young.

RUTH: Poor Elvira.

CHARLES: That remark is getting monotonous.

RUTH (*crosses up stage a pace*): Poor Charles, then.

CHARLES: That's better.

RUTH: And later on, Poor Ruth, I expect.

CHARLES: You have no faith, Ruth. I really do think you should try to have a little faith.

RUTH: I shall strain every nerve.

CHARLES: Life without faith is an arid business.

RUTH: How beautifully you put things, dear.

CHARLES: I aim to please.

RUTH: If I died, I wonder how long it would be before you married again?

CHARLES: You won't die—you're not the dying sort.

RUTH: Neither was Elvira.

CHARLES: Oh yes, she was, now that I look back on it—she had a certain ethereal, not quite of this world quality—nobody could call you even remotely ethereal.

RUTH: Nonsense—she was of the earth earthy.

CHARLES: Well she is now, anyhow.

RUTH: You know that's the kind of observation that shocks people.

CHARLES: It's discouraging to think how many people are shocked by honesty and how few by deceit.

RUTH: Write that down, you might forget it.

CHARLES: You underrate me.

RUTH: Anyhow it was a question of bad taste more than honesty.

CHARLES: I was devoted to Elvira. We were married for five years. She died. I missed her very much. That was seven years ago. I have now—with your help, my love—risen above the whole thing.

RUTH: Admirable. But if tragedy should darken our lives—(a bell rings)—I still say—with prophetic foreboding—poor Ruth!

CHARLES: That's probably the Bradmans.

RUTH: It might be Madame Arcati.

CHARLES: No, she'll come on her bicycle—she always goes everywhere on her bicycle.

RUTH: It really is very spirited of the old girl.

CHARLES: Shall I go, or shall we let Edith have her fling?

RUTH: Wait a minute and see what happens.

There is a slight pause.

CHARLES: Perhaps she didn't hear.

RUTH: She's probably on one knee in a pre-sprinting position waiting for cook to open the kitchen door.

There is the sound of a door banging and EDITH *is seen scampering across the hall.*

CHARLES: Steady, Edith.

EDITH (*dropping to a walk*): Yes, sir.

After a moment, DR. *and* MRS. BRADMAN *come into the room.* CHARLES *goes forward to meet them.* DR. BRADMAN *is a pleasant-looking middle-aged man.* MRS. BRADMAN *is fair and rather faded.* MRS. BRADMAN *comes to* RUTH *above sofa and shakes hands.* DR. BRADMAN *shakes hands with* CHARLES.

EDITH: Dr. and Mrs. Bradman.

DR. BRADMAN: We're not late, are we? I only got back from the hospital about half an hour ago.

CHARLES: Of course not—Madame Arcati isn't here yet.

MRS. BRADMAN: That must have been her we passed coming down the hill—I said I thought it was.

RUTH: Then she won't be long. I'm so glad you were able to come.

MRS. BRADMAN: We've been looking forward to it— I feel really quite excited. . . .

DR. BRADMAN: I guarantee that Violet will be good —I made her promise.

MRS. BRADMAN: There wasn't any need—I'm absolutely thrilled. I've only seen Madame Arcati two or three times in the village—I mean I've never seen her do anything at all peculiar, if you know what I mean?

CHARLES (*at cocktail table*): Dry Martini?

DR. BRADMAN: By all means.

CHARLES (*mixing it*): She certainly is a strange

woman. It was only a chance remark of the Vicar's about seeing her up on the Knoll on Midsummer Eve dressed in sort of Indian robes that made me realise that she was psychic at all. Then I began to make enquiries —apparently she's been a professional in London for years.

MRS. BRADMAN: It is funny, isn't it? I mean anybody doing it as a profession.

DR. BRADMAN: I believe it's very lucrative.

MRS. BRADMAN: Do you believe in it, Mrs. Condomine—do you think there's anything really genuine about it at all?

RUTH: I'm afraid not—but I do think it's interesting how easily people allow themselves to be deceived. . . .

MRS. BRADMAN: But she must believe it herself, mustn't she—or is the whole business a fake?

CHARLES: I suspect the worst. A real professional charlatan. That's what I am hoping for anyhow—the character I am planning for my book must be a complete impostor, that's one of the most important factors of the whole story.

DR. BRADMAN: What exactly are you hoping to get from her?

CHARLES: Jargon, principally—a few of the tricks of the trade—I haven't been to a séance for years. Ruth? I want to refresh my memory.

DR. BRADMAN: Then it's not entirely new to you?

CHARLES (*hands drinks to* DR. *and* MRS. BRADMAN): Oh no—when I was a little boy an aunt of mine used to come and stay with us—she imagined that she was a medium and used to go off into the most elaborate trances after dinner. My mother was fascinated by it.

MRS. BRADMAN: Was she convinced?

CHARLES: Good heavens, no—she just naturally disliked my aunt and loved making a fool of her. (*Gets cocktail for himself.*)

DR. BRADMAN (*laughing*): I gather that there were never any tangible results?

CHARLES: Oh, sometimes she didn't do so badly. On one occasion when we were all sitting round in the pitch dark with my mother groping her way through Chaminade at the piano, my aunt suddenly gave a shrill scream and said that she saw a small black dog by my chair, then someone switched on the lights and sure enough there it was.

MRS. BRADMAN: But how extraordinary.

CHARLES: It was obviously a stray that had come in from the street. But I must say I took off my hat to Auntie for producing it, or rather for utilising it—even mother was a bit shaken.

MRS. BRADMAN: What happened to it?

CHARLES: It lived with us for years.

RUTH: I sincerely hope Madame Arcati won't produce any livestock—we have so very little room in this house.

MRS. BRADMAN: Do you think she tells fortunes? I love having my fortune told.

CHARLES: I expect so——

RUTH: I was told once on the pier at Southsea that I was surrounded by lilies and a golden seven—it worried me for days.

All laugh.

CHARLES: We really must all be serious, you know, and pretend that we believe implicitly, otherwise she won't play.

RUTH: Also, she might really mind—it would be cruel to upset her.

DR. BRADMAN: I shall be as good as gold.

RUTH: Have you ever attended her, Doctor—professionally, I mean?

DR. BRADMAN: Yes—she had influenza in January—she's only been here just over a year, you know. I must say she was singularly unpsychic then—I always understood that she was an authoress.

CHARLES: Oh yes, we originally met as colleagues at one of Mrs. Wilmot's Sunday evenings in Sandgate. . . .

MRS. BRADMAN: What sort of books does she write?

CHARLES: Two sorts. Rather whimsical children's stories about enchanted woods filled with highly conversational flora and fauna, and enthusiastic biographies of minor royalties, very sentimental, reverent and extremely funny.

There is the sound of the front-door bell.

RUTH: Here she is.

DR. BRADMAN: She knows, doesn't she, about to-night? You're not going to spring it on her.

CHARLES: Of course—it was all arranged last week—I told her how profoundly interested I was in anything to do with the occult, and she blossomed like a rose.

RUTH: I really feel quite nervous—as though I were going to make a speech.

EDITH is seen sedately going towards the door.

CHARLES: You go and meet her, darling.

Meanwhile EDITH has opened the door, and MADAME ARCATI's voice, very high and clear, is heard.

MADAME ARCATI: I've leant my bike up against that little bush, it will be *perfectly* all right if no one touches it.

EDITH: Madame Arcati.

RUTH: How nice of you to have come all this way.

> MADAME ARCATI *enters. She is a striking woman, dressed not too extravagantly but with a decided bias towards the barbaric. She might be any age between forty-five and sixty-five.* RUTH *ushers her in.* RUTH *and* CHARLES *greet her simultaneously.*

CHARLES (*advancing*): My dear Madame Arcati!

MADAME ARCATI: I'm afraid I'm rather late, but I had a sudden presentiment that I was going to have a puncture so I went back to fetch my pump (MADAME ARCATI *takes off cloak and hands it to* RUTH *who puts it on chair*) and then of course I didn't have a puncture at all.

CHARLES: Perhaps you will on the way home.

MADAME ARCATI (*crosses to shake hands with* DR. BRADMAN. *Greeting him*): Doctor Bradman—the man with the gentle hands!

DR. BRADMAN: I'm delighted to see you looking so well. This is my wife.

> MADAME ARCATI *shakes hands with* MRS. BRADMAN *over back of sofa.*

MADAME ARCATI: We are old friends—we meet coming out of shops.

CHARLES: Would you like a cocktail?

MADAME ARCATI (*peeling off some rather strange-looking gloves*): If it's a dry Martini, yes—if it's a concoction, no. Experience has taught me to be very wary of concoctions.

CHARLES: It is a dry Martini.

MADAME ARCATI: How delicious. It was wonderful cycling through the woods this evening—I was deafened with bird-song.

RUTH: It's been lovely all day.

MADAME ARCATI: But the evening's the time—mark my words. (*She takes the cocktail* CHARLES *gives her.*) Thank you. Cheers! Cheers!

RUTH: Don't you find it very tiring bicycling everywhere?

MADAME ARCATI: On the contrary—it stimulates me—I was getting far too sedentary in London, that horrid little flat with the dim lights—they had to be dim, you know, the clients expect it.

MRS. BRADMAN: I must say I find bicycling very exhausting.

MADAME ARCATI: Steady rhythm—that's what counts. Once you get the knack of it you need never look back —on you get and away you go.

MRS. BRADMAN: But the hills, Madame Arcati— pushing up those awful hills——

MADAME ARCATI: Just knack again—down with your head, up with your heart, and you're over the top like a flash and skimming down the other side like a dragon-fly. This is the best dry Martini I've had for years.

CHARLES: Will you have another?

MADAME ARCATI (*holding out her glass*): Certainly. You're a very clever man. Anybody can write books, but it takes an artist to make a dry Martini that's dry enough.

RUTH: Are you writing anything nowadays, Madame Arcati?

MADAME ARCATI: Every morning regular as clock-work, seven till one.

CHARLES (*gives* MADAME ARCATI *a cocktail from above sofa*): Is it a novel or a memoir?

MADAME ARCATI: It's a children's book—I have to finish it by the end of October to catch the Christmas sales. It's mostly about very small animals, the hero is a moss beetle.

MRS. BRADMAN *laughs nervously*.

I had to give up my memoir of Princess Palliatani because she died in April—I talked to her about it the other day and she implored me to go on with it, but I really hadn't the heart.

MRS. BRADMAN (*incredulously*): You *talked* to her about it the other day?

MADAME ARCATI: Yes, through my control, of course. She sounded very irritable.

MRS. BRADMAN: It's funny to think of people in the spirit world being irritable, isn't it? I mean, one can hardly imagine it, can one?

CHARLES: We have no reliable guarantee that the after life will be any less exasperating than this one, have we?

MRS. BRADMAN (*laughing*): Oh, Mr. Condomine, how *can* you?

RUTH: I expect it's dreadfully ignorant of me not to know—but who was Princess Palliatani?

MADAME ARCATI: She was originally a Jewess from Odessa of quite remarkable beauty. It was an accepted fact that people used to stand on the seats of railway stations to watch her whizz by.

CHARLES: She was a keen traveller?

MADAME ARCATI: In her younger days, yes—later on she married a Mr. Clarke in the Consular Service and settled down for a while. . . .

RUTH: How did she become Princess Palliatani?

MADAME ARCATI: That was years later. Mr. Clarke

passed over and left her penniless with two strapping girls. . . .

RUTH: How unpleasant.

MADAME ARCATI: And so there was nothing for it but to obey the beckoning finger of adventure and take to the road again—so off she went, bag and baggage, to Vladivostock.

CHARLES: What an extraordinary place to go!

MADAME ARCATI: She had cousins there. Some years later she met old Palliatani who was returning from a secret mission in Japan. He was immediately staggered by her beauty and very shortly afterwards married her. From then on her life became really interesting.

DR. BRADMAN: I should hardly have described it as dull before.

RUTH: What happened to the girls?

MADAME ARCATI: She neither saw them nor spoke to them for twenty-three years.

MRS. BRADMAN: How extraordinary.

MADAME ARCATI: Not at all. She was always very erratic emotionally.

The double doors of the dining-room open and EDITH *comes in.*

EDITH (*nervously*): Dinner is served, Mum.

RUTH: Thank you, Edith—— Shall we——?

EDITH *retires backwards into the dining-room.*

ALL *rise.*

MADAME ARCATI: No red meat, I hope?

RUTH: There's meat, but I don't think it will be very red—would you rather have an egg or something?

MADAME ARCATI: No, thank you—it's just that I make it a rule never to eat red meat before I work—it sometimes has an odd effect. . . .

CHARLES: What sort of effect?

MADAME ARCATI: Oh, nothing of the least importance—if it isn't very red it won't matter much—anyhow, we'll risk it.

> MADAME ARCATI *goes out first with* RUTH *followed by* MRS. BRADMAN, DR. BRADMAN *and* CHARLES.

RUTH: Come along, then—Mrs. Bradman—Madame Arcati—you're on Charles's right. . . .

> *They all move into the dining-room as the lights fade on the scene.*

ACT I

SCENE II

When the lights go up again, dinner is over, and RUTH, MRS. BRADMAN *and* MADAME ARCATI *are sitting having their coffee;* MRS. BRADMAN *on pouffe down stage right.* MADAME ARCATI *on right end of sofa,* RUTH *on left end of sofa. All with coffee cups.*

MADAME ARCATI: . . . on her mother's side she went right back to the Borgias which I think accounted for a lot one way or another—even as a child she was given to the most violent destructive tempers—very inbred, you know.

MRS. BRADMAN: Yes, she must have been.

MADAME ARCATI: My control was quite scared the other day when we were talking—I could hear it in her voice—after all, she's only a child. . . .

RUTH: Do you always have a child as a control?

MADAME ARCATI: Yes, they're generally the best—some mediums prefer Indians, of course, but personally I've always found them unreliable.

RUTH: In what way unreliable?

MADAME ARCATI: Well, for one thing they're frightfully lazy and also, when faced with any sort of difficulty, they're rather apt to go off into their own tribal language which is naturally unintelligible—that generally spoils everything and wastes a great deal of time. No, children are undoubtedly more satisfactory, particularly when they get to know you and understand your ways. Daphne has worked with me for years.

MRS. BRADMAN: And she still goes on being a child—I mean, she doesn't show signs of growing any older?

MADAME ARCATI (*patiently*): Time values on the 'Other Side' are utterly different from ours.

MRS. BRADMAN: Do you feel funny when you go off into a trance?

MADAME ARCATI: In what way funny?

RUTH (*hastily*): Mrs. Bradman doesn't mean funny in its comic implication, I think she meant odd or strange——

MADAME ARCATI: The word was an unfortunate choice.

MRS. BRADMAN: I'm sure I'm very sorry.

MADAME ARCATI: It doesn't matter in the least—please don't apologise.

RUTH: When did you first discover that you had these extraordinary powers?

MADAME ARCATI: When I was quite tiny. My mother was a medium before me, you know, and so I had every opportunity of starting on the ground floor as you might say. I had my first trance when I was four years old and my first ectoplasmic manifestation when I was five and a half—what an exciting day that was, I shall never forget it—of course the manifestation itself was quite small and of very short duration, but, for a child of my tender years, it was most gratifying.

MRS. BRADMAN: Your mother must have been so pleased.

MADAME ARCATI (*modestly*): She was.

MRS. BRADMAN: Can you foretell the future?

MADAME ARCATI: Certainly not. I disapprove of fortune-tellers most strongly.

MRS. BRADMAN (*disappointed*): Oh really—why?

MADAME ARCATI: Too much guesswork and fake mixed up with it—even when the gift is genuine—and it only very occasionally is—you can't count on it.

RUTH: Why not?

MADAME ARCATI: Time again—time is the reef upon which all our frail mystic ships are wrecked.

RUTH: You mean, because it has never yet been proved that the past and the present and the future are not one and the same thing.

MADAME ARCATI: I long ago came to the conclusion that nothing has ever been definitely proved about anything.

RUTH: How very wise.

MADAME ARCATI *hands her cup to* RUTH. MRS. BRADMAN *puts her cup behind her on small table down stage right*. EDITH *comes in with a tray of drinks. She puts tray down on centre table by* RUTH. RUTH *moves a coffee cup and a vase to make room for it*. RUTH *takes off cigarette-box and ash-tray from table and gives them to* EDITH *who puts them on drinks table*.

I want you to leave the dining-room just as it is for to-night, Edith—you can clear the table in the morning.

EDITH: Yes'm.

RUTH: And we don't want to be disturbed for the next hour or so for any reason whatsoever—is that clear?

EDITH: Yes'm.

RUTH: And if anyone should telephone, just say we are out and take a message.

MRS. BRADMAN: Unless it's an urgent call for George.

RUTH: Unless it's an urgent call for Dr. Bradman.

EDITH: Yes'm.

      EDITH *goes out swiftly.*

RUTH: There's not likely to be one, is there?

MRS. BRADMAN: No, I don't think so.

MADAME ARCATI: Once I am off it won't matter, but an interruption during the preliminary stages might be disastrous.

MRS. BRADMAN: I wish the men would hurry up—I'm terribly excited.

MADAME ARCATI: Please don't be—it makes everything very much more difficult.

      CHARLES *and* DR. BRADMAN *come out of the dining-room. They are smoking cigars.*

CHARLES (*cheerfully*): Well, Madame Arcati—the time is drawing near.

MADAME ARCATI: Who knows? It may be receding!

CHARLES: How very true.

DR. BRADMAN: I hope you feel in the mood, Madame Arcati.

MADAME ARCATI: It isn't a question of mood—it's a question of concentration.

RUTH: You must forgive us being impatient. We

can perfectly easily wait though, if you're not quite ready to start . . .

MADAME ARCATI: Nonsense, my dear, I'm absolutely ready. (*She rises.*) Heigho, heigho, to work we go!

CHARLES: Is there anything you'd like us to do?

MADAME ARCATI: Do?

CHARLES: Yes—hold hands or anything?

MADAME ARCATI: All that will come later.

She goes to window and opens it. The others rise.

First a few deep, deep breaths of fresh air—(*over her shoulder.*) You may talk if you wish, it will not disturb me in the least. (*She flings open the windows wide and inhales deeply and a trifle noisily.*)

RUTH (*with a quizzical glance at* CHARLES): Oh dear!

CHARLES (*putting his finger to his lips warningly*): An excellent dinner, darling—I congratulate you.

RUTH: The mousse wasn't quite right.

CHARLES: It looked a bit hysterical but it tasted delicious.

MADAME ARCATI: That cuckoo is very angry.

CHARLES: I beg your pardon?

MADAME ARCATI: I said that cuckoo is very angry . . . listen. . . .

They all listen obediently.

CHARLES: How can you tell?

MADAME ARCATI: Timbre. . . . No moon—that's as well, I think—there's mist rising from the marshes. . . . (*A thought strikes her.*) There's no need for me to light my bicycle lamp, is there? I mean, nobody is likely to fall over it?

RUTH: No, we're not expecting anybody else.

MADAME ARCATI: Good-night, you foolish bird. (*She closes the windows.*) You have a table.

CHARLES: Yes. We thought that one would do.

MADAME ARCATI (*she puts her hands on the small table below piano and then points to the centre table*): I think the one that has the drinks on it would be better.

DR. BRADMAN: Change over.

CHARLES (*to* RUTH): You told Edith we didn't want to be disturbed?

RUTH: Yes, darling.

MADAME ARCATI (*crosses down stage of séance table over to mantelpiece. Walking about the room—twisting and untwisting her hands*): This is a moment I always hate.

RUTH: Are you nervous?

MADAME ARCATI: Yes. When I was a girl I always used to be sick.

DR. BRADMAN: How fortunate that you grew out of it.

RUTH: Children are always much more prone to be sick than grown-ups, though, aren't they? I know I could never travel in a train with any degree of safety until I was fourteen.

MRS. BRADMAN *brings pouffé over to table.*

(*Still walking.*) Little Tommy Tucker sings for his supper, what shall he have but Brown bread and butter? I despise that because it doesn't rhyme at all—but Daphne loves it.

DR. BRADMAN: Who's Daphne?

RUTH: Daphne is Madame Arcati's control—she's a little girl.

DR. BRADMAN: Oh, I see—yes, of course.

CHARLES: How old is she?

MADAME ARCATI: Rising seven when she died.

MRS. BRADMAN: And when was that?

MADAME ARCATI: February the sixth, 1884.

MRS. BRADMAN: Poor little thing.

DR. BRADMAN: She must be a bit long in the tooth by now, I should think.

MADAME ARCATI (*at fireplace. Stops walking and addresses* DR. BRADMAN): You should think, Dr. Bradman, but I fear you don't—at least, not profoundly enough.

MRS. BRADMAN: Do be quiet, George—you'll put Madame Arcati off.

MADAME ARCATI: Don't worry, my dear—I am quite used to sceptics—they generally turn out to be the most vulnerable and receptive in the long run.

RUTH: You'd better take that warning to heart, Dr. Bradman.

DR. BRADMAN: Please forgive me, Madame Arcati— I assure you I am most deeply interested.

MADAME ARCATI: It is of no consequence—— Will you all sit round the table please, and place your hands downwards on it.

RUTH: Come, Mrs. Bradman——

CHARLES: What about the lights?

MADAME ARCATI: All in good time, Mr. Condomine, sit down, please.

> *The four of them sit down at each side of a small square table.* MADAME ARCATI *surveys them critically, her head on one side. She is whistling a little tune. Sings.*

The fingers should be touching . . . that's right. . . . I presume that that is the gramophone, Mr. Condomine?

CHARLES (*half rising*): Yes—would you like me to start it? It's an electric one.

MADAME ARCATI: Please stay where you are—I can manage. (*She goes over to the gramophone and looks over the records.*) Now let me see—what have we here—

Brahms—oh, dear me, no—Rachmaninoff—too florid—
where is the dance music?

RUTH: They're the loose ones on the left.

MADAME ARCATI: I see. (*She stoops down and produces a
pile of dance records.*)

CHARLES: I'm afraid they're none of them very
new.

MADAME ARCATI: Daphne is really more attached to
Irving Berlin than anybody else—she likes a tune she
can hum—ah, here's one—'Always' . . .

CHARLES (*half jumping up again*): 'Always'!

RUTH: Do sit down, Charles—what is the matter?

CHARLES (*subsiding*): Nothing—nothing at all.

MADAME ARCATI: The light switch is by the door?

RUTH: Yes, all except the small one on the desk, and
the gramophone.

MADAME ARCATI: Very well—I understand.

RUTH: Charles, do keep still.

MRS. BRADMAN: Fingers touching, George—remember what Madame Arcati said.

MADAME ARCATI: Now there are one or two things
that I should like to explain, so will you all listen
attentively.

RUTH: Of course.

MADAME ARCATI: Presently, when the music begins,
I am going to switch out the lights. I may then either
walk about the room for a little or lie down flat—in due
course I shall draw up this dear little stool and join you
at the table—I shall place myself between you and your
wife, Mr. Condomine, and rest my hands lightly upon
yours—I must ask you not to address me or move or do
anything in the least distracting—is that quite, quite
clear?

CHARLES: Perfectly.

MADAME ARCATI: Of course, I cannot guarantee that anything will happen at all—Daphne may be unavailable —she had a head cold very recently, and was rather under the weather, poor child. On the other hand, a great many things might occur—one of you might have an emanation, for instance, or we might contact a poltergeist which would be extremely destructive and noisy. . . .

RUTH (*anxiously*): In what way destructive?

MADAME ARCATI: They throw things, you know.

RUTH: I didn't know.

MADAME ARCATI: But we must cross that bridge when we come to it, mustn't we?

CHARLES: Certainly—by all means.

MADAME ARCATI: Fortunately an Elemental at this time of the year is most unikely. . . .

RUTH: What do Elementals do?

MADAME ARCATI: Oh, my dear, one can never tell— they're dreadfully unpredictable . . . usually they take the form of a very cold wind. . . .

MRS. BRADMAN: I don't think I shall like that——

MADAME ARCATI: Occasionally reaching almost hurricane velocity——

RUTH: You don't think it would be a good idea to take the more breakable ornaments off the mantelpiece before we start?

MADAME ARCATI (*indulgently*): That really is not necessary, Mrs. Condomine—I assure you I have my own methods of dealing with Elementals.

RUTH: I'm so glad.

MADAME ARCATI: Now /then—are you ready to empty your minds?

Dr. Bradman: Do you mean we're to try to think of nothing?

Madame Arcati: Absolutely nothing, Dr. Bradman. Concentrate on a space or a nondescript colour that's really the best way. . . .

Dr. Bradman: I'll do my damndest.

Madame Arcati: Good work! I will now start the music.

> *She goes to the gramophone, puts on the record of 'Always', and begins to walk about the room; occasionally she moves into an abortive little dance step, and once, on passing a mirror on the mantelpiece, she surveys herself critically for a moment and adjusts her hair. Then with sudden speed, she runs across the room and switches off the lights.*

Mrs. Bradman: Oh, dear!

Madame Arcati: Quiet—please. . . .

> *Presently in the gloom* Madame Arcati, *after wandering about a little, draws up a stool and sits at the table between* Charles *and* Ruth. *The gramophone record comes to an end. There is dead silence.*

Is there anyone there? . . . (*A long pause.*) . . . Is there anyone there? . . . (*Another longer pause.*) . . . One rap for yes—two raps for no—now then—Is there anyone there? . . .

> *After a shorter pause, the table gives a little bump.*

Mrs. Bradman (*involuntarily*): Oh!

Madame Arcati: Sshhh! . . . Is that you, Daphne? (*The table gives a louder bump.*) Is your cold better, dear? (*The table gives two loud bumps very quickly.*) Oh, I'm so sorry—are you doing anything for it? (*The table bumps several times.*) I'm afraid she's rather fretful. . . . (*There is a silence.*) Is there anyone there who wishes to speak to

anyone here? (*After a pause the table gives one bump.*) Ah!
Now we're getting somewhere. . . . No, Daphne,
don't do that, dear, you're hurting me . . . Daphne,
dear, please . . . Oh, oh, oh! . . . be good, there's a
dear child. . . . You say there is someone there who
wishes to speak to someone here? (*One bump.*) Is it me?
(*Two sharp bumps.*) Is it Dr. Bradman? (*Two bumps.*) Is
it Mrs. Bradman? (*Two bumps.*) Is it Mrs. Condomine?
(*Several very loud bumps, which continue until* MADAME
ARCATI *shouts it down.*) Stop it! Behave yourself! Is it
Mr. Condomine? (*There is dead silence for a moment, and
then a very loud single bump.*) There's someone who wishes
to speak to you, Mr. Condomine. . . .

CHARLES: Tell them to leave a message.

The table bangs about loudly.

MADAME ARCATI: I really must ask you not to be
flippant, Mr. Condomine. . . .

RUTH: Charles, how can you be so idiotic—you'll
spoil everything.

CHARLES: I'm sorry—it slipped out.

MADAME ARCATI: Do you know anybody who has
passed over recently?

CHARLES: Not recently, except my cousin in the
Civil Service, and he wouldn't be likely to want to
communicate with me—we haven't spoken for years.

MADAME ARCATI (*hysterically*): Are you Mr. Condomine's cousin in the Civil Service? (*The table bumps
violently several times.*) I'm afraid we've drawn a blank.
. . . Can't you think of anyone else? Rack your
brains. . . .

RUTH (*helpfully*): It might be old Mrs. Plummett, you
know—she died on Whit Monday. . . .

CHARLES: I can't imagine why old Mrs. Plummett

should wish to talk to me—we had very little in common.

RUTH: It's worth trying, anyhow.

MADAME ARCATI: Are you old Mrs. Plummett? (*The table remains still.*)

RUTH: She was very deaf—perhaps you'd better shout——

MADAME ARCATI (*shouting*): Are you old Mrs. Plummett? (*Nothing happens.*) There's nobody there at all.

MRS. BRADMAN: How disappointing—just as we were getting on so nicely.

DR. BRADMAN: Violet, be quiet.

MADAME ARCATI (*rises*): Well, I'm afraid there's nothing for it but for me to go into a trance. I had hoped to avoid it because it's so exhausting—however, what must be must be. Excuse me a moment while I start the gramophone again. (*She comes to gramophone.*)

CHARLES (*in a strained voice*): Not 'Always'—don't play 'Always'——

RUTH: Why ever not, Charles? Don't be absurd.

MADAME ARCATI (*gently*): I'm afraid I must—it would be imprudent to change horses in midstream if you know what I mean. . . . (*She re-starts the gramophone.*)

CHARLES: Have it your own way.

> MADAME ARCATI *starts to moan and comes back slowly to stool and sits—then in the darkness a child's voice is heard reciting rather breathlessly:* 'Little Tommy Tucker'.

DR. BRADMAN: That would be Daphne—she ought to have had her adenoids out.

MRS. BRADMAN: George—please——

> MADAME ARCATI *suddenly gives a loud scream and falls off the stool on to the floor.*

CHARLES: Good God!

RUTH: Keep still, Charles. . . .

> CHARLES *subsides. Everyone sits in silence for a moment, then the table starts bouncing about.*

MRS. BRADMAN: It's trying to get away . . . I can't hold it. . . .

RUTH: Press down hard.

> *The table falls over with a crash.*

There now!

MRS. BRADMAN: Ought we to pick it up or leave it where it is?

DR. BRADMAN: How the hell do I know?

MRS. BRADMAN: There's no need to snap at me.

> *A perfectly strange and very charming voice says:* "Leave it where it is."

CHARLES: Who said that?

RUTH: Who said what?

CHARLES: Somebody said: "Leave it where it is."

RUTH: Nonsense, dear.

CHARLES: I heard it distinctly.

RUTH: Well, nobody else did—did they?

MRS. BRADMAN: I never heard a sound.

CHARLES: It was you, Ruth—you're playing tricks.

RUTH: I'm not doing anything of the sort. I haven't uttered.

> *There is another pause, and then the voice says:* "Good evening, Charles."

CHARLES (*very agitated*): Ventriloquism—that's what it is—ventriloquism. . . .

RUTH (*irritably*): What is the matter with you?

CHARLES: You must have heard that—one of you must have heard that!

RUTH: Heard *what*?

CHARLES: You mean to sit there solemnly and tell me that none of you heard anything at all?

DR. BRADMAN: I certainly didn't.

MRS. BRADMAN: Neither did I—I wish I had. I should love to hear something.

RUTH: It's you who are playing the tricks, Charles—you're acting to try to frighten us . . .

CHARLES (*breathlessly*): I'm not—I swear I'm not.

The voice speaks again. It says: "It's difficult to think of what to say after seven years, but I suppose good evening is as good as anything else."

CHARLES (*intensely*): Who are you?

The voice says: "Elvira, of course—don't be so silly."

CHARLES *rises and goes to light-switch centre, then down stage right to fireplace. Others all rise.* MADAME ARCATI *on floor.*

CHARLES: I can't bear this for another minute. . . . (*He rises violently.*) Get up, everybody—the entertainment's over.

He rushes across the room and switches on the lights.

RUTH: Oh, Charles, how tiresome of you—just as we were beginning to enjoy ourselves.

CHARLES: Never again—that's all I can say. Never, never again as long as I live. . . .

RUTH: What on earth's the matter with you?

CHARLES: Nothing's the matter with me—I'm just sick of the whole business, that's all.

DR. BRADMAN: Did you hear anything that we didn't hear really?

CHARLES (*with a forced laugh*): Of course not—I was only pretending . . .

RUTH: I know you were . . .

MRS. BRADMAN: Oh dear . . . look at Madame Arcati!
    MADAME ARCATI *is lying on the floor with her feet
    up on the stool from which she fell. She is obviously quite
    unconscious.*

RUTH: What are we to do with her?

CHARLES: Bring her round—bring her round as soon
as possible.

DR. BRADMAN (*going over and kneeling down beside her*): I
think we'd better leave her alone.

RUTH: But she might stay like that for hours.

    DR. BRADMAN, *kneeling left of* MADAME ARCATI,
    RUTH *above her.* MRS. BRADMAN, *to left of* DR.
    BRADMAN, CHARLES *to right of* MADAME ARCATI,
    below sofa.

DR. BRADMAN (*after feeling her pulse and examining her
eye*): She's out all right.

CHARLES (*almost hysterically*): Bring her round! It's
dangerous to leave her like that. . . .

RUTH: Really, Charles, you are behaving most
peculiarly.

CHARLES (*kneels right of* MADAME ARCATI, *shaking her
violently*): Wake up, Madame Arcati—wake up—it's
time to go home.

DR. BRADMAN: Here—go easy, old man . . .

    RUTH *goes to drinks table left pours brandy.*
    CHARLES *and* DR. BRADMAN *lift* MADAME ARCATI
    and put her in arm-chair. MRS. BRADMAN *takes
    stool from her feet and puts it back under piano.*

CHARLES: Get some brandy—give her some brandy
—lift her into the chair—help me, Bradman . . .

    RUTH *pours out some brandy while* CHARLES *and* DR.
    BRADMAN *lift* MADAME ARCATI *laboriously into an
    arm-chair.*

(*Leaning over her.*) Wake UP, Madame Arcati—Little Tommy Tucker, Madame Arcati!

> RUTH *brings brandy to above arm-chair.* CHARLES *takes it and gives some to* MADAME ARCATI *on her right.* DR. BRADMAN *patting her hand on her left.* MRS. BRADMAN *above* DR. BRADMAN.

RUTH: Here's the brandy.

> MADAME ARCATI *gives a slight moan and a shiver.*

CHARLES (*forcing some brandy between her lips*): Wake up!——

> MADAME ARCATI *gives a prolonged shiver and chokes slightly over the brandy.*

MRS. BRADMAN: She's coming round.

RUTH: Be careful, Charles—you're spilling it all down her dress.

MADAME ARCATI (*opening her eyes*): Well, that's that.

RUTH (*solicitously*): Are you all right?

MADAME ARCATI: Certainly I am—never felt better in my life.

CHARLES: Would you like some more brandy?

MADAME ARCATI: So that's the funny taste in my mouth—well, really! Fancy allowing them to give me brandy, Doctor Bradman, you ought to have known better—brandy on top of a trance might have been catastrophic. Take it away, please—I probably shan't sleep a wink to-night as it is.

CHARLES: I know I shan't.

RUTH: Why on earth not?

> CHARLES *crosses away to right to fireplace and takes cigarette.*

CHARLES: The whole experience has unhinged me.

MADAME ARCATI: Well, what happened—was it satisfactory?

RUTH: Nothing much happened, Madame Arcati, after you went off.

MADAME ARCATI: Something happened all right, I can feel it—— (MADAME ARCATI *rises and crosses to fireplace—sniffs.*) No poltergeist, at any rate—that's a good thing. Any apparitions?

DR. BRADMAN: Not a thing.

MADAME ARCATI: No ectoplasm?

RUTH: I'm not quite sure what it is, but I don't think so.

MADAME ARCATI: Very curious. I feel as though something tremendous had taken place.

RUTH: Charles pretended he heard a voice, in order to frighten us.

CHARLES: It was only a joke.

MADAME ARCATI: A very poor one, if I may say so—— (*Round above sofa to right centre.*) Nevertheless, I am prepared to swear that there is someone else psychic in this room apart from myself.

RUTH: I don't see how there can be really, Madame Arcati.

MADAME ARCATI: I do hope I haven't gone and released something—however, we are bound to find out within a day or two—if any manifestation should occur or you hear any unexpected noises—you might let me know at once.

RUTH: Of course we will—we'll telephone immediately.

MADAME ARCATI: I think I really must be on my way now.

RUTH: Wouldn't you like anything before you go?

MADAME ARCATI: No, thank you—I have some

Ovaltine all ready in a saucepan at home—it only needs hotting up.

DR. BRADMAN: Wouldn't you like to leave your bicycle here and let us drive you?

MRS. BRADMAN: I honestly do think you should, Madame Arcati, after that trance and everything—you can't be feeling quite yourself.

MADAME ARCATI: Nonsense, my dear, I'm as fit as a fiddle—always feel capital after a trance—rejuvenates me. Good-night, Mrs. Condomine.

RUTH: It was awfully sweet of you to take so much trouble.

MADAME ARCATI: I'm so sorry so little occurred— it's that cold of Daphne's, I expect—you know what children are when they have anything wrong with them —we must try again some other evening.

    MADAME ARCATI *crosses above* RUTH *to right of* MRS. BRADMAN.

RUTH: That would be lovely.

MADAME ARCATI (*shaking hands with* MRS. BRADMAN): Good-night, Mrs. Bradman.

MRS. BRADMAN: It was thrilling, it really was—I felt the table absolutely shaking under my hands.

    MADAME ARCATI *crosses above* MRS. BRADMAN *to* DR. BRADMAN *and shakes hands*.

MADAME ARCATI: Good-night, Doctor.

DR. BRADMAN: Congratulations, Madame Arcati.

MADAME ARCATI: I am fully aware of the irony in your voice, Dr. Bradman. As a matter of fact you'd be an admirable subject for telepathic hypnosis—a great chum of mine is an expert—I should like her to look you over.

DR. BRADMAN: I'm sure I should be charmed.

MADAME ARCATI: Good-night, everyone—next time we must really put our backs into it!

> *With a comprehensive smile and a wave of the hand, she goes out, followed by* CHARLES.
>
> RUTH *sinks down into sofa, laughing helplessly.*
>
> MRS. BRADMAN *comes and sits left of arm-chair.*
> DR. BRADMAN *picks up séance table and puts desk chair back up stage right, then comes back and puts pouffe back in position down stage right. He then returns to left centre.*

RUTH: Oh dear! . . . oh dear! . . .

MRS. BRADMAN (*beginning to laugh too*): Be careful, Mrs. Condomine—she might hear you.

RUTH: I can't help it—I really can't—I've been holding this in for ages.

MRS. BRADMAN: She certainly put you in your place, George, and serve you right.

RUTH: She's raving mad, of course—mad as a hatter.

MRS. BRADMAN: But do you really think she *believes*?

DR. BRADMAN: Of course not—the whole thing's a put up job—I must say, though, she shoots a more original line than they generally do.

RUTH: I should think that she's probably half convinced herself by now.

DR. BRADMAN: Possibly—the trance was genuine enough—but that, of course, is easily accounted for.

RUTH: Hysteria?

DR. BRADMAN: Yes—a form of hysteria, I should imagine.

MRS. BRADMAN: I do hope Mr. Condomine got all the atmosphere he wanted for his book.

RUTH: He might have got a great deal more if he hadn't spoiled everything by showing off. . . . I'm really very cross with him.

At this moment ELVIRA *comes in through the closed french windows. She is charmingly dressed in a sort of negligée. Everything about her is grey; hair, skin, dress, hands, so we must accept the fact that she is not quite of this world. She passes between* DR. *and* MRS. BRADMAN *and* RUTH *while they are talking. None of them see her. She goes up stage and sits soundlessly on a chair. She regards them with interest, a slight smile on her face.*

I suddenly felt a draught—there must be a window open.

DR. BRADMAN (*looking*): No—they're shut.

MRS. BRADMAN (*laughing*): Perhaps it was one of those what you may call 'ems that Madame Arcati was talking about.

DR. BRADMAN: Elementals.

RUTH (*also laughing again*): Oh no, it couldn't be—she distinctly said that it was the wrong time of the year for Elementals.

CHARLES *comes in, to arm-chair centre.*

CHARLES: Well, the old girl's gone pedalling off down the drive at the hell of a speed—we had a bit of trouble lighting her lamp.

MRS. BRADMAN: Poor thing.

CHARLES: I've got a theory about her, you know—I believe she is completely sincere.

RUTH: Charles! How could she be?

CHARLES: Wouldn't it be possible, Doctor? Some form of self-hypnotism?

DR. BRADMAN: It might be . . . as I was explaining to your wife just now, there are certain types of hysterical subjects. . . .

MRS. BRADMAN: George dear—it's getting terribly late, we really must go home—you have to get up so early in the morning.

DR. BRADMAN: You see? The moment I begin to talk about anything that really interests me, my wife interrupts me. . . .

MRS. BRADMAN: You know I'm right, darling—it's past eleven.

DR. BRADMAN (*crosses up stage to* CHARLES *centre*): I'll do a little reading up on the whole business—just for the fun of it.

CHARLES: You must have a drink before you go.

DR. BRADMAN: No, really, thank you—Violet's quite right, I'm afraid. I have got to get up abominably early to-morrow—I have a patient being operated on in Canterbury.

> MRS. BRADMAN *crosses to* RUTH *below sofa.* RUTH *rises.*

MRS. BRADMAN: It has been a thrilling evening— I shall never forget—it was sweet of you to include us.

DR. BRADMAN: Good-night, Mrs. Condomine— thank you so much.

CHARLES: You're sure about the drink?

DR. BRADMAN: Quite sure, thanks.

RUTH: We'll let you know if we find any poltergeists whirling about.

DR. BRADMAN: I should never forgive you if you didn't.

MRS. BRADMAN: Come along, darling . . .

> BRADMANS *exit, followed by* CHARLES.
> RUTH *crosses to piano, leans over* ELVIRA *and gets cigarette and lights it, then crosses back to fireplace.*
> CHARLES *comes back into the room.*

RUTH: Well, darling?

CHARLES (*to above left end of sofa. Absently*): Well?

RUTH: Would you say the evening had been profitable?

CHARLES: Yes—I suppose so.

RUTH: I must say it was extremely funny at moments.

CHARLES: Yes—it certainly was.

RUTH: What's the matter?

CHARLES: The matter?

RUTH: Yes—you seem odd somehow—do you feel quite well?

CHARLES: Perfectly. I think I'll have a drink. (*Moves up stage to drinks table and pours whisky-and-soda.*) Do you want one?

RUTH: No, thank you, dear.

CHARLES (*pouring himself out a drink*): It's rather chilly in this room.

RUTH: Come over by the fire.

CHARLES: I don't think I'll make any notes to-night —I'll start fresh in the morning.

> CHARLES *turns with glass in hand, sees* ELVIRA *and drops his glass on the floor.*

CHARLES: My God!

RUTH: Charles!

ELVIRA: That was very clumsy, Charles dear.

CHARLES: Elvira!—then it's true—it was you!

ELVIRA: Of course it was.

RUTH (*starts to go to* CHARLES): Charles—darling Charles—what are you talking about?

CHARLES (*to* ELVIRA): Are you a ghost?

ELVIRA (*crosses below sofa to fire*): I suppose I must be —it's all very confusing.

RUTH (*comes to right of* CHARLES, *becoming agitated*): Charles—what do you keep looking over there for? Look at me—what's happened?

CHARLES: Don't you see?

RUTH: See what?

CHARLES: Elvira.

RUTH (*staring at him incredulously*): Elvira!!

CHARLES (*with an effort at social grace*): Yes—Elvira, dear, this is Ruth—Ruth, this is Elvira.

> RUTH *tries to take his arm.* CHARLES *retreats down stage left.*

RUTH (*with forced calmness*): Come and sit down, darling.

CHARLES: Do you mean to say you can't see her?

RUTH: Listen, Charles—you just sit down quietly by the fire and I'll mix you another drink. Don't worry about the mess on the carpet—Edith can clean it up in the morning. (*She takes him by the arm.*)

CHARLES (*breaking away*): But you must be able to see her—she's there—look—right in front of you—there——

RUTH: Are you mad? What's happened to you?

CHARLES: You can't see her?

RUTH: If this is a joke, dear, it's gone quite far enough. Sit down for God's sake and don't be idiotic.

CHARLES (*clutching his head*): What am I to do—what the hell am I to do!

ELVIRA: I think you might at least be a little more pleased to see me—after all, you conjured me up.

CHARLES (*above table left centre*): I didn't do any such thing.

ELVIRA: Nonsense, of course you did. That awful child with the cold came and told me you wanted to see me urgently.

CHARLES: It was all a mistake—a horrible mistake.

RUTH: Stop talking like that, Charles—as I told you before, the joke's gone far enough.

CHARLES: I've gone mad, that's what it is—I've just gone raving mad.

RUTH (*pours out brandy and brings it to* CHARLES *below piano*): Here—drink this.

CHARLES (*mechanically—taking it*): This is appalling!

RUTH: Relax.

CHARLES: How can I relax? I shall never be able to relax again as long as I live.

RUTH: Drink some brandy.

CHARLES (*drinking it at a gulp*): There, now—are you satisfied?

RUTH: Now sit down.

CHARLES: Why are you so anxious for me to sit down —what good will that do?

RUTH: I want you to relax—you can't relax standing up.

ELVIRA: African natives can—they can stand on one leg for hours.

CHARLES: I don't happen to be an African native.

RUTH: You don't happen to be a *what*?

CHARLES (*savagely*): An African native!

RUTH: What's that got to do with it?

CHARLES: It doesn't matter, Ruth—really it doesn't matter—we'll say no more about it.

    CHARLES *crosses to arm-chair and sits.* RUTH *comes up stage of him.*

CHARLES: See, I've sat down.

RUTH: Would you like some more brandy?

CHARLES: Yes, please.

    RUTH *goes up to drinks table with glass.*

ELVIRA: Very unwise—you always had a weak head.

CHARLES: I could drink you under the table.

RUTH: There's no need to be aggressive, Charles—I'm doing my best to help you.

CHARLES: I'm sorry.

RUTH (*crosses to up stage of* CHARLES *with brandy*): Here—drink this—and then we'll go to bed.

ELVIRA: Get rid of her, Charles—then we can talk in peace.

CHARLES: That's a thoroughly immoral suggestion, you ought to be ashamed of yourself.

RUTH: What is there immoral in that?

CHARLES: I wasn't talking to you.

RUTH: Who were you talking to, then?

CHARLES: Elvira, of course.

RUTH: To hell with Elvira!

ELVIRA: There now—she's getting cross.

CHARLES: I don't blame her.

RUTH: What don't you blame her for?

CHARLES (*rises and backs down stage left a pace*): Oh, God!

RUTH: Now look here, Charles—I gather you've got some sort of plan behind all this. I'm not quite a fool. I suspected you when we were doing that idiotic séance . . .

CHARLES: Don't be so silly—what plan could I have?

RUTH: I don't know—it's probably something to do with the characters in your book—how they, or one of them would react to a certain situation—I refuse to be used as a guinea-pig unless I'm warned beforehand what it's all about.

CHARLES (*moves a couple of paces towards* RUTH): Elvira is here, Ruth—she's standing a few yards away from you.

RUTH (*sarcastically*): Yes, dear, I can see her distinctly —under the piano with a zebra!

CHARLES: But, Ruth . . .

RUTH: I am not going to stay here arguing any longer . . .

ELVIRA: Hurray!

CHARLES: Shut up!

RUTH (*incensed*): How dare you speak to me like that!

CHARLES: Listen, Ruth—please listen——

RUTH: I will not listen to any more of this nonsense —I am going up to bed now, I'll leave you to turn out the lights. I shan't be asleep—I'm too upset. So you can come in and say good-night to me if you feel like it.

ELVIRA: That's big of her, I must say.

CHARLES: Be quiet—you're behaving like a gutter-snipe.

RUTH (*icily*): That is all I have to say. Good-night, Charles.

> RUTH *walks swiftly out of the room without looking at him again.*

CHARLES (*follows* RUTH *to door*): Ruth . . .

ELVIRA: That was one of the most enjoyable half-hours I have ever spent.

CHARLES (*puts down glass on drinks table*): Oh, Elvira— how could you!

ELVIRA: Poor Ruth!

CHARLES (*staring at her*): This is obviously a hallucination, isn't it?

ELVIRA: I'm afraid I don't know the technical term for it.

CHARLES (*comes down stage to centre*): What am I to do?

ELVIRA: What Ruth suggested—relax.

CHARLES (*crosses below chair to sofa*): Where have you come from?

ELVIRA: Do you know, it's very peculiar, but I've sort of forgotten.

CHARLES: Are you to be here indefinitely?

ELVIRA: I don't know that either.

CHARLES: Oh, my God!

ELVIRA: Why, would you hate it so much if I was?

CHARLES: Well, you must admit it would be embarrassing?

ELVIRA: I don't see why, really—it's all a question of adjusting yourself—anyhow I think it's horrid of you to be so unwelcoming and disagreeable.

CHARLES: Now look here, Elvira . . .

ELVIRA (*near tears*): I do—I think you're mean.

CHARLES: Try to see my point, dear—I've been married to Ruth for five years, and you've been dead for seven . . .

ELVIRA: Not dead, Charles—'passed over'. It's considered vulgar to say 'dead' where I come from.

CHARLES: Passed over, then.

ELVIRA: At any rate now that I'm here, the least you can do is to make a pretence of being amiable about it . . .

CHARLES: Of course, my dear, I'm delighted in one way . . .

ELVIRA: I don't believe you love me any more.

CHARLES: I shall always love the memory of you.

ELVIRA (*crosses slowly down stage left above sofa by armchair*): You mustn't think me unreasonable, but I really am a little hurt. You called me back—and at great inconvenience I came—and you've been thoroughly churlish ever since I arrived.

CHARLES (*gently*): Believe me, Elvira, I most emphatically did not send for you—there's been some mistake.

ELVIRA (*irritably*): Well, somebody did—and that child said it was you—I remember I was playing backgammon with a very sweet old Oriental gentleman—I think his name was Genghis Khan—and I'd just thrown double sixes, and then the child paged me and the next thing I knew I was in this room . . . perhaps it was your subconscious.

CHARLES: You must find out whether you are going to stay or not, and we can make arrangements accordingly.

ELVIRA: I don't see how I can.

CHARLES: Well, try to think—isn't there anyone that you know, that you can get in touch with over there—on the other side, or whatever it's called—who could advise you?

ELVIRA: I can't think—it seems so far away—as though I'd dreamed it . . .

CHARLES: You must know somebody else besides Genghis Khan.

ELVIRA (*to arm-chair a pace*): Oh, Charles . . .

CHARLES: What is it?

ELVIRA: I want to cry, but I don't think I'm able to . . .

CHARLES: What do you want to cry for?

ELVIRA: It's seeing you again—and you being so irascible like you always used to be . . .

CHARLES: I don't mean to be irascible, Elvira . . .

ELVIRA: Darling—I don't mind really—I never did.

CHARLES: Is it cold—being a ghost?

ELVIRA: No—I don't think so.

CHARLES: What happens if I touch you?

ELVIRA: I doubt if you can. Do you want to?

CHARLES (*sits left end of sofa*): Oh, Elvira. . . . (*He buries his face in his hands.*)

ELVIRA (*to left arm of sofa*): What is it, darling?

CHARLES: I really do feel strange, seeing you again . . .

ELVIRA (*moves to right below sofa and round above it again to left arm*): That's better.

CHARLES (*looking up*): What's better?

ELVIRA: Your voice was kinder.

CHARLES: Was I ever unkind to you when you were alive?

ELVIRA: Often . . .

CHARLES: Oh, how can you! I'm sure that's an exaggeration.

ELVIRA: Not at all—you were an absolute pig that time we went to Cornwall and stayed in that awful hotel —you hit me with a billiard cue——

CHARLES: Only very, very gently. . . .

ELVIRA: I loved you very much.

CHARLES: I loved you too . . . (*He puts out his hand to her and then draws it away.*) No, I can't touch you— isn't that horrible?

ELVIRA: Perhaps it's as well if I'm going to stay for any length of time . . . (*Sits left arm of sofa.*)

CHARLES: I suppose I shall wake up eventually . . . but I feel strangely peaceful now.

ELVIRA: That's right. Put your head back.

CHARLES (*doing so*): Like that?

ELVIRA (*stroking his hair*): Can you feel anything . . .?

CHARLES: Only a very little breeze through my hair . . .

ELVIRA: Well, that's better than nothing.

CHARLES (*drowsily*): I suppose if I'm really out of my mind they'll put me in an asylum.

ELVIRA: Don't worry about that—just relax——

CHARLES (*very drowsily indeed*): Poor Ruth . . .

ELVIRA (*gently and sweetly*): To hell with Ruth.

    Curtain.

THE CURTAIN FALLS

ACT II

Scene I

It is about nine-thirty the next morning. The sun is pouring in through the open french windows.

> *Breakfast table set left centre below piano.* Ruth *sitting left of table back to window reading 'The Times'.* Charles *comes in and crosses to window—he kisses her.*

Charles: Good morning, darling.

Ruth (*with a certain stiffness*): Good morning, Charles.

Charles (*going to the open window and taking a deep breath*): It certainly is.

Ruth: What certainly is what?

Charles: A good morning—a tremendously good morning—there isn't a cloud in the sky and everything looks newly washed.

Ruth (*turning a page of 'The Times'*): Edith's keeping your breakfast hot—you'd better ring.

Charles (*crosses to mantelpiece and rings bell up stage*): Anything interesting in *The Times*?

Ruth: Don't be silly, Charles.

Charles (*sitting at the table and pouring himself out some coffee*): I intend to work all day.

Ruth: Good.

Charles (*comes back to breakfast table*): It's extraordinary about daylight, isn't it?

Ruth: How do you mean?

CHARLES: The way it reduces everything to normal.

RUTH: Does it?

CHARLES (*sits right of table opposite* RUTH—*firmly*): Yes—it does.

RUTH: I'm sure I'm very glad to hear it.

CHARLES: You're very glacial this morning.

RUTH: Are you surprised?

CHARLES: Frankly—yes. I expected more of you.

RUTH: Well, really!

CHARLES: I've always looked upon you as a woman of perception and understanding.

RUTH: Perhaps this is one of my off days.

> EDITH *comes in with some bacon and eggs and toast— comes to above table between* CHARLES *and* RUTH.

CHARLES (*cheerfully*): Good morning, Edith.

EDITH: Good morning, sir.

CHARLES: Feeling fit?

EDITH: Yes, sir—thank you, sir.

CHARLES: How's cook?

EDITH: I don't know, sir—I haven't asked her.

CHARLES: You should. You should begin every day by asking everyone how they are—it oils the wheels.

EDITH: Yes, sir.

CHARLES: Greet her from me, will you?

EDITH: Yes, sir.

RUTH: That will be all for the moment, Edith.

EDITH: Yes'm.

> EDITH *goes out*.

RUTH: I wish you wouldn't be facetious with the servants, Charles—it confuses them and undermines their morale.

CHARLES: I consider that point of view retrogressive, if not downright feudal.

RUTH: I don't care what you consider it, I have to run the house and you don't.

CHARLES: Are you implying that I couldn't?

RUTH: You're at liberty to try.

CHARLES: I take back what I said about it being a good morning—it's a horrid morning.

RUTH: You'd better eat your breakfast while it's hot.

CHARLES: It isn't.

RUTH (*putting down 'The Times'*): Now look here, Charles—in your younger days this display of roguish flippancy might have been alluring—in a middle-aged novelist it's nauseating.

CHARLES: Would you like me to writhe at your feet in a frenzy of self-abasement.

RUTH: That would be equally nauseating but certainly more appropriate.

CHARLES: I really don't see what I've done that's so awful.

RUTH: You behaved abominably last night. You wounded me and insulted me.

CHARLES: I was the victim of an aberration.

RUTH: Nonsense—you were drunk.

CHARLES: Drunk?

RUTH: You had four strong dry Martinis before dinner—a great deal too much Burgundy at dinner—heaven knows how much Port and Kummel with Dr. Bradman while I was doing my best to entertain that mad woman—and then two double brandies later—I gave them to you myself—of course you were drunk.

CHARLES: So that's your story, is it?

RUTH: You refused to come to bed and finally when I came down at three in the morning to see what had happened to you, I found you in an alcoholic coma on the sofa with the fire out and your hair all over your face.

CHARLES: I was not in the least drunk, Ruth. Something happened to me last night—something very peculiar happened to me.

RUTH: Nonsense.

CHARLES: It isn't nonsense—I know it looks like nonsense now in the clear remorseless light of day, but last night it was far from being nonsense—I honestly had some sort of hallucination . . .

RUTH: I would really rather not discuss it any further.

CHARLES: But you must discuss it—it's very disturbing.

RUTH: There I agree with you. It showed you up in a most unpleasant light—I find that extremely disturbing.

CHARLES: I swear to you that during the séance I was convinced that I heard Elvira's voice——

RUTH: Nobody else did.

CHARLES: I can't help that—I did.

RUTH: You couldn't have.

CHARLES: And later on I was equally convinced that she was in this room—I saw her distinctly and talked to her. After you'd gone up to bed we had quite a cosy little chat.

RUTH: And you seriously expect me to believe that you weren't drunk?

CHARLES: I *knew* I wasn't drunk. If I'd been all that drunk I should have a dreadful hangover now, shouldn't I?

RUTH: I'm not at all sure that you haven't.

CHARLES: I haven't got a trace of a headache—my tongue's not coated—look at it—(*he puts out his tongue.*)

RUTH: I've not the least desire to look at your tongue, kindly put it in again.

CHARLES (*rises, crosses to mantelpiece and lights cigarette*): I know what it is—you're frightened.

RUTH: Frightened! Rubbish. What is there to be frightened of?

CHARLES: Elvira. You wouldn't have minded all that much even if I had been drunk—it's only because it was all mixed up with Elvira.

RUTH: I seem to remember last night before dinner telling you that your views of female psychology were rather didactic. I was right. I should have added that they were puerile.

CHARLES: That was when it all began.

RUTH: When what all began?

CHARLES (*moves up to above right end of sofa*): We were talking too much about Elvira—it's dangerous to have somebody very strongly in your mind when you start dabbling with the occult.

RUTH: She certainly wasn't strongly in my mind.

CHARLES: She was in mine.

RUTH: Oh, she was, was she?

CHARLES (*crosses to face* RUTH *at breakfast table*): You tried to make me say that she was more physically attractive than you, so that you could hold it over me.

RUTH: I did not. I don't give a hoot how physically attractive she was.

CHARLES: Oh yes, you do—your whole being is devoured with jealousy.

RUTH (*rises*): This is too much!

CHARLES (*sits in arm-chair*): Women! My God, what I think of women!

RUTH: Your view of women is academic to say the least of it—just because you've always been dominated by them it doesn't necessarily follow that you know anything about them.

CHARLES: I've never been dominated by anyone.

RUTH (*crosses to below right breakfast chair*): You were hag-ridden by your mother until you were twenty-three —then you got into the clutches of that awful Mrs. Whatever her name was——

CHARLES: Mrs. Winthrop-Llewelyn.

RUTH (*clears plates on breakfast table and works round with her back to* CHARLES *to above table*): I'm not interested. Then there was Elvira—she ruled you with a rod of iron.

CHARLES: Elvira never ruled anyone, she was much too elusive—that was one of her greatest charms. . . .

RUTH: Then there was Maud Charteris——

CHARLES: My affair with Maud Charteris lasted exactly seven and a half weeks and she cried all the time.

RUTH: The tyranny of tears—then there was——

CHARLES: If you wish to make an inventory of my sex life, dear, I think it only fair to tell you that you've missed out several episodes—I'll consult my diary and give you the complete list after lunch.

RUTH: It's no use trying to impress me with your routine amorous exploits. . . . (*Crosses up stage centre.*)

CHARLES: The only woman in my whole life who's ever attempted to dominate me is you—you've been at it for years.

RUTH: That is completely untrue.

CHARLES: Oh no, it isn't. You boss me and bully me and order me about—you won't even allow me to have an hallucination if I want to.

RUTH (*comes down stage to* CHARLES *above sofa*): Charles, alcohol will ruin your whole life if you allow it to get hold of you, you know.

CHARLES (*rises and comes up stage above chair to face* RUTH): Once and for all, Ruth, I would like you to understand that what happened last night was nothing whatever to do with alcohol. You've very adroitly rationalised the whole affair to your own satisfaction, but your deductions are based on complete fallacy. I am willing to grant you that it was an aberration, some sort of odd psychic delusion brought on by suggestion or hypnosis—I was stone cold sober from first to last and extremely upset into the bargain.

RUTH: *You* were upset indeed? What about me?

CHARLES: You behaved with a stolid, obtruse lack of comprehension that frankly shocked me!

RUTH: I consider that I was remarkably patient. I shall know better next time.

CHARLES: Instead of putting out a gentle comradely hand to guide me—you shouted staccato orders at me like a sergeant-major.

RUTH: You seem to forget that you gratuitously insulted me.

CHARLES: I did not.

RUTH: You called me a guttersnipe—you told me to shut up—and when I quietly suggested that we should go up to bed you said, with the most disgusting leer, that it was an immoral suggestion.

CHARLES (*exasperated*): I was talking to Elvira!

RUTH: If you were I can only say that it conjures up a fragrant picture of your first marriage.

CHARLES: My first marriage was perfectly charming and I think it's in the worst possible taste for you to sneer at it.

RUTH: I am not nearly so interested in your first marriage as you think I am. It's your second marriage that is absorbing me at the moment—it seems to me to be on the rocks.

CHARLES: Only because you persist in taking up this ridiculous attitude.

RUTH: My attitude is that of any normal woman whose husband gets drunk and hurls abuse at her.

CHARLES (*crosses to fireplace below sofa, shouting*): I was not drunk!

RUTH: Be quiet, they'll hear you in the kitchen.

CHARLES: I don't care if they hear me in the Folkestone Town Hall—I was not drunk!

RUTH: Control yourself, Charles.

CHARLES: How can I control myself in the face of your idiotic damned stubbornness? It's giving me claustrophobia.

RUTH: You'd better ring up Doctor Bradman.

    EDITH *comes in with a tray to clear away the breakfast things.*

EDITH: Can I clear, please'm?

RUTH: Yes, Edith. (*Crosses to window.*)

EDITH: Cook wants to know about lunch, mum.

RUTH (*coldly*): Will you be in to lunch, Charles?

CHARLES: Please don't worry about me—I shall be perfectly happy with a bottle of gin in my bedroom.

RUTH: Don't be silly, dear. (*To* EDITH.) Tell cook we shall both be in.

EDITH: Yes'm.

RUTH (*conversationally—after a long pause*): I'm going into Hythe this morning—is there anything you want?

CHARLES: Yes, a great deal—but I doubt if you could get it in Hythe.

RUTH: Tell cook to put Alka-Seltzer down on my list, will you, Edith.

EDITH: Yes'm.

RUTH (*at the window—after another long pause*): It's clouding over.

CHARLES: You have a genius for understatement.

> *In silence, but breathing heavily,* EDITH *staggers out with the tray.*

RUTH (*as she goes*): Don't worry about the table, Edith—I'll put it away.

EDITH: Yes'm.

> *When* EDITH *has gone* CHARLES *goes over to* RUTH.

CHARLES (*coming over to breakfast table to* RUTH *who is folding cloth*): Please, Ruth—be reasonable.

RUTH: I'm perfectly reasonable.

CHARLES: I wasn't pretending—I really did believe that I saw Elvira and when I heard her voice I was appalled.

RUTH: You put up with it for five years.

> RUTH *puts chairs back up stage right and down left.*
> CHARLES *takes table off stage centre.*

CHARLES: When I saw her I had the shock of my life —that's why I dropped the glass.

RUTH: But you *couldn't* have seen her.

CHARLES: I know I couldn't have but I *did*.

RUTH (*puts chair up right*): I'm willing to concede then that you imagined you did.

CHARLES: That's what I've been trying to explain to you for hours. (*Crosses to mantelpiece.*)

RUTH (*to centre below arm-chair*): Well then, there's obviously something wrong with you.

CHARLES (*sits on left arm of sofa*): Exactly—there is something wrong with me—something fundamentally wrong with me—that's why I've been imploring your sympathy and all I got was a sterile temperance lecture.

RUTH: You had been drinking, Charles—there's no denying that.

CHARLES: No more than usual.

RUTH: Well, how do you account for it then?

CHARLES (*frantically*): I can't account for it—that's what's so awful.

RUTH (*practically*): Did you feel quite well yesterday —during the day I mean?

CHARLES: Of course I did.

RUTH: What did you have for lunch?

CHARLES: You ought to know, you had it with me.

RUTH (*thinking*): Let me see now, there was lemon sole and that cheese thing——

CHARLES: Why should having a cheese thing for lunch make me see my deceased wife after dinner?

RUTH: You never know—it was rather rich.

CHARLES: Why didn't you see your dead husband then? You had just as much of it as I did.

RUTH: This is not getting us anywhere at all.

CHARLES: Of course it isn't, and it won't as long as you insist on ascribing supernatural phenomena to colonic irritation.

RUTH: Supernatural grandmother.

CHARLES: I admit she'd have been much less agitating.

RUTH (*standing at back of arm-chair*): Perhaps you ought to see a nerve specialist.

CHARLES: I am not in the least neurotic and never have been.

RUTH: A psycho-analyst then.

CHARLES: I refuse to endure months of expensive humiliation only to be told at the end of it that at the age of four I was in love with my rocking-horse.

RUTH: What do you suggest then?

CHARLES: I don't suggest anything—I'm profoundly uneasy.

RUTH (*sits in arm-chair*): Perhaps there's something pressing on your brain.

CHARLES: If there were something pressing on my brain I should have violent headaches, shouldn't I?

RUTH: Not necessarily, an uncle of mine had a lump the size of a cricket ball pressing on his brain for years and he never felt a thing.

CHARLES: I know I should know if I had anything like that. (*Rises and goes over to fireplace.*)

RUTH: He didn't.

CHARLES: What happened to him?

RUTH: He had it taken out and he's been as bright as a button ever since.

CHARLES: Did he have any sort of delusions—did he think he saw things that weren't there?

RUTH: No, I don't think so.

CHARLES: Well, what the hell are we talking about him for then? It's sheer waste of valuable time.

RUTH: I only brought him up as an example.

CHARLES: I think I'm going mad.

RUTH: How do you feel now?

CHARLES: Physically, do you mean?

RUTH: Altogether.

CHARLES (*after due reflection*): Apart from being worried I feel quite normal.

RUTH: Good. You're not hearing or seeing anything in the least unusual?

CHARLES: Not a thing.

> ELVIRA *enters by windows carrying a bunch of grey roses. She crosses to writing-table up stage right and throws zinnias into waste-paper basket and puts her roses into the vase. The roses are as grey as the rest of her.*

ELVIRA: You've absolutely ruined that border by the sundial—it looks like a mixed salad.

CHARLES: Oh, my God!

RUTH: What's the matter now?

CHARLES: She's here again!

RUTH: What do you mean?—who's here again?

CHARLES: Elvira.

RUTH: Pull yourself together and don't be absurd.

ELVIRA: It's all those nasturtiums—they're so vulgar.

CHARLES: I like nasturtiums.

RUTH: You like what?

ELVIRA (*putting her grey roses into a vase*): They're all right in moderation but in a mass like that they look beastly.

CHARLES (*crosses over to right of* RUTH *centre*): Help me, Ruth—you've got to help me——

RUTH (*rises and retreats a pace to left*): What did you mean about nasturtiums?

CHARLES (*takes* RUTH'S *hands and comes round to left of her*): Never mind about that now—I tell you she's here again.

ELVIRA (*comes to above sofa*): You have been having a

nice scene, haven't you? I could hear you right down the garden.

CHARLES: Please mind your own business.

RUTH: If you behaving like a lunatic isn't my business nothing is.

ELVIRA: I expect it was about me, wasn't it? I know I ought to feel sorry but I'm not—I'm delighted.

CHARLES: How can you be so inconsiderate?

RUTH (*shrilly*): Inconsiderate!—I like that I must say——

CHARLES: Ruth—darling—please . . .

RUTH: I've done everything I can to help—I've controlled myself admirably—and I should like to say here and now that I don't believe a word about your damned hallucination—you're up to something, Charles —there's been a certain furtiveness in your manner for weeks—why don't you be honest and tell me what it is?

CHARLES: You're wrong—you're dead wrong—I haven't been in the least furtive—I——

RUTH: You're trying to upset me—— (*Breaks away from* CHARLES *to right centre.*) For some obscure reason you're trying to goad me into doing something that I might regret—I won't stand for it any more—you're making me utterly miserable. (*Crosses to sofa and falls into right end of it—she bursts into tears.*)

CHARLES (*crosses to* RUTH *right*): Ruth—please . . .

RUTH: Don't come near me——

ELVIRA: Let her have a nice cry—it'll do her good. (*Saunters round to down stage left.*)

CHARLES: You're utterly heartless!

RUTH: Heartless!

CHARLES (*wildly*): I was not talking to you—I was talking to Elvira.

RUTH: Go on talking to her then, talk to her until you're blue in the face but don't talk to me——

CHARLES (*crosses to* ELVIRA *down stage left*): Help me, Elvira——

ELVIRA: How?

CHARLES: Make her see you or something.

ELVIRA: I'm afraid I couldn't manage that—it's technically the most difficult business—frightfully complicated, you know—it takes years of study——

CHARLES: You are here, aren't you? You're not an illusion?

ELVIRA: I may be an illusion but I'm most definitely here.

CHARLES: How did you get here?

ELVIRA: I told you last night—I don't exactly know——

CHARLES: Well you must make me a promise that in future you only come and talk to me when I'm alone——

ELVIRA (*pouting*): How unkind you are—making me feel so unwanted—I've never been treated so rudely . . .

CHARLES: I don't mean to be rude, but you must see——

ELVIRA: It's all your own fault for having married a woman who is incapable of seeing beyond the nose on her face—if she had a grain of real sympathy or affection for you she'd believe what you tell her.

CHARLES: How could you expect anybody to believe this?

ELVIRA: You'd be surprised how gullible people are —we often laugh about it on the other side.

RUTH, *who has stopped crying and been staring at* CHARLES *in horror, suddenly gets up.*

RUTH *rises*, CHARLES *crosses to her down stage right.*

RUTH (*gently*): Charles——

CHARLES (*surprised at her tone*): Yes, dear——

RUTH: I'm awfully sorry I was cross——

CHARLES: But, my dear——

RUTH: I understand everything now—I do really——

CHARLES: You do?

RUTH (*patting his arm reassuringly*): Of course I do.

ELVIRA: Look out—she's up to something——

CHARLES: Will you please be quiet.

RUTH: Of course, darling—we'll all be quiet, won't we? We'll be as quiet as little mice.

CHARLES: Ruth dear, listen——

RUTH: I want you to come upstairs with me and go to bed——

ELVIRA: The way that woman harps on bed is nothing short of erotic.

CHARLES: I'll deal with you later——

RUTH: Very well, darling—come along.

CHARLES: What are you up to?

RUTH: I'm not up to anything—I just want you to go quietly to bed and wait there until Doctor Bradman comes——

CHARLES: No, Ruth—you're wrong——

RUTH (*firmly*): Come, dear——

ELVIRA: She'll have you in a strait-jacket before you know where you are——

CHARLES (*comes to* ELVIRA—*frantically*): Help me— you must help me——

ELVIRA (*enjoying herself*): My dear, I would with pleasure, but I can't think how——

CHARLES: I can. (*Back to* RUTH.) Listen, Ruth——

RUTH: Yes, dear?

CHARLES: If I promise to go to bed will you let me stay here for five minutes longer?

RUTH: I really think it would be better——

CHARLES: Bear with me—however mad it may seem —bear with me for just five minutes longer——

RUTH (*leaving go of him*): Very well—what is it?

CHARLES: Sit down.

RUTH (*sitting down*): All right—there.

CHARLES: Now listen—listen carefully——

ELVIRA: Have a cigarette, it will soothe your nerves.

CHARLES: I don't want a cigarette.

RUTH (*indulgently*): Then you shan't have one, darling.

CHARLES: Ruth, I want to explain to you clearly and without emotion that beyond any shadow of doubt, the ghost or shade or whatever you like to call it of my first wife Elvira, is in this room now.

RUTH: Yes, dear.

CHARLES: I know you don't believe it and are trying valiantly to humour me but I intend to prove it to you.

RUTH: Why not lie down and have a nice rest and you can prove anything you want to later on.

CHARLES: She may not be here later on.

ELVIRA: Don't worry—she will!

CHARLES: Oh God!

RUTH: Hush, dear.

CHARLES (*to* ELVIRA): Promise you'll do what I ask?

ELVIRA: That all depends what it is.

CHARLES (*between them both, facing up stage*): Ruth— you see that bowl of flowers on the piano?

RUTH: Yes, dear—I did it myself this morning.

ELVIRA: Very untidily if I may say so.

CHARLES: You may not.

RUTH: Very well—I never will again—I promise.

CHARLES: Elvira will now carry that bowl of flowers to the mantelpiece and back again. You will, Elvira, won't you—just to please me?

ELVIRA: I don't really see why I should—you've been quite insufferable to me ever since I materialised.

CHARLES: Please.

ELVIRA: All right, I will just this once—not that I approve of all these Maskelyne and Devant carryings on. (*She goes over to the piano.*)

CHARLES (*crosses to mantelpiece*): Now, Ruth—watch carefully.

RUTH (*patiently*): Very well, dear.

CHARLES: Go on, Elvira—take it to the mantelpiece and back again.

> ELVIRA *takes bowl of pansies off piano—brings it slowly down stage below arm-chair to fire then suddenly pushes it towards* RUTH's *face, who jumps up.*

RUTH (*furiously*): How dare you, Charles! You ought to be ashamed of yourself.

CHARLES: What on earth for?

RUTH (*hysterically*): It's a trick—I know perfectly well it's a trick—you've been working up to this—it's all part of some horrible plan. . . .

CHARLES: It isn't—I swear it isn't—Elvira—do something else for God's sake——

ELVIRA: Certainly—anything to oblige.

RUTH (*becoming really frightened*): You want to get rid of me—you're trying to drive me out of my mind——

CHARLES: Don't be so silly.

RUTH: You're cruel and sadistic and I'll never forgive you. . . .

ELVIRA *waltzes with chair from down stage left and puts it back and stands above window.*

*Making a dive for the door—crosses between arm-chair and sofa—*CHARLES *follows and catches her up stage left.* I'm not going to put up with this any more——

CHARLES (*holding her*): You must believe it—you must——

RUTH: Let me go immediately . . .

CHARLES: That was Elvira—I swear it was——

RUTH (*struggling*): Let me go . . .

CHARLES: Ruth—please——

RUTH *breaks away to windows.* ELVIRA *shuts them in her face and crosses quickly to mantelpiece.* RUTH *turns.*

RUTH (*looking at* CHARLES *with eyes of horror*): Charles —this is madness—sheer madness—it's some sort of auto-suggestion, isn't it—some form of hypnotism, swear to me it's only that—(*rushes to* CHARLES *centre*)— swear to me it's only that.

ELVIRA (*taking an expensive vase from the mantelpiece and crashing it into the grate*): Hypnotism my foot!

RUTH *gives a scream and goes into violent hysterics as the* CURTAIN FALLS

ACT II

SCENE II

The time is late on the following afternoon.

When the curtain rises RUTH *is sitting alone at the tea-table, which is set in front of the fire. After a moment or two she gets up and, frowning thoughtfully, goes over to the mantelpiece and takes a cigarette out of a box.*

As she returns to the table the front-door bell rings. She hears it and straightens herself as though preparing for a difficult interview.

EDITH *enters.*

EDITH: Madame Arcati.

　　　EDITH *steps aside and* MADAME ARCATI *comes in.*
　　　EDITH *goes out.*

　　　MADAME ARCATI *is wearing a tweed coat and skirt and a great many amber beads and, possibly, a beret.*

MADAME ARCATI: My dear Mrs. Condomine—I came directly I got your message.

RUTH: That was very kind of you.

MADAME ARCATI (*briskly*): Kind—nonsense—nothing kind about it—I look upon it as an outing.

RUTH: I'm so glad—will you have some tea?

MADAME ARCATI: China or Indian?

RUTH: China.

MADAME ARCATI: Good. I never touch Indian, it upsets my vibrations.

RUTH: Do sit down.

　　　RUTH *sits left end of sofa and pours tea.*

MADAME ARCATI (*turning her head and sniffing*): I find this room very interesting—very interesting indeed—I noticed it the other night.

RUTH: I'm not entirely surprised.

MADAME ARCATI (*sitting down and pulling off her gloves*): Have you ever been to Cowden Manor?

RUTH: No, I'm afraid I haven't.

MADAME ARCATI: That's very interesting too—strikes you like a blow between the eyes the moment you walk into the drawing-room. Two lumps of sugar please and no milk at all.

RUTH: I am profoundly disturbed, Madame Arcati, and I want your help.

MADAME ARCATI: Aha! I thought as much. What's in these sandwiches?

RUTH: Cucumber.

MADAME ARCATI: Couldn't be better. (*She takes one.*) Fire away.

RUTH: It's most awfully difficult to explain——

MADAME ARCATI: Facts first—explanations afterwards.

RUTH: It's the facts that are difficult to explain—they're so fantastic——

MADAME ARCATI: Facts very often are. Take creative talent for instance, how do you account for that? Look at Shakespeare and Michael Angelo! Try to explain Mozart snatching sounds out of the air and putting them down on paper when he was practically a baby—facts—plain facts. I know it's the fashion nowadays to ascribe it all to glands but my reply to that is fiddlededee.

RUTH: Yes, I'm sure you're quite right.

MADAME ARCATI: There are more things in heaven and earth than are dreamt of in your philosophy, Mrs. Condomine.

RUTH: There certainly are.

MADAME ARCATI: Come now—take the plunge—out with it. You've heard strange noises in the night no doubt—boards creaking—doors slamming—subdued moaning in the passages—is that it?

RUTH: No—I'm afraid it isn't.

MADAME ARCATI: No sudden gusts of cold wind, I hope?

RUTH: No, it's worse than that.

MADAME ARCATI: I'm all attention.

RUTH (*with an effort*): I know it sounds idiotic but the other night—during the séance—something happened——

MADAME ARCATI: I knew it! Probably a poltergeist, they're enormously cunning you know, they sometimes lie doggo for days . . .

RUTH: You know that my husband was married before?

MADAME ARCATI: Yes—I have heard it mentioned.

RUTH: His first wife, Elvira, died comparatively young . . .

MADAME ARCATI (*sharply*): Where?

RUTH: Here—in this house—in this very room.

MADAME ARCATI (*whistling*): Whew! I'm beginning to see daylight——

RUTH: She was convalescing after pneumonia and one evening she started to laugh helplessly at one of the B.B.C. musical programmes and died of a heart attack.

MADAME ARCATI: And she materialised the other evening—after I had gone?

RUTH: Not to me, but to my husband.

MADAME ARCATI *rises*.

MADAME ARCATI (*impulsively*): Capital—capital—oh, but that's splendid!

RUTH (*coldly*): From your own professional standpoint I can see that it might be regarded as a major achievement——

MADAME ARCATI (*delighted*): A triumph, my dear! Nothing more nor less than a triumph!

RUTH: But from my own personal point of view it is, to say the least of it, embarrassing.

MADAME ARCATI (*walking about the room*): At last—at last—a genuine materialisation!

RUTH: Please sit down again, Madame Arcati . . .

MADAME ARCATI: How could anyone sit down at a moment like this—it's tremendous! I haven't had such a success since the Sudbury case . . .

RUTH (*sharply*): Nevertheless I must insist upon you sitting down and controlling your natural exuberance. I appreciate fully your pride in your achievement but I would like to point out that it has made my position in this house untenable and that I hold you entirely responsible.

MADAME ARCATI (*comes to arm-chair and sits— contrite*): Forgive me, Mrs. Condomine—I am being abominably selfish—how can I help you?

RUTH: How? By sending her back immediately to where she came from, of course.

MADAME ARCATI: I'm afraid that that is easier said than done.

RUTH: Do you mean to tell me that she is liable to stay here indefinitely?

MADAME ARCATI: It's difficult to say—I fear it depends largely on her.

RUTH: But my dear Madame Arcati. . . .

MADAME ARCATI: Where is she now?

RUTH: My husband has driven her into Folkestone— apparently she was anxious to see an old friend of hers who is staying at the Grand.

    MADAME ARCATI *produces note-book from bag and takes notes through following speeches.*

MADAME ARCATI: Forgive this formality, but I shall have to make a report to the Psychical Research people . . .

RUTH: I would be very much obliged if there were no names mentioned.

MADAME ARCATI: The report will be confidential.

RUTH: This is a small village you know, and gossip would be most undesirable.

MADAME ARCATI: I quite understand. You say she is visible only to your husband?

RUTH: Yes.

MADAME ARCATI: Visible only to husband. Audible too—I presume?

RUTH: Extremely audible.

MADAME ARCATI: Extremely audible. Your husband was devoted to her?

RUTH (*with slight irritation*): I believe so!

MADAME ARCATI: Husband devoted.

RUTH: It was apparently a reasonable happy marriage . . .

MADAME ARCATI: Oh, tut tut!

RUTH: I beg your pardon?

MADAME ARCATI: When did she pass over?

RUTH: Seven years ago.

MADAME ARCATI: Aha! That means she must have been on the waiting list.

RUTH: Waiting list?

MADAME ARCATI: Yes, otherwise she would have got beyond the materialisation stage by now. She must have marked herself down for a return visit and she'd never have been able to manage it unless there were a strong influence at work . . .

RUTH: Do you mean that Charles—my husband—wanted her back all that much?

MADAME ARCATI: Possibly, or it might have been her own determination. . . .

RUTH: That sounds much more likely.

MADAME ARCATI: Would you say that she was a woman of strong character?

RUTH (*with rising annoyance*): I really don't know, Madame Arcati—I never met her. Nor am I particularly interested in how and why she got here, I am solely concerned with the question of how to get her away again as soon as possible.

MADAME ARCATI: I fully sympathise with you, Mrs. Condomine, and I assure you I will do anything in my power to help—but at the moment I fear I cannot offer any great hopes.

RUTH: But I always understood that there was a way of exorcising ghosts—some sort of ritual?

MADAME ARCATI: You mean the old Bell and Book method?

RUTH: Yes—I suppose I do.

MADAME ARCATI: Poppycock, Mrs. Condomine. It was quite effective in the old days of genuine religious belief but that's all changed now, I believe the decline of faith in the Spirit World has been causing grave concern. . . .

RUTH (*impatiently*): Has it indeed?

MADAME ARCATI: There was a time of course when a drop of holy water could send even a poltergeist scampering for cover, but not any more—'Ou sont les neiges d'Antan?'

RUTH: Be that as it may, Madame Arcati, I must beg of you to do your utmost to dematerialise my husband's first wife as soon as possible.

MADAME ARCATI: The time has come for me to admit to you frankly, Mrs. Condomine, that I haven't the faintest idea how to set about it.

RUTH (*rises*): Do you mean to sit there and tell me that having mischievously conjured up this ghost or spirit or whatever she is and placed me in a hideous position you are unable to do anything about it at all?

MADAME ARCATI: Honesty is the best policy.

RUTH: But it's outrageous! I ought to hand you over to the police. (*Crosses to fireplace.*)

MADAME ARCATI: You go too far, Mrs. Condomine.

RUTH (*furiously*): I go too far indeed? Do you realise what your insane amateur muddling has done?

MADAME ARCATI: I have been a professional since I was a child, Mrs. Condomine—'Amateur' is a word I cannot tolerate.

RUTH: It seems to me to be the highest height of amateurishness to evoke malignant spirits and not be able to get rid of them again.

MADAME ARCATI (*with dignity*): I was in a trance. Anything might happen when I am in a trance.

RUTH: Well all I can suggest is that you go into another one immediately and get this damned woman out of my house.

MADAME ARCATI: I can't go into trances at a moment's notice—it takes hours of preparation—in addition to which I have to be extremely careful of my diet for days beforehand. To-day, for instance, I happened to lunch with friends and had pigeon pie which, plus these cucumber sandwiches, would make a trance out of the question.

RUTH: Well, you'll have to do something.

MADAME ARCATI: I will report the whole matter to the Society for Psychical Research at the earliest possible moment.

RUTH: Will they be able to do anything?

MADAME ARCATI: I doubt it. They'd send an investigation committee, I expect, and do a lot of questioning and wall tapping and mumbo jumbo and then they'd have a conference and you would probably have to go up to London to testify——

RUTH (*near tears*): It's too humiliating—it really is.

MADAME ARCATI (*rises and goes to* RUTH): Please try not to upset yourself—nothing can be achieved by upsetting yourself.

RUTH: It's all very fine for you to talk like that, Madame Arcati—you don't seem to have the faintest realisation of my position.

MADAME ARCATI: Try to look on the bright side.

RUTH: Bright side indeed! If your husband's first wife suddenly appeared from the grave and came to live in the house with you, do you suppose you'd be able to look on the bright side?

MADAME ARCATI: I resent your tone, Mrs. Condomine, I really do.

RUTH: You most decidedly have no right to—you are entirely to blame for the whole horrible situation.

MADAME ARCATI: Kindly remember that I came here the other night on your own invitation.

RUTH: On my husband's invitation.

MADAME ARCATI: I did what I was requested to do, which was to give a séance and establish contact with the other side—I had no idea that there was any ulterior motive mixed up with it.

RUTH: Ulterior motive?

MADAME ARCATI: Your husband was obviously eager to get in touch with his former wife. If I had been aware of that at the time I should naturally have consulted you beforehand—after all 'Noblesse oblige'!

RUTH: He had no intention of trying to get in touch with anyone—the whole thing was planned in order for him to get material for a mystery story he is writing about a homicidal medium.

MADAME ARCATI (*drawing herself up*): Am I to understand that I was only invited in a spirit of mockery?

RUTH: Not at all—he merely wanted to make notes of some of the tricks of the trade.

MADAME ARCATI (*incensed*): Tricks of the trade! Insufferable! I've never been so insulted in my life. I feel we have nothing more to say to one another, Mrs. Condomine—Good-bye. (*Turns away*.)

RUTH: Please don't go—please——

MADAME ARCATI (*turns and faces* RUTH): Your attitude from the outset has been most unpleasant, Mrs. Condomine. Some of your remarks have been discourteous in the extreme and I should like to say without umbrage, that if you and your husband were foolish enough to tamper with the unseen for paltry motives and in a spirit of ribaldry, whatever has happened to you is your own fault and, to coin a phrase, as far as I'm concerned you can stew in your own juice!

MADAME ARCATI *goes majestically from the room.*

RUTH (*puts out cigarette in ash-tray on small table*): Damn—Damn—Damn!

After a moment or two CHARLES *comes in with* ELVIRA.

CHARLES: What on earth was Madame Arcati doing here?

RUTH: She came to tea.

CHARLES: Did you ask her?

RUTH: Of course I did.

76

CHARLES: You never told me you were going to.

RUTH: You never told me you were going to ask Elvira to live with us.

CHARLES: I didn't.

ELVIRA (*sauntering over to the tea-table*): Oh, yes, you did, darling—it was your sub-conscious.

CHARLES: What was the old girl so cross about—she practically cut me dead.

RUTH: I told her the truth, about why we invited her the other night.

CHARLES: That was quite unnecessary and most unkind.

RUTH: She needed taking down a bit, she was blowing herself out like a pouter pigeon.

CHARLES: Why did you ask her to tea?

ELVIRA: To get me exorcised, of course. Oh, dear, I wish I could have a cucumber sandwich—I did love them so.

CHARLES: Is that true, Ruth?

RUTH: Is what true?

CHARLES: What Elvira said.

RUTH: You know perfectly well I can't hear what Elvira says.

CHARLES: She said that you got Madame Arcati here to try to get her exorcised. Is that true?

RUTH: We discussed the possibilities.

ELVIRA (*sits in arm-chair with her legs over left arm*): There's a snake in the grass for you.

CHARLES: You had no right to do such a thing without consulting me.

RUTH: I have every right—this situation is absolutely impossible and you know it.

CHARLES: If only you'd make an effort and try to be a

77

little more friendly to Elvira we might all have quite a jolly time.

RUTH: I have no wish to have a jolly time with Elvira.

ELVIRA: She's certainly very bad tempered, isn't she? I can't think why you married her.

CHARLES: She's naturally a bit upset—we must make allowances.

ELVIRA: I was never bad tempered though, was I, darling? Not even when you were beastly to me——

CHARLES: I was never beastly to you.

RUTH (*exasperated*): Where is Elvira at the moment?

CHARLES: In the chair by the table.

RUTH: Now look here, Elvira—I shall have to call you Elvira, shan't I? I can't very well go on saying Mrs. Condomine all the time, it would sound too silly. . . .

ELVIRA: I don't see why.

RUTH: Did she say anything?

CHARLES: She said she'd like nothing better.

ELVIRA (*giggling*): You really are sweet, Charles, darling—I worship you.

RUTH: I wish to be absolutely honest with you, Elvira. . . .

ELVIRA: Hold on to your hats, boys!

RUTH: I admit I did ask Madame Arcati here with a view to getting you exorcised and I think that if you were in my position you'd have done exactly the same thing—wouldn't you?

ELVIRA: I shouldn't have done it so obviously.

RUTH: What did she say?

CHARLES: Nothing—she just nodded and smiled.

RUTH (*with a forced smile*): Thank you, Elvira—that's

generous of you. I really would so much rather that there were no misunderstandings between us. . . .

CHARLES: That's very sensible, Ruth—I agree entirely.

RUTH (*to* ELVIRA): I want, before we go any further, to ask you a frank question. Why did you really come here? I don't see that you could have hoped to have achieved anything by it beyond the immediate joke of making Charles into a sort of astral bigamist.

ELVIRA: I came because the power of Charles's love tugged and tugged and tugged at me. Didn't it, my sweet?

RUTH: What did she say?

CHARLES: She said that she came because she wanted to see me again.

RUTH: Well, she's done that now, hasn't she?

CHARLES: We can't be inhospitable, Ruth.

RUTH: I have no wish to be inhospitable, but I should like to have just an idea of how long you intend to stay, Elvira?

ELVIRA: I don't know—I really don't know! (*She giggles.*) Isn't it awful?

CHARLES: She says she doesn't know.

RUTH: Surely that's a little inconsiderate?

ELVIRA: Didn't the old spiritualist have any constructive ideas about getting rid of me?

CHARLES: What did Madame Arcati say?

RUTH: She said she couldn't do a thing.

ELVIRA (*rises and crosses to window*): Hurray!

CHARLES: Don't be upset, Ruth dear—we shall soon adjust ourselves, you know—you must admit it's a unique experience—I can see no valid reason why we shouldn't get a great deal of fun out of it.

RUTH: Fun! Charles, how can you—you must be out of your mind!

CHARLES: Not at all—I thought I was at first—but now I must say I'm beginning to enjoy myself.

RUTH (*bursting into tears*): Oh, Charles—Charles. . . .

ELVIRA: She's off again.

CHARLES: You really must not be so callous, Elvira—try to see her point a little——

RUTH: I suppose she said something insulting. . . .

CHARLES: No, dear, she didn't do anything of the sort.

RUTH: Now look here, Elvira. . . .

CHARLES: She's over by the window now.

RUTH: Why the hell can't she stay in the same place?

ELVIRA: Temper again—my poor Charles, what a terrible life you must lead.

CHARLES: Do shut up, darling, you'll only make everything worse.

RUTH: Who was that 'darling' addressed to—her or me?

CHARLES: Both of you.

RUTH *rises*.

RUTH (*stamping her foot*): This is intolerable!

CHARLES: For heaven's sake don't get into another state.

RUTH (*furiously*): I've been doing my level best to control myself ever since yesterday morning and I'm damned if I'm going to try any more, the strain is too much. She has the advantage of being able to say whatever she pleases without me being able to hear her, but she can hear me all right, can't she, without any modified interpreting?

CHARLES: Modified interpreting! I don't know what you mean.

RUTH: Oh, yes, you do—you haven't told me once what she really said—you wouldn't dare. Judging from her photograph she's the type who would use most unpleasant language. . . .

CHARLES: Ruth—you're not to talk like that.

RUTH: I've been making polite conversation all through dinner last night and breakfast and lunch to-day—and it's been a nightmare—and I am not going to do it any more. I don't like Elvira any more than she likes me and what's more I'm certain that I never could have, dead or alive. If, since her untimely arrival here the other evening, she had shown the slightest sign of good manners, the slightest sign of breeding, I might have felt differently towards her, but all she has done is try to make mischief between us and have private jokes with you against me. I am now going up to my room and I shall have my dinner on a tray. You and she can have the house to yourselves and joke and gossip with each other to your heart's content. The first thing in the morning I am going up to London to interview the Psychical Research Society and if they fail me I shall go straight to the Archbishop of Canterbury. . . .

> *Exit* RUTH.

CHARLES (*making a movement to follow her*): Ruth . . .

ELVIRA: Let her go—she'll calm down later on.

CHARLES: It's unlike her to behave like this—she's generally so equable.

ELVIRA: No, she isn't, not really, her mouth gives her away—it's a hard mouth, Charles.

CHARLES: Her mouth's got nothing to do with it—I resent you discussing Ruth as though she were a horse.

ELVIRA: Do you love her?

CHARLES: Of course I do.

ELVIRA: As much as you loved me?

CHARLES: Don't be silly—it's all entirely different.

ELVIRA: I'm so glad. Nothing could ever have been quite the same, could it?

CHARLES: You always behaved very badly.

ELVIRA: Oh, Charles!

CHARLES: I'm grieved to see that your sojourn in the other world hasn't improved you in the least.

ELVIRA (*curls up in right end of sofa*): Go on, darling— I love it when you pretend to be cross with me. . . .

CHARLES: I'm going up to talk to Ruth.

ELVIRA: Cowardy custard.

CHARLES: Don't be idiotic. I can't let her go like that —I must be a little nice and sympathetic to her.

ELVIRA: I don't see why! If she's set on being disagreeable I should just let her get on with it.

CHARLES: The whole business is very difficult for her —we must be fair.

ELVIRA: She should learn to be more adaptable.

CHARLES: She probably will in time—it's been a shock——

ELVIRA: Has it been a shock for you too, darling?

CHARLES: Of course—what did you expect?

ELVIRA: A nice shock?

CHARLES: What do you want, Elvira?

ELVIRA: Want? I don't know what you mean.

CHARLES: I remember that whenever you were overpoweringly demure it usually meant that you wanted something.

ELVIRA: It's horrid of you to be so suspicious. All I want is to be with you.

CHARLES: Well you are.

ELVIRA: I mean alone, darling. If you go and

pamper Ruth and smarm her over, she'll probably come flouncing down again and our lovely quiet evening together will be spoilt.

CHARLES: You're incorrigibly selfish.

ELVIRA: Well, I haven't seen you for seven years—it's only natural that I should want a little time alone with you—to talk over old times. I'll let you go up just for a little while if you really think it's your duty.

CHARLES: Of course it is.

ELVIRA (*smiling*): Then I don't mind.

CHARLES: You're disgraceful, Elvira.

ELVIRA: You won't be long, will you? You'll come down again very soon?

CHARLES: I shall probably dress for dinner while I'm upstairs—you can read the *Tatler* or something.

ELVIRA: Darling, you don't have to dress—for me.

CHARLES: I always dress for dinner.

ELVIRA: What are you going to have? I should like to watch you eat something really delicious. . . .

CHARLES (*moves up to door*): Be a good girl now—you can play the gramophone if you like.

ELVIRA (*demurely*): Thank you, Charles.

    CHARLES *goes out.*

    ELVIRA *gets up, looks in the gramophone cupboard, finds the record of 'Always' and puts it on.*

    She starts to waltz lightly round the room to it.

    EDITH *comes in to fetch the tea-tray. She sees the gramophone playing by itself and so she turns it off and puts the record back in the cupboard. While she is picking up the tray* ELVIRA *takes the record out and puts it on again.*

    EDITH *gives a shriek, drops the tray and rushes out of the room.* ELVIRA *continues to waltz gaily.*

CURTAIN

ACT II

Scene III

The time is evening several days later.

When the curtain rises Mrs. Bradman *is sitting in an arm-chair.* Ruth *is standing by the window drumming on the pane with her fingers.*

Mrs. Bradman: Does it show any signs of clearing?

Ruth: No, it's still pouring.

Mrs. Bradman: I do sympathise with you, really I do—it's really been quite a chapter of accidents, hasn't it?

Ruth: It certainly has.

Mrs. Bradman: That happens sometimes, you know—everything seems to go wrong at once—exactly as though there were some evil forces at work. I remember once when George and I went away for a fortnight's holiday not long after we were married—we were dogged by bad luck from beginning to end—the weather was vile—George sprained his ankle—I caught a terrible cold and had to stay in bed for two days—and to crown everything the lamp fell over in the sitting-room and set fire to the treatise George had written on hyperplasia of the abdominal glands.

Ruth: How dreadful! (*Absently.*)

Mrs. Bradman: He had to write it all over again—every single word.

Ruth: You're sure you wouldn't like a cocktail or some sherry or anything?

Mrs. Bradman: No, thank you—really not—George

84

will be down in a minute and we've got to go like lightning—we were supposed to be at the Wilmot's at seven and it's nearly that now.

RUTH (*coming away from the window*): I think I'll have a little sherry—I feel I need it. (*Moves up to table and pours sherry.*)

MRS. BRADMAN: Don't worry about your husband's arm, Mrs. Condomine—I'm sure it's only a sprain.

RUTH: It's not his arm I'm worried about.

MRS. BRADMAN: And I'm sure Edith will be up and about again in a few days. . . .

RUTH: My cook gave notice this morning.

MRS. BRADMAN: Well, really! Servants are awful, aren't they? Not a shred of gratitude—at the first sign of trouble they run out on you—like rats leaving a sinking ship.

RUTH: I can't feel that your simile was entirely fortunate, Mrs. Bradman.

MRS. BRADMAN (*flustered*): Oh, I didn't mean that, really I didn't!

DR. BRADMAN *comes in.*

DR. BRADMAN: Nothing to worry about, Mrs. Condomine—it's only a slight strain. . . .

RUTH: I'm so relieved.

DR. BRADMAN: He made a good deal of fuss when I examined it—men are much worse patients than women, you know—particularly highly strung men like your husband.

RUTH: Is he so highly strung, do you think?

DR. BRADMAN: Yes, as a matter of fact I wanted to talk to you about that. I'm afraid he's been over-working lately.

RUTH (*frowning*): Overworking?

DR. BRADMAN: He's in rather a nervous condition—nothing serious, you understand——

RUTH: What makes you think so?

DR. BRADMAN: I know the symptoms. Of course the shock of his fall might have something to do with it, but I certainly should advise a complete rest for a couple of weeks——

RUTH: You mean he ought to go away?

DR. BRADMAN: I do. In cases like that a change of atmosphere can work wonders.

RUTH: What symptoms did you notice?

DR. BRADMAN: Oh, nothing to be unduly alarmed about—a certain air of strain—an inability to focus his eyes on the person he is talking to—a few rather marked irrelevancies in his conversation.

Ruth: I see. Can you remember any specific example?

DR. BRADMAN: Oh, he suddenly shouted 'What are you doing in the bathroom?' and then, a little later, while I was writing him a prescription he suddenly said 'For God's sake behave yourself!'

MRS. BRADMAN: How extraordinary.

RUTH (*nervously*): He often goes on like that—particularly when he's immersed in writing a book——

DR. BRADMAN: Oh, I am not in the least perturbed about it really—but I do think a rest and a change would be a good idea.

RUTH: Thank you so much, Doctor. Would you like some sherry?

DR. BRADMAN: No, thank you—we really must be off.

RUTH: How is poor Edith?

DR. BRADMAN: She'll be all right in a few days—she's still recovering from the concussion.

MRS. BRADMAN: It's funny, isn't it, that both your housemaid and your husband should fall down on the same day, isn't it?

RUTH: Yes, if that sort of thing amuses you.

MRS. BRADMAN (*giggling nervously*): Of course I didn't mean it like that, Mrs. Condomine.

DR. BRADMAN: Come along, my dear—you're talking too much as usual.

MRS. BRADMAN: You are horrid, George.

MRS. BRADMAN *rises and crosses to* RUTH.
Good-bye, Mrs. Condomine——

RUTH (*shaking hands*): Good-bye.

DR. BRADMAN (*also shaking hands*): I'll pop in and have a look at both patients some time to-morrow morning.

RUTH: Thank you so much.

CHARLES *comes in. His left arm is in a sling.* ELVIRA *follows him in.*

DR. BRADMAN: Well—how does it feel?

CHARLES: All right.

DR. BRADMAN: It's only a slight sprain, you know.

CHARLES: Is this damned sling really essential?

DR. BRADMAN: It's a wise precaution—it will prevent you using your left hand except when it's really necessary.

CHARLES: I had intended to drive into Folkestone this evening.

DR. BRADMAN: It would be much better if you didn't.

CHARLES: It's extremely inconvenient——

RUTH: You can easily wait and go to-morrow, Charles.

ELVIRA: I can't stand another of those dreary evenings at home, Charles—it'll drive me dotty—and I haven't seen a movie for seven years. . . .

CHARLES: Let me be the first to congratulate you.

DR. BRADMAN (*kindly*): What's that, old man?

RUTH (*with intense meaning*): Charles, dear—try to be sensible I implore you.

CHARLES: Sorry—I forgot.

DR. BRADMAN: You can drive the car if you promise to go very slowly and carefully. Your gear change is on the right, isn't it?

CHARLES: Yes.

DR. BRADMAN: Well, use your left hand as little as possible.

CHARLES: All right.

RUTH: You'd much better stay at home.

DR. BRADMAN: Couldn't you drive him in?

RUTH (*stiffly*): I'm afraid not—I have lots to do in the house and there's Edith to be attended to.

DR. BRADMAN: Well, I'll leave you to fight it out among yourselves. (*To* CHARLES.) But remember if you do insist on going—carefully does it—the roads are very slippery anyhow. Come along, Violet.

MRS. BRADMAN: Good-bye again—good-bye, Mr. Condomine.

CHARLES: Good-bye.

CHARLES *follows the* BRADMANS *off*.

RUTH (*left alone, at fire, speaks to* ELVIRA *right down stage*): You really are infuriating, Elvira—surely you could wait and go to the movies another night.

ELVIRA *takes rose out of vase on centre table and throws it at* RUTH *and runs out of windows*.

(*Picking up the rose and putting it back in the vase.*) And stop behaving like a schoolgirl—you're old enough to know better.

CHARLES (*comes in*): What?

RUTH (*puts rose back in vase*): I was talking to Elvira.

CHARLES: She isn't here.

RUTH: She was a moment ago—she threw a rose at me.

CHARLES: She's been very high-spirited all day. I know this mood of old. It usually meant that she was up to something.

> *Pause.* RUTH *shuts door and then comes across below sofa to* CHARLES.

RUTH: You're sure she isn't here?

CHARLES: Quite sure.

RUTH: I want to talk to you.

CHARLES: Oh God!

RUTH: I must—it's important.

CHARLES: You've behaved very well for the last few days, Ruth—you're not going to start making scenes again, are you?

RUTH: I resent that air of patronage, Charles. I have behaved well, as you call it, because there was nothing else to do, but I think it only fair to warn you that I offer no guarantee for the future. My patience is being stretched to its uttermost.

CHARLES: As far as I can see the position is just as difficult for Elvira as it is for you—if not more so. The poor little thing comes back trustingly after all those years in the other world and what is she faced with? Nothing but brawling and hostility!

RUTH: What did she expect?

CHARLES: Surely even an ectoplasmic manifestation has the right to expect a little of the milk of human kindness?

RUTH: Milk of human fiddlesticks.

CHARLES: That just doesn't make sense, dear.

RUTH (*comes to* CHARLES *and leans over him*): Elvira is about as trusting as a puff-adder.

CHARLES: You're granite, Ruth—sheer unyielding granite.

RUTH: And a good deal more dangerous into the bargain.

CHARLES: Dangerous? I never heard anything so ridiculous. How could a poor lonely wistful little spirit like Elvira be dangerous?

RUTH: Quite easily—and she is. She's beginning to show her hand.

CHARLES: How do you mean—in what way?

RUTH: This is a fight, Charles—a bloody battle—a duel to the death between Elvira and me. Don't you realise that?

CHARLES: Melodramatic hysteria.

RUTH: It isn't melodramatic hysteria—it's true. Can't you see?

CHARLES: No, I can't. You're imagining things— jealousy causes people to have the most curious delusions.

RUTH (*pause*): I am making every effort not to lose my temper with you, Charles, but I must say you are making it increasingly difficult for me.

CHARLES: All this talk of battles and duels——

RUTH: She came here with one purpose and one purpose only—and if you can't see it you're a bigger fool than I thought you.

CHARLES: What purpose could she have had beyond a natural desire to see me again? After all you must remember that she was extremely attached to me, poor child.

RUTH: Her purpose is perfectly obvious. It is to get you to herself for ever.

CHARLES: That's absurd—how could she?

RUTH: By killing you off, of course.

CHARLES: Killing me off. You're mad!

RUTH: Why do you suppose Edith fell down the stairs and nearly cracked her skull?

CHARLES: What's Edith got to do with it?

RUTH: Because the whole of the top stair was covered with axle grease—Cook discovered it afterwards.

CHARLES: You're making this up, Ruth. . . .

RUTH: I'm not. I swear I'm not. Why do you suppose when you were lopping that dead branch off the pear tree that the ladder broke? Because it had been practically sawn through on both sides?

CHARLES (*rises*): But why should she want to kill me? I could understand her wanting to kill you, but why me?

RUTH: If you were dead it would be her final triumph over me. She'd have you with her for ever on her damned astral plane and I'd be left high and dry. She's probably planning a sort of spiritual re-marriage. I wouldn't put anything past her.

CHARLES (*really shocked*): Ruth!

RUTH: Don't you see now?

CHARLES: She couldn't be so sly, so wicked—she couldn't.

RUTH: Couldn't she just?

CHARLES: I grant you that as a character she was always rather light and irresponsible but I would never have believed her capable of low cunning——

RUTH: Perhaps the spirit world has deteriorated her.

CHARLES: Oh Ruth!

RUTH: For heaven's sake stop looking like a wounded spaniel and concentrate—this is serious.

CHARLES: What are we to do?

RUTH: You're not to let her know that we suspect a thing—behave perfectly ordinarily—as though nothing had happened. I'm going to Madame Arcati immediately—I don't care how cross she is, she's got to help us—even if she can't get rid of Elvira she must have some technical method of rendering her harmless. If a trance is necessary she shall go into a trance if I have to beat her into it. I'll be back in a half an hour—tell Elvira I've gone to see the vicar——

CHARLES: This is appalling. . . .

RUTH: Never mind about that—remember now, don't give yourself away by so much as a flick of an eyelid——

ELVIRA *comes in from the garden.*

CHARLES: Look out. . . .

RUTH: What?

CHARLES: I merely said it's a nice look out.

ELVIRA: What's a nice look out?

CHARLES: The weather, Elvira—the glass is going down and down and down—it's positively macabre.

ELVIRA: I find it difficult to believe that you and Ruth, at this particular moment, can't think of anything more interesting to talk about than the weather.

RUTH (*rises*): I can't stand this any more. I really can't.

CHARLES: Ruth dear—please. . . .

ELVIRA: Has she broken out again?

RUTH: What did she say?

CHARLES: She asked if you had broken out again.

RUTH: How dare you talk like that, Elvira?

CHARLES: Now then, Ruth. . . .

RUTH (*with dignity*): Charles and I were not talking about the weather, Elvira, as you so very shrewdly suspected. I should loathe you to think that we had any secrets from you.

> RUTH *addressing* ELVIRA *up stage.* CHARLES *motions that she is behind her.* RUTH *turns and addresses her down stage.* ELVIRA *crosses below her to above sofa.*

(*Repeats.*) And so I will explain exactly what we were talking about. I was trying to persuade him *not* to drive you into Folkestone this evening, it will be bad for his arm and you can perfectly easily wait until to-morrow. However as he seems to be determined to place your wishes before mine in everything, I have nothing further to say. I'm sure I hope you both enjoy yourselves.

> *She goes out and slams the door.*

ELVIRA: Oh, Charles—have you been beastly to her?

CHARLES: No—Ruth doesn't like being thwarted any more than you do.

ELVIRA: She's a woman of sterling character. It's a pity she's so ungiving.

CHARLES: As I told you before—I would rather not discuss Ruth with you—it makes me uncomfortable.

ELVIRA: I won't mention her again. Are you ready?

CHARLES: What for?

ELVIRA: To go to Folkestone of course.

CHARLES: I want a glass of sherry first.

ELVIRA: I don't believe you want to take me at all.

CHARLES: Of course I want to take you, but I still think it would be more sensible to wait until to-morrow—it's a filthy night.

ELVIRA (*crosses and flings herself into arm-chair—crossly*): How familiar this.

CHARLES: In what way familiar?

ELVIRA: All through our married life I only had to suggest something for you immediately to start hedging me off——

CHARLES: I'm not hedging you off, I merely said . . .

ELVIRA: All right—all right—we'll spend another cosy intimate evening at home with Ruth sewing away at that hideous table centre and snapping at us like a terrier.

CHARLES: Ruth is perfectly aware that the table centre is hideous. It happens to be a birthday present for her mother——

ELVIRA: It's no use trying to defend Ruth's taste to me—it's thoroughly artsy craftsy and you know it.

CHARLES: It is not artsy craftsy.

ELVIRA: She's ruined this room—look at those curtains and that awful shawl on the piano. . . .

CHARLES: Lady Mackinley sent it to us from Burma.

ELVIRA: Obviously because it had been sent to her from Birmingham.

CHARLES (*crosses to right of* ELVIRA): If you don't behave yourself I shan't take you into Folkestone ever.

ELVIRA (*coaxingly*): Please, Charles—don't be elderly and grand with me! Please let's go now.

CHARLES: Not until I've had my sherry.

ELVIRA: You are tiresome, darling—I've been waiting about for hours. . . .

CHARLES: A few more minutes won't make any difference then. (*He pours himself out some sherry.*)

ELVIRA (*petulantly, flinging herself into a chair*): Oh, very well.

CHARLES: Besides the car won't be back for a half an hour at least.

ELVIRA (*sharply*): What do you mean?

CHARLES (*sipping his sherry nonchalantly*): Ruth's taken it—she had to go and see the vicar. . . .

ELVIRA (*jumping up—in extreme agitation*): What!!

CHARLES: What on earth's the matter?

ELVIRA: You say *Ruth's* taken the car?

CHARLES: Yes—to go and see the vicar—but she won't be long.

ELVIRA (*rises*): Oh, my God!—Oh, my God!

CHARLES: Elvira!

ELVIRA: Stop her—you must stop her at once. . . .

CHARLES: Why—what for? . . .

ELVIRA (*jumping up and down*): Stop her—go out and stop her immediately.

CHARLES: It's too late now—I heard her go a couple of minutes ago. . . .

ELVIRA (*retreats backwards slowly towards window—CHARLES comes to her*): Oh Oh Oh Oh!!!

CHARLES: What are you going on like this for? What have you done?

ELVIRA (*frightened*): Done!—I haven't done anything——

CHARLES: Elvira—you're lying.

ELVIRA (*backing away from him*): I'm not lying—what is there to lie about?

CHARLES: What are you in such a state for?

ELVIRA (*almost hysterical*): I'm not in a state—I don't know what you mean. . . .

CHARLES: You've done something dreadful——

ELVIRA: Don't look at me like that, Charles—I haven't—I swear I haven't. . . .

CHARLES (*striking his forehead*): My God the car!

ELVIRA: No, Charles—no. . . .

CHARLES: Ruth was right—you did want to kill me—you've done something to the car. . . .

ELVIRA (*howling like a banshee*): Oh—oh—oh—oh!

CHARLES (*steps towards her again*): What did you do—answer me?

> *At this moment the telephone rings.*

CHARLES (*at telephone*): Hallo—hallo—yes, speaking. . . . I see . . . the bridge at the bottom of the hill . . . thank you—— No, I'll come at once.

> *He slowly puts back the receiver. As he does so the door bursts open. ELVIRA stands facing door.*

ELVIRA (*obviously retreating from someone*): Well, of all the filthy low-down tricks. (*She shields her head with her hands and screams.*) Ow—stop it—Ruth—leave go——

> *She runs out of the room and slams the door. It opens again immediately and slams again. CHARLES stares aghast.*

CURTAIN

ACT III

Scene I

The time is evening a few days later.

> CHARLES *is standing before the fire drinking his after-dinner coffee. He is in deep mourning. He finishes his coffee, puts the cup down on the mantelpiece, lights a cigarette and settles himself comfortably in an arm-chair. He adjusts a reading lamp and with a sigh of well-being, opens a novel and begins to read it. There is a ring at the front-door bell. With an exclamation of annoyance he puts down the book, gets up and goes out into the hall. After a moment or so* MADAME ARCATI *comes in.* CHARLES *follows her and shuts the door.* MADAME ARCATI *is wearing the strange, rather barbaric evening clothes that she wore in Act I.*

MADAME ARCATI: I hope you will not consider this an intrusion, Mr. Condomine.

CHARLES: Not at all—please sit down, won't you?

MADAME ARCATI: Thank you. (*She sits.*)

CHARLES: Would you like some coffee—or a liqueur?

MADAME ARCATI: No, thank you. I had to come, Mr. Condomine.

CHARLES (*politely*): Yes?

MADAME ARCATI: I felt a tremendous urge—like a rushing wind and so I hopped on my bike and here I am.

CHARLES: It was very kind of you.

MADAME ARCATI: No, no, no—not kind at all—it was my duty—I know it strongly.

CHARLES: Duty?

97

MADAME ARCATI: I reproach myself bitterly, you know.

CHARLES: Please don't—there is no necessity for that. (*Sits in arm-chair.*)

MADAME ARCATI: I allowed myself to get into a huff the other day with your late wife. I rode all the way home in the grip of temper, Mr. Condomine—I have regretted it ever since.

CHARLES: My dear Madame Arcati . . .

MADAME ARCATI (*holding up her hand*): Please let me go on. Mine is the shame, mine is the blame—I shall never forgive myself. Had I not been so impetuous— had I listened to the cool voice of reason—much might have been averted. . . .

CHARLES: You told my wife distinctly that you were unable to help her—you were perfectly honest— Over and above the original unfortunate mistake I see no reason for you to reproach yourself.

MADAME ARCATI: I threw up the sponge—in a moment of crisis I threw up the sponge instead of throwing down the gauntlet. . . .

CHARLES: Whatever you threw, Madame Arcati, I very much fear nothing could have been done—it seems that circumstances have been a little too strong for all of us.

MADAME ARCATI: I cannot bring myself to admit defeat so easily—it is gall and wormwood to me—I could have at least concentrated—made an effort.

CHARLES: Never mind.

MADAME ARCATI: I do mind. I cannot help it. I mind with every fibre of my being. I have been thinking very carefully, I have also been reading up a good deal during the last few dreadful days. . . . I gather that we are alone?

CHARLES (*looking round*): My first wife is not in the room, she is upstairs lying down, the funeral exhausted her. I imagine that my second wife is with her but of course I have no way of knowing for certain.

MADAME ARCATI: You have remarked no difference in the texture of your first wife since the accident?

CHARLES: No, she seems much as usual, a little under the weather, perhaps, a trifle low spirited, but that's all.

MADAME ARCATI: Well that washes that out.

CHARLES: I'm afraid I don't understand.

MADAME ARCATI: Just a little theory I had. In the nineteenth century there was a pretty widespread belief that a ghost who participated in the death of a human being, disintegrated automatically——

CHARLES: How do you know that Elvira was in any way responsible for Ruth's death?

MADAME ARCATI: Elvira—such a pretty name—it has a definite lilt to it, hasn't it? (*She hums for a moment.*) Elvira—El-vi-ira. . . .

CHARLES (*rather agitated*): You haven't answered my question. How did you know?

MADAME ARCATI: It came to me last night, Mr. Condomine—it came to me in a blinding flash—I had just finished my Ovaltine and turned the light out when I suddenly started up in bed with a loud cry—"Great Scott!" I said—"I've got it!"—after that I began to put two and two together. At three in the morning—with my brain fairly seething—I went to work on my crystal for a little but it wasn't very satisfactory—cloudy, you know——

CHARLES (*moving about uneasily*): I would be very much obliged if you would keep any theories you have regarding my wife's death to yourself, Madame Arcati. . . .

MADAME ARCATI: My one desire is to help you. I feel I have been dreadfully remiss over the whole affair —not only remiss but untidy.

CHARLES: I am afraid there is nothing whatever to be done.

MADAME ARCATI (*triumphantly*): But there is—there is! (*She produces a piece of paper from her bag and brandishes it.*) I have found a formula—here it is! I copied it out of Edmondson's *Witchcraft and its Byways*.

CHARLES (*irritably*): What the hell are you talking about?

MADAME ARCATI (*rises*): Pluck up your heart, Mr. Condomine . . . all is not lost!

CHARLES (*rises*): Now look here, Madame Arcati——

MADAME ARCATI: You are still anxious to de-materialise your first wife, I suppose?

CHARLES (*in a lower voice, with a cautious look towards the door*): Of course I am—I'm perfectly furious with her but——

MADAME ARCATI: But what?

CHARLES: Well—she's been very upset for the last few days—you see apart from me being angry with her which she always hated even when she was alive, Ruth, my second wife, has hardly left her side for a moment— you must see that she's been having a pretty bad time what with one thing and another. . . .

MADAME ARCATI: Your delicacy of feeling does you credit but I must say, if you will forgive my bluntness, that you are a damned fool, Mr. Condomine.

CHARLES (*away to left by gramophone. Stiffly*): You are at liberty to think whatever you please.

MADAME ARCATI: Now, now, now—don't get on your high horse—there's no sense in that, is there? I have a formula here that I think will be able to get rid of her without hurting her feelings in the least. It's extremely simple and requires nothing more than complete concentration from you and a minor trance from me—I may even be able to manage it without lying down.

CHARLES: Honestly I would rather——

At this moment the door opens and ELVIRA *comes quickly into the room. She is obviously very upset.*

ELVIRA: Charles——

CHARLES: What on earth's the matter?

ELVIRA (*seeing* MADAME ARCATI): Oh! What's she doing here?

CHARLES: She came to offer me her condolences.

ELVIRA: They should have been congratulations.

CHARLES: Please don't say things like that, Elvira—it is in the worst possible taste. Madame Arcati—allow me to introduce my first wife Elvira——

MADAME ARCATI: How do you do?

ELVIRA: What does she want, Charles—send her away. (*She walks about the room.*)

MADAME ARCATI: In what part of the room is she at the moment?

CHARLES: She's moving about rather rapidly. I'll tell you when and where she settles.

ELVIRA: She's the one who got me here in the first place, isn't she?

CHARLES: Yes.

ELVIRA: Well, please tell her to get me away again as soon as possible—I can't stand this house another minute.

CHARLES: Really, Elvira—I'm surprised at you.

ELVIRA (*nearly in tears*): I don't care how surprised you are—I want to go home—I'm sick of the whole thing.

CHARLES: Don't be childish, Elvira.

ELVIRA: I'm not being childish—I mean it.

MADAME ARCATI (*by fireplace. Sniffing*): Very interesting—very interesting—I smell ectoplasm strongly!

ELVIRA: What a disgusting thing to say.

MADAME ARCATI: Where is she now?

CHARLES: Here—close to me.

MADAME ARCATI (*mystically—stretching out her hands*): Are you happy, my dear——?

ELVIRA (*stamping her foot*): Tell the silly old bitch to mind her own business.

MADAME ARCATI (*in a sing-song voice*): Was the journey difficult? Are you weary?

ELVIRA: She's dotty.

CHARLES: Just a moment, Madame Arcati. . . .

MADAME ARCATI (*with her eyes shut*): This is wonderful—wonderful——

ELVIRA: For God's sake tell her to go into the other room, Charles. I've got to talk to you.

CHARLES: Madame Arcati. . . .

MADAME ARCATI: Just a moment. I almost have contact—I can sense the vibrations—this is magnificent. . . .

CHARLES: Go on, Elvira—don't be a spoilsport—give her a bit of encouragement.

ELVIRA: If you'll promise to get her into the other room.

CHARLES: All right.

    ELVIRA *crosses to* MADAME ARCATI *and blows gently into her ear.*

MADAME ARCATI (*jumping*): Yes, yes—again—again——

ELVIRA (*blowing in the other ear*): How's that?

MADAME ARCATI (*clasping and unclasping her hands in a frenzy of excitement*): This is first-rate—it really is first-rate. Absolutely stunning!

CHARLES: I'm so glad you're pleased.

ELVIRA: Please get rid of her. Ruth will be in in a minute.

CHARLES: Madame Arcati, would you think it most frightfully rude if I asked you to go into the dining-room for a moment? My first wife wishes to speak to me alone.

MADAME ARCATI: Oh, must I? It's so lovely being actually in the room with her.

CHARLES: Only for a few minutes—I promise she'll be here when you come back.

MADAME ARCATI: Very well. Hand me my bag, will you—it's on the settee.

ELVIRA (*picking it up and handing it to her*): Here you are.

MADAME ARCATI (*taking it and blowing her a kiss*): Oh, you darling—you little darling.

> MADAME ARCATI *humming ecstatically, goes into the dining-room and shuts the door.*

ELVIRA: How good is she really?

CHARLES: I don't know.

ELVIRA: Do you think she really could get me back again?

CHARLES: But, my dear child . . .

ELVIRA: And don't call me your dear child—it's smug and supercilious.

CHARLES: There's no need to be rude.

ELVIRA: The whole thing's been a failure—a miserable dreary failure—and oh! what high hopes I started out with.

CHARLES: You can't expect much sympathy from me, you know. I am perfectly aware that your highest hope was to murder me.

ELVIRA: Don't put it like that, it sounds so beastly.

CHARLES: It is beastly. It's one of the beastliest ideas I've ever heard.

ELVIRA: There was a time when you'd have welcomed the chance of being with me for ever.

CHARLES: Your behaviour has shocked me immeasurably, Elvira—I had no idea you were so unscrupulous.

ELVIRA (*bursting into tears*): Oh, Charles. . . .

CHARLES: Stop crying.

ELVIRA: They're only ghost tears—they don't mean anything really—but they're very painful.

CHARLES: You've brought all this on yourself, you know.

ELVIRA: That's right—rub it in. Anyhow it was only because I loved you—the silliest thing I ever did in my whole life was to love you—you were always unworthy of me.

CHARLES: That remark comes perilously near impertinence, Elvira.

ELVIRA: I sat there, on the other side, just longing for you day after day. I did really—all through your affair with that brassy-looking woman in the South of France I went on loving you and thinking truly of you—then you married Ruth and even then I forgave you and tried to understand because all the time I believed deep inside that you really loved me best . . . that's why I put myself down for a return visit and had to fill in all those forms and wait about in draughty passages for hours—if only you'd died before you met Ruth everything might have been all right—she's absolutely ruined you—I hadn't been in the house a day before I realised that. Your books aren't a quarter as good as they used to be either.

CHARLES (*incensed*): That is entirely untrue. . . . Ruth helped me and encouraged me with my work which is a damned sight more than you ever did.

ELVIRA: That's probably what's wrong with it.

CHARLES: All you ever thought of was going to parties and enjoying yourself.

ELVIRA: Why shouldn't I have fun? I died young, didn't I?

CHARLES: You needn't have died at all if you hadn't been idiotic enough to go out on the river with Guy Henderson and get soaked to the skin.

ELVIRA: So we're back at Guy Henderson again, are we?

CHARLES: You behaved abominably over Guy Henderson and it's no use pretending that you didn't.

ELVIRA: Guy adored me—and anyhow he was very attractive.

CHARLES: You told me distinctly that he didn't attract you in the least.

ELVIRA: You'd have gone through the roof if I'd told you that he did.

CHARLES: Did you have an affair with Guy Henderson?

ELVIRA: I would rather not discuss it if you don't mind.

CHARLES: Answer me—did you or didn't you?

ELVIRA: Of course I didn't.

CHARLES: You let him kiss you though, didn't you?

ELVIRA: How could I stop him—he was bigger than I was.

CHARLES (*furiously*): And you swore to me——

ELVIRA: Of course I did. You were always making scenes over nothing at all.

CHARLES: Nothing at all——

ELVIRA: You never loved me a bit really—it was only your beastly vanity.

CHARLES: You seriously believe that it was only vanity that upset me when you went out in the punt with Guy Henderson?

ELVIRA: It was not a punt—it was a little launch.

CHARLES: I didn't care if it was a three-masted schooner you had no right to go!

ELVIRA: You seem to forget *why* I went! You seem to forget that you had spent the entire evening making sheep's eyes at that overblown harridan with the false pearls.

CHARLES: A woman in Cynthia Cheviot's position would hardly wear false pearls.

ELVIRA: They were practically all she was wearing.

CHARLES: I am pained to observe that seven years in the echoing vaults of eternity have in no way impaired your native vulgarity.

ELVIRA: That was the remark of a pompous ass.

CHARLES: There is nothing to be gained by continuing this discussion.

ELVIRA: You always used to say that when you were thoroughly worsted.

CHARLES: On looking back on our married years, Elvira, I see now, with horrid clarity, that they were nothing but a mockery.

ELVIRA: You invite mockery, Charles—it's something to do with your personality, I think, a certain seedy grandeur.

CHARLES: Once and for all, Elvira——

ELVIRA: You never suspected it but I laughed at you steadily from the altar to the grave—all your ridiculous petty jealousies and your fussings and fumings——

CHARLES: You were feckless and irresponsible and morally unstable—I realised that before we left Budleigh Salterton.

ELVIRA: Nobody but a monumental bore would have thought of having a honeymoon at Budleigh Salterton.

CHARLES: What's the matter with Budleigh Salterton?

ELVIRA: I was an eager young bride, Charles—I wanted glamour and music and romance—all I got was potted palms, seven hours every day on a damp golf course and a three-piece orchestra playing 'Merrie England'.

CHARLES: It's a pity you didn't tell me so at the time.

ELVIRA: I did—but you wouldn't listen—that's why I went out on the moors that day with Captain Bracegirdle. I was desperate.

CHARLES: You swore to me that you'd gone over to see your aunt in Exmouth!

ELVIRA: It was the moors.

CHARLES: With Captain Bracegirdle?

ELVIRA: With Captain Bracegirdle.

CHARLES (*furiously*): I might have known it—what a fool I was—what a blind fool! Did he make love to you?

ELVIRA (*sucking her finger and regarding it thoughtfully*): Of course.

CHARLES: Oh, Elvira!

ELVIRA: Only very discreetly—he was in the cavalry, you know. . . .

CHARLES: Well, all I can say is that I'm well rid of you.

ELVIRA: Unfortunately you're not.

CHARLES: Oh yes I am—you're dead and Ruth's dead —I shall sell this house lock, stock and barrel and go away.

ELVIRA: I shall follow you.

CHARLES: I shall go a long way away—I shall go to South America—you'll hate that, you were always a bad traveller.

ELVIRA: That can't be helped—I shall have to follow you—you called me back.

CHARLES: I did *not* call you back!

ELVIRA: Well somebody did—and it's hardly likely to have been Ruth.

CHARLES: Nothing in the world was further from my thoughts.

ELVIRA: You were talking about me before dinner that evening.

CHARLES: I might just as easily have been talking about Joan of Arc but that wouldn't necessarily mean that I wanted her to come and live with me.

ELVIRA: As a matter of fact she's rather fun.

CHARLES: Stick to the point.

ELVIRA: When I think of what might have happened if I'd succeeded in getting you to the other world after all—it makes me shudder, it does honestly . . . it would be nothing but bickering and squabbling for ever and ever and ever. I swear I'll be better off with Ruth— at least she'll find her own set and not get in my way.

CHARLES: So I get in the way, do I?

ELVIRA: Only because I was idiotic enough to imagine that you loved me, and I sort of felt sorry for you.

CHARLES: I'm sick of these insults—please go away.

ELVIRA: There's nothing I should like better—I've always believed in cutting my losses. That's why I died.

CHARLES: Of all the brazen sophistry——

ELVIRA: Call that old girl in again—set her to work —I won't tolerate this any longer—I want to go home.

> ELVIRA *starts to cry.*

CHARLES: For heaven't sake don't snivel.

ELVIRA (*stamping her foot*): Call her in—she's got to get me out of this.

CHARLES (*going to the dining-room door*): I quite agree— and the sooner the better. (*He opens the door.*) Madame Arcati—would you please come in now?

> CHARLES *goes out.* MADAME ARCATI *comes in followed by* CHARLES.

MADAME ARCATI (*eagerly*): Is the darling still here?

CHARLES (*grimly*): Yes, she is.

MADAME ARCATI: Where—tell me where?

CHARLES: Over by the piano—blowing her nose.

MADAME ARCATI (*approaches piano above* ELVIRA): My dear—oh, my dear——

ELVIRA: Stop her fawning on me, Charles, or I shall break something.

CHARLES: Elvira and I have discussed the whole situation, Madame Arcati, and she wishes to go home immediately.

MADAME ARCATI: Home?

CHARLES: Wherever she came from.

MADAME ARCATI: You don't think she would like to

stay a few days longer—while I try to get things a little more organised?

ELVIRA: No—no—I want to go now.

MADAME ARCATI: I could come and be here with her —I could bring my crystal——

ELVIRA: God forbid!

CHARLES: We are both agreed that she must go as soon as possible. Please strain every nerve, Madame Arcati—make every effort—you said something about a formula—what is it?

MADAME ARCATI (*reluctantly*): Well—if you insist——

CHARLES: I most emphatically do insist.

ELVIRA (*wailing*): Oh, Charles . . .

CHARLES: Shut up.

MADAME ARCATI: I can't guarantee anything, you know—I'll do my best but it may not work.

CHARLES: What is the formula?

MADAME ARCATI: Nothing more than a little verse really—it fell into disuse after the seventeenth century— I shall need some pepper and salt——

CHARLES: There's some pepper and salt in the dining-room—I'll get it.

He goes.

MADAME ARCATI: We ought of course to have some Shepherd's Wort and a frog or two but I think I can manage without.

> MADAME ARCATI *talks to* ELVIRA *as though she were standing by piano.*

You won't be frightened, dear, will you? It's absolutely painless.

CHARLES (*coming back with the cruet*): Will this be enough?

MADAME ARCATI: Oh yes—I only need a little—put it on the table please. Now then, let me see—— (*She fumbles in her bag for the paper and her glasses.*) Ah, yes—— (*To* CHARLES.) Sprinkle it, will you—just a soupçon—there, right in the middle——

> CHARLES *does so.*

ELVIRA: This is going to be a flop—I can tell you that here and now.

MADAME ARCATI: Now a few snapdragons out of that vase, there's a good chap.

> CHARLES *brings flowers.*

CHARLES: Here you are.

ELVIRA: Merlin does all this sort of thing at parties and bores us all stiff with it.

MADAME ARCATI: Now then—the gramophone—in the old days of course they used a zither or reed pipes—we'd better have the same record we had before, I think.

ELVIRA: I'll get it.

> ELVIRA *gets record and gives it to* MADAME ARCATI, *then crosses to mantelpiece.*

CHARLES: Whatever you think best, Madame Arcati.

MADAME ARCATI (*watching, fascinated*): Oh, if only that Mr. Emsworth of the Psychical Research Society could see this—he'd have a fit, he would, really! Don't start it yet, dear. Now then—sit down, please, Mr. Condomine, rest your hands on the table but don't put your fingers in the pepper—I shall turn out the lights myself—— Oh, Shucks, I'd nearly forgotten—— (*She goes to the table and makes designs in the sprinkled pepper and salt with her forefinger.*) One triangle—(*She consults the paper.*) One half circle and one little dot—there!

III

ELVIRA: This is waste of time—she's a complete fake.

CHARLES: Anything's worth trying.

ELVIRA: I'm as eager for it to succeed as you are—don't make any mistake about that. But I'll lay you ten to one it's a dead failure.

MADAME ARCATI: Now, if your wife would be kind enough to lie down on the sofa——

CHARLES: Go on, Elvira——

ELVIRA (*lying down*): This is sheer nonsense—don't blame me if I get the giggles.

CHARLES: Concentrate—think of nothing.

MADAME ARCATI (*she faces* ELVIRA's *feet instead of her head*): That's right—quite right—hands at the sides—legs extended—breathe steadily—one two—one two—one two—is she comfortable?

CHARLES: Are you comfortable, Elvira?

ELVIRA: No.

CHARLES: She's quite comfortable.

MADAME ARCATI: I shall join you in a moment, Mr. Condomine—I may have to go into a slight trance, but if I do, pay no attention—Now first the music and away we go! (*Crosses to gramophone and starts it.*)

> MADAME ARCATI *turns on the gramophone and stands quite still by the side of it with her hands behind her head for a little—then suddenly, with great swiftness, she runs to the door and switches out the lights. Her form can dimly be discerned moving about in the darkness.*
> CHARLES *gives a loud sneeze.*

ELVIRA (*giggling*): Oh dear—it's the pepper.

CHARLES: Damn!

MADAME ARCATI: Hold on to yourself—concentrate——

MADAME ARCATI *recites in a sing-song voice.*

'Ghostly spectre—ghoul or fiend
Never more be thou convened
Shepherd's Wort and Holy Rite
Banish thee into the night.'

ELVIRA: What a disagreeable little verse.

CHARLES: Be quiet, Elvira.

MADAME ARCATI (*pulls up chair down stage left and sits opposite* CHARLES): Sshh! (*There is silence.*) Is there anyone there? . . . Is there anyone there?—one rap for yes—two raps for no—— Is there anyone there? . . . (*The table gives a loud bump.*) Aha—— Good Stuff! Is that you, Daphne? . . . (*The table gives another bump.*) I'm sorry to bother you, dear, but Mrs. Condomine wants to return. (*The table bumps several times very quickly.*) Now then, Daphne. . . . Did you hear what I said? (*After a pause the table gives one bump.*) Can you help us? . . . (*There is another pause, then the table begins to bump violently without stopping.*) Hold tight, Mr. Condomine—it's trying to break away—— Oh—oh—oh —(*the table falls over with a crash. She falls off chair and pulls over table on to her.*)

CHARLES: What's the matter, Madame Arcati?—are you hurt?

MADAME ARCATI (*wailing*): Oh—oh—oh——

    CHARLES *rushes to door and turns on lights then back to* MADAME ARCATI *and kneels above her.*

CHARLES: What on earth's happening?

    MADAME ARCATI *is lying on the floor with the table upside down on her back.* CHARLES *hurriedly lifts it off.* (*Shaking her.*) Are you hurt, Madame Arcati?

ELVIRA (*rises and comes and looks at* MADAME ARCATI *then crosses back to fireplace*): She's in one of her damned trances again and I'm here as much as ever I was.

CHARLES (*shaking* MADAME ARCATI): For God's sake wake up.

ELVIRA: Leave her alone—she's having the whale of a time.

MADAME ARCATI (*moaning*): Oh—oh—oh——

ELVIRA: If I ever do get back I'll strangle that bloody little Daphne. . . .

MADAME ARCATI (*sitting up suddenly*): What happened?

CHARLES: Nothing—nothing at all.

> MADAME ARCATI *rises.* CHARLES *rises and picks up table.*

MADAME ARCATI (*dusting herself*): Oh, yes, it did—I know something happened.

CHARLES: You fell over—that's all that happened.

MADAME ARCATI: Is she still here?

CHARLES: Of course she is.

MADAME ARCATI: Something must have gone wrong.

ELVIRA: Make her do it properly. I'm sick of being messed about like this.

CHARLES: Be quiet—she's doing her best.

MADAME ARCATI: Something happened—I sensed it in my trance—I felt it—it shivered through me.

> *Suddenly the window curtains blow out almost straight and* RUTH *walks into the room. She is still wearing the brightly-coloured clothes in which we last saw her but now they are entirely grey. So is her hair and her skin.*

RUTH (*enters from windows and goes straight to* CHARLES *centre*): Once and for all, Charles—what the hell does this mean?

THE LIGHTS FADE

ACT III

SCENE II

When the lights go up again several hours have elapsed.
The whole room is in slight disarray. There are birch
branches and evergreens laid on the floor in front of the
doors and crossed birch branches pinned rather untidily
on to the curtains. The furniture has been moved about a
bit. On the Bridge table there is a pile of playing-cards,
MADAME ARCATI'S crystal and a Ouija board. Also a
plate of sandwiches and two empty beer mugs.
MADAME ARCATI is asleep on the sofa. RUTH is
leaning on the mantelpiece. CHARLES sitting on back of
sofa. ELVIRA sitting on piano-stool above séance table.

RUTH: Well—we've done all we can—I must say I
couldn't be more exhausted.

ELVIRA: It will be daylight soon.
    The clock strikes five, very slowly.

RUTH: That clock's always irritated me—it strikes far
too slowly.

CHARLES: It was a wedding present from Uncle
Walter.

RUTH: Whose Uncle Walter?

CHARLES: Elvira's.

RUTH: Well all I can say is he might have chosen
something a little more decorative.

ELVIRA: If that really were all you could say, Ruth,
I'm sure it would be a great comfort to us all.

RUTH (*grandly*): You can be as rude as you like,
Elvira. I don't mind a bit—as a matter of fact I should
be extremely surprised if you weren't.

ELVIRA (*truculently*): Why?

RUTH: The reply to that is really too obvious.

CHARLES: I wish you two would stop bickering for one minute.

RUTH: This is quite definitely one of the most frustrating nights I have ever spent.

ELVIRA: The reply to that is pretty obvious, too.

RUTH: I'm sure I don't know what you mean.

ELVIRA: Skip it.

RUTH (*crosses to* ELVIRA): Now listen to me, Elvira. If you and I have got to stay together indefinitely in this house—and it looks unpleasantly likely—we had better come to some sort of an arrangement.

ELVIRA: What sort of an arrangement?

CHARLES: You're *not* going to stay indefinitely in this house.

RUTH: With you, then—we shall have to be with you.

CHARLES: I don't see why—why don't you take a cottage somewhere?

RUTH: You called us back.

CHARLES: I've already explained until I'm black in the face that I did nothing of the sort.

RUTH: Madame Arcati said you did.

CHARLES: Madame Arcati's a muddling old fool.

ELVIRA: I could have told you that in the first place.

RUTH: I think you're behaving very shabbily, Charles.

CHARLES: I don't see what I've done.

RUTH: We have all agreed that as Elvira and I are dead that it would be both right and proper for us to dematerialise again as soon as possible. That, I admit.

We have allowed ourselves to be subjected to the most humiliating hocus-pocus for hours and hours without complaining. . . .

CHARLES: Without complaining?

RUTH: We've stood up—we've lain down—we've concentrated. We've sat interminably while that tiresome old woman recited extremely unflattering verses at us. We've endured five séances—we've watched her fling herself in and out of trances until we're dizzy and at the end of it all we find ourselves exactly where we were at the beginning. . . .

CHARLES: Well, it's not my fault.

RUTH: Be that as it may, the least you could do is to admit failure gracefully and try and make the best of it—your manners are boorish to a degree.

CHARLES (*rises*): I'm just as exhausted as you are. I've had to do all the damned table tapping, remember.

RUTH: If she can't get us back, she can't and that's that. We shall have to think of something else.

CHARLES: She *must* get you back—anything else is unthinkable.

ELVIRA: There's gratitude for you!

CHARLES: Gratitude?

ELVIRA: Yes, for all the years we've both devoted to you—you ought to be ashamed.

CHARLES: What about all the years I've devoted to you?

ELVIRA: Nonsense—we've waited on you hand and foot—haven't we, Ruth?—You're exceedingly selfish and always were.

CHARLES: In that case I fail to see why you were both so anxious to get back to me.

RUTH: You called us back. And you've done nothing

but try to get rid of us ever since we came—hasn't he, Elvira?

ELVIRA: He certainly has.

RUTH: And now, owing to your idiotic inefficiency, we find ourselves in the most mortifying position— we're neither fish, flesh nor fowl nor whatever it is.

ELVIRA: Good red herring.

RUTH: It can't be.

CHARLES: Well, why don't you do something about it? Why don't you go back on your own?

RUTH: We can't—you know perfectly well we can't.

CHARLES: Isn't there anybody on the other side who can help?

RUTH: How do I know? I've only been there a few days . . . ask Elvira.

ELVIRA: I've already told you that's no good—if we got Cagliostro, Mesmer, Merlin, Gil de Retz and the Black Douglas in a row they couldn't do a thing—the impetus has got to come from here. . . . Perhaps darling Charles doesn't want us to go quite enough.

CHARLES: I certainly do.

ELVIRA: Well, you must have a very weak will then. I always suspected it.

RUTH: It's no use arguing any more—wake up, Madame Arcati.

ELVIRA: Oh, not another séance—please not another séance.

CHARLES: Please wake up, Madame Arcati. . . .

RUTH: Shake her.

CHARLES: It might upset her.

RUTH: I don't care if it kills her.

CHARLES: Please wake up, Madame Arcati. . . .

MADAME ARCATI (*waking*): What time is it?

CHARLES: Ten past five!

MADAME ARCATI: What time did I go off? (*She sits up.*)

CHARLES: Over an hour ago.

MADAME ARCATI (*reaching for her bag*): Curious . . . very curious. Forgive me for a moment, I must just make a note of that for my diary. (*She takes a book out of her bag and scribbles in it.*) Are they still here?

CHARLES: Yes.

MADAME ARCATI: How disappointing.

CHARLES: Have you any suggestions?

MADAME ARCATI (*rising briskly*): We mustn't give up hope—chin up—never give in—that's my motto.

RUTH: This schoolgirl phraseology's driving me mad.

MADAME ARCATI: Now then. . . .

CHARLES: Now then what?

MADAME ARCATI: What do you say we have another séance and really put our shoulders to the wheel?— Make it a real rouser?

ELVIRA: For God's sake not another séance.

MADAME ARCATI: I might be able to materialise a trumpet if I tried hard enough—better than nothing, you know—I feel as fit as a fiddle after my rest.

ELVIRA: I don't care if she materialises a whole symphony orchestra—I implore you not to let her have another séance.

CHARLES: Don't you think, Madame Arcati, that perhaps we've had enough séances? After all they haven't achieved much, have they?

MADAME ARCATI: Rome wasn't built in a day, you know.

CHARLES: I know it wasn't, but . . .

MADAME ARCATI: Well then—cheer up—away with melancholy.

CHARLES: Now listen, Madame Arcati . . . before you go off into any further trances I really think we ought to discuss the situation a little.

MADAME ARCATI: Good—an excellent idea—and while we're doing it I shall have another of these delicious sandwiches—I'm as hungry as a hunter. (*Crosses to table and gets sandwich.*)

CHARLES: Would you like some more beer?

MADAME ARCATI: No, thank you—better not.

CHARLES: Very well—I think I'll have a small whisky-and-soda.

MADAME ARCATI: Make it a double and enjoy yourself.

> CHARLES *goes to the drink table and mixes himself a whisky-and-soda.*

RUTH: One day I intend to give myself the pleasure of telling Madame Arcati exactly what I think of her.

CHARLES: She's been doing her best.

MADAME ARCATI: Are the girls getting despondent?

CHARLES: I'm afraid they are, rather.

MADAME ARCATI: We'll win through yet—don't be downhearted. (*Sits on sofa.*)

RUTH: If we're not very careful she'll materialise a hockey team.

MADAME ARCATI: Now then, Mr. Condomine—the discussion—fire away.

CHARLES (*crosses and sits on pouffé down stage right*): Well, my wives and I have been talking it over and they are both absolutely convinced that I somehow or other called them back.

MADAME ARCATI: Very natural.

CHARLES: I am equally convinced that I did not.

MADAME ARCATI: Love is a strong psychic force, Mr. Condomine—it can work untold miracles—a true love call can encompass the universe——

CHARLES (*hastily*): I'm sure it can but I must confess to you frankly that although my affection for both Elvira and Ruth is of the warmest I cannot truthfully feel that it would come under the heading that you describe.

ELVIRA: I should just think not indeed.

MADAME ARCATI: You may not know your own strength, Mr. Condomine.

CHARLES (*firmly*): I did *not* call them back—either consciously or sub-consciously.

MADAME ARCATI: But, Mr. Condomine. . . .

CHARLES: That is my final word on the subject.

MADAME ARCATI: Neither of them could have appeared unless there had been somebody—a psychic subject—in the house, who wished for them . . .

CHARLES: Well, it wasn't me.

ELVIRA: Perhaps it was Doctor Bradman—I never knew he cared.

MADAME ARCATI: Are you sure?—Are you really sure?

CHARLES: Absolutely positive.

MADAME ARCATI (*throws sandwich over her head and rises*): Great Scott, I believe I've been barking up the wrong tree!

CHARLES: How do you mean?

MADAME ARCATI: The Sudbury case!

CHARLES: I don't understand.

MADAME ARCATI: There's no reason why you should—it was before your day—I wonder—oh, I wonder . . .

CHARLES: What was the Sudbury case? I wish you'd explain.

MADAME ARCATI: It was the case that made me famous, Mr. Condomine—it was what you might describe in theatrical parlance as my first smash hit! I had letters from all over the world about it—especially India.

CHARLES: What did you do?

MADAME ARCATI: I de-materialised old Lady Sudbury after she'd been firmly entrenched in the private chapel for over seventeen years.

CHARLES: How?—Can you remember how?

MADAME ARCATI: Chance—a fluke—I happened on it by the merest coincidence.

CHARLES: What fluke—what was it?

MADAME ARCATI: Wait—all in good time. (*She begins to walk about the room.*) Now let me see—who was in the house during our first séance?

CHARLES: Only the Bradmans, Ruth and me and yourself.

MADAME ARCATI: Ah, yes—yes—to be sure—but the Bradmans weren't here last night, were they?

CHARLES: No.

MADAME ARCATI: Quickly—my crystal——

CHARLES (*gets crystal from table and gives it to* MADAME ARCATI): Here . . .

MADAME ARCATI (*shaking it crossly*): Damn the thing, it gives me the pip. It's cloudy again. (*She looks again.*) Ah!—that's better—it's there again—it's there again— I'm beginning to understand.

CHARLES: I wish I was. What's there again?

MADAME ARCATI: A bandage . . . a white bandage —hold on to a white bandage. . . .

CHARLES: I haven't got a white bandage.

MADAME ARCATI: Shhh!

ELVIRA: She's too good, you know—she ought to be in a circus.

> MADAME ARCATI *runs across and leaps on to pouffé. She advances to the middle of the room and raises her arms slowly—she begins to intone.*

MADAME ARCATI: Be you in nook or cranny answer me,
> Be you in Still-room or closet answer me,
> Be you behind the panel, above the stairs
> Beneath the eaves—waking or sleeping,
> Answer me!

That ought to do it or I'm a Dutchman.

CHARLES: Do what?

MADAME ARCATI: Hush—wait——

> MADAME ARCATI *crosses to window and picks up bunch of garlic and crosses to writing-desk, making cabalistic signs. She picks up one of the birch branches and waves it solemnly to and fro.*

RUTH (*rises and comes to gramophone down stage left*): For God's sake don't let her throw any more of that garlic about—it nearly made me sick last time.

CHARLES: Would you like the gramophone on or the lights out or anything?

MADAME ARCATI: No, no—it's near—it's very near——

ELVIRA: If it's a ghost I shall scream.

RUTH: I hope it's nobody we know—I shall feel so silly.

Suddenly the door opens and EDITH *comes into the room. She is wearing a pink flannel dressing-gown and bedroom slippers. Her head is bandaged.*

EDITH: Did you ring, sir?

MADAME ARCATI: The bandage! The white bandage!

CHARLES: No, Edith.

EDITH: I'm sorry, sir—I could have sworn I heard the bell—or somebody calling—I was asleep—I don't rightly know which it was. . . .

MADAME ARCATI: Come here, child.

EDITH: Oh! (*She looks anxiously at* CHARLES.)

CHARLES: Go on—go to Madame Arcati—it's quite all right.

MADAME ARCATI: Who do you see in this room, child?

EDITH: Oh dear. . . .

MADAME ARCATI: Answer please.

EDITH (*falteringly*): You, Madame. (*She stops.*)

MADAME ARCATI: Go on.

EDITH: The Master.

MADAME ARCATI: Anyone else?

EDITH: Oh, no, Madame. . . .

MADAME ARCATI (*inflexibly*): Look again.

EDITH (*imploringly, to* CHARLES): I don't understand, sir—I——

MADAME ARCATI: Come, child—don't beat about the bush—look again.

ELVIRA *moves across to fireplace.* RUTH *follows.* EDITH *follows them with her eyes.*

RUTH: Do concentrate, Elvira, and keep still.

ELVIRA: I can't. . . .

MADAME ARCATI: Do you see anyone else now?

EDITH (*slyly*): Oh no, Madame.

MADAME ARCATI: She's lying.

EDITH: Oh, Madame!

MADAME ARCATI: They always do.

CHARLES: They?

MADAME ARCATI (*sharply*): Where are they now?

EDITH: By the fireplace—— Oh!

CHARLES: She can see them—do you mean she can see them?

MADAME ARCATI: Probably not very clearly—but enough——

EDITH (*bursting into tears*): Let me go—I haven't done nothing nor seen nobody—let me go back to bed.

MADAME ARCATI: Give her a sandwich.

     CHARLES *goes to table and gets sandwich for* EDITH.

EDITH (*drawing away*): I don't want a sandwich. I want to go back to bed.

CHARLES (*handing* EDITH *the plate*): Here, Edith.

MADAME ARCATI: Nonsense—a big healthy girl like you saying no to a delicious sandwich—I never heard of such a thing—sit down.

EDITH (*to* CHARLES): Please, sir, I . . .

CHARLES: Please do as Madame Arcati says, Edith.

EDITH (*sitting down and sniffing*): I haven't done nothing wrong.

CHARLES: It's all right—nobody said you had.

RUTH: If she's been the cause of all this unpleasantness I'll give her a week's notice to-morrow.

ELVIRA: You may not be here to-morrow——

MADAME ARCATI: Look at me, Edith.

     EDITH *obediently does so.*

Cuckoo—cuckoo—cuckoo——

EDITH (*jumping*): Oh dear—what's the matter with her? Is she barmy?

MADAME ARCATI: Here, Edith—this is my finger—look—(*She waggles it.*) Have you ever seen such a long, long, long finger—look now, it's on the right—now it's on the left—backwards and forwards it goes—see—very quietly backwards and forwards—tic-toc—tic-toc—tic-toc.

ELVIRA: The mouse ran up the clock.

RUTH: Be *quiet*—you'll ruin everything.

 MADAME ARCATI *whistles a little tune close to* EDITH'S *face—then she snaps her fingers.* EDITH *looks stolidly in front of her without flinching.* MADAME ARCATI *stands back.*

MADAME ARCATI: Well—so far so good—she's off all right.

CHARLES: Off?

MADAME ARCATI: She's a Natural—just the same as the Sudbury case—it really is the most amusing coincidence. Now then—would you ask your wives to stand close together, please.

CHARLES: Where?

MADAME ARCATI: Over there by you.

CHARLES: Elvira—Ruth——

RUTH: I resent being ordered about like this.

ELVIRA: I don't like this at all—I don't like any of it—I feel peculiar.

CHARLES: I'm afraid I must insist.

ELVIRA: It would serve you right if we flatly refused to do anything at all.

MADAME ARCATI: Are you sorry for having been so mischievous, Edith?

EDITH (*cheerfully*): Oh yes, Madame.

MADAME ARCATI: You know what you have to do now, don't you, Edith?

EDITH: Oh yes, Madame.

RUTH: I believe it's going to work whatever it is—Oh, Charles.

CHARLES: Shhh!

RUTH: This is good-bye, Charles.

ELVIRA: Tell her to stop for a minute—there's something I want to say before I go.

CHARLES: You should have thought of that before—it's too late now.

ELVIRA: Of all the mean, ungracious——

RUTH: Charles—Listen a moment. . . .

MADAME ARCATI (*in a shrill voice*): Lights!

> MADAME ARCATI *rushes to the door and siwtches off the lights. In the dark* EDITH *is singing* 'Always' *in a very high cockney voice.*

ELVIRA (*in the dark*): I saw Captain Bracegirdle again, Charles—several times—I went to the Four Hundred with him twice when you were in Nottingham, and I must say I couldn't have enjoyed it more . . . etc.

RUTH: Don't think you're getting rid of us quite so easily, my dear—you may not be able to see us but we shall be here all right—I consider that you have behaved atrociously over the whole miserable business, and I should like to say here and now . . . etc.

> *Her voice fades into a whisper and then disappears altogether.*

MADAME ARCATI (*exultantly*): Splendid—Hurrah!—We've done it! That's quite enough singing for the moment, Edith.

CHARLES (*after a pause*): Shall I put on the lights?

MADAME ARCATI: No, I will.

> CHARLES *crosses to window and pulls curtains. Daylight floods into the room.* RUTH *and* ELVIRA

have disappeared. EDITH *is sitting still on the chair.*

CHARLES: They've gone—they've really gone.

MADAME ARCATI: Yes—I think we've really pulled it off this time.

CHARLES: You'd better wake her up, hadn't you? She might bring them back again.

MADAME ARCATI (*clapping her hands in* EDITH's *face*): Wake up, child!

EDITH (*nearly jumping out of the chair*): Good 'Eavens! Where am I?

CHARLES: It's all right, Edith—you can go back to bed now.

EDITH: Why, it's morning.

CHARLES: Yes—I know it is.

EDITH: But I *was* in bed—how did I get down 'ere?

CHARLES: I rang, Edith—I rang the bell and you answered it—didn't I, Madame Arcati?

EDITH: Did I drop off? Do you think it's my concussion again? Oh dear!

CHARLES: Off you go, Edith, and thank you very much. (*He presses a pound note into her hand.*) Thank you very much, indeed.

EDITH: Oh, sir, whatever for? (*She looks at him in sudden horror.*) Oh, sir!!

She bolts from the room.

CHARLES (*surprised*): What on earth did she mean by that?

MADAME ARCATI: Golly, what a night! I'm ready to drop in my tracks.

CHARLES: Would you like to stay here—there's the spare room, you know.

MADAME ARCATI: No, thank you—each to his own nest—I'll pedal home in a jiffy—it's only seven miles.

CHARLES: I'm deeply grateful to you, Madame Arcati. I don't know what arrangements you generally make, but I trust you will send in your account in due course.

MADAME ARCATI: Good heavens, Mr. Condomine—it was a pleasure—I wouldn't dream of such a thing.

CHARLES: But really I feel that all those trances . . .

MADAME ARCATI: I enjoy them, Mr. Condomine, thoroughly. I always have since a child.

CHARLES: Perhaps you'd give me the pleasure of lunching with me one day soon?

MADAME ARCATI: When you come back—I should be delighted.

CHARLES: Come back?

MADAME ARCATI *crosses to table and kneels to pick up cards on floor.*

MADAME ARCATI (*lowering her voice*): Take my advice, Mr. Condomine, and go away immediately.

CHARLES: But, Madame Arcati! You don't mean that . . .?

MADAME ARCATI: This must be an unhappy house for you—there must be memories both grave and gay in every corner of it—also—— (*She pauses.*)

CHARLES: Also what?

MADAME ARCATI (*thinking better of it*): There are more things in heaven and earth, Mr. Condomine. (*She places her finger to her lips.*) Just go—pack your traps and go as soon as possible. (*Rises and goes to* CHARLES.)

CHARLES (*also in lowered tones*): Do you mean that they may still be here?

MADAME ARCATI (*she nods and then nonchalantly whistles a little tune*): Quien sabe, as the Spanish say. (*She collects her bag and her crystal.*)

MADAME ARCATI *goes to table and collects crystal, cards and Ouija board.*

CHARLES (*looking furtively round the room*): I wonder— I wonder. I'll follow your advice, Madame Arcati. Thank you again.

MADAME ARCATI: Well, good-bye, Mr. Condomine —it's been fascinating—from first to last—fascinating. Do you mind if I take just one more sandwich to munch on my way home? (*Gets sandwich from table.*)

CHARLES: By all means.

MADAME ARCATI *goes to the door.* CHARLES *follows her to see her safely out.*

MADAME ARCATI (*as they go*): Don't trouble—I can find my way. Cheerio once more and Good Hunting!

CHARLES *watches her into the hall and then comes back into the room. He prowls about for a moment as though he were not sure that he was alone.*

CHARLES (*comes in. Softly*): Ruth—Elvira—are you there? (*A pause.*) Ruth—Elvira—I know damn well you're there—(*Another pause.*) I just want to tell you that I'm going away so there's no point in your hanging about any longer—I'm going a long way away—somewhere where I don't believe you'll be able to follow me —in spite of what Elvira said I don't think spirits can travel over water. Is that quite clear, my darlings? You said in one of your more acid moments, Ruth, that I had been hag-ridden all my life! How right you were— but now I'm free, Ruth dear, not only of Mother and Elvira and Mrs. Winthrop Llewelyn, but free of you too and I should like to take this farewell opportunity of saying I'm enjoying it immensely——

The vase on mantelpiece falls on to hearth-stone and smashes.

Aha—I thought so—you were very silly, Elvira, to imagine that I didn't know all about you and Captain Bracegirdle—I did. But what you didn't know was that I was extremely attached to Paula Westlake at the time!

The picture above piano crashes to the ground.

I was reasonably faithful to you, Ruth, but I doubt if it would have lasted much longer—you were becoming increasingly domineering, you know, and there's nothing more off-putting than that is there?

The clock strikes sixteen very quickly.

Good-bye for the moment, my dears. I expect we are bound to meet again one day, but until we do I'm going to enjoy myself as I've never enjoyed myself before.

A sofa cushion is thrown into the air towards CHARLES.

You can break up the house as much as you like—I'm leaving it anyhow. Think kindly of me and send out good thoughts——

The curtains are pulled up and down and the gramophone lid opens and shuts. The overmantel begins to shake and tremble as though someone were tugging at it.

Nice work, Ruth—get Elvira to help you . . . persevere.

A figure from above right book-shelves falls off on to floor.

Good-bye again—parting is such *sweet* sorrow!

A vase from book-shelves up stage falls. The curtains fall. Gramophone starts playing 'Always' very quickly and loudly. He goes out of the room just as the overmantel crashes to the floor and the curtain pole comes tumbling down.

CURTAIN

131

PRESENT LAUGHTER

A Light Comedy in Three Acts

CHARACTERS:

GARRY ESSENDINE
LIZ ESSENDINE
MORRIS DIXON
HENRY LYPPIATT
JOANNA LYPPIATT
MONICA REED
FRED
MISS ERIKSON
DAPHNE STILLINGTON
LADY SALTBURN
ROLAND MAULE

The action of the play passes in GARRY ESSENDINE'S *studio in London.*

ACT I

Morning.

ACT II

Scene I.   Evening.   Three days later.
Scene II.   The next morning.

ACT III

Evening.   A week later.
Time: The Present.

ACT I

The scene is GARRY ESSENDINE's *Studio in London. On stage right there is a door leading into the spare bedroom. Above this is an alcove and hall leading to the front door. Just below and on the left of this is a staircase leading to* GARRY's *bedroom. Under the stairs is a service door, below it, a large window and below that another door leading into the office. Down stage right is a fireplace. The furnishing is comfortable, if a trifle eccentric.*

When the curtain rises it is about 10.30 a.m. *The studio is rather dim as the curtains are drawn.* DAPHNE STILLINGTON *comes out of the spare room. She is a pretty girl of about twenty-three or four. She is wearing a man's dressing-gown and pyjamas. She wanders about until she finds the telephone and then, almost furtively, dials a number.*

DAPHNE (*at telephone*): Hallo—hallo! Is that you Saunders? Can I speak to Miss Cynthia? . . . all right I'll hold on . . . hallo . . . Cynthia darling it's Daphne . . . yes . . . are you alone? Listen I'm you know where. . . . Yes I did. . . . No he isn't awake yet. . . . There's nobody about at all. . . . No, in the spare room, I've only just got up I'm not dressed or anything. . . . I can't go on about it now someone might come in. . . . If anybody rings up from home will you swear to say that I stayed with you. . . . Darling you promised. . . . In that case say I'm in the bath or something. . . . Yes, as soon as I'm dressed in about an hour I should think. . . . Of course . . . I can't wait to tell you. . . . All right.

She puts down the telephone and goes over towards the service door. She has nearly reached it when MISS ERIKSON *comes through it.* MISS ERIKSON *is a thin, vague-looking Swedish housekeeper. She is wearing a chintz smock, gloves and very tattered bedroom slippers. She is smoking a cigarette.*

DAPHNE (*a trifle nervously*): Good morning.

MISS E. (*betraying no surprise*): Good morning.

She goes over to the windows and draws the curtains.

DAPHNE (*following her*): What time is Mr. Essendine going to be called?

MISS E.: He will ring.

DAPHNE: What time does he usually ring?

MISS E.: That depends what time he went to bed.

She goes over to the fireplace. DAPHNE *follows her.*

DAPHNE (*in a rush*): I'm afraid we were rather late last night you see we were at a party and Mr. Essendine very kindly said he'd drive me home and then I found I'd forgotten my latch key and I knew I shouldn't be able to make any of the servants hear because they sleep at the top of the house so Mr. Essendine said I could stay the night here and—and so I did.

MISS E.: If you were very late he will probably sleep until the afternoon.

DAPHNE: Oh dear. Couldn't you call him?

MISS E.: Alas no, we can never call him.

DAPHNE: Well, do you think I could have some coffee or orange juice or something?

MISS E.: I will see.

She goes out through the service door. DAPHNE *left*

*alone sits down rather gloomily on the edge of the sofa.
After a few moments* FRED *enters.* FRED *is* GARRY'S
*valet. He is smartly dressed and wears a black alpaca
coat.* DAPHNE *gets up from the sofa.*

DAPHNE: Good morning.

FRED: Good morning.

DAPHNE: Have *you* any idea what time Mr. Essendine
will wake up?

FRED: Might be any time, he didn't leave no note.

DAPHNE: Couldn't you call him? It's nearly eleven
o'clock.

FRED: The whole place goes up in smoke if we wake
him by accident let alone call 'im.

DAPHNE: Well, do you think I could have some
breakfast?

FRED: What would you fancy?

DAPHNE: Coffee, please, and some orange juice.

FRED: Rightyo.

FRED *goes off again.* DAPHNE *wanders about finally
ending up once more on the sofa.* MONICA REED,
GARRY'S *secretary comes in from the hall. She is in her
hat and coat and carries a bundle of letters.* MONICA *is a
pleasant, rather austere woman in the early forties.*

DAPHNE: Good morning.

MONICA: Good morning. I am Mr. Essendine's
secretary. Is there anything I can do for you?

DAPHNE: Well, I'm afraid it's rather awkward—you
see, Mr. Essendine drove me home last night from a
party and I idiotically forgot my latch-key and so he very
sweetly said I could stay here—in the spare room.

MONICA: I hope you were warm enough.

DAPHNE: Oh yes, quite, thank you.

MONICA: It's liable to be a bit nippy in the spare room.

DAPHNE: I kept the heater on.

MONICA: Very sensible.

DAPHNE: And now I was wondering if somebody could tell Mr. Essendine that I'm—well—here.

MONICA: I expect he'll remember when he wakes up.

DAPHNE: Have you any idea when that will be?

MONICA: I'm afraid not. If he didn't leave any special time to be called he might sleep on indefinitely.

DAPHNE: I don't want to go away without saying good-bye and thanking him.

MONICA: If I were you I should have some breakfast and dress and if he isn't awake by then you can leave a message for him. Have you asked for any breakfast?

DAPHNE: Yes, I think the man's bringing it.

MONICA: Have you known Mr. Essendine long?

DAPHNE: Well, no, not exactly—I mean of course I've known *him* for ages. I think he's wonderful but we actually only met last night for the first time at Maureen Jarratt's party.

MONICA (*quizzically*): I see.

DAPHNE: I think he's even more charming off the stage than on, don't you?

MONICA (*with a slight smile*): I can never quite make up my mind.

DAPHNE: Have you been with him for a long while?

MONICA: Just on seventeen years.

DAPHNE (*enthusiastically*): How wonderful! I expect you know him better than anybody.

MONICA: Less intimately than some, better than most.

DAPHNE: Is he happy, do you think? I mean really happy?

MONICA: I don't believe I've ever asked him.

DAPHNE: He has a sad look in his eyes every now and then.

MONICA: Oh, you noticed that, did you?

DAPHNE: We talked for hours last night. He told me all about his early struggles.

MONICA: Did he by any chance mention that Life was passing him by?

DAPHNE: I think he did say something like that.

MONICA (*taking off her hat and coat*): Oh dear!

DAPHNE: Why?

MONICA: I only wondered.

DAPHNE: You've no idea how I envy you, working for him, but then I expect everybody does. It must be absolute heaven.

MONICA: It's certainly not dull.

DAPHNE: I hope you don't think it's awful me staying here for the night—I mean it does look rather bad, doesn't it?

MONICA: Well, really, Miss—Miss——?

DAPHNE: Stillington. Daphne Stillington.

MONICA: Miss Stillington—it's hardly my business, is it?

DAPHNE: No, I suppose not, but I wouldn't like you to think——

MONICA: Seventeen years is a long time, Miss Stillington. I gave up that sort of thinking in the Spring of Nineteen Twenty Two.

DAPHNE: Oh, I see.

> FRED *comes out of the service door with a tray of orange juice, coffee and toast.*

FRED: Will you 'ave it in here, Miss, or in the bedroom?

DAPHNE: Here, please.

MONICA: I think it would really be more comfortable for you in the bedroom. The studio becomes rather active round about eleven. People call you know, and the telephone rings. . . .

DAPHNE: Very well.

MONICA: I'll let you know the minute he wakes up.

DAPHNE: Thank you so much.

> FRED *takes the tray into the bedroom.* DAPHNE *follows him.* MONICA *goes into the office and comes out again to meet* FRED *emerging from the bedroom.*

MONICA: Is there any soap in that bathroom?

FRED: Yes, but the tap's a bit funny. You 'ave to go on turning it till Kingdom come.

MONICA: Did you tell her?

FRED: She'll find out for herself.

MONICA: You'd better send Miss Erikson in to her.

FRED: She's gone to the grocers but I'll tell 'er when she comes back.

MONICA: Were you here last night?

FRED: No. She's news to me.

MONICA: If he hasn't rung by twelve we'd better wake him.

FRED: You know what 'appened last time!

MONICA: It can't be helped. He's got to lunch out, anyhow.

FRED: Well, if the balloon goes up don't blame me.

> *At this moment* GARRY ESSENDINE *appears at the top of the stairs. He is in his pyjamas and his hair is tousled.*

GARRY (*furiously*): I suppose it's of no interest to any

of you that I have been awakened from deep deep sleep by everybody screaming like banshees! What's going on?

MONICA: I've been talking to Miss Stillington.

GARRY: Who the hell is Miss Stillington?

MONICA: She's in the spare room.

GARRY (*coming down*): I didn't ask where she was, I asked who she was?

MONICA: We might look her up in the telephone book.

FRED: She forgot her latch-key if you know what I mean.

GARRY: Go away, Fred, and get me some coffee.

FRED: Rightyo.

GARRY: And don't say Rightyo.

FRED: Very good, sir. (*He goes.*)

MONICA: You met her at a party and brought her home here and told her about your early struggles and she stayed the night.

GARRY: She's a darling. I remember now. I'm mad about her. What did you say her name was?

MONICA: Stillington. Daphne Stillington.

GARRY: I knew it was Daphne, but I hadn't the faintest idea it was Stillington. How did she look to you?

MONICA: Restive.

GARRY: Poor sweet, I hope you were nice to her. Has anybody given her anything to eat?

MONICA: Fred took her some coffee and orange juice.

GARRY: What's she doing now?

MONICA: I don't know, drinking it, I suppose.

GARRY: It's awful, isn't it? What are we to do?

MONICA: She wants to say good-bye to you and to thank you.

GARRY: Whatever for?

MONICA: That, Garry dear, I am in no position to say.

GARRY: Why didn't you tell her to dress quietly like a mouse and go home? You know perfectly well it's agony here in the morning with everybody banging about.

MONICA: You might have thought of that before you asked her to stay the night.

GARRY: She had to stay the night. She'd lost her key.

MONICA: The sooner we turn that spare room into a library the better.

GARRY: She's probably sobbing her heart out.

MONICA: Why don't you go and see.

GARRY: Lend me a comb and I will.

MONICA (*taking a comb out of her bag*): Here.

GARRY (*taking it and going over to a looking-glass*): Good God, I look ninety-eight.

MONICA: Never mind.

GARRY: In two years from now I shall be bald as a coot and then you'll be sorry.

MONICA: On the contrary I shall be delighted. There will be fewer eager, gently-bred débutantes ready to lose their latch-keys for you when you've got a toupee perched on the top of your head, and life will be a great deal simpler.

GARRY (*thoughfully*): I shall never wear a toupee, Monica, however bald I get. Perhaps on the stage I might have a little front piece but in life, never. I intend to grow old with distinction.

MONICA: Well, I'm sure that will be a great relief to all of us.

GARRY: Here's your sordid little comb.

MONICA (*taking it and putting it back in her bag*): Now, do go and do a nice good-bye scene, there's a dear and get rid of her as quickly as possible. We've got to do the morning mail and Morris might appear at any minute and we can't have her littering up the place and getting in everybody's way.

GARRY: I haven't done my exercises yet.

MONICA: You can do those after she's gone.

GARRY: I can't go into that spare room in my pyjamas, it's like an ice-box.

MONICA: The heater's on. It's been on all night.

GARRY: Very extravagant.

DAPHNE *comes out of the spare room.*

DAPHNE: Garry! I thought I heard your voice.

GARRY (*tenderly*): My dear!

MONICA: If you want me I shall be in the office, Garry.

GARRY (*with great politeness*): Thank you Monica.

MONICA: You won't forget, will you, that a quarter to twelve Mr. Roderick is coming to discuss your special broadcast on the seventeenth?

GARRY: No, Monica.

MONICA: And that at twelve sharp Morris is coming to discuss what understudies you are going to take to Africa.

GARRY: No, Monica.

MONICA: And that at twelve-thirty you have given an appointment to Mr. Roland Maule.

GARRY: I shall remember.

MONICA: I'm so glad. Good-bye Miss Stillington. I do hope we shall meet again.

DAPHNE: Good-bye.

MONICA *goes into the office and shuts the door firmly.*
DAPHNE *runs to* GARRY *and flings her arms round him.*

DAPHNE (*burying her face in his shoulder*): Garry. Oh, Garry!

GARRY (*depositing her in a chair*): Darling.

DAPHNE: I'm ridiculously happy.

GARRY: I'm so glad, darling.

DAPHNE: Are you?

GARRY: Happy?

DAPHNE (*taking his hand*): Yes.

GARRY (*gently withdrawing his hand and turning away*): There's something awfully sad about happiness, isn't there?

DAPHNE: What a funny thing to say.

GARRY: It wasn't meant to be funny.

DAPHNE: Don't you trust me?

GARRY: Trust you? Of course I trust you. Why shouldn't I?

DAPHNE: I've been in love with you for such a long time.

GARRY (*rising*): Don't—don't say that.

DAPHNE: Why? What's the matter?

GARRY: Don't love me too much, Daphne! Promise me you won't. You'll only be unhappy. No good can come of loving anyone like me—I'm not worthy of it, really I'm not.

DAPHNE: You're more worthy of it than anybody in the whole world.

GARRY: Foolish child.

DAPHNE: I'm not a child. I'm twenty-four.

GARRY (*smilingly*): Twenty-four! If only I were younger—— If only you were older——

DAPHNE: What does age matter when people love each other?

GARRY: I wonder how tragically often that has been said.

DAPHNE: It's true.

GARRY: Look at me, Daphne. Look at me kindly. Clearly and honestly—look at the lines on my face—my thinning hair—look at my eyes!

DAPHNE: You're not so very old.

GARRY (*with a touch of asperity*): I didn't say I was so very old, Daphne. I merely said look at me. As a matter of fact I'm only just forty.

DAPHNE: What's forty?

GARRY: Too old for twenty-four.

DAPHNE: You mean you don't love me?

GARRY: I don't mean any such thing.

DAPHNE: Do you love me? Say it—— Do you?

GARRY: Of course I do.

DAPHNE: Say it.

GARRY: I love you, Daphne.

DAPHNE: Oh, darling——

GARRY (*taking both her hands in his*): But this is good-bye!

DAPHNE (*aghast*): Good-bye?

GARRY: It must be. It's inevitable. Not for my sake, my dear, but for yours. Last night—suddenly—a spark was struck! The flame burned brightly—that was happiness—tremendous, wonderful happiness, something to be remembered always——

DAPHNE (*weeping*): You're different this morning—

you don't love me—you didn't mean any of the things you said last night.

GARRY: Youth never understands. That's what's so absolutely awful about Youth—it never, never understands.

DAPHNE (*with spirit*): I don't know what you're talking about.

GARRY: Listen to me, my dearest. You're not in love with me—the real me. You're in love with an illusion, the illusion that I gave you when you saw me on the stage. Last night I ran a terrible risk. I ran the risk of breaking that dear young illusion for ever—but I didn't—— Oh, thank God I didn't—— It's still there —I can see it in your eyes—but never again—never, never again—that's all I can dare to hope for now— moments like last night—that's why I'm so lonely sometimes, so desperately lonely—but I have learned one bitter lesson in my life and that lesson is to be able to say Good-bye——

DAPHNE: But, Garry——

GARRY: Let me go on——

DAPHNE: But I really don't see why——

GARRY: "We meet not as we parted
          We feel more than all may see;
          My bosom is heavy hearted
          And thine full of doubt for me
          One moment has bound the free.

          That moment has gone for ever
          Like lightning that flashed and died
          Like a snowflake upon the river
          Like a sunbeam upon the tide,
          Which the dark shadows hide——"

DAPHNE: But, Garry——

GARRY: Be quiet for a minute, darling——

> "That moment from time was singled
> As the first of a life of pain
> The cup of its joy was mingled
> Delusion too sweet though vain
> Too sweet to be mine again."

There now, that was Shelley. Don't you think it's beautiful?

DAPHNE: Yes, but——

GARRY: There was nothing Shelley didn't know about love, not a thing! All the sadness, all the joy, all the unbearable pain——

DAPHNE: I don't see why love should be so miserable.

GARRY (*laughing bitterly*): That's because you're young, my sweet—young and eager and greedy for life——

DAPHNE: You said last night that I was the one that you had been searching for always and that now that you had found me you would never let me go.

GARRY (*with beautiful simplicity*): That was perfectly true. I never shall let you go. You will be here in my heart for ever.

DAPHNE (*weeping again*): Oh, Garry——

GARRY (*tenderly putting his arm round her*): Don't cry—please, please, don't cry—I can't bear it——

DAPHNE (*clinging to him*): How can you say that I'm only in love with an illusion and not the real you at all——

GARRY: Because it's true.

DAPHNE: It isn't—it isn't——— It was the real you last night, you weren't on the stage—you weren't acting——

GARRY: I'm always acting—watching myself go by —that's what's so horrible—I see myself all the time eating, drinking, loving, suffering—sometimes I think I'm going mad——

DAPHNE: I could help you if only you'd let me.

GARRY (*rising and striding about the room*): If only you could, but it's too late——

DAPHNE: It isn't—I swear it isn't——— You see, I'll prove it to you.

GARRY (*very quietly*): Listen my dear. It isn't that I don't love you, I do—I knew it the first moment that I took you in my arms last night but my life is not my own—I am not free like other men to take happiness when it comes to me—I belong to the public and to my work. In two weeks time I am going away to Africa with a repertory of six plays—do you understand what that means? The work, the drudgery, the nerve strain? That is my job, the one thing to which I must be faithful. When I come back, if I come back, I shall look at you again and I shall know—in the first glance— whether you have waited for me or not—please come here now and kiss me once, just once and then go——

DAPHNE (*running to him*): Oh, Garry——— Oh, darling——

GARRY (*kissing her passionately with his eyes tight shut*): Au revoir, my sweet—not good-bye—just au revoir.

> *He gently disentangles her from him and goes sadly to the window where he stands, obviously a prey to emotion, with his back to her. She looks at him uncertainly for a moment and then goes weeping into the bedroom and shuts*

the door. FRED *comes out of the service door with a breakfast tray.*

FRED: Do you want your coffee here or upstairs?

GARRY: Anywhere—put it anywhere.

FRED: I'd have brought it in before but I 'eard all the weeping and wailing going on and thought I'd better wait.

GARRY: Put the tray down Fred and go away.

FRED: Rightyo.

He puts the tray on the table by the fire and goes off whistling. MONICA *comes out of the office with a tray of opened letters. The telephone rings.*

GARRY (*irritably*): My God, there's no peace—no peace anywhere——

MONICA (*going to the telephone*): I switched it in here because we've got to go through the mail and I can't keep darting in and out of the office all the time. (*At telephone.*) Hallo—hallo, Mr. Essendine's secretary speaking. . . . No, I'm afraid he's not available at the moment, is there anything I can do? . . . Well, he's very busy just now, I think perhaps it would be better if you wrote. . . . No, I'm sorry that's quite impossible . . . very well. . . . Not at all. . . . Goodbye. (*She hangs up.*)

GARRY: Who was that?

MONICA: A Mr. Bramble.

GARRY: Never heard of him.

MONICA: He said you promised to look at his invention.

GARRY (*sitting down at the table*): What sort of an invention?

MONICA: I haven't the faintest idea.

MISS ERIKSON *comes out of the service door.*

MISS E.: Fred said I was to go and speak to the young lady.

GARRY: Very well, Miss Erikson.

MISS E.: What shall I say to her?

GARRY: I really don't know.

MISS E.: I have been to the grocer's and——

GARRY: That's as good an opening gambit as any.

MONICA: Just see that she has everything she wants, Miss Erikson, and turn on a bath for her.

MISS E.: Alas, that I cannot do, the tap makes no water.

GARRY: Do the best you can.

MISS E.: I will try. (*She goes into the spare room.*)

MONICA: There's nothing much this morning. I'll go through them quickly.

GARRY: The coffee tastes of curry powder.

MONICA: Never mind.

GARRY: I wish I had a French chef instead of a Scandinavian Spiritualist.

MONICA: You could never get rid of Miss Erikson, she worships you.

GARRY: Everybody worships me, it's nauseating.

MONICA: There's hell to pay if they don't.

GARRY: What's that blue letter?

MONICA: Sylvia Laurie, she says she must see you before you go away.

GARRY: Well, she can't.

MONICA: And there's another one from Lady Worrall. Lunch on Friday or dinner on Tuesday.

GARRY: Neither.

MONICA (*handing him a letter*): You'd better read this one yourself, it's from that young man you forced to go to the Slade School, he's very unhappy.

GARRY: I didn't force him, he asked me for my advice and I gave it to him.

MONICA: Well, he says he's hedged in by obsolete conventions, that his inspiration's withered and that it's all your fault.

GARRY (*reading the letter*): He's a bloody fool. I knew it the first moment I clapped eyes on him.

MONICA: In that case it would have been wiser not to have let him think that you minded so passionately about his career.

GARRY: If people don't want my advice why the hell do they come and badger me? (*He gives her back the letter.*) Put it in Mount Pleasant.

MONICA: We'll have to go through Mount Pleasant before you go, it's overflowing. Here's a postcard I can't make head or tail of.

GARRY (*turning it round in his hands*): It's from Brazil.

MONICA: I know, it says so on the stamp.

GARRY (*reading*): I've done what you said and its nearly finished—I can't read the signature, it looks like Pickett.

MONICA: Can you remember anyone called Pickett that you sent to Brazil to finish something?

GARRY (*giving her the postcard*): Tear it up, people should write legibly or not at all.

MONICA: Not at all would be lovely.

The telephone rings. MONICA *goes over to it.*

MONICA (*at telephone*): Hallo—Mr. Essendine's secretary speaking. . . . Oh, Tony . . . all right, hold on, he's just here. . . . It's Tony, he wants to know what you thought of the play last night . . .

GARRY *gets up and takes the telephone from her.*

MISS ERIKSON *comes out of the spare room. The*

following conversation take place simultaneously.

GARRY (*at telephone*): Tony. . . . That was a pretty thing, wasn't it? . . . What persuaded Laura to do it? . . . Yes, but it wasn't even a good part . . . all that turgid nonsense. . . . It would have been easier to understand if they'd put a synopsis in the programme. . . . Medieval my foot, they just looked like bananas! . . . No, I haven't read any of them. . . . It's insufferable—if they think that ramping and roaring's good acting, I'm thankful I'm going to Africa. . . . About six o'clock, Liz will probably be here, I think she's coming back to-day. . . . all right. (*He hangs up.*)

MONICA: Is Miss Stillington nearly dressed?

MISS E.: Yes, but she is crying, which makes her slow. The bath was on the blink.

MONICA: You'd better go upstairs, Garry.

GARRY: Where's Fred?

MONICA: Tell Fred Mr. Essendine wants his bath, Miss Erikson.

MISS E.: I will tell him.

> MISS ERIKSON *goes off. After a moment* FRED *comes on and goes upstairs.*

GARRY: You'd better come up, we can do the rest of the letters while I'm in the bath.

MONICA: There are only two more. An invitation from Gertrude Lovat, she's giving a coming out dance for that pimply-looking daughter of hers——

GARRY: Polite refusal.

MONICA: And rather a complicated letter from some boy scouts.

GARRY: Good God!

MONICA: Apparently you're a patron of their

dramatic club which I must say I'd completely forgotten and they're giving a performance of *Laughter in Heaven,* and want you to send them a message.

GARRY (*going upstairs*): All right—send them one.

MONICA: What shall I say?

GARRY (*patiently*): Monica dear, don't tell me that you have arrived at the age of forty-three and are unable to send a message.

GARRY *goes off.* MISS ERIKSON *comes on again and collects the breakfast tray. The telephone rings.* MONICA *goes to answer it.*

MONICA (*at telephone*): Hallo—Oh Henry—Yes, he's in but he's just gone to have his bath. . . . To-day? I thought you weren't going until the end of the week. . . . Yes, of course. . . . He's not lunching until half-past. . . . All right, I'll tell him. . . .

MONICA *hangs up the telephone and picks up the tray of letters. There is a ring at the front-door bell.* MISS ERIKSON *comes out of the service door and goes to answer it.* LIZ's *voice is heard saying,* "Hallo, Miss Erikson— is everybody in?" *After a moment she comes in.* MISS ERIKSON *follows her and goes off again.* LIZ *is a charming-looking woman in the thirties. She is well-dressed but not elaborate. She carries two parcels.*

LIZ: Good morning, Monica dear.

MONICA: Liz! We thought you weren't coming back until to-night.

LIZ: I came over on the Ferry, loaded with gifts like an Eastern potentate. Here's one for you.

MONICA (*taking the parcel that* LIZ *gives her*): How lovely.

LIZ: It's a bottle of scent and very expensive.

MONICA: Thanks ever so much, Liz, you're a darling.

Liz: What's God up to?

Monica: In the bath.

Liz: I've brought him a dressing-gown.

Monica: How thoughtful—he's only got eighteen.

Liz: Don't be acid, Monica, you know he loves peacocking about in something new. It's nice and thin and highly suitable for Africa.

She puts the other parcel on the piano and takes off her hat and coat.

Miss Erikson looked more peculiar than ever this morning. Is her spiritualism getting worse?

Monica: She got in touch with a dead friend at a séance on Sunday night and all he said was, 'No, No, No', and 'Christmas Day'! It upset her very much.

Liz: I do hope she won't get any dottier and do something awful.

Monica: I don't think she will. Hers is quite a tranquil madness.

The telephone rings.

Monica (*going to it*): That damned thing never stops. 'Hallo—hallo—— Morris?—No, he's in the bath. . . . Liz is here if you want to talk to her—yes, she's just arrived. . . .' Here, Liz, it's Morris.

Monica gives Liz the telephone and, while she's talking, opens her present.

Liz (*at telephone*): Good morning, dear. . . . No, on the Ferry. . . . Yes, I saw the play twice. . . . We shall have to alter the end for England, but I talked to Vallion and he didn't seem to mind what happened as long as Garry played it. . . . I told him your idea about Janet playing Eloise and he said that although he knew she was a formidable actress he'd rather have someone who looked less like a guinea-pig? . . . Cochon d'Inde.

. . . Yes, dear, pig of India. . . . He's a very sweet little man and I adore him. . . . No, I'm lunching with poor Violet but I'll come to the office directly afterwards if you like. . . . Yes, I'll get rid of her, you needn't be frightened. . . . All right. (*She hangs up.*)

MONICA (*with her bottle of scent*): This looks wonderful, Liz, I shan't open it until I get home.

FRED *comes down the stairs.*

LIZ: Hallo, Fred—how's everything?

FRED: Bit of a lash up, Miss, as usual.

LIZ: Do you think I could have a cup of coffee—I feel a sinking.

FRED: Rightyo, Miss.

FRED *goes off through the service door.*

LIZ: It's very resolute of Fred to go on calling me Miss, isn't it?

MONICA: I think he has a sort of idea that when you gave up being Garry's wife you automatically reverted to maidenhood.

LIZ: It's a very pretty thought.

DAPHNE *comes out of the spare room in an evening dress and cloak. She is no longer crying but looks depressed. She jumps slightly on seeing* LIZ.

DAPHNE: Oh!

MONICA: I'm so awfully sorry about the bath, Miss Stillington.

DAPHNE: It didn't matter a bit.

MONICA: This is Mrs. Essendine—Miss Stillington.

DAPHNE: Oh!

LIZ (*amiably*): How do you do.

DAPHNE (*shattered*): Mrs. Essendine. Do you mean . . . I mean . . . Are you Garry's wife?

LIZ: Yes.

DAPHNE: Oh—I thought he was divorced.

LIZ: We never quite got round to it.

DAPHNE: Oh, I see.

LIZ: But please don't look agitated—I upped and left him years ago.

MONICA (*a trifle wickedly*): Miss Stillington lost her key last night and so she slept in the spare room.

LIZ (*to* DAPHNE): You poor dear, you must be absolutely congealed!

DAPHNE: Do you think I could get a taxi?

MONICA: I'll ring up for one.

LIZ: No, don't do that, my car's downstairs, it can take you wherever you want to go.

DAPHNE: It's most awfully kind of you.

LIZ: Not at all, the chauffeur's got bright red hair and his name's Frobisher—you can't miss him.

DAPHNE: Thank you very much indeed—you're sure it's not inconvenient?

LIZ (*briskly*): Not in the least—Just tell him to come straight back here after he's dropped you.

DAPHNE (*still floundering*): Oh—yes—of course I will —thank you again . . . good-bye.

LIZ (*shaking hands*): Good-bye—I do hope you haven't caught cold.

DAPHNE (*laughing nervously*): No, I don't think so— good-bye.

MONICA: I'll see you out.

DAPHNE: Please don't trouble——

MONICA: It's no trouble at all.

> MONICA *goes into the hall with* DAPHNE. LIZ *lights a cigarette.* FRED *comes in with a cup of coffee.*

FRED: Would you like anything with it, Miss?

LIZ: No, thank you, Fred, just the coffee.

FRED: I'll tell his nibs you're here—I don't think he knows.

LIZ: Thank you, Fred.

FRED *bounds upstairs.* MONICA *comes back.*

LIZ: Has that been going on long or is it new?

MONICA: Quite new—I found it wandering about in Garry's pyjamas.

LIZ: Poor little thing, how awful for her to be faced with me like that, you ought to have pretended I was someone else.

MONICA: Serve her right, she ought to be ashamed of herself.

LIZ: She seemed to be what is known as a 'lady'. It's all very odd, isn't it?

MONICA: That type's particularly idiotic and the woods are full of them, they go shambling about London without hats and making asses of themselves.

LIZ: Very discouraging.

MONICA: I don't mind if only they'd leave Garry alone, it makes the mornings so complicated. I think it's time we all went for him again—if only out of consideration for Africa.

LIZ: He's not really nearly as flamboyant as he pretends to be, he's just incapable of saying 'No' or 'Good-bye'.

MONICA: He *says* 'Good-bye' often enough, but he always managed to give the impression that he doesn't really mean it, that's what causes all the trouble.

LIZ: I'll have a go at him, after all he's turned forty now, it's high time he relaxed.

MONICA: If you think a big scene's necessary we can get Morris and Henry too, and have a real rouser the night before he sails. It's generally more effective when we all do it together.

LIZ: Morris is awfully hysterical these days and Henry's not nearly so reliable since he married Joanna.

MONICA: Do you like her? Joanna?

LIZ: She's a lovely creature, but tricky. Yes, I think I like her all right.

MONICA: I don't.

LIZ: You never would, darling, she's not your cup of tea at all.

GARRY, *in shirt and trousers, comes downstairs.*

GARRY: Who isn't?

LIZ: Joanna.

GARRY: She's not bad, a bit predatory perhaps, but then as far as I can see everybody's predatory in one way or another.

LIZ: I shall give it up for Lent.

GARRY (*kissing her absently*): Good morning, darling, where's my present?

LIZ: On the piano.

GARRY: It's not another glass horse, is it, to go with Lord Baldwin?

LIZ: No, it's a dressing-gown for Africa.

GARRY (*opening it*): How wonderful, just what I wanted. . . . (*He shakes it out.*) It's absolutely charming . . . thank you, darling, I'm mad about it. (*He puts it on over his shoulders and looks at it in the glass.*) It really is perfect taste, the best sort of Colonial propaganda!

MONICA: Henry rang up, he's going to Brussels to-day and he's coming in to see you before he goes.

GARRY: All right.

MONICA: So is Morris, I think.

LIZ: Go away then, Monica, I must talk to Garry before Morris gets here, it's important.

MONICA: You'd better hurry, Mr. Maule will be here in a minute.

GARRY: Who's he?

MONICA: You know perfectly well, he's the young man who wrote that mad play half in verse and caught you on the telephone and you were so busy being attractive and unspoiled by your great success that you promised him an appointment.

GARRY: I can't see him—you ought to protect me from things like that.

MONICA: You must see him, he's coming all the way from Uckfield, and it serves you right for snatching the telephone when I wasn't looking.

GARRY: I've noticed a great change in you lately, Monica. I don't know whether it's because you've given up cramming yourself with potatoes or what it is but you're getting nastier with every day that passes. Go away.

MONICA (*gathering up her bottle of scent*): I'm going.

GARRY: Who gave you that?

MONICA: Liz.

GARRY: Most unsuitable.

MONICA: I shall be in the office if you want me.

GARRY: Of course you'll be in the office, spinning awful plots and intrigues against me.

MONICA: I will if I can think of any.

GARRY: Go away—go away—go away——

MONICA: Do try and persuade him to have some electric treatments on his hair, Liz, it's getting terribly thin.

MONICA *goes into the office.*

GARRY (*shouting after her*): Switch the telephone off.

MONICA (*off*): All right.

GARRY: Now then, tell me all about everything.

LIZ: I saw the play.

GARRY: Good?

LIZ: Yes, very. We shall have to change it a bit, but Vallion's quite willing to let us do what we like. But I don't want to go on about it now until I've mulled it over a little more. I'm seeing Morris after lunch.

GARRY: I've told him I can't open until November. I must have a holiday after Africa. So there's lots of time.

LIZ: Now I want to talk to you about something else.

GARRY: I don't like that tone at all. What's on your mind?

LIZ: You. Your general behaviour.

GARRY: Really, Liz! What have I done now?

LIZ: Don't you think it's time you started to relax?

GARRY: I don't know what you're talking about.

LIZ: Who was that poor little creature I saw here this morning in evening dress?

GARRY: She'd lost her latch-key.

LIZ: They often do.

GARRY: Now listen to me, Liz——

LIZ: You're over forty, you know.

GARRY: Only just.

LIZ: And in my humble opinion all this casual scampering about is rather undignified.

GARRY: Scampering indeed. You have a genius for putting things unpleasantly.

LIZ: Don't misunderstand me, I'm not taking a moral view, I gave that up as hopeless years ago, I'm merely basing my little homily on reason, dignity, position and, let's face it, age.

GARRY: Perhaps you'd like me to live in a bath-chair!

LIZ: It would certainly have its compensations.

GARRY: It's all very fine for you to come roaring back from Paris where you've been up to God knows what and start to bully me——

LIZ: I'm not bullying you.

GARRY: Yes, you are. You're sitting smug as be damned on an awful little cloud and blowing down on me.

LIZ: Don't bluster.

GARRY: Who went away and left me a prey to everybody? Answer me that!

LIZ: I did thank God.

GARRY: Well then.

LIZ: Would you have liked me to have stayed?

GARRY: Certainly not, you drove me mad.

LIZ: Well, stop shilly shallying about then and pay attention.

GARRY: This, to date, is the most irritating morning of my life.

LIZ: I can remember better ones.

GARRY: Where were we?

LIZ: Be good, there's a darling—I mean it.

GARRY: Mean what?

LIZ: Exactly this. You have reached a moment in life when a little restraint would be becoming. You are no longer a debonair, irresponsible juvenile. You are an eminent man advancing, with every sign of reluctance, into middle age.

GARRY: May God forgive you.

LIZ: Never mind about that, listen. We all know about your irresistible fascination. We've watched it going on monotonously for twenty years.

161

GARRY: I met you for the first time exactly eleven years ago next August, and you were wearing a very silly hat.

LIZ: Will you be serious. Your behaviour naturally affects all of us. Morris, Henry, Monica and me. You're responsible for us and we're responsible for you. You never lose an opportunity of lecturing us and wagging your finger in our faces when we happen to do something you don't approve of.

GARRY: And am I right or am I not? Answer me that!

LIZ: Oh, you're fine when dealing with other people's problems, but when it comes to your own you're not so hot.

GARRY: Of all the base ingratitude!——

LIZ: I think the time has come for you to look very carefully at yourself and see how much you really need all this buccaneering. I personally don't believe it's nearly as necessary to you as you think it is. Think what fun it would be to be *un*attractive for a minute or two. Why you might take to it like a duck to water, and anyhow, it would be a wonderful change.

GARRY: Dear Liz. You really are very sweet.

LIZ (*crossly*): Oh dear, I might just as well have been talking Chinese.

GARRY: Don't be cross, Liz dear. I do see what you mean, honestly I do.

LIZ: That's rather sudden, isn't it? After your belligerence of a few moments ago?

GARRY (*coaxingly*): Surely I may be allowed a little change of mood?

LIZ: You're acting again.

GARRY: You've said some very cruel things to me. I'm upset.

LIZ (*turning away*): If only you were.

GARRY: Seriously though, don't you think you've been a bit too hard on me? I admit I'm a trifle feckless every now and then, but I really don't do much harm to anybody.

LIZ: You do harm to yourself and to the few, the very few, who really mind about you.

GARRY: I suppose you've discussed all this with Monica and Morris and Henry?

LIZ: I haven't yet, but I will unless I see some signs of improvement.

GARRY: Blackmail, hey?

LIZ: You know how you hate it when we all make a concerted pounce.

GARRY (*with exasperation, walking about*): The thing that astonishes me in life is people's arrogance! It's fantastic. Look at you all! Gossiping in corners, whispering behind your fans, telling me what to do and what not to do. It's downright sauce, that's what it is. What happens if I relax my loving hold on any of you for a minute?—Disaster! I happen to go to New York to play a three months season. Henry immediately gets pneumonia, goes to Biarritz to recover, meets Joanna and marries her! I go away for a brief holiday at San Tropez for a month in 1937 and when I come back, what do I find? You and Morris between you have bought the dullest Hungarian play ever written and put it into rehearsal with Phoebe Lucas in the leading part. Phoebe Lucas playing a glamorous courtesan with about as much sex appeal as a haddock! How long did it run? One week! And that was only because the press said it was lascivious.

LIZ: Isn't all this a little beside the point?

GARRY: Certainly not. Twenty years ago Henry put all his money into *The Lost Cavalier*. And who played it for eighteen months to capacity with extra matinees? I did. And who started his whole career as a producer in that play? Morris!

LIZ: I wish you'd stop asking questions and answering them yourself, it's making me giddy.

GARRY: Where would they have been without me? Where would Monica be now if I hadn't snatched her away form that sinister old aunt of hers and given her a job?

LIZ: With the sinister old aunt.

GARRY: And you! One of the most depressing, melancholy actresses on the English stage. Where would you be if I hadn't forced you to give up acting and start writing?

LIZ: Regent's Park.

GARRY: Good God, I even had to marry you to do it.

LIZ: Yes, and a fine gesture that turned out to be.

GARRY: Well, I was in love with you longer than anyone else, you can't grumble.

LIZ: I never grumbled. I believe in going through any experience however shattering.

GARRY: You adored me, you know you did.

LIZ: I still do, dear. You're so chivalrous, rubbing it in how dependent we all are on you for every breath we take.

GARRY: I didn't say that.

LIZ: You're just as dependant on us, anyway, now. We stop you being extravagant and buying houses every five minutes. We stopped you, in the nick of time, from playing Peer Gynt.

GARRY: I still maintain I should have been magnificent as Peer Gynt.

LIZ: Above all we stop you from overacting.

GARRY: You have now gone too far, Liz, I think you had better go away somewhere.

LIZ: I've only just come back.

GARRY (*shouting*): Monica!—Monica!—— Come here at once.

MONICA (*entering*): What on earth's the matter?

GARRY: Have you or have you not ever seen me overact.

MONICA: Frequently.

GARRY: It's a conspiracy!—I knew it!

MONICA: As a matter of fact you're overacting now.
    She goes off.

GARRY: Very well—I give in—everybody's against me—It doesn't matter about me—Oh no—I'm only the breadwinner. It doesn't matter how much I'm wounded and insulted! It doesn't matter that my timorous belief in myself should be subtly undermined.

LIZ: Your belief in yourself is about as timorous as Napoleon's.

GARRY: And look what happened to him. He died forsaken and alone on a beastly little island in the middle of the sea.

LIZ: Islands have that in common.

GARRY: You're trying to be funny now because you're ashamed. You're ashamed because you know perfectly well that you've hurt me unbearably. I doubt if any of you would care a fig if I were exiled for ever to-morrow. You'd probably be delighted. I expect that's why I'm being forced to go to Africa.

LIZ: You're longing to go, and you know it. But

oh, darling, do be careful when you're there for heaven's sake, and don't go having affairs with everybody and showing off and letting down the whole thing.

GARRY: I shall live like a monk. I shall spend all my time in a sad, dilapidated hotel all by myself and I won't speak to a living soul, and if I die of melancholia perhaps you'll be satisfied.

LIZ: Now then, about Morris. I want you to concentrate for a minute.

GARRY: How can I concentrate. You come here and say the most awful things to me, tear the heart out of my bosom and jump up and down on it and then say calmly, 'Now then, about Morris' as though you'd been discussing the weather.

LIZ: I'm very worried.

GARRY: Serve you right.

LIZ: About Morris!

GARRY (*exasperated*): What about Morris? What's wrong?

LIZ: I'm not definitely sure that anything is really, but I've heard things.

GARRY: What kind of things?

LIZ: I think you'll have to do a little of your famous finger wagging. It's—it's Joanna.

GARRY: Joanna?

LIZ: Apparently Morris is in love with her. I don't know how far it's gone, or any details, but I do know that if its true something ought to be done about it and at once.

GARRY: Morris and Joanna! He must be mad. Who told you?

LIZ: Bobbie first, when we were driving out from

Versailles, but I didn't pay much attention to that because we all know he's the world's mischief maker, anyhow. But about two nights later Louise tackled me in Maxims. She'd just arrived from here and was in a state about it. You know how she adores Henry.

GARRY: Does Henry suspect anything?

LIZ: I don't think so, but then he never would, would he? Until it was shoved under his nose.

GARRY: He ought never to have married her, I always said it was a grave mistake. You can't introduce stereotyped diamond studded syrens into a closely-knit group like us without asking for trouble.

LIZ: I don't think she's as stereotyped as all that, but she's dangerous all right.

GARRY: I've always run a mile from her. Morris! He couldn't be such a fool, could he?

LIZ: He's been looking a bit mournful for some time. I've had a feeling that something was wrong.

GARRY (*getting up and walking about*): Oh, God, it's too tiresome, really, it is—just as I'm going away and everything—it might bust up the whole business.

LIZ: If Henry finds out it certainly will.

GARRY: What are we to do?

LIZ: You'd better first of all find out from Morris whether it's true or not, and if it is, how far it's gone, then read the riot act and get him away—take him to Africa with you—anything.

The front door bell rings.

GARRY: There's that beastly young man from Uckfield and here am I trembling like a leaf. I can't face him. I can't!

LIZ: You've got to if you promised.

GARRY: My life is one long torment and nobody even remotely cares.

LIZ: It might not be the young man at all, it might be Morris.

GARRY: To hell with Morris! To hell with everybody.

LIZ: Don't be idiotic. You know as well as I do that if there is any truth in this Joanna business it'll land us all in the most sordid complications and probably wreck everything. You've got to find out. And if you don't I shall, I'm seeing him at two-thirty.

GARRY: He'd never tell you a thing, he'd only get into a rage and ask you to mind your own business.

LIZ: I shall be in until one-fifteen, telephone me when he's gone.

GARRY: He won't go, I'm lunching with him. I can't give you a detailed report of his love life over the telephone with him in the room.

LIZ: Dial my number by mistake and just say, 'I'm so sorry it's a wrong number' then I shall know.

GARRY: What will you know?

LIZ: That everything's all right. But if you say I'm so *terribly* sorry it's a wrong number I'll know that everything's all wrong and be round in a flash to back you up.

GARRY: Intrigue! My whole existence is enmeshed in intrigue.

LIZ: Have you got that clear? Will you promise to do it?

GARRY: All right. (*The bell rings again.*) I'll tell you another fascinating thing about my life if you're interested. Nobody in any circumstances ever answers a

bell under a half an hour. (*He shouts.*) Miss Erikson——
Fred——

LIZ: I'm going now, remember I shall be in until I hear from you. Poor Violet can wait.

GARRY: Poor Violet never does anything else. Miss Erikson!—Fred!!

MISS ERIKSON *comes hurriedly out of the service door.*

GARRY: The front door bell, Miss Erikson, has been pealing incessantly for twenty minutes.

MISS E.: Alas, yes, but there's a woman at the back door with a tiny baby.

GARRY: What does she want?

MISS E.: I do not know, there was no time to ask her.

MISS ERIKSON *goes out into the hall.*

GARRY: Most of the silver's gone by now, I expect.

LIZ: She'd be better advised to settle for some bread and cheese.

GARRY *runs to the office door, opens it and shouts.*

GARRY: Monica, there's a woman at the back door with a tiny baby! Go and deal with her.

MONICA (*entering*): What does she want?

GARRY (*with frigid patience*): That can only be discovered by asking her. Kindly do so.

MONICA: There's no need to snap at me.

MONICA *goes off through the service door.* LIZ *puts on her hat and coat.* MISS ERIKSON *re-enters.*

MISS E. (*announcing*): Mr. Maule.

ROLAND MAULE *enters. He is an earnest young man with glasses. He is obviously petrified with nerves but endeavouring to hide it by assuming an air of gruff defiance.* MISS ERIKSON *goes off.*

GARRY (*advancing, with great charm*): How do you do.

ROLAND: How do you do.

GARRY: This is my wife—Mr. Maule. She just popped in for a minute and is now about to pop out again.

ROLAND: Oh.

LIZ: I know you have an appointment with Garry and I wouldn't interrupt it for the world, so I'll say good-bye.

ROLAND: Good-bye.

LIZ: Don't forget, Garry, I'll be sitting by the telephone.

GARRY: All right.

> LIZ *goes out.* GARRY *motions* ROLAND *into a chair.*

GARRY: Do sit down, won't you?

ROLAND (*sitting*): Thank you.

GARRY: Cigarette?

ROLAND: No, thank you.

GARRY: Don't you smoke?

ROLAND: No.

GARRY: Drink?

ROLAND: No, thank you.

GARRY: How old are you?

ROLAND: Twenty-five, why?

GARRY: It doesn't really matter—I just wondered.

ROLAND: How old are you?

GARRY: Forty in December—Jupiter, you know—very energetic.

ROLAND: Yes, of course. (*He gives a nervous, braying laugh.*)

GARRY: You've come all the way from Uckfield?

ROLAND: It isn't very far.

GARRY: Well, it sort of sounds far, doesn't it?

ROLAND (*defensively*): It's quite near Lewes.

GARRY: Then there's nothing to worry about, is there?

MONICA *comes in.*

MONICA: It's a sweet little thing but it looks far from well.

GARRY: What did she want?

MONICA: Her sister.

GARRY: Well, we haven't got her, have we?

MONICA: She lives two doors down in the Mews, it was all a mistake.

GARRY: This is my secretary, Miss Reed—Mr. Maule.

MONICA: How do you do—I have your script in the office if you'd like to take it away with you.

ROLAND: Thank you very much.

MONICA: I'll put it in an envelope.

MONICA *goes into the office and shuts the door.*

GARRY: I want to talk to you about your play.

ROLAND (*gloomily*): I expect you hated it.

GARRY: Well, to be candid, I thought it was a little uneven.

ROLAND: I thought you'd say that.

GARRY: I'm glad I'm running so true to form.

ROLAND: I mean it really isn't the sort of thing you would like, is it?

GARRY: In that case why on earth did you send it to me?

ROLAND: I just took a chance. I mean I know you only play rather trashy stuff as a rule, and I thought you just might like to have a shot at something deeper.

GARRY: What is there in your play that you consider so deep, Mr. Maule? Apart from the plot which is completely submerged after the first four pages.

ROLAND: Plots aren't important, it's ideas that matter. Look at Chekov.

GARRY: In addition to ideas I think we might concede Chekov a certain flimsy sense of psychology, don't you?

ROLAND: You mean my play isn't psychologically accurate?

GARRY (*gently*): It isn't very good, you know, really, it isn't.

ROLAND: I think it's very good indeed.

GARRY: I understand that perfectly, but you must admit that my opinion, based on a lifelong experience of the theatre, might be the right one.

ROLAND (*contemptuously*): The commercial theatre.

GARRY: Oh, dear. Oh, dear. Oh, dear!

ROLAND: I suppose you'll say that Shakespeare wrote for the commercial theatre and that the only point of doing anything with the drama at all is to make money! All those old arguments. What you don't realise is that the theatre of the future is the theatre of ideas.

GARRY: That may be, but at the moment I am occupied with the theatre of the present.

ROLAND (*heatedly*): And what do you do with it? Every play you appear in is exactly the same, superficial, frivolous and without the slightest intellectual significance. You have a great following and a strong personality, and all you do is prostitute yourself every night of your life. All you do with your talent is to wear dressing-gowns and make witty remarks when you might be really helping people, making them think! Making them feel!

GARRY: There can be no two opinions about it. I am having a most discouraging morning.

ROLAND (*rising and standing over* GARRY): If you want to live in people's memories, to go down to posterity as an important man, you'd better do something about it quickly. There isn't a moment to be lost.

GARRY: I don't give a hoot about posterity. Why should I worry about what people think of me when I'm dead as a doornail, anyway? My worst defect is that I am apt to worry too much about what people think of me when I'm alive. But I'm not going to do that any more. I'm changing my methods and you're my first experiment. As a rule, when insufferable young beginners have the impertinence to criticise me, I dismiss the whole thing lightly because I'm embarrassed for them and consider it not quite fair game to puncture their inflated egos too sharply. But this time my highbrow young friend you're going to get it in the neck. To begin with, your play is not a play at all. It's a meaningless jumble of adolescent, pseudo intellectual poppycock. It bears no relation to the theatre or to life or to anything. And you yourself wouldn't be here at all if I hadn't been bloody fool enough to pick up the telephone when my secretary wasn't looking. Now that you are here, however, I would like to tell you this. If you wish to be a playwright you just leave the theatre of to-morrow to take care of itself. Go and get yourself a job as a butler in a repertory company if they'll have you. Learn from the ground up how plays are constructed and what is actable and what isn't. Then sit down and write at least twenty plays one after the other, and if you can manage to get the twenty-first produced for a Sunday night performance you'll be damned lucky!

ROLAND (*hypnotised*): I'd no idea you were like this. You're wonderful!

173

GARRY (*flinging up his hands*): My God!

ROLAND: I'm awfully sorry if you think I was impertinent, but I'm awfully glad too because if I hadn't been you wouldn't have got angry and if you hadn't got angry I shouldn't have known what you were really like.

GARRY: You don't in the least know what I'm really like.

ROLAND: Oh, yes, I do—now.

GARRY: I can't see that it matters, anyway.

ROLAND: It matters to me.

GARRY: Why?

ROLAND: Do you really want to know?

GARRY: What on earth are you talking about?

ROLAND: It's rather difficult to explain really.

GARRY: What is difficult to explain?

ROLAND: What I feel about you.

GARRY: But——

ROLAND: No, please let me speak—you see, in a way I've been rather unhappy about you—for quite a long time—you've been a sort of obsession with me. I saw you in your last play forty-seven times, one week I came every night, in the pit, because I was up in town trying to pass an exam.

GARRY: Did you pass it?

ROLAND: No, I didn't.

GARRY: I'm not entirely surprised.

ROLAND: My father wants me to be a lawyer, that's what the exam was for, but actually I've been studying psychology a great deal because I felt somehow that I wasn't at peace with myself and gradually, bit by bit, I began to realise that you signified something to me.

GARRY: What sort of something?

ROLAND: I don't quite know—not yet.

GARRY: That 'not yet' is one of the most sinister remarks I've ever heard.

ROLAND: Don't laugh at me, please. I'm always sick if anyone laughs at me.

GARRY: You really are the most peculiar young man.

ROLAND: I'm all right now though, I feel fine!

GARRY: I'm delighted.

ROLAND: Can I come and see you again?

GARRY: I'm afraid I'm going to Africa.

ROLAND: Would you see me if I came to Africa too?

GARRY: I really think you'd be happier in Uckfield.

ROLAND: I expect you think I'm mad but I'm not really, I just mind deeply about certain things. But I feel much better now because I think I shall be able to sublimate you all right.

GARRY: Good. Now I'm afraid I shall have to turn you out because I'm expecting my manager and we have some business to discuss.

ROLAND: It's all right. I'm going immediately.

GARRY: Shall I get you your script?

ROLAND: No, no—tear it up—you were quite right about it—it was only written with part of myself, I see that now. Good-bye.

GARRY: Good-bye.

> ROLAND *goes out.* GARRY *waits until he hears the door slam and then runs to the office door.*

GARRY: Monica.

MONICA (*entering*): Has he gone?

GARRY: If ever that young man rings up again get rid of him at all costs. He's mad as a hatter.

MONICA: Why, what did he do?

GARRY: He started by insulting me and finished by sublimating me.

MONICA: Poor dear, you look quite shattered. Have a glass of sherry.

GARRY: Those are the first kind words I've heard this morning.

MONICA: I think I'll have a nip too. (*She pours out two glasses of sherry. The front door bell rings.*)

GARRY: That's Morris. What time is it?

MONICA: Twenty-to-one. Here—(*she gives him his sherry*)—I'll let him in.

> MONICA *goes into the hall.* MISS ERIKSON *runs on through the service door.*

GARRY: It's all right, Miss Erikson. Miss Reed's gone to the door.

> MISS ERIKSON *goes off again. There is the sound of voices outside.* HENRY *and* MORRIS *come in followed by* MONICA. HENRY *is rather dapper and neat. His age is about forty.* MORRIS *is a trifle younger, tall and good-looking and a little grey at the temples.*

HENRY: There's a strange young man sitting on the stairs.

GARRY: What's he doing?

HENRY: Crying.

MORRIS: What have you been up to, Garry?

GARRY: I haven't been up to anything. I merely told him what I thought of his play.

HENRY: I'm glad to see you haven't lost your touch.

MONICA: Sherry, Morris?

MORRIS: Thanks. (MONICA *gives him some.*)

MONICA: Henry?

HENRY: Is it the same sherry that you always have?

MONICA: Yes.

HENRY: No, thank you.

GARRY: Why, what's the matter with it?

HENRY: Nothing much, it's just not very nice.

GARRY: You ought never to have joined the Athenæum Club, it was disastrous.

HENRY: I really don't see why.

GARRY: It's made you pompous.

HENRY: It can't have. I've always been too frightened to go into it.

MORRIS: Henry's quite right about the sherry, it's disgusting.

GARRY: If anybody complains about anything else I shall go mad. This studio's been like a wailing wall all the morning.

MORRIS: Liz is back.

GARRY: How nice of you to let me know, Morris, I really must try to get in touch with her.

MORRIS: What's the matter with the old boy, Monica? He seems remarkably crochety.

MONICA: Liz went for him a bit and then I told him he overacted, he really has had rather a beastly time, and then that dotty young man on top of everything.

MORRIS: Never mind, Garry—God's in his heaven and all's right with the world—I've got some lovely bad news for you.

GARRY: What?

MORRIS: Nora Fenwick can't come to Africa.

GARRY: Why not? What's the matter with her?

MORRIS: She's broken her leg.

GARRY (*exasperated*): Well, really——! ! !

HENRY: It isn't actually so terribly important.

GARRY: Oh, not at all, it couldn't matter less! It

merely means that I've got to spend all the voyage out rehearsing a new woman in six different character parts! How did the silly bitch do it?

MORRIS: She fell down at Victoria Station.

GARRY: She'd no right to be at Victoria Station. Who can we get?

HENRY: Morris wants Beryl Willard, but I don't think she's quite right.

GARRY (*dangerously*): So you want Beryl Willard, do you!

MORRIS: Why not? She's extremely competent.

GARRY (*with intense quietness*): I agree with you. Beryl Willard is extremely competent. She has been extremely competent for well over forty years. In addition to her competence she has contrived, with uncanny skill, to sustain a spotless reputation for being the most paralysing, epoch-making, monumental, world-shattering, God-awful bore that ever drew breath!

MORRIS: Now really, Garry, I don't see——

GARRY (*warming up*): You don't see? Very well I will explain further, just one thing and it's this. No prayer, no bribe, no threat. No power, human or divine, would induce me to go to Africa with Beryl Willard. I wouldn't go as far as Wimbledon with Beryl Willard.

MONICA: What he's trying to say is that he doesn't care for Beryl Willard.

MORRIS: All right, she's out. Whom do you suggest?

HENRY: Just a minute, if you're going to start one of those casting arguments I'm going. I've got to catch a plane for Brussels, I only wanted to let you know that you can't have the Mayfair Theatre for the French play in the autumn.

GARRY: Why not?

HENRY: Because Robert's got it for the whole season, starting in September.

GARRY: Why did you let him? You knew I wanted it.

HENRY: The Forum's much nicer, anyhow, and the capacity's bigger.

GARRY: It's a conspiracy! You've both of you been trying to get me into that underheated morgue for years.

MORRIS: It's being done up and re-decorated.

GARRY: It'll have to be rebuilt brick by brick before I set foot in it.

HENRY: Arrange it later, will you, Morris, he's obviously in one of his states this morning. I can't stop now.

GARRY: What are you going to Brussels for, anyhow?

HENRY: Business. Nice ordinary straightforward business. Nothing to do with the theatre at all. I can't wait to get there. Good-bye, Sweetie. Try to be a little more amiable when I come back. Good-bye, Monica— good-bye, Morris—— By the way, you might call up Joanna, she's all alone.

MORRIS: I have. I'm taking her to the opening at the Haymarket to-morrow night.

HENRY: Fine—good-bye.

HENRY *goes out*. MONICA *goes towards the office.*

MONICA: Do you want me any more?

GARRY: Why, what are you going to do?

MONICA: I'm going to write to Beryl Willard and ask her to come and live with you.

MONICA *goes off.*

GARRY: So you're taking Joanna to the Haymarket to-morrow night, are you?

MORRIS: Yes, why?

GARRY: Why not! Why not, indeed?

MORRIS: What on earth do you mean?

GARRY: I think I shall come too.

MORRIS: All right, that'll be grand. I've got a box, there's lots of room.

GARRY: Why have you been so mournful lately?

MORRIS: I haven't been in the least mournful.

GARRY: Oh, yes, you have. Liz has noticed it and so have I.

MORRIS: Well, you're both quite wrong. I'm perfectly happy.

GARRY (*irritably, walking about the room*): Oh, Morris!

MORRIS: What the devil's the matter?

GARRY: You like Joanna, don't you?

MORRIS: Of course I do, she's a darling.

GARRY: I wouldn't call her a darling exactly, but then I don't see very much of her. I gather you do.

MORRIS: What are you getting at?

GARRY: People are talking, Morris.

MORRIS (*with an edge on his voice*): What about?

GARRY: About you and Joanna.

MORRIS: Rubbish!

GARRY: It's perfectly true and you know it.

MORRIS: I don't know anything of the sort.

GARRY: Are you in love with her?

MORRIS: In love with Joanna? Of course I'm not.

GARRY: Are you preparing to be? I can generally tell when you're about to embark on one of your emotional rampages.

MORRIS: Well, I like that, I must say. What about you?

GARRY: Never mind about me for a moment, nobody could accuse me of being emotional, anyway.

MORRIS: Couldn't they just! Look at Sylvia Laurie! You carried on like a maniac over her for weeks. All that sobbing and screaming.

GARRY: That was years ago.

MORRIS: Never mind when it was. It was! And if that wasn't emotional I should like to know what is. You wore us all to shreds.

GARRY: I notice that you've turned the conversation very adroitly into an attack on me.

MORRIS: Now listen, Garry——

GARRY: Do you swear to me that you haven't had an affair with Joanna?

MORRIS: I'm damned if I'll be cross-questioned like this.

GARRY: Have you or haven't you?

MORRIS: Mind your own business.

GARRY: My God if this isn't my business nothing is. If you're fooling about with Joanna on the side and Henry finds out do you realise what it will mean?

MORRIS: I refuse to go on with this conversation.

GARRY: You can refuse until you're blue in the face, you're going to listen to me.

MORRIS: I'm not.

He makes a move towards the door. GARRY *grabs him by the arm.*

GARRY: It's true then, is it?

MORRIS (*shaking him off*): Leave me alone.

GARRY: Sit down, this really is serious.

MORRIS: I've no intention of submitting to one of

your famous finger wagging tirades—I'm sick to death
of them.

GARRY: Many years ago, Morris, very many years
ago, before you were so sick to death of them, you
might just as well admit that they helped you consider-
ably.

MORRIS: Of course I admit it, and so what?

GARRY: We've never lied to each other about
anything really vital to us, have we?

MORRIS: No.

GARRY: And it would be rather foolish, after all
those turbulent years, to start now, wouldn't it?

MORRIS: All right, all right, but nobody has as far as
I can see.

GARRY: I'm not going to ask you one more question.
I'm not even going to bellow at you, much, but that all
depends upon whether or not you annoy me. I am,
however, going to make you see one thing clearly, and
it's this. You and Henry and Monica and Liz and I
share something of inestimable importance to all of us,
and that something is mutual respect and trust. God
knows it's been hard won. We can look back on years
and years of bloody conflict with ourselves and with
each other. But now, now that we're all middle-aged we
can admit, with a certain mellow tranquillity, that it's
been well worth it. Here we are, five people closely
woven together by affection and work and intimate
knowledge of each other. It's too important a 'set up'
to risk breaking for any outside emotional reason
whatsoever. Joanna is alien to us. She doesn't really
belong to us and never could. Henry realises that
perfectly well, he's nobody's fool, and to do him justice
he has never tried to force her on us. But don't believe

for a minute that Joanna isn't a potential danger because she is! She's a hundred per cent female, exceedingly attractive and ruthlessly implacable in the pursuit of anything she wants. If she could succeed in wreaking havoc among all of us I am quite certain she would leave no stone unturned. She's a scalp hunter, that baby, if ever I saw one, and all I implore you is this. Be careful! You needn't even answer me but BE CAREFUL! Is that clear?

MORRIS (*rising*): Quite. I think I'll have a little more sherry.

He goes over and helps himself.

GARRY: Give me some too, I need it.

MORRIS (*bringing him some*): Here you are.

GARRY: Thanks. (*He glances at his watch.*) Good heavens, it's past one, I forgot to telephone up for a table.

MORRIS: There's no need, we can always go upstairs.

GARRY: Upstairs smells of potted shrimps, it won't take a minute to ring up.

He goes to the telephone and dials a number.

GARRY (*at telephone, with a radiant smile*): Oh, I'm so sorry, it's a wrong number.

He hangs up and, as he is dialling again,

THE CURTAIN FALLS

ACT II

SCENE I

The time is midnight.

> *Three days have elapsed since Act I.*
>
> *When the curtain rises the studio is pleasantly but not too brightly lit.* GARRY, *wearing a dressing-gown over his evening clothes, is playing the piano. There is a whisky and soda by him which he sips occasionally.*
>
> *Presently* FRED *enters from the service door. He is very smartly dressed in a dinner-jacket and he carries a soft black hat.*

FRED: Well, I'm off now. Got everything you want?

GARRY: You're very dressy! Where are you going?

FRED: Tagani's.

GARRY: Where's that?

FRED (*laconically*): Tottenham Court Road.

GARRY: Is it a dance hall or a night club or what?

FRED: Bit of all sorts really. Doris works there.

GARRY: What does she do?

FRED: Sings a couple of numbers and does a dance with a skipping rope.

GARRY: Very enjoyable.

FRED: I think it's a bit wet if you ask me, but still it goes down all right.

GARRY: Are you going to marry Doris?

FRED: Me marry? What a hope!

GARRY: You know you really are dreadfully immoral, Fred.

FRED (*cheerfully*): That's right!

GARRY: I know for a fact that you've been taking advantage of Doris for over two years now.

FRED: Why not? She likes it, I like it and a good time's 'ad by all.

GARRY: Do you really mind about her at all? I mean do you ever think about her when she's not there?

FRED (*complacently*): She always is there—when I want her.

GARRY: What will she do when we go to Africa?

FRED: She'll manage. She's got a couple of blokes running round after her now. Quite posh one of 'em is, in the silk business.

GARRY: Oh, I see, she's communal.

FRED: Will you ring in the morning as usual or do you want to be called?

GARRY: I'll ring. Has Miss Erikson gone?

FRED: Oh, yes, she went early. She 'ad a come over about six o'clock and 'opped it. She's gone to 'er friend in Hammersmith. They turn out all the lights, play the gramophone and talk to an Indian.

GARRY: I suppose if it makes her happy it's all right.

FRED: She's a good worker even if she is a bit scatty, and you can't 'ave everything, can you? Will that be all?

GARRY: Yes, thank you, Fred. Enjoy yourself.

FRED: Same to you—be good.

> FRED *goes out jauntily.* GARRY *continues to play the piano. Presently the telephone rings.* GARRY *answers it.*

GARRY: 'Allo, 'allo? . . . Who is that speaking? (*His voice changes.*) Oh, Liz. . . . No, I've been in about half an hour. . . . Yes, dear, quite alone, I'm turning over a new leaf, hadn't you heard? . . . Yes, with both of them, and I went to supper with them at the Savoy afterwards and Morris and I dropped her home. . . . No, I didn't go on about it any more, I thought it wiser not. You sound a little sceptical. . . . No, as a matter of fact she was very charming, she's quite intelligent, you know, and I must say she's a permanent pleasure to the eye. . . . All right. . . . No, I've got to lunch with Tony. . . . Very well, about eleven. . . . Yes, of course, I'm going straight to bed now. . . . Good-night, darling.

> *He hangs up. He goes over to the piano, finishes his drink, takes a book off the table, switches off the lights and is halfway upstairs when the front door bell rings. He mutters "Damn" softly, comes down and switches on the lights again and goes out into the hall and is heard to say "Joanna!" in a surprised voice. She comes in and he follows her.* JOANNA *is an exquisitely gowned woman in the early thirties. She has a great deal of assurance and considerable charm.*

JOANNA: I can't tell you how relieved I am that you're in. I've done the most idiotic thing.

GARRY: Why, what's happened?

JOANNA: I've forgotten my latch-key!

GARRY: Oh, Joanna!

JOANNA: It's no good looking at me like that—I'm not in the least inefficient as a rule, this is the first time I've ever done such a thing in my life. I'm in an absolute fury. I had to dress in the most awful rush to dine with Freda and go to the Toscanni concert and I left it in my other bag.

GARRY: And I suppose the servants sleep at the top of the house.

JOANNA: They do more than sleep, they apparently go off into a coma. I've been battering on the door for nearly half an hour.

GARRY: Would you like a drink?

JOANNA: Very much indeed—I'm exhausted.
    She takes off her cloak.

GARRY (*mixing a drink for her and himself*): We must decide what's best to be done.

JOANNA: I went to a call office and rang up Liz but she must be out because there wasn't any reply.

GARRY (*looking at her*): You rang up Liz and there wasn't any reply!

JOANNA: Yes, and as I hadn't any more coppers and the taxi man hadn't either, I came straight here.

GARRY: Cigarette?

JOANNA (*taking one*): Thank you—— You're looking very whimsical, don't you believe me?

GARRY (*lighting her cigarette*): Of course I believe you, Joanna, why on earth shouldn't I?

JOANNA: I don't know, you always look at me as though you didn't trust me an inch. It's a shame because I'm so nice really.

GARRY (*smiling*): I'm sure you are, Joanna.

JOANNA: I know that voice, Garry, you've used it in every play you've ever been in.

GARRY: Complete naturalness on the stage is my strong suit.

JOANNA: You've never liked me really, have you?

GARRY: No, not particularly.

JOANNA: I wonder why.

GARRY: I always had a feeling you were rather tiresome.

JOANNA: In what way tiresome?

GARRY: Oh, I don't know. There's a certain arrogance about you, a little too much self assurance.

JOANNA: You don't care for competition, I see.

GARRY: You're lovely-looking, of course, I've always thought that.

JOANNA (*smiling*): Thank you.

GARRY: If perhaps a little too aware of it.

JOANNA (*doing up her face in the glass from her bag*): You're being conventionally odious but somehow it doesn't quite ring true. But then you never do quite ring true, do you? I expect it's because you're an actor, they're always apt to be a bit papier mâché.

GARRY: Just puppets, Joanna dear, creatures of tinsel and sawdust, how clever of you to have noticed it.

JOANNA: I wish you'd stop being suave, just for a minute.

GARRY: What would you like me to do, fly into a tantrum? Burst into tears?

JOANNA (*looking down*): I think I should like you to be kind.

GARRY: Kind?

JOANNA: Yes. At least kind enough to make an effort to overcome your perfectly obvious prejudice against me.

GARRY: I'm sorry it's so obvious.

JOANNA: I'm not quite an idiot, although I must say you always treat me as if I were. I know you resented me marrying Henry, you all did, and I entirely see why you should have, anyhow at first. But after all that's five years ago, and during that time I've done my best not to obtrude myself, not to encroach on any special preserves. My reward has been rather meagre, from you particularly, nothing but artificial politeness and slightly frigid tolerance.

GARRY: Poor Joanna.

JOANNA (*rising*): I see my appeal has fallen on stony ground. I'm so sorry.

GARRY: What is all this? What are you up to?

JOANNA: I'm not up to anything.

GARRY: Then sit down again.

JOANNA: I'd like you to call me a taxi.

GARRY: Nonsense, there's nothing you'd hate more. You came here for a purpose, didn't you?

JOANNA: Of course I did. I lost my key, I knew you had a spare room and——

GARRY: Well?

JOANNA: I wanted to get to know you a little better.

GARRY: I see.

JOANNA: Oh, no, you don't. I know exactly what you think. Of course I can't altogether blame you. In your position as one of the world's most famous romantic comedians, it's only natural that you should imagine that every woman is anxious to hurl herself at your head. I'm sure, for instance, that you don't believe for a moment that I've lost my latch-key!

GARRY: You're good—— My God, you're good!

JOANNA: What's the number of the taxi rank—I'll ring up myself.

GARRY: Sloane 2664.

JOANNA *dials the number and waits a moment.*

JOANNA: "Hallo—hallo. . . . Is that Sloane 2664?— Oh, I'm so sorry it's the wrong number."

GARRY *collapses on to the sofa laughing.*
What are you laughing at?

GARRY: You, Joanna.

JOANNA (*dialling again*): You're enjoying yourself enormously, aren't you?

GARRY (*jumping up and taking the telephone out of her hand*): You win.

JOANNA: Give me that telephone and don't be so infuriating.

GARRY: Have another drink?

JOANNA: No, thank you.

GARRY: Just one more cigarette?

JOANNA: No.

GARRY: Please—I'm sorry.

JOANNA *rises and walks back to the sofa in silence.*

JOANNA: I wish you were really sorry.

GARRY (*handing her another cigarette*): Maybe I am.

JOANNA: I could cry now, you know, very effectively, if only I had the technique.

GARRY: Technique's terribly important.

JOANNA: Oh, dear.

GARRY (*lighting her cigarette*): Conversation seems to have come to a standstill.

JOANNA: I think perhaps I would like another drink after all, a very small one. You make me feel extraordinarily self-conscious. Of course that's one of your most renowned gifts, isn't it—frightening people?

GARRY (*pouring out a drink*): You're not going to pretend that I frighten you.

JOANNA: Freda Lawson's terrified out of her life of you, she told me so the other day.

GARRY: I can't imagine why, I hardly know her.

JOANNA: It's personality, I expect, plus a reputation for being—well—(*she laughs*)—rather ruthless.

GARRY (*giving her her drink*): Amorously or socially?

JOANNA: Both.

GARRY: Well—How are we doing?

JOANNA: Better, I think.

GARRY: That's a very pretty dress.

JOANNA: I wore it for Toscanni.

GARRY: He frightens people too, when they play wrong notes.

JOANNA: You look strangely young every now and then. It would be nice to know what you were really like, under all the trappings.

GARRY: Just a simple boy, stinking with idealism.

JOANNA: Sentimental too, almost Victorian at moments.

GARRY: I spend hours at my sampler.

JOANNA: Are you happy on the whole?

GARRY: Ecstatically.

JOANNA: You never get tired of fixing people's lives, of being the Boss, of everybody adoring you and obeying you?

GARRY: Never. I revel in it.

JOANNA: I suspected that you did, but I wasn't sure.

GARRY: Would you like me to play you something?

JOANNA: No, thank you.

GARRY: Why ever not? You must be mad!

JOANNA: Not mad, just musical.

GARRY: Snappy, too. Quite rude in fact.

JOANNA: Yes, that was rather rude, wasn't it? I'm sorry.

GARRY: Never mind. What shall we do now?

JOANNA: Do? Is there any necessity to do anything?

GARRY: I don't know, my social sense tells me that something is demanded and I'm not quite sure what it is. That's why I suggested playing to you.

JOANNA: There's always the radio.

GARRY: Not here there isn't!

JOANNA: I'm so glad I'm adult. You must be pretty shattering to the young and inexperienced.

GARRY: Is that a subtle allusion to my charm?

JOANNA: You glitter so brightly. You're so gaily caparisoned—all the little bells tinkling.

GARRY: I sound like a circus horse.

JOANNA: You are rather like a circus horse as a matter of fact! Prancing into the ring to be admired, jumping, with such assurance, through all the paper hoops.

GARRY: Now listen, Joanna. You've got to make up your mind. This provocative skirmishing is getting me down. What do you want?

JOANNA: I want you to be what I believe you really are, friendly and genuine, someone to be trusted. I want you to do me the honour of stopping your eternal performance for a little, ring down the curtain, take off your make-up and relax.

GARRY: Everyone keeps on telling me to relax.

JOANNA: One can hardly blame them.

GARRY: Shouldn't I be very vulnerable, dear Delilah, shorn of my nice silky hair?

JOANNA: Why are you so afraid of being vulnerable? Wouldn't it be rather a relief? To be perpetually on guard must be terribly tiring.

GARRY: I was right about you from the first.

JOANNA: Were you?

GARRY: You're as predatory as hell!

JOANNA: Garry!

GARRY: You got the wretched Henry when he was convalescent, you've made a dead set at Morris, and now by God you're after me! Don't deny it—I can see it in your eye. You suddenly appear out of the night reeking with the lust of conquest, the whole atmosphere's quivering with it! You had your hair done this afternoon, didn't you? and your nails and probably your feet too! That's a new dress, isn't it? Those are new shoes! You've never worn those stockings before in your life! And your mind, even more expertly groomed to vanquish than your body. Every word, every phrase, every change of mood cunningly planned. Just the right amount of sex antagonism mixed with subtle flattery, just the right switch over, perfectly timed, from provocative implication to wistful diffidence. You want to know what I'm really like do you, under all the glittering veneer? Well, this is it. This is what I'm really like—— Fundamentally honest! When I'm driven into a corner I tell the truth, and the truth at the moment is that I know you, Joanna. I know what you're after, I can see through every trick. Go away from me! Leave me alone!

JOANNA (*laughing*): Curtain!

GARRY (*at the drink table*): Damn it, there isn't any more soda-water.

JOANNA: Take it neat, darling.

GARRY: How dare you call me darling.

JOANNA: Because I think you are a darling—I always have.

GARRY: Go away immediately.

JOANNA: You're really the reason I married Henry.

GARRY: Are there no depths to which you won't descend?

JOANNA: Absolutely none. I'm in love with you—I've been in love with you for over seven years now, it's high time something was done about it.

GARRY (*striding about*): This is the end!

JOANNA (*calmly*): No, my sweet, only the beginning.

GARRY: Now listen to me, Joanna——

JOANNA: I think you'd better listen to me first.

GARRY: I shall do no such thing.

JOANNA (*rising, calmly and with great firmness*): You must, it's terribly important to all of us. Please sit down.

GARRY: I'd rather walk about if you don't mind.

JOANNA: Sit down, dear sweet Garry, please sit down. You must concentrate, things aren't nearly as bad as they look. I've got to explain and I can't if you're whirling about all the time.

GARRY (*flinging himself on to the sofa*): This is dreadful!

JOANNA: First of all I want you to promise me to answer one question absolutely truthfully. Will you?

GARRY: What is it?

JOANNA: Will you promise?

GARRY: Yes—all right—go on.

JOANNA: If you had never seen me in your life before, if we had met for the first time to-night, if I were in no way concerned with anyone you know, would you have made love to me? Would you have wanted me?

GARRY: Yes.

JOANNA: Well, that's that. Now then——

GARRY: Look here, Joanna——

JOANNA: Shut up! You must be fair, you must let me explain. When I said just now that you were the reason I married Henry, that was only partly true. I'm devoted to Henry, much fonder of him really than he is of me. He was madly in love with me for the first two years, but he isn't now. You stood between us. Not only in my heart but in his. He hated your thinly-veiled disapproval of me, and it gradually strangled his love for me. That's the worst of people like you with damned dominant personalities, you not only affect others when they're actually with you, but when they're away from you as well. Henry has been lightly unfaithful to me eleven times to my certain knowledge during the last three years. He's probably having a high old time in Brussels at this very moment.

GARRY: You're lying, Joanna.

JOANNA: I'm not lying. I don't mind enough to lie. Henry's a darling and I wouldn't leave him for anything in the world, we get on perfectly, better now really than we did before, but you're the one I'm in love with and always have been. I don't want to live with you, God forbid! You'd drive me mad in a week, but you are to me the most charming, infuriating, passionately attractive man I have ever known in my life——

GARRY (*bitterly*): What about Morris?

JOANNA: Morris? Don't be so idiotic, he was only a step nearer you.

GARRY: Is he in love with you? Has there been anything between you?

JOANNA: Of course there hasn't. He's quite sweet, but he doesn't attract me in the least, and never could.

GARRY: Do you swear that?

JOANNA: There's no need for me to swear it, you can see, can't you? And even if you can't see you must at least be able to feel that what I'm saying is the truth. We're neither of us exactly adolescent, we both know enough by experience that when our instincts are pushing us with all their force in one direction that it's foolish and painful to rush off in the other.

GARRY: Are you so sure it's foolish?

JOANNA: It's the most foolish thing in the world to

store up regrets. Who could you and I possibly harm by loving each other for a little?

GARRY: Please may I get up now?

JOANNA: Yes.

GARRY (*prowling about*): How was the Toscanni concert?

JOANNA: Glorious. (*She sits down.*) He played the Eighth and the Seventh.

GARRY: Personally I prefer the Fifth.

JOANNA: I like the Ninth best of all.

GARRY (*casually sitting beside her on the sofa*): There's nothing like the dear old Ninth.

JOANNA: I love the Queen's Hall, don't you? It's so uncompromising.

GARRY (*taking her hand*): I love the Albert Hall much more.

JOANNA (*leaning against him*): I wonder why. I always find it depressing.

GARRY (*taking her in his arms*): Not when they do 'Hiawatha', surely?

JOANNA (*dreamily*): Even then.

GARRY (*his mouth on hers*): I won't hear a word against the Albert Hall.

The lights fade and the Curtain falls.

ACT II

SCENE II

The time is about ten-thirty the next morning. The curtains are drawn and the studio is dim. JOANNA comes out of the spare room wearing pyjamas and the same dressing-

gown that DAPHNE *wore in Act I. She wanders round the room for a bit looking for a bell.* MISS ERIKSON *comes out of the service door.*

JOANNA (*brightly*): Good morning.

MISS E.: Good morning.

JOANNA: Is Mr. Essendine awake yet?

MISS E.: He has not rung.

She goes over and draws the curtains.

JOANNA: I wonder if you'd be very kind and tell him that I am awake.

MISS E.: Alas, no. He would be crazy with anger.

JOANNA: Would he, indeed! I shall be crazy with anger myself unless I have some breakfast. I have been ringing that bell in there for hours.

MISS E. (*straightening the furniture and patting the sofa cushions*): It does not work.

JOANNA: Oddly enough that dawned on me after a while.

MISS E.: It is the mice, they eat right through the wires, they are very destructive.

FRED *comes out of the service door.*

JOANNA: Good morning.

FRED: Good morning, Miss—— (*He recognises her.*) Oh, dear!

JOANNA: I beg your pardon?

FRED: You're Mrs. Lyppiatt, aren't you?

JOANNA: Yes, I am.

FRED (*whistling*): Whew!

He goes off again through the service door.

JOANNA: That I gather was Mr. Essendine's valet. Does he always behave like that?

MISS E.: He was a steward on a very large ship.

JOANNA: Most of the ship's stewards I've met have good manners.

MISS E.: He is the only one I know.

JOANNA (*peremptorily*): I would like some china tea, some thin toast without butter and a soft boiled egg, please.

MISS E.: We have no tea and no eggs either, but I will make the toast with pleasure.

JOANNA: Is there any coffee?

MISS E.: Yes, we have coffee.

JOANNA: Well, please bring me some as quickly as you can.

MISS E.: I will tell Fred.

JOANNA: And as he was on such a very large ship perhaps he could do something about the tap in that bathroom.

MISS E.: Alas, he was not a bathroom steward.

> MISS ERIKSON *goes off and just as* JOANNA, *with an exclamation of irritation is about to go back into the spare room,* MONICA *comes in from the hall in a hat and coat. As in Act I she carries a bundle of letters.*

JOANNA: Good morning, Monica.

MONICA (*horrified*): Joanna!

JOANNA: Thank heaven you've come, I've had such a complicated chat with the housekeeper.

MONICA: Did you stay the night here?

JOANNA: Yes, wasn't it sweet of Garry to let me? I did the most idiotic thing. I lost my latch-key.

MONICA: You lost your latch-key?

JOANNA: I was in absolute despair and then I suddenly thought of Garry.

MONICA: You suddenly thought of Garry!

JOANNA: Why do you keep repeating everything I say?

MONICA: I don't know, it seems easier than saying anything else.

JOANNA: Why, Monica, you actually look as if you disapproved of my staying the night here!

MONICA: I think it was tactless to say the least of it.

JOANNA: In heaven's name why? It was a perfectly natural thing to do in the circumstances.

MONICA: When is Henry coming home?

JOANNA: To-morrow morning by the eleven o'clock plane. Is there anything else you'd like to know?

MONICA (*slowly*): No, I don't think I want to know anything else at all.

JOANNA: I must say, Monica, I really do resent your manner a little bit, anyone would think I'd done something awful.

MONICA: Obviously you are a better judge of that than I.

JOANNA: It's quite astounding to think that anyone as close to Garry as you have been for so many years should have a prurient mind.

MONICA: I'm sure you must be shocked to the marrow.

JOANNA (*with great poise*): I really don't feel equal to continuing this rather strained conversation before I've had some coffee. Perhaps you'd be kind enough to hurry it up for me.

MONICA: I always knew it.

JOANNA (*irritably*): Always knew what?

MONICA: That you'd cause trouble. I'll see about your coffee. (*The front door bell rings.*) There's somebody at the door, you'd better go back into the spare room.

JOANNA (*sitting on the sofa*): I'm quite happy here, thank you.

MONICA: As you please.

> *She goes into the hall. After a moment's pause she comes in again followed by* LIZ. LIZ, *to whom the news has only just been broken, is wearing a set expression. She is however quite calm.*

LIZ: Good morning, Joanna. This *is* a surprise.

JOANNA: Liz! I tried to get you for hours last night. I'd lost my latch-key and was in the most awful state. But you weren't in.

LIZ: I was in from ten o'clock onwards. You must have been ringing the wrong number.

JOANNA: I rang the number you gave me.

LIZ (*sweetly*): Then I must have given you the wrong number.

MONICA: If you want me, Liz, I shall be in the office.

LIZ: I do want you, Monica, so don't budge.

> FRED *comes in with a tray.*

JOANNA (*with rather overdone relief*): Ah, breakfast.

FRED: Where will you 'ave it?

JOANNA: Here, please.

FRED (*to* LIZ): Good morning, Miss.

LIZ: Good morning, Fred. I think it would be more comfortable for Mrs. Lyppiatt to have her coffee in the spare room.

JOANNA (*firmly*): I'd rather have it here if you don't mind. I like to see what's going on.

LIZ: Put it down there for the moment, Fred, we will decide later where Mrs. Lyppiatt is going to have her coffee.

JOANNA: I've already decided, Liz, but it's sweet of you to take so much trouble.

LIZ: That will be all, thank you, Fred.

FRED: Rightyo, Miss—— Give us a shout if you want anything.

LIZ: Thanks—I will.

FRED *vanishes through the service door.*

JOANNA (*pouring out her coffee*): I understand he used to be a steward on a liner.

LIZ (*to* MONICA): I suppose Garry hasn't been called yet, has he?

MONICA: No, I don't think so. Shall I go and wake him now?

LIZ: No, not yet.

JOANNA: He ought to be wakened at once, Liz. It's disgraceful lying in bed on a lovely morning like this— so unhealthy. He'll be getting fat and flabby if he's not careful.

MONICA (*in heartfelt tones*): I wish to God he would.

JOANNA: I wonder what she put in this coffee, apart from the coffee, I mean.

MONICA: Weed killer if she had any sense.

JOANNA: You're really being remarkably offensive, Monica. One always hears that the secretaries of famous men are rather frustrated and dragon-like. It's funny that you should turn out to be so true to type.

MONICA: The only thing that's frustrating me at the moment is a wholesome fear of the gallows.

LIZ: I think after all perhaps you had better go into the office, Monica. This situation is becoming rather tense.

JOANNA: For no reason at all as far as I can see, unless you all have the most unpleasant minds.

MONICA: All right, Liz.

LIZ: I'll come in in a minute.

MONICA *goes into the office and slams the door.*

JOANNA: Poor thing, she's ever so much more faded than when I first met her. I suppose she's mad about Garry like all of us?

LIZ: All of *us*, JOANNA?

JOANNA: I must say he is enchanting. We had the most lovely talk last night.

LIZ: I think it would be better if neither Henry nor Morris knew you stayed the night here, Joanna.

JOANNA: Good heavens, why? Henry wouldn't mind a bit.

LIZ: I wouldn't be too sure if I were you, anyhow, Morris would.

JOANNA: Morris? What on earth has Morris to do with it?

LIZ (*with irritation*): Oh, really, Joanna.

JOANNA: I haven't the faintest idea what you're talking about.

LIZ: Now listen, we haven't much time to waste fencing with each other. I know perfectly well that you have been unfaithful to Henry with Morris so you needn't trouble to deny it any further.

JOANNA: It's the most abominable lie——

LIZ: Unfortunately I dined quietly with Morris last night, upstairs at the Ivy. He was very upset and became rather hysterical, as you know he sometimes does, and he told me everything.

JOANNA (*grimly*): So he told you everything, did he?

LIZ: It's quite natural that he should. We're very old friends, you know. All of us!

JOANNA: How dare he discuss me with you, or with anybody.

LIZ: Don't be silly, Joanna.

JOANNA (*bitterly*): A charming constellation of

gossipy little planets circling round the great glorious sun.

Liz: I was coming to that.

Joanna: What do you mean?

Liz: I don't wish to know anything about what happened last night, but I'll tell you one thing. The great glorious sun is not going to get tangled up in this if I can stop it. And I can.

Joanna: I should be interested to know how?

Liz: I don't think Garry would like to know that you had been Morris's mistress as well as Henry's wife. I don't think Morris would like to know that you have been Garry's mistress, which I suspect you have.

Joanna: Mistress indeed. Melodramatic nonsense.

Liz: And I don't think Henry would like to know anything about any of it.

Joanna: Are you trying to blackmail me?

Liz: Yes, I am.

Joanna: You mean that you'd be low enough to tell Garry?

Liz: Yes. And Morris, and Henry. I'll tell them all unless you do as I say.

Joanna: I suppose you're still in love with Garry yourself?

Liz: Not in the least, but even if I were it's entirely beside the point. I certainly love him. I love Henry and Morris too. We've all been devoted to one another for many years, and it would take more than you to break it up permanently. But I'm not taking any risks of you even upsetting it temporarily. You're going to do what I tell you.

Joanna: And what if I don't?

Liz: You'll be out, my dear, with all of us, for ever.

With Garry most of all—quite soon. You wouldn't like that you know. It would be very shaming to your vanity.

JOANNA: You're very sure.

LIZ: Absolutely positive. I know Garry very well, you know. After all I've had every opportunity.

JOANNA: It's a pity you ever left him.

LIZ: For him, yes, I think it is.

JOANNA: And why should you imagine that I should mind—so terribly—even if I were 'out' with all of you as you put it?

LIZ: Principally because you made such a terrific effort to get in. You'd have had better results and much quicker too if you hadn't been so determined to be alluring.

JOANNA: I've never been talked to like this in my life.

LIZ: Well, make the most of it. There isn't much time. What are you going to do?

JOANNA: Do? I'm not going to do anything.

LIZ: Are you going to be sensible and do what I ask you or not?

JOANNA: You haven't asked me anything yet.

LIZ: I want you to promise me that you won't see Garry again before he goes to Africa.

JOANNA: Well, really!

LIZ: Will you promise that?

JOANNA: No, certainly not. It's nonsense. And even if I did how do I know that I can trust you? And Monica? What about her?

LIZ: Monica won't say a word, and I won't, either if you swear not to see Garry again before he goes to Africa.

JOANNA: I'm bound to see him again. How can I avoid it?

LIZ: You can be ill. You can go to Paris. Anywhere.

JOANNA: I have no intention of doing any such thing.

LIZ: Very well. (*She goes to the service door and calls.*) Fred—Fred.

JOANNA: It will be you who's breaking everything up, not me.

FRED *enters*.

FRED: Did you call, Miss?

LIZ: Go and wake Mr. Garry immediately, will you.

FRED: Rightyo.

He starts to go upstairs when the front door bell rings.

LIZ: You'd better answer the door first. (*To* JOANNA.) It's Morris. He told me last night he was coming to see Garry at eleven.

JOANNA (*as* FRED *goes into the hall*): Look here, Liz——

LIZ: I'm glad, really, it'll be more convenient.

JOANNA (*rising hurriedly*): I can't face him. It'll be too unpleasant. I'll do what you say.

LIZ: You swear it? You swear you won't see him again? You'll go away?

JOANNA: Yes, yes—I swear it.

LIZ: Quickly, get into the spare room. Don't come out until I tell you.

JOANNA darts into the spare room and shuts the door.

LIZ swiftly sits down at the table and is sipping JOANNA'*s coffee.* FRED *comes back.*

FRED: It's a Mr. Maule. He says he has an appointment.

LIZ: Mr. what?

FRED: Maule. He looks a bit wet to me.

LIZ: Oh, dear—well, I suppose you'd better show him in—Miss Reed can deal with him—I'll tell her.

FRED: Rightyo.

> FRED *goes back into the hall.* LIZ *flies over to the office door.*

LIZ (*in an urgent whisper*): Monica—Monica——

MONICA (*appearing*): What is it?

LIZ: A Mr. Maule is here.

MONICA: He's no right to be, he's raving mad.

FRED (*announcing*): Mr. Maule.

> ROLAND MAULE *enters.*

ROLAND (*nervously*): Good morning.

LIZ: Good morning.

ROLAND: We met before, do you remember?

LIZ: Yes, very well—just the other day.

MONICA: Have you an appointment with Mr. Essendine?

ROLAND: Oh, yes, indeed. I spoke to him on the telephone last night. He told me I was to come at ten-thirty. I fear I'm a little late.

MONICA: I'm afraid you can't see him just at the moment. Could you come back later?

ROLAND: Isn't there anywhere I could wait?

MONICA: Go into the office for a moment and I'll find out when Mr. Essendine can see you.

ROLAND: It's very kind of you—thanks very much.

MONICA: Not at all—this way.

> MONICA *puts him into the office and shuts the door.*

FRED: Oughtn't I to have let 'im in?

MONICA: I don't know. He says Mr. Garry told

him to come, although I can hardly believe he did. You'd better go and wake him and ask him.

LIZ: No, Monica. Don't wake Garry yet. I'd rather he slept on a bit.

MONICA: All right, Fred. We'll call him later.

FRED: It's all the same to me.

FRED goes off through the service door.

LIZ: Listen, Monica. I've guaranteed that you and I won't say a word to Henry or Morris or anybody about her being here if she swears not to see Garry again before he goes.

MONICA: Did she?

LIZ: Yes, she did. But Morris will be here at any moment and it's going to be awkward. There's a telephone in the spare room, isn't there?

MONICA: Yes.

LIZ: Is it the same number as this, or different?

MONICA: It's the private wire. This one is an extension of the office.

LIZ: What's the number?

MONICA: You know it—the private line—Sloane 2642.

The front door bell rings.

LIZ: There he is. Leave this to me. I'll explain later.

She rushes over to the spare room and goes in, closing the door behind her. MONICA *goes to the office and opens the door.*

MONICA: Oh, Mr. Maule, what are you doing?

She goes in and shuts the door. FRED *comes through the service door and goes into the hall.* GARRY *appears at the top of the stairs, fully dressed, with a hat on. He creeps down stairs and meets* MORRIS *face to face.*

MORRIS: Garry! Where are you going?

GARRY (*a little flustered*): Out.

MORRIS: Out where?

GARRY: Just out. I suppose I can go out if I want to, can't I?

FRED: I never even knew you was up! You are a dark 'orse and no mistake.

GARRY: Don't be impertinent, Fred, and go away.

FRED: All right—all right. The gentleman's in the office and the lady's in the spare room if you 'appen to want either of 'em.

FRED *goes off cheerfully.*

GARRY: What's he talking about! The boy's off his rocker.

MORRIS: Lady! Really, Garry, you're impossible. Who is it?

GARRY: I would be so very very much obliged if everybody would mind their own God-damned business.

MORRIS: For heaven's sake get rid of her—I've got to talk to you—I'm in a bad way——

GARRY: What's the matter?

MORRIS: Get rid of her first whoever she is. She's probably got her ear clamped to the keyhole.

GARRY: How can I get rid of her, she may be in the bath.

MORRIS: Tell her to hurry, then.

GARRY: Now look here, Morris——

MORRIS: If you won't—I will.

He strides over to the bedroom door.

GARRY: Morris—I forbid you to go near that room.

MORRIS (*loudly, knocking on the door*): Will you please come out—as soon as you can?

LIZ (*entering and closing the door behind her*): I'm coming —I was only just powdering my nose.

MORRIS: Liz! It's you!

LIZ: Of course. Who did you think it was?

MORRIS: What on earth were you making such a fuss about, Garry?

GARRY: I make a fuss? I don't know what you mean!

LIZ: Why are you so completely dressed so very suddenly? You were asleep a few minutes ago!

GARRY: Oh, no, I wasn't. I most gravely doubt whether I shall ever be able to sleep again.

LIZ: Perhaps your conscience was troubling you.

GARRY: I cannot for the life of me imagine why everybody is so absolutely beastly to me! I'm bullied and cross-questioned and ordered about from morning till night. I can't wait to get to Africa! To be away from the lot of you.

LIZ: It won't be exactly unrelieved sadness for us.

MORRIS: For God's sake stop bickering both of you. I'm in the most awful state.

GARRY: What about?

MORRIS: Liz knows—I told her last night.

GARRY: What does Liz know? What did you tell her last night?

LIZ: Pull yourself together, Morris. Have a drink or something. Try not to be silly.

MORRIS: I don't want a drink. If I have a drink it will make it much worse. It always does.

GARRY: This is a most fascinating little conversation, but I must say I should appreciate the full flavour of it more if I had just an inkling as to what it was all about.

MORRIS: I haven't slept for three nights, Garry—

ever since you talked to me the other morning.

Liz: Oh, dear!

Garry: Why not?

Morris: It's bad enough getting one of my awful obsessions. You know what I'm like when I get an obsession. God knows you've helped me through enough of them, but this time I've made an utter fool of myself and lied to you into the bargain.

Garry (*sharply*): Lied to me? You mean?

Morris: Joanna and I love each other, Garry.

Garry (*after a slight pause—looking at* Liz): Oh!

Morris: It's been going on for several months, but we made a pact that we'd lie about it to everyone, whatever happened, in order not to make an awful mess and upset everything. But I'm not used to lying to you —I never have before, and it's been absolutely driving me mad ever since. Yesterday afternoon I couldn't bear it any longer and I told Joanna I was going to tell you. She was furious, and said she'd never speak to me again if I did and went away and left me. I've been trying to find her ever since. She's disappeared. Her servants say she hasn't been home all night. I'm so terrified that something has happened to her.

Liz: Perhaps it has.

Morris: You don't like her, Liz, you never did. I'm not sure that I do really, but I love her.

Liz: The whole thing's very fragrant, isn't it, Garry? You needn't fuss any more, Morris. Joanna spent the night with me.

Morris: Spent the night with you!

Liz (*viciously*): Yes, on the sofa. She lost her latch-key. She's there now. I told her I'd tell you to ring her up if I saw you.

MORRIS: I'll go round now.

LIZ: You'd better ring up first and see if she's still there—she may have gone out. I'll get the number for you.

She dials a number. GARRY *watches her, fascinated. She speaks.*

Hallo—Maggie? Is Mrs. Lyppiatt still there?—all right. . . . Here you are, Morris——

She hands him the telephone and comes over to GARRY.

LIZ (*quietly to* GARRY): You unutterable fool!

MORRIS (*at telephone*): Joanna! . . . Yes, it's me, Morris. . . . I've been terribly worried, why didn't you tell me you were with Liz. . . .

GARRY (*hissing to* LIZ): How did you get her out?

LIZ: She's not out, she's in there, on the other line.

MORRIS: . . . I thought something had happened to you. . . . Yes, I'm at the studio. . . . No, only Liz and Garry. . . . Yes, I have, I had to. . . . How can you be so cruel! . . . Listen, Joanna . . . I must see you . . . Joanna! . . .

(*To* LIZ *and* GARRY.)

She's hung up!

GARRY: Serve you right.

MORRIS (*frantically*): I must see her—I must see her—— What am I to do?

GARRY: Control yourself and don't be hysterical.

MORRIS: I'm going to Liz's flat now.

GARRY: You're not. You're coming with me.

MORRIS: Coming with you? Where to?

GARRY (*at random*): Hampstead Heath.

MORRIS: It's cruel and heartless of you to try to be funny at a moment like this, when you know I'm utterly miserable.

GARRY: I'm not trying to be funny at all. What's the matter with Hampstead Heath? Anybody'd think I'd suggested taking you to Devil's Island.

LIZ: Be quiet, Garry. Listen, Morris. It really would be better if you didn't try to see Joanna in your present state. Have a drink and calm down—you can see her later in the day.

> LIZ *pours out a drink for* MORRIS *and hands it to him*.

GARRY (*violently*): I'm surrounded by lies and intrigue and sickening emotionalism! I tell you here and now I'm not going to put up with it for a minute longer. My whole life is spent in trying to help people, in giving them wise, sensible advice, in trying to shield them from the buffets of Fate and what's the result? They batten on me! They drain every ounce of vitality out of me until I'm a nerveless wreck and then expect me to go tramping all over darkest Africa in order to make money for them. It's not good enough. I'm sick to death of the whole business. If ever I attempt to snatch a little happiness for myself, a little gaiety, a little relaxation, I'm accused of being immoral and undignified and letting down my position. Position indeed! I have no more position than a little frightened beetle, cringing into the shadows, trying frantically to hide away from the blinding, merciless light of criticism that is for ever beating down upon me. . . .

MONICA (*entering*): Did you or did you not give an appointment to Mr. Maule this morning?

GARRY: I most emphatically did not. He terrifies the life out of me.

MONICA: Well, he's here——

> ROLAND *comes out of the office*.

ROLAND: I'm afraid I told a wicked lie about the appointment but I must see you—it's very, very important.

MONICA: Oh, Mr. Maule, you promised to stay in the office.

ROLAND (*ignoring her*): I want to tell you that it's all right.

GARRY: What's all right?

ROLAND (*eagerly*): About what I felt about you—I've got the whole thing straightened out.

GARRY: I'm absolutely delighted, and I congratulate you from the bottom of my heart, but you really must go away now.

There is a ring at the front door bell.

MONICA: Please go now, Mr. Maule. Mr. Essendine is in the middle of a conference.

GARRY: Like hell I am. (*The bell rings again, insistently.*) Fred;—Miss Erikson!—There is somebody at the door. I have not the remotest idea who it is but I strongly suspect that it is a mad cripple from Stoke Poges who is passionately in love with me!

MONICA: I'll go.

She goes into the hall.

LIZ: Mr. Maule, I really do think it would be better if you were to come back later.

ROLAND: Couldn't I stay a little longer, you see every moment I'm near him I get smoother and smoother and smoother, my whole rhythm improves tremendously.

HENRY *comes in very quickly, followed by* MONICA. *He is obviously in a state of great agitation.*

HENRY: Where's Joanna? She's disappeared.

GARRY: I thought you weren't coming back until to-morrow.

HENRY: She hasn't been home all night, nobody knows where she is.

LIZ: It's all right, Henry, she stayed with me.

HENRY: But I rang up Maggie and she said she hadn't seen her.

LIZ: There's a reason for that, I'll explain later.

HENRY: Something's happened. I had a presentiment in the aeroplane.

GARRY: I always have a presentiment in an aeroplane, a presentiment that I'm going to be sick! I think I'm going to be sick now!

HENRY: But why did Maggie say——

LIZ: Ring her up if you don't believe me, Monica get my flat on the telephone——

MONICA *goes to the telephone and proceeds to dial the number.*

ROLAND (*going to* HENRY *and shaking hands with him*): How do you do, my name is Roland Maule.

HENRY (*abstractedly*): How do you do.

ROLAND (*shaking hands with* MORRIS): Roland Maule, I don't think we've met.

GARRY: Please go away, Mr. Maule.

MONICA (*at telephone*): Hallo—Joanna!—Hold on a minute. Henry wants to speak to you—— Yes, he's here—— In the studio. . . . (*She hands the telephone to* HENRY.)

HENRY: . . . Darling—you gave me the most awful fright—No, I got through everything yesterday, and there was no sense in staying—I sent a telegram. . . . No, I couldn't think what had happened. . . . Yes, we're all here. . . . No, I think I shall have to lunch with Morris, there's some difficulty about a theatre for Garry for the play in the autumn. . . . Are you coming back to the house? . . . All right I'll be in to change in about half an hour. . . Very well, darling —I'll tell her—— (*To* Liz.) She says she's going out in a minute.

Liz: Tell her to stay where she is, I'll pop in and see her presently.

Henry (*at telephone*): Liz says do stay where you are and she'll be round presently—— What! . . . Joanna, whatever is the matter? (*To* Liz.) She says she feels as if she were in a French Farce and is sick to death of it, she sounds upset.

Liz: That's the telephone, it never stops ringing. Tell her to shut it off.

Henry (*at telephone*): Liz says you're to shut off the telephone. . . . Joanna. . . . Hallo. . . . (*To everyone.*) She's hung up.

> *During the preceding conversation the front door bell has rung again.* Fred *has come out of the service door and gone to answer it. He now returns from the hall.*

Fred: There's a Lady Saltburn outside, Miss Reed, she says she has an appointment for eleven-thirty.

Garry: Who?

Monica (*horrified*): Good heavens! What's to-day?

Garry: Black Thursday.

Monica: Thursday—I'd completely forgotten—Lady Saltburn's niece—You promised you'd give her an audition and recommend her to the R.A.D.A. or something, don't you remember?

Garry: No, I do not. She must be sent away immediately.

Monica: We can't send Lady Saltburn away, she gave us fifty pounds for the Footlights Fund.

Garry: How can I possibly listen to people's nieces

this morning? I'm on the verge of a nervous break-down already.

HENRY: Why, what's happened?

GARRY: Too much, Henry! Far, far too much!

MONICA: You must see her, it won't take a minute, it would be most terribly rude not to, after all you promised. Ask her in, Fred.

FRED: Rightyo. (*He goes into the hall.*)

ROLAND (*with his braying laugh*): It's all very exciting, isn't it?

MORRIS: We'd better go—I'll come back later, Garry—Liz, Henry——

HENRY: All right. We'll go to Liz's flat and talk to Joanna, it's only just round the corner.

MORRIS (*in a panic*): No—I must go to the office and you must come with me—it's urgent.

FRED (*announcing*): Lady Saltburn. Miss Stillington.

GARRY (*bitterly*): Thank you, Monica, you're a great comfort to me!

> LADY SALTBURN *enters accompanied by* DAPHNE STILLINGTON. LADY SALTBURN *is a majestic but rather effusive society woman.* DAPHNE *is wearing a set expression of social poise. There is a glint in her eye.*

LADY S. (*advancing to* GARRY): Mr. Essendine, this is so charming of you.

GARRY (*shaking hands*): Not at all—it's a pleasure.

LADY S.: This is my niece Daphne. I believe you knew her mother years ago, she died you know—in Africa.

GARRY (*shaking hands with* DAPHNE): How do you do.

DAPHNE: I've been longing to meet you Mr. Essendine. (*With intensity.*) I've loved everything you've ever done.

216

GARRY: How very nice of you.

LADY S.: Daphne simply wouldn't give me any peace until I had rung up your secretary and absolutely implored her for an appointment. She's so tremendously keen, you know——

GARRY: She must be. (*He shoots* DAPHNE *a look of fury.*) I must introduce you to everybody. My wife, my secretary, Miss Reed. . . .

LADY S.: How do you do—How do you do, you were so kind on the telephone.

GARRY: Mr. Dixon—Mr. Lyppiatt—and Mr. Maule.

LADY S.: How do you do. This is quite a peep behind the scenes, isn't it, Daphne, dear?

DAPHNE: This is the most thrilling moment of my life, Mr. Essendine. I've always wondered what you'd be like close to.

LADY S.: You mustn't embarrass Mr. Essendine, Daphne.

DAPHNE: I'm sure he understands—don't you, Mr. Essendine?

GARRY: Of course, my dear, I understand perfectly, but I'm afraid I can only give you just a few minutes— you see I'm terribly busy just now making arrangements for my tour—(*he shoots a look at* LADY SALTBURN)—in Africa.

LADY S.: I'd no idea you were going to Africa, how very interesting. You really must pay a visit to my brother-in-law, he lives on the top of the most beautiful mountain.

HENRY (*to* LADY SALTBURN): I do hope you'll forgive us, but we really must go now—we have to go to the office—Good-bye.

LADY S.: How sad—Good-bye.

HENRY: Morris? Liz?

LIZ: I'm staying here for a little—I'll come later.

MORRIS: Good-bye, Lady Saltburn—(*he bows to* DAPHNE)—Good-bye.

GARRY: Good-bye, Mr. Maule.

ROLAND: I'm staying too.

> MORRIS *and* HENRY *go out.* MONICA *and* LIZ *exchange glances of relief.*

MONICA: Won't you sit down, Lady Saltburn?

LADY S.: Thank you so much. (*She does so.*) Are you ready, Daphne? You know how busy Mr. Essendine is —I'm sure it's very sweet of him to see us at all— We mustn't impose on him.

DAPHNE (*almost defiantly*): Yes—I'm ready.

GARRY: What are you going to do?

DAPHNE (*looking into his eyes*): Nothing very much— I'll try not to bore you. You see, I want you to hear me so very much—it means everything to me—you will hear me, won't you—you can hear me, can't you?— And you're not angry, are you?

LADY S.: Daphne—really! What are you talking about?

DAPHNE: Mr. Essendine understands, don't you, Mr. Essendine?

GARRY: Mr. Essendine understands everything. He spends his whole life understanding absolutely everything and what nobody else seems to understand is that the strain of it is driving him step by step to a suicide's grave!

LIZ: Don't be affected, Garry.

GARRY: My wife, Lady Saltburn, left me several years ago. Gnawing regret has embittered her.

ROLAND: There's nothing worse than regret. Look at Chekov! He knew.

GARRY: We have no time at the moment to look at Chekov, Mr. Maule. (*To* DAPHNE.) Please don't be nervous. What are you going to do, sing?

DAPHNE: I'm not nervous, but I wish you weren't so many miles away. I'm not going to sing—I'm just going to say a few lines——

GARRY (*sitting down*): Very well—fire away.

    DAPHNE *stands by the piano and looks at him fixedly. She begins.*

DAPHNE: "We meet not as we parted
        We feel more than all may see;
        My bosom is heavy hearted
        And thine full of doubt for me
        One moment has bound the free.

      "That moment has gone for ever
        Like lightning that flashed and died
        Like a snowflake upon the river
        Like a sunbeam upon the tide
        Which the dark shadows hide.

      "That moment from time was singled
        As the first of a life of pain
        The cup of its joy was mingled
        Delusion too sweet though vain
        Too sweet to be mine again . . ."

    During the last verse JOANNA *comes swiftly out of the spare room. She is wearing her evening dress and cloak of the night before. She is obviously extremely angry.*

JOANNA (*furiously*): That room is like a frigidaire and

I have no intention of staying in it one minute longer. Will somebody kindly call me a taxi.

DAPHNE (*breaking off*): Oh!—Oh, dear!

LIZ: You'd better take my car, Joanna, it's downstairs.

DAPHNE (*violently*): The chauffeur's got red hair and his name's Frobisher!

LADY S.: Daphne!

JOANNA: Thank you very much. (*To* GARRY.) I shan't see you again, Garry, as I am going to Paris tomorrow for a month, so this is good-bye. I do hope that when you go to Africa you will be wise enough to take all your staunch, loyal satellites with you. It's too dangerous for a little tinsel star to go twinkling off alone and unprotected. Please don't imagine that I haven't enjoyed the circus enormously. I have. But in the circuses I've been used to it was always the ringmaster who cracked the whip, not the clowns. Goodbye!

> *She sweeps out.* DAPHNE *gives a loud cry and faints dead away.* LADY SALTBURN *and* MONICA *run to her.*

ROLAND (*exultantly*): This is splendid! Splendid! I feel reborn.

GARRY: Oh, go to hell!

CURTAIN

ACT III

A week has passed since the preceding act. The time is
between nine and ten in the evening. GARRY *is leaving for*
Africa first thing in the morning so there are various
trunks and suitcases about. There has been a farewell
cocktail party so there is a buffet table with remains on it
and the whole place is dotted with glasses and ash-trays.
GARRY, *with the inevitable dressing-gown over his suit, is*
enjoying a light meal at a Bridge table.
MONICA *is seated on the sofa with a large tray of letters*
on her lap, around her on the sofa are scattered several
more. At her feet is a waste-paper basket.
When the curtain rises MONICA *is reading a letter aloud.*

MONICA (*reading*): . . . I shall never forget those
lovely days in Madeira and our picnics on the rocks,
what fun we had. It really was wonderful getting to
know you intimately like that without you being
surrounded by crowds of people all the time. I can
never begin to tell you how much it meant to me. Now
for my exciting news. I am coming to England.
Imagine! The first time for seven years. I arrive on the
twenty-eighth and shall be in London for three whole
weeks staying at the Rubens Hotel. You remember you
told me to let you know a good time beforehand if I
should be coming so I am doing so. I am so longing to
see you again. With my love and many many glorious
memories. Yours Winnie.

GARRY: Poor Winnie. When's it dated?
MONICA: November the seventh.

GARRY: Over six months ago. She must be gone by now.

MONICA: You told me to put it into 'Mount Pleasant.'

GARRY: Well, it's too late to answer it.

MONICA (*tearing it up*): Much. She'd probably have been an awful nuisance anyhow. Don't forget your ship stops at Madeira in a few days' time. You'd better lock yourself in your cabin.

GARRY: Not at all. If I run into her I shall say I never got the letter and that it's my secretary's fault.

MONICA: Here's one signed 'Joe'.

GARRY: Joe what?

MONICA: Just 'Joe'. It's dated February the second.

GARRY: Let's look.

MONICA (*handing it to him*): He seems to have met you in the South of France.

GARRY: I do get about, don't I? (*Looking at the letter.*) Oh, it's Joe.

MONICA (*patiently*): That's what I said.

GARRY: Joe was wonderful. I met him in a bar in Marseilles. He's dark green and comes from Madras. What does he want?

MONICA: It's at the end, after the bit about his sister having a baby.

GARRY: Oh, yes—well, why didn't you send him one?

MONICA: Because I didn't consider that 'Joe, Madras', was sufficient address.

GARRY: I'm damned if I can remember his other name.

MONICA (*taking it from him and tearing it up*): Well, he's out of luck then, isn't he?

GARRY: What's that large packet?

MONICA: Those are all from that madwoman in

Herne Bay. You said you'd read them sometime because they might be interesting psychologically.

GARRY: Well, I haven't time now. You'd better keep them though for evidence in case she murders me some day.

MONICA: I don't think she wants to murder you, merely to live with you.

GARRY (*ruminatively*): Herne Bay. I don't think I've ever been to Herne Bay.

MONICA: Never mind about Herne Bay now dear, we've got too much to do.

GARRY: I wonder if I shall ever see Green England again.

MONICA: I see no reason why you shouldn't.

GARRY: I might die of some awful tropical disease or be bitten by a snake.

MONICA: I doubt if there are many snakes in the larger cities.

GARRY: I can see myself under a mosquito net, fighting for breath——

MONICA: Who with?

GARRY: You have no imagination, Monica. Just a flat literal mind. It must be very depressing for you.

MONICA: I get by.

GARRY: How many more are there to do?

MONICA: About twenty.

GARRY: I can't bear it. Put them back in 'Mount Pleasant' until I come back.

MONICA: You seemed to be in doubt just now as to whether you were coming back.

GARRY: Well, I can't answer letters if I'm dead, can I?

MONICA: There are just one or two here that you've got to answer dead or alive.

GARRY: Not a moment's peace ever in my life—not even a tranquil hour when I can say farewell to my books and pictures . . . I slave and slave. . . .

MONICA: Nonsense, you've got the whole evening to say farewell to your books and pictures, but before you do you've got to tell me what to say to this awful old Admiral in Rugby.

GARRY: What's he doing in Rugby, anyhow, it's not a Naval Base.

MONICA: He's retired.

GARRY: If you ask me that's all to the good. What does he want?

MONICA (*with letter*): It seems that you met his son at a dance in Edinburgh when you were up there with *Laughter in Heaven* and swore to him that if he left the Navy you'd give him a job on the stage.

GARRY: I never said such a thing.

MONICA (*grimly*): He has left the Navy.

GARRY: Well, give him some letters of introduction to people, don't just sit there.

MONICA: I don't know anything about him, what does he look like?

GARRY: Absolutely marvellous, if it's the one I think it is, vast strapping shoulders and tiny, tiny hips like a wasp——

MONICA: Can he act?

GARRY: How do I know, don't be so silly.

MONICA: And what happens if it isn't the one you think it is?

GARRY: He'll probably be very short and stumpy with no legs at all and projecting teeth. Give him the introductions, anyhow.

MONICA: Very well. Now there's just one more that

must be dealt with. It's from Sarah Lady Walsingham, she's written very civilly to know whether you'll give the prizes at a charity costume ball she's giving on November the twelfth. There will be Royalty present.

GARRY: Why can't they give the prizes?

MONICA: Because she's asked you, I suppose—you can't all give them.

GARRY: Polite refusal.

MONICA: What excuse can I give? I can't say you won't be here because you will. She's written so long in advance.

GARRY: Wily old devil!

MONICA: I really think you must say yes, she was awfully nice to us over that special matinée.

GARRY: Oh, her! She's a darling—of course I will—say I'll be charmed.

> FRED *comes in through the service door. He's in evening dress again.*

FRED: 'Ave you finished with the tray? I want to be getting along.

GARRY: Is everything packed?

FRED: All except the last minute stuff, we can pop that in in the morning.

GARRY: Is this poor Doris's swan song?

FRED: 'Ow d'you mean?

GARRY: Nothing, Fred—it couldn't matter less.

FRED (*taking the tray*): She's coming to the station to-morrow morning to see us off, you don't mind, do you?

GARRY: I can't wait.

> FRED *disappears with the tray.*

MONICA (*gathering up the letters*): I must be going home now.

GARRY: Don't leave me alone—I feel depressed.

MONICA: You were screaming for peace just now. I'll be here first thing in the morning.

GARRY: I wish you were coming with me. I shall be utterly lost with some dreary temporary African.

MONICA: Is Liz coming to the station?

GARRY (*turning away*): No.

MONICA: Why don't you go round and see her?

GARRY: You know perfectly well. She's still in a rage. I haven't seen her for a week.

MONICA: Have you tried?

GARRY: Of course I have. I've telephoned her three times. Each time she spoke to me kindly and remotely as if I were an idiot child. I'm not sure she didn't spell some of the words out to me.

MONICA: Would you like me to have a go at her?

GARRY: No. If she wants to behave like an outraged governess with chilblains she can get on with it.

MONICA: I see her point you know. You really did go a little too far.

GARRY: For heaven's sake don't you start on me too.

MONICA (*with a slight smile*): I'll take these into the office.

> *She goes into the office with the letters.* FRED *comes out of the service door with his hat.*

FRED: Nothing more you want?

GARRY: No, Fred.

FRED: This place looks a fair lash-up, don't it? 'Ow many did we 'ave?

GARRY: I don't know, about sixty I should think.

FRED: Well, between 'em all they put away enough gin to float the *Queen Mary*.

GARRY: You'd better call me at eight in the morning. We have to leave the house at ten.

FRED: Rightyo.

GARRY: Good-night, Fred—enjoy yourself.

FRED: Same to you—be good.

FRED *goes off.* GARRY *walks about the room emptying the ash-trays into the waste-paper basket.* MONICA *comes out of the office in her hat and coat.*

MONICA: By the way, you'd better be careful if the telephone rings. Roland Maule has been calling up all the week.

GARRY: I think I'd almost welcome him to-night. At least he'd be interesting psychologically.

MONICA: So would Rasputin.

GARRY: I feel dreadfully flat. I suppose one always does before going away.

MONICA: It's your own fault that you're alone, you know, you refused all offers. You pleaded for a few hours solitude, and said you'd throw yourself out of the window if you didn't get it, and that then we should all be sorry.

GARRY: I'm quite sure you wouldn't.

MONICA: Now, now, now, you're getting a big boy, you know. You'll be forty-two next birthday. Just fancy!

GARRY: Forty-one.

MONICA (*kissing him*): Good-night, dear. See you in the morning.

GARRY: I do envy you, Monica, you're so unruffled and efficient. You go churning through life like some frightening old warship.

MONICA: Thank you, dear, that sounds most attractive. Good-night.

GARRY: Good-night.

    MONICA *goes off. He continues to empty the ash-trays. The telephone rings. He flies to it.*

GARRY: Hallo, hallo. . . . No, it isn't.

    He hangs up. MISS ERIKSON *comes out of the service door in her hat and coat.*

MISS E.: I am going away now, Mr. Essendine. Have you everything you want?

GARRY: Frankly, Miss Erikson, No. I have nothing that I want.

MISS E.: Oh, what a pity.

GARRY: Have you? Have any of us—got what we want?

MISS E. (*with a little laugh*): Oh, Mr. Essendine, you are only acting! For a moment you made me quite upset.

GARRY: You lead a strange life, Miss Erikson, do you enjoy it?

MISS E.: Yes, indeed.

GARRY: Tell me about it from A to Z.

MISS E.: Do you mind if I pinch a cigarette?

GARRY: Pinch anything you like, Miss Erikson.

MISS E. (*taking several*): I smoke so much and I am always running out. It is most silly.

GARRY: Where are you going now, for instance?

MISS E.: I am going to my friend in Hammersmith. She is a German.

GARRY: Is she a spy?

MISS E.: Yes, I think so, but she is very kind.

GARRY: I understand from Fred that she is a medium as well?

MISS E.: Oh dear, yes. Sometimes she makes a trance and it is very surprising. She will lie on the ground for many hours making noises.

GARRY: What kind of noises?

MISS E.: They are different. Sometimes she will sing high, high up like a bird and at other times she may make a little bark. Often she is very ill.

GARRY: I'm not at all surprised.

MISS E.: Well, I must be pushing off now.

GARRY: Thank you very much, Miss Erikson, it's been most interesting.

MISS E.: Not at all—good-night.

GARRY: Good-night.

> MISS ERIKSON *goes out. He flings himself on the sofa with a book and tries to read. Presently he throws it down and goes to the telephone. He dials a number and waits. It obviously doesn't reply. He hangs up and wanders about the room. The front door bell rings. He jumps slightly and then goes to open it. In the hall his voice is heard saying* 'DAPHNE'. *She comes in carrying a small dressing-case. She is wearing a travelling coat and hat. She is rather nervous but obviously determined.*

GARRY (*apprehensively*): Daphne, my dear—this really is very sweet of you—to come and say good-bye.

DAPHNE (*in a strained voice*): I haven't come to say good-bye.

GARRY: What do you mean?

DAPHNE: I'm coming with you. I bought my ticket this afternoon.

GARRY: You what!!

DAPHNE: I've run away—I left a note for my aunt—you see, I know something now—I've known it all the week really, ever since that awful morning when I fainted—I know that you need me as much as I need you—No, please, don't say anything for a moment—I've thought it all over very carefully. I know I'm

very much younger than you, and all that, but I can help
you and look after you. . . .

GARRY: Daphne, dear, this is really too absurd.
You must go home at once.

DAPHNE (*taking off her hat*): I knew you'd say that.

GARRY: Please put your hat on again and don't be silly.

DAPHNE: I know you better than you think I do. I
know when you're acting and when you're not. You're
acting now.

GARRY: I'm not doing anything of the sort.

DAPHNE: You were acting when you pretended to be
cross when I came and recited. But when you said
good-bye to me so sweetly, that other morning, then
you weren't acting. The mask was off then, wasn't it—
wasn't it?

GARRY: Now listen, my dear child. . . .

DAPHNE: I felt ashamed on Thursday at first,
ashamed at playing a trick on you by making Auntie
ring up for an audition but when I was here I was
glad. . . .

GARRY: Oh, so you were glad, were you?

DAPHNE (*exultantly*): Yes, I was. I think that's why I
fainted. You see I suddenly realised the truth.

GARRY: What truth?

DAPHNE: How desperately lonely you really were,
in spite of all those people round you, in spite of all your
success—I knew how deep your longing must be to
have someone really to love you, to be with you, when I
saw that dreadful prostitute come out of the spare room
in that tawdry evening dress.

GARRY (*with chilling grandeur*): That was not a prostitute. It was the wife of one of my dearest friends!

DAPHNE: No, Garry—you can't deceive me—I know.

GARRY: Once and for all, Daphne, I wish to say loudly and clearly that I am not acting. I am speaking with the utmost sincerity of which I am capable when I order you to put on your hat, get into a taxi and go straight back to your Aunt.

DAPHNE: No—you needn't be frightened—I won't make any demands on you whatever. I don't want you to marry me or anything like that. I don't believe that real love should be bound by Church or Law. I'm just coming with you, that's all. I've got quite a lot of money in the bank and the manager said he'd wire for them to open an account for me in Johannesburg. I'll just be there when you want me, when you're tired and lonely and want someone to put their arms round you. I won't even see you on the boat if you don't want me to. I'm not a very good sailor, anyhow.

The front door bell rings.

GARRY: That's the front door bell.

DAPHNE: Who is it?

GARRY: How do I know? You'd better go into the spare room.

DAPHNE: No, Garry, please, not the spare room.

GARRY: All right, the office then, go quickly.

DAPHNE: Get rid of them soon, promise, whoever it is.

GARRY: Here's your hat—don't argue.

He shoves her into the office and goes into the hall. The following dialogue is heard off stage.

ROLAND: Forgive me—I must see you.

GARRY: I'm very sorry you can't—I'm just going to bed.

ROLAND: I'm afraid I must insist. You see it's a matter of life and death.

GARRY: Please come back at once.

ROLAND *comes in followed by* GARRY.

GARRY: This is really insupportable. What the hell do you mean by forcing yourself into my house like this.

ROLAND: That's right—shout—shout—you're magnificent when you're angry!

GARRY: I'll tell you something young man—you're just raving bloody mad, that's all that's the matter with you. You ought to be shut up. You ought to be in a strait-jacket.

ROLAND: Oh, no I'm not. You're the one who's mad.

GARRY: Will you please leave this house immediately?

ROLAND: I'm afraid I can't—it's quite impossible—I've burnt my boats.

GARRY: Burnt your what?

ROLAND (*simply*): Boats.

GARRY: What are you talking about.

ROLAND: I told a wicked lie just now when I said it was a matter of life and death. It isn't really quite as bad as that but it's very, very serious—for me I mean—perhaps for us both.

GARRY: If you're not out of this house by the time I've counted ten I shall telephone for the police.

ROLAND: I shan't let you. I'm tremendously strong, you know, I can lift the heaviest things imaginable without turning a hair.

GARRY (*changing his manner*): Now look here, Mr. Maule.

ROLAND: You may call me Roland.

GARRY: Well, Roland, I want to put this situation to you reasonably and quietly. This is my last night in England and I have a great deal to do——

ROLAND: You said just now that you were going to bed.

GARRY: Be that as it may, Roland——

ROLAND (*interrupting*): I know you think I'm mad, and I really don't blame you a bit, but I assure you I'm not at all. I merely have an exceptional brain in many ways, a brain incidentally that can be of inestimable service to you. As I told you the other day you signify a great deal to me. You are, in fact, part of me.

GARRY: I'm sure I'm very flattered, Roland.

ROLAND: I wonder if I could have a biscuit?

GARRY: By all means, there are some in that dish, help yourself.

ROLAND: Thank you. (*He takes a biscuit.*) I promise you faithfully I'll go when I've finished this biscuit. I have booked a room at the Grosvenor Hotel. After all there's no valid reason is there why I shouldn't be acting being mad just as you're acting being sane?

GARRY: I am not acting.

ROLAND: You are always acting. That's what is so fascinating and you are so used to it that you don't even know it yourself. I am always acting too. I have been acting mad with you because it amuses me to see you put on a surprised face. I am absolutely devoted to your face in every mood.

GARRY: I suppose you wouldn't like to act getting the hell out of here, would you?

ROLAND (*laughing wildly*): That's wonderful!

GARRY: Listen, what exactly do you want, really?

ROLAND: To be with you. That's why I'm coming to Africa.

GARRY: That's why you're what!!

ROLAND: I bought a ticket to-day, it's steerage, but it's better than nothing. I have given up my law studies and left Uckfield for good. That's why I'm rather excitable to-night. You needn't be frightened that I shall get in your way or make any demands on you.

GARRY: You mean you don't expect me to marry you!

There is a ring at the door bell.

GARRY: There's somebody at the door. Do be a good boy and go away now, will you? You promised you would when you'd finished your biscuit.

ROLAND (*with complete sincerity*): Please don't send me away—please don't send me away! You're too great a person to be unkind. Please let me stay with you. I can protect you from a whole lot of things you don't know anything about.

GARRY: Such as?

ROLAND: Yourself—all your dangerous vibrations— you're surrounded by pitfalls, every step you take is fraught with peril but your head is in the stars and you can't see——

The door bell rings again.

GARRY: It's extremely kind of you to take such a keen interest in me, Roland, but if you really care so deeply you will do what I ask you and go quietly back to Uckfield.

ROLAND: I shall never go back to Uckfield. The last train's gone now, anyway.

GARRY: Well, go to the Grosvenor Hotel then.

ROLAND: I'm not going to allow you to turn me away. You'll regret it your whole life long if you do. I have a profound conviction about it that nothing will shake——

ROLAND suddenly rushes into the spare room, slams the door and turns the key in the lock. GARRY bangs helplessly on the door. The front door bell rings insistently.

GARRY: Come out of that room immediately! Mr. Maule—Roland—Come out at once. . . . Oh, my God! . . .

> *He goes out into the hall to open the front door. After a moment* JOANNA *enters with a small dressing-case and a jewel case. She puts them down firmly and looks at* GARRY *with a smile.*

JOANNA: Hallo, darling.

GARRY: What is the meaning of this, Joanna?

JOANNA: Don't you know?

GARRY: Yes, I do. You're coming to Africa with me. You bought your ticket this afternoon. You're not going to make any demands on me and you're not a good sailor.

JOANNA: I'm a perfect sailor.

> GARRY *goes to the telephone. He dials a number.*

JOANNA: What are you doing?

GARRY: Ringing up Henry. (*At telephone.*) Hallo—hallo—— Oh, I'm so terribly terribly terribly sorry it's a wrong number!

> *He hangs up.*

JOANNA: It's no good doing that, he's not in.

GARRY (*with a grim smile*): It doesn't matter now.

JOANNA: Darling. Underneath this rather taut, strained manner of yours, deep down inside, aren't you just a little bit glad to see me?

GARRY: Absolutely delighted. It will settle things once and for all.

JOANNA: That's what I thought.

GARRY: When did you get back from Paris?

JOANNA: This afternoon. Did you get my telegram saying good-bye?

GARRY: Yes, Monica read it out to me.

JOANNA: I meant her to.

GARRY: I understood that you were going to stay in Paris for a month.

JOANNA: No, you didn't, darling, you knew perfectly well I wouldn't. I must say I tried for the first few days, to put you out of my mind. I railed against you, said the most dreadful things that you weren't there to hear, then I remembered——

GARRY: What did you remember?

JOANNA: I remembered what you said to me the other night. You said 'It doesn't matter what comes after this, what circumstances combine against us, what tears are shed! This is magic, the loveliest magic that I've ever known!'

GARRY: That's out of the second act of *Love Is So Simple*.

JOANNA (*smiling*): Yes—I recognised it. I saw the play several times, you know.

GARRY: In that case why did you believe it?

JOANNA: I didn't. But the fact of your saying it proved something to me. It proved that you are no more sincere emotionally than I am, that you no longer need or desire the pangs of love, but are perfectly willing to settle for the fun of love. It's an adult point of view and I salute it. I couldn't agree with you more.

GARRY: That, to date, is the most immoral statement I've ever heard in my life.

JOANNA: It's true though, isn't it?

GARRY: No, it is not.

JOANNA: There's no need to be testy, my darling.

GARRY: How dare you, Joanna! It's women like you who undermine the whole integrity of civilisation!

JOANNA: What's that out of?

GARRY: It's not out of anything.

JOANNA: As I told you the other night I've always wanted you. I've always known instinctively that we were right for each other. If we had met years ago it wouldn't have worked, we'd have got caught, tied up with each other and been utterly miserable. Now it's all right, we meet on the same terms. You need me. The people round you are no longer enough. I need you. You're the first man I've ever met who's worthy of my steel. I can't guarantee that we shall be domestically happy together, but we'll have a good time.

GARRY: Well, I'll be damned!

JOANNA: You were quite right when you said just now, with remarkable clairvoyance, that I was coming to Africa with you. I am. I've got the Bridal suite, it was all there was left. In addition to that I've written a note to Henry telling him everything. He's dining with Morris at the Athenæum. They can read it together. (*There is a ring at the door bell.*) Who's that?

GARRY: With any luck it's the Lord Chamberlain.

> GARRY *runs out into the hall.* JOANNA *takes off her hat and arranges her hair in front of the mirror.* LIZ *comes quickly in followed by* GARRY. *She betrays no surprise upon seeing* JOANNA.

LIZ: Hallo, Joanna.

JOANNA: Good evening, Liz dear, how nice you look.

LIZ: Thank you so much. I do my best.

JOANNA: I think it only fair to tell you. I'm sailing with Garry to-morrow.

LIZ: What fun, so am I.

GARRY: What!

LIZ: I decided this afternoon.

GARRY: It's certainly a big day for the Union Castle Line.

LIZ: I've sent Maggie down to Southampton to-night with my luggage.

GARRY: So Maggie's coming too?

LIZ: Of course, I couldn't move without Maggie.

JOANNA (*perfectly controlled but obviously angry*): If I may say so Liz I think that's rather silly of you.

LIZ: I really don't see why. It'll be charming. We can all eat at the same table and do our life-boat drill together.

GARRY: Joanna has written a note to Henry and Morris explaining everything.

LIZ: Good, then they'll probably be coming too.

GARRY: I should like to take this opportunity of saying that I wish I were dead.

LIZ: Nonsense, darling, you'll enjoy the voyage enormously. There won't be a dull moment.

JOANNA: You imagine you're being very clever, Liz, don't you?

LIZ: I've learnt in a hard school.

JOANNA: Personally I think you're making the greatest mistake in your life. It's always foolish not to have the courage to admit defeat.

LIZ: You're being very high-handed, Joanna and, for a woman of your experience, a trifle obtuse. You seem to imagine that I'm competing with you. I assure you I'm doing nothing of the sort. It's very important for all of us that this African tour of Garry's should be a success. Obviously there is no way of preventing you coming if you want to but you'd better realise before it's too late that from the social and publicity angle you will be there as a friend of mine.

There is a ring at the front door bell.

GARRY: I give you just three guesses as to who that is!

JOANNA: The gathering of the clans.

LIZ: I'll go, Garry.

LIZ *goes quickly into the hall.*

JOANNA (*viciously*): Perhaps I've been wrong about you, after all. You haven't got the guts of a rabbit!

GARRY: I'm very glad I haven't, I'm sure they'd be extremely inadequate.

HENRY *and* MORRIS *come in.* LIZ *follows behind them. Both of them are palpably in a fury.*

HENRY: Is it true? That's all I want to know. Is it true?

MORRIS (*just a trifle intoxicated*): False, friend! False, friend!

GARRY: Come come Morris, you're not in the Athenæum now.

HENRY: It's no good trying to be flippant. This is a miserable, disgusting situation and you know it.

MORRIS: A stab in the back, that's what it is, a low-down stab in the back.

GARRY: Not too low down, I hope.

LIZ: Shut up, Morris.

HENRY: I've had a note from Joanna. I suppose you know that, don't you?

JOANNA: Yes, he does. I've just told him.

HENRY: Is what she says in it true?

GARRY: How do I know? I haven't read it.

HENRY: Don't prevaricate. She says that you've been lovers and that you're going away together to-morrow. Is that true?

JOANNA: Perfectly true.

HENRY (*ignoring her*): Answer me, Garry.

GARRY (*dangerously*): I'll tell you what's true and what's not true all right and you can stop bouncing up and down like a rubber ball and listen——

LIZ (*warningly*): Be careful, Garry.

GARRY: Careful! I've been a damn sight too careful with the lot of you for years!

HENRY: You haven't answered my question yet. I want to hear it from your own lips before I decide what to do.

GARRY: Decide what to do indeed! What can you do?

HENRY: Have you or have you not been Joanna's lover?

GARRY: Yes, I have.

MORRIS: You miserable cad!

GARRY (*to* JOANNA): You came here the other night absolutely determined to get me, didn't you? And you were plausible and superficially alluring enough to succeed. You certainly roused my curiosity very cleverly but it takes more than cleverness to touch my heart or my mind.

MORRIS (*violently*): You haven't got a heart or a mind. You haven't got one decent instinct in you. You're morally unstable and false through and through!

GARRY (*full out*): For the love of God stop being theatrical!!

LIZ (*collapsing on to the sofa*): Oh dear.

GARRY: You should never have married Joanna in the first place, Henry, I always told you it was a grave mistake.

HENRY (*furiously*): You have the damned impertinence to stand there after seducing my wife and——

GARRY: Look here, Henry, it's high time we got down to brass tacks. I didn't seduce your wife and well you know it. You're taking up a very high and mighty attitude over the whole thing but I'm perfectly convinced that if you face the facts honestly for a minute you'll discover that you don't really mind in the least. Morris is the one who minds. For the moment.

HENRY: Morris! What do you mean!

LIZ: Oh Garry, that was disgraceful of you.

GARRY: Disgraceful my foot! I'm sick to death of everybody lying and intriguing and acting all over the place.

JOANNA: All right, you win, Garry. I wouldn't have believed anyone in the world could sink so low.

GARRY (*lighting a cigarette*): Fiddlesticks!

HENRY: What did you mean about Morris? Answer me!

GARRY: I mean that Morris and Joanna have been carrying on an abortive little ding-dong under your silly nose for months.

MORRIS: I'll never speak to you again until the day I die!

GARRY: Well, we can have a nice chat then, can't we?

HENRY: Morris—Joanna. . . . Is this true?

GARRY: Of course it's true. It hasn't lasted quite so long as your rather dreary affair with Elvira Radcliffe— that's been hiccuping along for nearly a year now.

JOANNA: Henry!

GARRY: And don't you pretend that you didn't know Joanna. You were absolutely delighted. It gave you room to expand!

HENRY: I told you about that in the deepest

confidence. How could you be so vile as to betray it.

GARRY: I'm sick to death of being stuffed with everybody's confidences. I'm bulging with them. You all of you come to me over and over again and pour your damned tears and emotions and sentiment over me until I'm wet through. You're all just as badly behaved as I am really, in many ways a great deal worse. You believe in your lachrymose amorous hangovers whereas I at least have the grace to take mine lightly. You wallow and I laugh because I believe now and I always have believed that there's far too much nonsense talked about sex. You, Morris, happen to like taking your paltry attachments seriously. You like suffering and plunging into orgies of jealousy and torturing yourself and everyone else. That's your way of enjoying yourself. Henry's technique is a little different, he plumps for the domestic blend. That's why he got tired of Joanna so quickly. Anyhow, he's beautifully suited with poor Elvira. She's been knee-deep in pasture ever since she left Roedean! Joanna's different again. She devotes a great deal of time to sex but not for any of the intrinsic pleasures of it, merely as a means to an end. She's a collector. A go-getter and attractive, unscrupulous pirate. I personally am none of these things. To me the whole business is vastly over-rated. I enjoy it for what it's worth and fully intend to go on doing so for as long as anybody's interested and when the time comes that they're not I shall be perfectly content to settle down with an apple and a good book!

MORRIS: Well, I'll be damned!

HENRY: Of all the brazen, arrogant sophistry I've ever listened to that takes the prize for all time!

MORRIS: You have the nerve to work yourself up

into a state of moral indignation about us when we all
know——

GARRY: I have not worked myself into anything at
all. I'm merely defending my right to speak the truth
for once.

HENRY: Truth! You wouldn't recognise the truth if
you saw it. You spend your whole life attitudinising
and posturing and showing off——

GARRY: And I should like to know where we should
all be if I didn't! I'm an artist, aren't I? Surely I may
be allowed a little license!

MORRIS: As far as I'm concerned, it's expired.

LIZ: For heaven's sake stop shouting all of you,
you'll have the roof off.

JOANNA (*rising*): I'm sick of this idiotic performance.
I'm going.

HENRY (*furiously to* GARRY): And kindly don't start
that old threadbare argument about none of us being
able to live and breathe if it wasn't for your glorious
talent.

GARRY: How dare you allude to my talent in that
nasty sarcastic tone, you ungrateful little serpent!

MORRIS: Anyhow, if it hadn't been for our restraining influence you'd be in the provinces by now.

GARRY: And what's the matter with the provinces,
may I ask? They've often proved to be a great deal
more intelligent than London.

HENRY: Be careful! Someone might hear.

GARRY: I suppose you'll be saying next that it's your
restraining influence that has allowed me to hold my
position as the idol of the public for twenty years——

MORRIS: You're not the idol of the public. They'll
come and see you in the right play and the right part,

and you've got to be good at that. Look what happened to you in *Pity the Blind*!

GARRY: I was magnificent in *Pity the Blind*.

MORRIS: Yes, for ten days.

HENRY: If it hadn't been for us you'd have done *Peer Gynt*.

GARRY: If I so much as hear *Peer Gynt* mentioned in this house again I swear before heaven that I shall produce it at Drury Lane.

HENRY: Not on my money you won't!

GARRY: Your money indeed! Do you think I'm dependent on your miserable money to put on plays? Why there are thousands of shrewd old gentlemen in the city who would be only too delighted to back me in anything I choose to do.

HENRY: I think it rather depends whether they are married or not.

GARRY: Oh, so we're back to that again, are we.

HENRY: No, we're not back to anything. This has been a most disgusting, degrading scene, and if it wasn't for the fact that Morris and I signed the contract for the Forum Theatre this morning we should both of us wash our hands of you for ever!

GARRY: You've what!!

LIZ: Now, Garry, for heaven's sake——

JOANNA (*loudly*): I'm going. Do you hear me all of you? I'm going—for good.

LIZ: Take my car, it's downstairs.

JOANNA (*going up to* GARRY): It's been a great evening for speaking the truth, hasn't it, and I should like to add just one little contribution to the entertainment before I leave. I consider you, Mr. Garry Essendine to be not only an overbearing, affected egomaniac, but the most unmitigated cad that it has ever been my misfortune to meet and I most devoutly hope that I shall never set eyes on you again as long as I live.

She gives him a ringing slap on the face and walks off.

GARRY (*not noticing it—to* HENRY): Do you mean to tell me that you signed a contract for that theatre when I particularly told you that no power on God's earth would induce me to play in it?

MORRIS: Now look here, Garry——

GARRY: I will not look there. It's nothing more nor less than the most outrageous betrayal of faith and I'm deeply, deeply angry. . . .

HENRY: As I told you the other day they are doing up the whole theatre, reseating the orchestra floor which will put over a hundred on to the capacity. In addition to that they're mad to have you there and have even consented to put a shower bath into your dressing-room——

GARRY: I don't care whether they've put a swimming bath in my dressing-room and a Squash Court and a Steinway Grand. I will not play a light French comedy to an auditorium that looks like a Gothic edition of Wembley Stadium.

LIZ: It won't look like that, honestly, darling, when they've redecorated it. I've seen the designs, they're really awfully good.

GARRY: So you're against me too, are you? The whole world's against me.

MORRIS: Really, Garry, I promise you——

GARRY (*brokenly*): Go away—go away all of you—I can't bear any more. I've got to face that dreadful sea voyage to-morrow and then those months of agonising drudgery all across the length and breadth of what is admitted to be by everybody, the most sinister continent there is. Go away from me—please go——

LIZ: Go on, both of you. I'll talk to him.

MORRIS: That performance wouldn't deceive a kitten. He's losing his grip. Come on, Henry.

HENRY: It's a pity they're pulling down the Lyceum.

HENRY *and* MORRIS *go out.*

GARRY: I think I should like a little sip of something to drink. I really do feel quite tired.

LIZ (*going to the drink table*): Whisky or brandy?

GARRY: Brandy I think. It's more stimulating.

LIZ: All right.

GARRY: You're not really coming to Africa with me, are you?

LIZ: Certainly I am. And not only to Africa. I'm coming back to you for good.

GARRY: I don't want you to come back to me. I'm perfectly happy as I am.

LIZ: That can't be helped. You behave abominably anyhow, but you won't be able to be quite so bad with me there.

GARRY: Liz, I implore you not to come back to me. Have you no sympathy? No heart?

LIZ: I'm thinking of the good of the firm. That reminds me. I must leave a note for Monica in the office. I want her to ring up the bank for me first thing in the morning.

GARRY (*remembering*): The office! My God!

LIZ: What's the matter?

GARRY (*in a hoarse whisper*): You've got a sofa, haven't you in your flat?

LIZ: Of course. What are you talking about?

GARRY: You're not coming back to me, dear, I'm coming back to you!

He does an elaborate pantomime pointing first to the office and then to the spare room. LIZ looks bewildered for a minute and then begins to laugh. GARRY quickly slips off his dressing-gown and puts on his coat end they tiptoe out together as the

CURTAIN FALLS

THIS HAPPY BREED

A Play in Three Acts

CHARACTERS:
FRANK GIBBONS
ETHEL, *his wife*
SYLVIA, *his sister*
VI
QUEENIE }*his children*
REG
MRS. FLINT, *his mother-in-law*
BOB MITCHELL
BILLY
SAM LEADBITTER
PHYLLIS BLAKE
EDIE

   The action of the play passes in the dining-room of the GIBBONS' *house, Number 17 Sycamore Road, Clapham Common.*

SCENES
ACT I

Scene   I.   June, 1919.
Scene II.   December, 1925.
Scene III.   May, 1926.

ACT II

Scene   I.   October, 1931.
Scene II.   November, 1931.
Scene III.   May, 1932.

ACT III

Scene   I.   December, 1936.
Scene II.   September, 1938.
Scene III.   June, 1939.

ACT I

Scene I

Time: *June, 1919.*

Scene: *The scene is the dining-room of Number 17 Sycamore Road, Clapham Common. On the right as you look at it there is a fireplace. At the back a french window opening on to a narrow stretch of garden. On the left downstage is the door leading into the hall and through which, when open, can be seen the staircase.*

The time is about eight-thirty in the evening, and, being June, it is still daylight. The french window is open and over the fence at the end of the garden can be seen a May tree in blossom.

The Gibbons *family have only just moved in and so the room is chaotic. There are pale squares on the wallpaper where the last tenant's pictures hung; a huddle of odd furniture; several packing-cases and odd parcels, etc. The only piece of furniture in position is a large sideboard which is against the wall on the left.*

Mrs. Flint *is sitting in a cane arm-chair by the empty fireplace. She is a woman of sixty, soberly dressed in black. She has worn her best clothes for the move as she didn't fancy packing them.* Ethel, *her daughter, a tall woman of thirty-four, is bustling about arranging furniture and undoing parcels. She looks rather hot and untidy as it has been a tiring day. From upstairs comes the sound of intermittent hammering.*

MRS. F. (*querulously*): What is Frank doing?

ETHEL: Putting up the curtains in the front bedroom.

MRS. F.: He'll have the house down in a minute.

ETHEL: They've got to be up before we go to bed to-night, we can't have the whole neighbourhood watching us undress, can we?

MRS. F.: They couldn't see right across the road.

ETHEL: Well, they've got to go up some time.

MRS. F.: Nobody's thought to put any up in my room, there's no blind either. I suppose I don't matter.

ETHEL: Oh, do shut up grumbling, Mother. You know perfectly well the blinds haven't come yet and your room is at the back, anyhow.

MRS. F.: A nice thing if Mr. Whatsisname next door 'appens to go out into the garden and looks up.

ETHEL: We'll send him a note asking him to keep his head down.

MRS. F.: It's all very fine to laugh.

ETHEL: I don't know what's the matter with you to-day, Mother, really I don't. Moving in's no picnic anyhow, and it only makes things worse to keep complaining all the time.

MRS. F.: Me complain? I like that, I must say. I've 'ad a splitting headache ever since two o'clock and I 'aven't so much as mentioned it—rushing about here, there and everywhere, and a fat lot of thanks I get.

ETHEL: It's all right, Mother, cheer up, you'll feel better when you've 'ad a nice cup of tea.

MRS. F.: If I ever *do* 'ave a nice cup of tea.

ETHEL: Well, the kettle's on, but Sylvia isn't back yet.

MRS. F. (*contemptuously*): Sylvia!

ETHEL: She 'ad to go to the U.K. Stores, you know, and that's quite a way.

MRS. F.: She wouldn't 'ave 'ad to do that if she 'adn't forgotten half the things we told her to order. That girl's getting sillier and sillier every breath she takes. I wouldn't be surprised if she 'adn't forgotten the number of the house and lost herself—her and her anæmia!

ETHEL: Well, she can't help her anæmia, can she, now?

MRS. F.: I don't know how you and Frank put up with her, and that's a fact.

ETHEL: Now you know as well as I do, Mother, I couldn't let my own sister-in-law live all by herself, could I? Specially after all she's been through.

MRS. F.: All she's been through, indeed.

ETHEL: I suppose you'll be saying next that she wasn't engaged to Bertie and he wasn't killed, and they've lived 'appy ever after!

MRS. F.: Sylvia 'asn't been through no more than anyone else has, not so much if the truth were known. What she needs is a job of work.

ETHEL: She couldn't stand it, she's too delicate, you know what the doctor said.

MRS. F.: That doctor'd say anything. Look how he went on over Queenie's whooping-cough, frightening us all to death.

ETHEL: Give us a hand with this little table. We can move it over by the window for the time being, it's not heavy.

MRS. F. (*rising reluctantly and helping with the table*): I'm not supposed to lift anything at all, you know—not anything.

ETHEL: All right, all right, now you can 'ave a nice sit down again.

MRS. F. (*sitting again*): This house smells a bit damp to me. I 'ope it isn't.

ETHEL: I don't see why it should be, it's not near any water.

MRS. F.: Well, you never know. Mrs. Willcox moved into that house in Leatherhead and before she'd been in it for three months she was in bed with rheumatic fever.

ETHEL: That's right, dear, look on the bright side.

MRS. F.: Isn't that the front door?

ETHEL: Yes. I gave Sylvia a key, she's probably lost it. I'll go and see.

MRS. F.: Perhaps she's been run over, and it's the police come to tell us.

> ETHEL *goes into the hall; after a moment she returns followed by* SYLVIA, *a pale woman of thirty-four, carrying a large parcel of groceries which she plumps down on the sideboard with a sigh.*

Well, you've taken your time, I must say. We thought something 'ad 'appened to you.

SYLVIA: I'd like to see you be any quicker with a lot like that to carry. (*She groans.*) Oo, my poor back!

MRS. F.: It was your feet this afternoon.

SYLVIA (*snappily*): Well, it's me back now, so there.

ETHEL (*gathering up the parcel*): I'll take this into the kitchen.

SYLVIA: This house smells a bit damp, if you ask me.

ETHEL (*as she goes out*): All houses smell damp when you first move in to 'em.

SYLVIA (*sinking down on to a packing-case*): Oh dear, I

thought I was going to have one of my attacks just as I turned into Abbeville Road. I 'ad to lean against a pillar box.

MRS. F.: I suppose you didn't think to remember my peppermints?

SYLVIA: Yes, I did. They're in my bag. (*She fumbles in her bag.*) Here . . .

MRS. F. (*taking them*): Well, thank 'eaven for small mercies—want one?

SYLVIA: No thanks, I daren't. What's that hammering?

MRS. F.: Frank. 'E's putting up the curtains in the front bedroom.

SYLVIA: I shall be glad when we're settled in and no mistake. What a day!

ETHEL (*returning*): There's no opener!

MRS. F.: Frank's got one on his penknife.

ETHEL (*going into the hall and shouting*): Frank—Frank.

FRANK (*upstairs*): What's up?

ETHEL: Chuck us down your penknife, we want the opener for the baked beans.

FRANK: 'Arf a mo' . . . here you are . . . coming down.

> *There is a moment's pause, and then the penknife falls at* ETHEL'S *feet. She comes back into the room.*

ETHEL: Here, Syl, go and fix 'em, there's a dear. I've got to get this room straight. Mother, you might go and help her. I've laid half the table and the saucepans are on the floor by the dresser.

SYLVIA (*taking opener*): No peace for the wicked.

ETHEL: Go on, Mother, you've sat there quite long enough.

MRS. F.: We ought to have kept Gladys an extra

day and made her 'elp us with the move. . . .

ETHEL: Gladys was more trouble than she was worth. I'd rather do for myself.

MRS. F.: All very fine for you. You're a young woman—wait till you get to my age . . . (*She gets up resentfully.*)

ETHEL: Go on, Mother—I'll be in in a minute. I put the butter on the window-sill.

SYLVIA *and* MRS. FLINT *go out.*

ETHEL, *left alone, continues straightening the room. She hums a little song to herself as she does so. After a few moments* FRANK *comes in. He is an ordinary-looking man of thirty-five. He carries a hammer and a bag of tintacks. These he puts down on the sideboard.*

FRANK: I just tacked 'em up for the time being. We'll 'ave to take 'em down again when the blinds come.

ETHEL: Supper'll be ready soon.

FRANK: You look tired. You've been doing too much.

ETHEL: Don't talk so silly.

FRANK: You've been at it all day, you know.

ETHEL: What do you expect me to do—sit down by the fire and read a nice book?

FRANK: All right, snappy!

He puts his arm round her shoulder and they stand looking out into the garden.

They haven't 'arf left that garden in a mess. Wait till I get after it. Bit of luck about that May tree, isn't it?

ETHEL: I never noticed it.

FRANK: You wouldn't.

ETHEL: Fat lot of time I've had to stand around looking at May trees.

FRANK: Where's Percy?

ETHEL: He started miaouing his 'ead off the moment we got here, so I let him out. He's up to no good, I shouldn't wonder.

FRANK: We ought to have 'ad him arranged when he was little.

ETHEL: Oh, Frank . . . (*She leans against him.*) D'you like it?

FRANK: Like what?

ETHEL: The house, silly, you haven't said a word.

FRANK: Of course I like it.

ETHEL: I can't hardly believe it, you know, not really, it's all been so quick. You being demobbed and coming home and getting the job through Mr. Baxter and now here we are moved in all inside of six weeks!

FRANK: Good old Baxter. We ought to drink his health.

ETHEL: We 'aven't got anything to drink it in except Sylvia's Wincarnis.

FRANK: Well, 'e'll 'ave to take the will for the deed.

ETHEL (*suddenly sitting down*): Oh, dear!

FRANK: What's up?

ETHEL: I don't know—I just can't get over not having that awful weight on me mind all the time.

FRANK: How d'you mean?

ETHEL: Oh, you know.

FRANK: Me perishing on a field of slaughter? What a chance!

ETHEL: There was a chance every minute of every day for four years and don't you forget it. I used to feel sick every time the postman came, every time the bell rang.

FRANK: Well, there's no sense in going on about it now, it's all over and done with.

ETHEL: We're lucky; it isn't so over and done with for some people. Look at poor old Mrs. Worsley, two sons gone and her husband, nothing left to live for, and Mrs. Cross with that boy she was so proud of done in for life, can't even feed himself properly. We're lucky all right, we ought to be grateful . . .

FRANK: Who to?

ETHEL: Now then, Frank . . .

FRANK: All right, I won't start any arguments—you can say your prayers till kingdom come if you like, but you can't expect me to, not after all I've seen. I don't 'old with a God who just singles a few out to be nice to, and lets all the others rot. 'E can get on with it for all I care.

ETHEL: It's wrong to talk like that, Frank, it's blasphemous.

FRANK: Sorry, old girl. I've got to talk the way I feel.

ETHEL: Well, I think you ought to feel different from what you do.

FRANK: That's as maybe, but you can't 'elp your feelings, can you? I'm back, aren't I, that's a fact. Instead of lying out there dead in a shell 'ole I'm standing 'ere alive. In Number 17 Sycamore Road, Clapham Common. That's another fact. It's nobody's fault, not mine or yours or God's or anyone's, it just 'appened like that.

ETHEL: You went to the war because it was your duty and it's no use you pretending you didn't.

FRANK: I went to the war because I wanted to.

ETHEL: Would you go again?

FRANK: I expect so.

ETHEL (*almost crying*): I wouldn't let you, see? Not again! I'd rather kill you with my own hands.

FRANK: That'd be just plain silly.

ETHEL: You give me a headache talking like that, it doesn't make sense.

FRANK: What does make sense, I'd like to know?

ETHEL (*heatedly*): Lots of things. There's me and the children, isn't there? There's your job, there's this house and the life we've got to live in it and you spoil everything by talking about war and saying you'd go again if anyone asked you to . . .

FRANK: I never said that at all.

ETHEL: Oh, yes, you did, you know you did, and I just can't bear to think of it—not after all I've been through, waiting for you and wondering about you— it's cruel to make me even think of it.

FRANK: What's the use of upsetting yourself, there isn't going to be another war, anyway.

ETHEL: There'll always be wars as long as men are such fools as to want to go to them.

FRANK (*gently, sitting down next to her*): Well, let's stop talking about it now, shall we? Everything's all right. You're here, I'm here, the children are fine, except for Queenie's tonsils, and we've got a home of our own at last. Everything's more than all right, it's wonderful.

ETHEL (*burying her head on his shoulder*): Oh, Frank . . .

FRANK: Poor old girl—living four years with your mother can't 'ave been all jam, I will say. I think I was better off in the trenches.

ETHEL (*muffled*): You ought to be ashamed, saying such things.

FRANK: Oh, your mother's all right in her way, but that house in Battersea, oh dear! It gave me the willies after five weeks, let alone four years. At least we've got a bath now that doesn't scratch the hide off of you.

ETHEL: Lend me your 'anky.

FRANK (*giving her his handkerchief*): Here you are.

ETHEL (*blowing her nose*): I must go and 'elp mother and Syl with the supper.

FRANK (*turning her round*): 'Ere, let's have a look at you.

ETHEL: What for?

FRANK: Just to see what's 'appened to your face. I don't seem to have 'ad time for a really good look since I've been back.

ETHEL: Stop it . . . leave off . . .

FRANK: 'Old still a minute.

ETHEL: Now see here, Frank Gibbons . . . (*She wriggles but without conviction.*)

FRANK: Well, it's not a bad face as faces go, I will say . . .

ETHEL: Thanks very much, I'm sure.

FRANK: And of course it's not quite as young as it was when I married it . . .

ETHEL: Leave 'old of me!

FRANK: But still taken by and large, I wouldn't change it! I might wipe some of the dirt off the side of it, but I wouldn't change it!

ETHEL (*struggling to get up*): Dirt—where?

FRANK (*firmly*): Keep still—'ere—— (*He rubs the side of her face with his handkerchief.*) That's better—now then——

ETHEL: Now then, what?

FRANK: Give us a kiss.

ETHEL: I'll do no such thing.

FRANK: Why not, may I ask?

ETHEL: Because we haven't got no time for fooling about and well you know it . . .

FRANK: Oh—turning nasty, are we? We'll soon see about that.

ETHEL: Frank Gibbons——

FRANK (*kissing her firmly*): Shut up.

> *At this moment* BOB MITCHELL *appears at the french window and taps politely. He is a pleasant-looking man of thirty-seven.* ETHEL *and* FRANK *jump up.*

BOB: I hope I don't intrude?

ETHEL: Oh, dear!

BOB: I live at number fifteen next door, and my missus and I thought if you needed anything in the way of groceries or what-not . . .

FRANK (*staring at him*): Well, I'll be damned!

ETHEL: Frank!

FRANK: Mitchell—Bob Mitchell!

BOB (*a little puzzled*): That's right.

FRANK: Don't you remember me—Frank Gibbons, the Buffs, B. Company, Festubert 1915?

BOB: My God! It's old Gibbo!

> *They rush at each other, shake hands and slap each other on the back.*

ETHEL: Well, I never . . .

FRANK: You old son of a gun . . .

BOB: My God, I thought you was dead as mutton after that night attack . . . when we'd gone on to Givenchy and left your lot in the mud . . .

FRANK: Me dead as mutton! I'm tougher than that— only one small 'ole through me leg in four years. . . . How did you make out?

BOB: Not so bad—got gassed in 1917, but I'm all right now—made me chest a bit weak, that's all.

FRANK: Well, I'll say it's a small world and no mistake.

ETHEL: Don't you think you'd better introduce me, Frank?

FRANK: Of course—this is my wife, Bob.

BOB: Pleased to meet you, Mrs. Gibbons.

ETHEL: It's a pleasure, I'm sure.

BOB: What a coincidence—I can't get over it.

FRANK: How long have you been here?

BOB: Over a year now—we took the house when I got me discharge in March 1918. I couldn't do any work for a while, but I had me pension and Nora, that's my missus, had a little put by, but now I'm doing fine— in the insurance business. (*To* ETHEL.) Nora would have come herself, but she's a bit under the weather to-night. You see, we're expecting a little stranger almost any day now, and . . .

ETHEL: It's not her first, is it?

BOB: Oh no—we've got a boy of fourteen, he wants to be a sailor, and we had a girl too, but she died in 1916 just after I'd gone back after me first leave . . .

FRANK: What a coincidence! What a coincidence! After four bloody years.

ETHEL: Frank!

FRANK: Well, if they weren't bloody, nothing was!

ETHEL: I'm afraid we haven't anything to offer you, Mr. Mitchell—you see, everything's upside down . . .

FRANK: He can stay and have whatever we're 'aving.

BOB: No thanks, all the same—I'll have to be getting back to Nora.

FRANK: We've got to celebrate this somehow . . .

BOB: I've got a bottle of Johnnie Walker next door—it won't take a minute . . .

ETHEL: You two stay here—I'll go and fetch Sylvia's Wincarnis.

She runs out.

FRANK: Oh, dear!

BOB: It won't take me a minute to get the whisky . . .

FRANK: Here, whose dugout d'you think this is? I'll pop in and 'ave one with you later.

BOB: Have you got a job yet?

FRANK: Yes—I had a bit of luck—a chap called Baxter in my regiment, he was drafted out to Arras in February and before the war he was running a sort of travel agency in Oxford Street—well, he got a Blighty one and was invalided 'ome, and believe it or not, 'e was the first one I run into when I got back last April. He'd started his business again, and things were beginning to pick up so he gave me a job.

BOB: Travel Agency—whew!

FRANK: Tours of the battlefields, I'll thank you.

BOB (*laughing*): That's a good one.

FRANK: Some people certainly do have queer ways of enjoying themselves.

BOB: You've got kids, haven't you? I remember you talking about them.

FRANK: Yes, three. Two girls and a boy. They're with Ethel's aunt in Broadstairs. We didn't want them under our feet while we were moving in.

BOB: How old are they?

FRANK: Reg, that's the boy, 'e's twelve; Queenie's thirteen, and Vi's fourteen.

BOB: My Billy's getting on for fifteen.

FRANK: Seems funny, this, doesn't it? When you think of the last time we 'ad a jaw—remember that canteen?

BOB: Just before Christmas, wasn't it? The night before you went up to the line. What was her name, that Lady Something-or-other behind the bar, the one that called you her poor dear . . .

FRANK: What was it?—I can see her now—a fair knockout she was.

BOB: What happened to old Shorty?

FRANK: You mean the little fat chap with red hair in my company?

BOB: That's him.

FRANK: 'E got 'is on the Somme, poor bastard, 'adn't been out of the trench two seconds when, wallop, out 'e went!

BOB: Nice and quick and no hurt feelings.

FRANK: You've said it.

> ETHEL *returns with a bottle of Wincarnis and two glasses.*

ETHEL: Here you are—supper will be ready in a minute—Are you sure you won't stay and take pot luck with us, Mr. Mitchell?

BOB: Thanks very much, Mrs. Gibbons, but I really must get back.

ETHEL: Will you ask your wife when it would be convenient for me to pop in and see her?

BOB: Any time—any time at all.

ETHEL: Well, I'll be saying good-night, Mr. Mitchell.

FRANK: Aren't you going to have a drop?

ETHEL: No, dear, it would spoil my supper—don't be long.

Bob: Don't forget—if there's anything you're wanting——

Ethel: Thank you very much, I'm sure. Good-night.

Bob: Good-night.

> Ethel *goes out.*

> Frank *pours out the Wincarnis.*

Frank (*handing a glass to* Bob): Here you are, old man.

Bob: Thanks.

Frank: It tastes a bit funny, but it's better than nothing.

Bob: Happy days!

Frank: Happy days!

> *They drink as—*

THE LIGHTS FADE

ACT I

Scene II

Time: *December, 1925.*

> *It is about three o'clock on Christmas afternoon. Christmas dinner is over.* Vi, Queenie, Reg, Sam Leadbitter *and* Phyllis Blake *are still sitting at the table wearing paper hats, having port and nuts and pulling crackers. The chairs of* Frank, Ethel, Sylvia *and* Mrs. Flint *are empty as they have retired to the rarely used front room in order to leave the young people alone.* Vi *is a pleasant, nondescript-looking girl of twenty;* Queenie, *who is a year younger, is prettier and a trifle flashy.* Reg, *aged eighteen, is a nice-looking,*

intelligent boy. SAM LEADBITTER, *who is about a year older than* REG, *is rather farouche in appearance. He is intense, without much humour, and slightly aware of intellectual superiority.* REG *admires him extravagantly.* PHYLLIS BLAKE, *who is a friend of* QUEENIE'S, *is a gentle, matter-of-fact girl of about eighteen. As the curtain rises,* REG *is starting to make a speech.*

REG: . . . I will now propose a toast to the two strangers within our gates . . .

QUEENIE: 'Ark at him!

VI: Shut up, Queenie.

REG (*ignoring the interruption*): Welcome, thrice welcome, Sam Leadbitter and Phyllis Blake.

> *He raises his glass of port and makes a signal for everyone to drink.*

QUEENIE: You ought to have mentioned the lady first.

REG (*grandly*): Sweeping aside the annoying interruptions of my young sister, who is being far too bossy as usual, I will now call upon my old and valued friend, Sam Leadbitter, to say a few words . . .

QUEENIE: Old and valued friend! You've only known 'im since August Bank Holiday—chuck us the nut crackers, Phyl——

VI: Speech—Speech—Speech! Oh, dear!

> *She giggles.*

REG: Come on, Sam.

QUEENIE: Get it off your chest, Sam, Edie'll be in to clear in a minute.

> *Amid loud applause* SAM *rises to his feet.*

SAM: Ladies and gentlemen—Comrades——

QUEENIE: Make up your mind.

REG: You're asking for it, you know, Queenie, and if you don't shut up being saucy, you'll get it! Go on, Sam, don't take no notice of her.

SAM: Comrades—in thanking you for your kind hospitality on this festive day, I would like to say that it is both a pleasure and a privilege to be here . . .

QUEENIE: Hear—hear——

SAM: Though as you know, holding the views I do, it's really against my principles to hobnob to any great extent with the bourgeoisie . . .

QUEENIE: What's that?

VI: I think it means common in a nice way.

REG: Order!

SAM: I cannot help but feel that to-day, what with being Christmas and one thing and another, it would be but right and proper to put aside all prejudice and class hatred . . .

QUEENIE: Very nice of you, I'm sure.

SAM: . . . As you well know, there are millions and millions of homes in this country to-day where Christmas is naught but a mockery, where there is neither warmth nor food nor even the bare necessities of life, where little children, old before their time, huddle round a fireless grate . . .

QUEENIE: They'd be just as well off if they stayed in the middle of the room then, wouldn't they?

REG: Shut up, Queenie, Sam's quite right.

SAM (*sternly*): That sort of remark, Queenie, springs from complacency, arrogance and a full stomach!

QUEENIE: You leave my stomach out of it!

SAM (*warming up*): It is people like you, apathetic, unthinking, docile supporters of a capitalistic system which is a disgrace to civilisation, who are responsible for at

least three-quarters of the cruel suffering of the world!
You never trouble to look below the surface of things,
do you? And for why? Because you and your whole
class are servers of Mammon! Money's all you think
about. As long as you can earn your miserable little
salaries and go to the pictures and enjoy yourselves and
have a roof over your head and a bed to sleep in and
food to eat, the rest of suffering humanity can go hang,
can't it? You'll accept any conditions, no matter how
degrading, as long as *you're* all right, as long as your
petty security isn't interfered with. It doesn't matter to
you that the greatest struggle for the betterment of
mankind that has ever been in the history of the world is
going on under your noses! Oh dear no, you haven't
even noticed it, you're too busy getting all weepy about
Rudolph Valentino to spare any tears for the workers
of the world whose whole lives are made hideous by
oppression, injustice and capitalistic greed!

VI: Don't get excited, Sam, Queenie didn't mean it.

SAM (*violently*): I am not excited. Queenie doesn't
mean anything to me, anyway . . .

QUEENIE: Pardon me all, while I go and commit
suicide!

SAM: . . . But what she represents, what she
symbolises means a great deal. She is only one of the
millions who, when the great day comes, will be swept
out of existence like so much chaff on the wind . . .

QUEENIE: Well, it's nice to know, isn't it?

SAM (*sitting down abruptly*): I've said my say, thank you
very much.

REG (*dutifully*): Hear, hear . . . bravo!

QUEENIE: I don't know what you're saying bravo
about, I'm sure. I think Sam's been very rude.

REG: You don't understand, Queenie; if you did, you wouldn't have kept interrupting all the time and trying to be funny. Sam's quite right in everything he says, only you just haven't got enough sense to see it.

QUEENIE: I suppose you understand all of it, don't you?

REG: No, I don't but I'm trying to.

QUEENIE: I suppose we shall soon be having you standing up on a soap-box in Hyde Park and making a fathead of yourself!

VI: Run and tell Edie we're ready for her to clear now, Queenie, say we'll help her—the boys can go into the front room, we've left Mum and Dad and Granny alone quite long enough.

REG (*with sarcasm*): Maybe if we asked her nicely, Aunt Sylvia'd sing us the 'Indian Love Lyrics'!

VI: And don't talk in that tone about poor Aunt Sylvia, she's not feeling well.

QUEENIE (*going out of the room*): She never is.

REG (*rising*): Come on, Sam. Come up to my room for a minute and have a cigarette.

VI: Better not let your father catch you.

SAM (*rising*): I'm sorry if I was rude, Vi.

VI (*beginning to pile up the plates*): It doesn't matter, Sam, only you can't expect everybody in the world to feel just the same as you do, you know.

REG (*hotly*): Sam's got more knowledge and intelligence than all of us put together.

VI: If that's the case, it wouldn't do him any harm to remember it once in a while and not shout so much.

REG (*irritably*): Come on, Sam.

    He slams out of the room followed rather sheepishly by
    SAM.

PHYLLIS: Can I help, Vi?

VI: Yes, Phyl, you might put the preserved fruits in the sideboard cupboard, the sweets can go in there too, but leave one dish out to take into the front room.

PHYLLIS (*complying*): Sam got quite upset, didn't he?

VI: He's a bit Bolshie, that's all that's the matter with him.

PHYLLIS: I didn't understand half of what he was talking about.

VI: I don't expect he understood much of it himself.

PHYLLIS: Reg thinks he's wonderful.

VI: Reg thinks anybody who can use a few long words is wonderful. He'll soon get over it.

> QUEENIE *re-enters, followed by* EDIE, *with a tray.* EDIE *is rather an unkempt girl of about twenty-five. During the following scene she and the girls manage to clear the table, change the tablecloths and generally tidy up the room.*

QUEENIE: Has Trotsky gone upstairs?

VI: You were awful, Queenie, if you hadn't of gone on at him the way you did, he wouldn't have got so excited.

QUEENIE (*busying herself*): Silly great fool.

VI: You needn't stay and wash up, Edie, you can slip along home, we can do it later.

EDIE: Thanks very much.

VI: How's your father's neck?

EDIE: Mother was up all night poulticing it, but it was still paining him terrible when I left this morning.

PHYLLIS: They say if you have one you generally have seven.

EDIE: Well, this is 'is third, so we only got four more to go.

Vi (*piling things on to the tray*): There's some crackers left in the box in the sideboard—you might care to take them home to your little brother.

Edie (*finding them*): Thanks ever so.

Queenie: Here—you can balance them on the top— that's right.

> Queenie *balances the box of crackers on the top of the loaded tray and* Edie *staggers out of the room with it.* Vi *and* Phyllis *fold up the tablecloth between them while* Queenie *gets the day cloth out of the sideboard drawer.*

Phyllis (*to* Vi): It has been nice you letting me come and spend my Christmas Day with you. I don't know what I'd have done all by myself in that house in Wandsworth with Auntie ill and everything.

Vi: Is she any better?

Phyllis: No, she just goes on about the same. Mrs. Watts is looking after her until seven so I don't have to get back till about then.

Queenie (*helping* Vi *to put on the day tablecloth*): One of our girls at the shop's mother has been bedridden for five years—can't even get up to wash herself. Just think of that.

Phyllis: What some people go through!

> *There is the sound of a tap at the window.*

Queenie: Good heavens, what's that? (*Going to the window.*) Only Mr. Mitchell come to talk to Dad, I expect.

> *She pulls back the curtain and opens the window. It is still more or less daylight, but there is a fog, so the outlook is rather gloomy.* Billy Mitchell *steps into the room. He is a nice-looking boy of about twenty-one. He is in sailor's rig only without his cap.*

271

Billy, what a surprise! I thought you was going back this morning.

BILLY: No, not till to-night. Hallo—Queen——

QUEENIE: Hallo.

BILLY: Better leave the window on the latch, Dad'll be in in a minute.

VI (*introducing*): Do you know Miss Blake . . . Mr. Mitchell.

BILLY (*shaking hands*): Pleased to meet you.

QUEENIE: Have a choc?

BILLY: No, thanks, I've been eating my head off. Where's Reg?

VI: Upstairs with Sam.

BILLY: Oh, he's here, is he?

QUEENIE: I'll say he is. I wonder you didn't hear him. He's been bellowing like a bull.

BILLY: Down with the dirty capitalists?

QUEENIE: That's right.

BILLY: I know all that stuff by heart—we got a couple of 'em in my ship, not bad chaps really, you know, just got everything a bit cock-eyed, that's all.

PHYLLIS: It must be lovely being a sailor.

BILLY: Well, I wouldn't go so far as to say lovely, exactly, but it's not bad, and you do get about. Join the Navy and see the world, you know.

QUEENIE: Go on—you've never been further than Southsea!

BILLY (*cheerfully*): Lots of time. Next year I'll probably be sent to the China station—think of that!

QUEENIE: Well, drop us a p.c. saying you've arrived safely.

PHYLLIS: China station sounds funny, doesn't it? Like as though it was on the Underground!

She giggles.

VI: We ought to go into the drawing-room now. Mum'll be wondering what's happened to us.

BILLY: Be a sport and go on in then, Vi, I want to talk to Queenie a minute.

VI: Oh, so that's how it is, is it?

QUEENIE: I don't know what you're talking about, I'm sure.

VI: Come on, Phyl, we know when we're not wanted.

QUEENIE: I don't see why we don't all go.

BILLY: I want to talk to you a minute, I just said so, didn't I?

QUEENIE: Maybe I don't want to talk to you!

BILLY: Well, if you're going to be high and mighty about it, it's all right with me. I only thought that as I was going back to duty to-night that . . .

VI: Of course Queenie'll stay for a minute, Billy, she's only putting on airs.

QUEENIE: You mind your own business Vi Gibbons. I'll talk to who I like when I like.

VI: Well, nobody's stopping you—come on, Phyl—— See you later, Billy, don't go without saying good-bye to Mum and Dad.

BILLY: You bet I won't.

> VI *and* PHYLLIS *go out, shutting the door after them.*
> QUEENIE *flounces over to the fire and sits down.*

QUEENIE: Well?

BILLY (*grinning*): Well, what?

QUEENIE: What is it you're so keen to talk to me about?

BILLY: I don't rightly know now, you being so upsiedupsie's put it right out of my head.

QUEENIE: I beg your pardon, I'm sure.

BILLY: Don't mention it—all in the day's work.

QUEENIE: Fancy asking Vi and Phyl to go out and leave us alone, you ought to have known better. I shall never hear the last of it.

BILLY: Oh, so that's what's worrying you, is it?

QUEENIE (*shrugging her shoulders*): It's not worrying me at all, I just thought it sounded sort of silly, that's all.

BILLY: I don't see what's silly about it. Vi knows we went to the Majestic on Friday night, and she saw us with her own eyes walking down Elm Park Road on Sunday—she must guess there's something doing.

QUEENIE: Well, if she does she's wrong, so there. There isn't.

BILLY: 'Ere, 'arf a minute—what's got into you, anyway? I haven't done anything wrong, have I?

QUEENIE: I don't like being taken for granted, no girl does.

BILLY: How d'you mean, taken for granted? You can't hold hands with someone all through *Desert Love* and the next minute expect them to treat you like the Empress of Russia!

QUEENIE: Oh, don't talk so silly.

BILLY: It's you that's silly.

QUEENIE (*getting up*): I think we'd better go into the drawing-room.

BILLY (*turning away*): All right, if that's the way you feel.

QUEENIE: Well, we're not doing much good here, are we? Just nagging at each other.

BILLY: Who started it?

QUEENIE: Oh—come on.

BILLY (*downcast*): Aren't you going to kiss me good-bye? We shan't be able to in there.

QUEENIE: I should think not, indeed.

BILLY: Look here, Queenie, if you think I oughtn't to have said that about wanting to talk to you alone in front of Vi, I'm sorry, see? I can't say more than that, now can I?

QUEENIE (*looking down*): No, I suppose not.

BILLY: Well then!

QUEENIE (*with an imperceptible movement towards him*): Oh, all right . . .

> *He takes her in his arms and kisses her.*

BILLY (*gently*): I do love you, Queenie—you know that, don't you?

QUEENIE (*resting her head on his shoulder*): Yes.

BILLY: And I wouldn't do anything to upset you—that is, not meaning to—you know that too, don't you?

QUEENIE: Oh, Billy—I wish you weren't going back so soon.

BILLY: Will you write to me every now and again? Even if it's only a post-card?

QUEENIE: If you'll write to me.

BILLY: That's easy. Promise?

QUEENIE: Yes cross my heart.

BILLY: You're the sweetest girl I ever met in all my life or ever will meet, either.

QUEENIE: That's easy to say, but how do you know?

BILLY: Never you mind, it's true. I've been thinking about you all the time, ever since that sick leave I had at Whitsun, when we went to Richmond Park—do you remember?

QUEENIE: Of course I do.

BILLY: A little later on, when I'm earning a bit more, do you think we might have a shot at getting married!

QUEENIE (*turning away*): Oh Bill, how do I know—you might be in China or anywhere—you might have forgotten all about me by then.

BILLY: More likely to be the other way round. A pretty kid like you, working at being a manicurist, talking to all sorts of different fellows all day long . . .

QUEENIE: It isn't all jam being a sailor's wife, is it?

BILLY: It wouldn't be so bad, if I get me promotion all right and get on—don't say anything now, just think it over . . .

QUEENIE (*with a rush*): Oh, Billy, I wouldn't be the right sort of wife for you, really I wouldn't. I want too much—I'm always thinking about the kind of things I want and they wouldn't be the kind of things you'd want me to want.

BILLY: How do you mean?

QUEENIE: Oh, I know it sounds silly, but I'm not like Vi, she's a quiet one. I'm different. Mum sometimes says that all I think of is having a good time, but it isn't only that . . .

BILLY: I don't see no harm in wanting to have a good time—that's what everybody wants in one way or another.

QUEENIE: I'll tell you something awful. I hate living here, I hate living in a house that's exactly like hundreds of other houses. I hate coming home from work in the Tube. I hate washing up and helping Mum darn Dad's socks and listening to Aunt Sylvia keeping on about how ill she is all the time, and what's more I know why I hate it too, it's because it's all so common! There! I expect you'll think I'm getting above myself, and I

wouldn't blame you—maybe I am, but I can't help it—
that's why I don't think I'd be a good wife for you,
however much I loved you—and I do . . . I really
do . . . Oh, Billy . . . (*She bursts into tears.*)

BILLY (*putting his arms round her*): Here, hold on, dear,
there isn't anything to cry about—I know what you
mean all right, it's only natural that you should feel that
way about things.

QUEENIE: You don't think I'm awful then, do you?
And mean?

BILLY: Of course I don't—come on now, cheer up,
you don't want to have red eyes on Christmas Day, do
you?

QUEENIE (*dabbing her eyes with her handkerchief*): I'm
sorry, Bill, please forgive me . . .

> *She suddenly kisses him and runs out of the room.*
>
> *He stands looking after her in perplexity for a moment,
> and then with a sigh goes up towards the window. He has
> nearly reached it when* FRANK *comes in. He hasn't really
> changed very much in the last six years. His figure is
> perhaps a shade thicker and his hair a shade greyer and
> thinner. At the moment he is still wearing the paper hat
> he got out of a cracker.*

FRANK: Billy! What are you doing in here all by
yourself?

BILLY: I've been talking to Queenie.

FRANK: Was that her rushing upstairs just now?

BILLY: Yes—I think it was.

FRANK (*quizzically*): Oh, I see.

BILLY: I just popped in to say good-bye——

FRANK: A bit miserable having to go back to work
on Christmas Day, isn't it?

BILLY: Oh, I dunno—it's all right once you're there.

FRANK: How old are you now, Billy?

BILLY: Getting on for twenty-one.

FRANK: Wish I was.

BILLY (*with an effort*): Mr. Gibbons——

FRANK: Yes, son?

BILLY: If in two or three years' time when I've worked my way up a bit Queenie and me got married, would you mind?

FRANK: If Queenie wanted to, it wouldn't matter whether I minded or not. She'd get her own way, she always does.

BILLY (*ruefully*): She's certainly got a will of her own all right.

FRANK: Anyway, a lot can happen between now and three years.

BILLY: You see I leave the ship I'm in now round about April and next commission I'll probably be drafted for foreign service. By the time I get back, I ought to be drawing higher pay if I've been behaving myself.

FRANK: What does Queenie think about it?

BILLY: That's the trouble—I think she thinks that being a sailor's wife might be rather hard going . . .

FRANK: She likes having a good time, our Queenie, but maybe she'll calm down later on, here's hoping, anyhow.

BILLY: If you get a chance, Mr. Gibbons, you might put in a good word for me every now and again.

FRANK (*smiling*): Righto, son, I'll do my best.

BILLY: Thanks, Mr. Gibbons. I think I'll be getting along now. Mother always gets a bit depressed on my last day of leave.

FRANK: How is she?

BILLY: As well as can be expected.

FRANK: Aren't you going into the front room?

BILLY: I'd rather not, if you don't mind.

FRANK: All right—I'll say good-bye for you.

BILLY: Thank you again, Mr. Gibbons.

FRANK: Go on, 'op it—good luck!

They shake hands solemnly.

BILLY *goes out through the french window.*

FRANK, *left alone, takes a Gold Flake out of a packet in his pocket, lights it, and balances it on the edge of the mantelpiece while he puts some more coal on the fire. Then he settles himself comfortably in an arm-chair. From the drawing-room comes the sound of the piano and* SYLVIA'S *voice singing 'When I Am Dying'. The door opens gently, and* ETHEL *slips into the room.*

ETHEL: Frank, you are awful creeping out like that. You knew Sylvia was going to sing.

FRANK: What about you?

ETHEL: I came to find you.

FRANK: Oh yes, we know all about that.

ETHEL: D'you want the light on?

FRANK: No, it's all right like this—come and sit down.

ETHEL (*sitting near him*): Edie's gone home; the girls are going to do the washing up after tea.

FRANK: Is Reg in there?

ETHEL: Yes, he came in a minute ago with that Sam Leadbitter.

FRANK (*chuckling*): What's the betting they've been smoking themselves silly up in Reg's room?

ETHEL: Well, it is Christmas. I don't think much of that Sam Leadbitter taken all round, he seems a bit soft to me.

FRANK: I wouldn't call him soft exactly.

ETHEL: Well, you know what I mean—all that talking big—he'll get himself into trouble one of these days, you mark my words.

FRANK: He'll grow out of it. I used to shoot me neck off to beat the band when I was his age.

ETHEL: Not like he does though, all that stuff about world revolution and the great day and down with everything—you had more sense than that. Anyhow I wouldn't mind so much if it wasn't for Reg taking every word he says as gospel—we'll be having him with long hair and a red tie soon if we're not careful.

FRANK: I shouldn't say a word if I was you, let 'em get it out of their systems.

ETHEL: It is wrong, isn't it? All that Bolshie business?

FRANK: Oh, there's something to be said for it, there's always something to be said for everything. Where they go wrong is trying to get things done too quickly. We don't like doing things quickly in this country. It's like gardening, someone once said we was a nation of gardeners, and they weren't far out. We're used to planting things and watching them grow and looking out for changes in the weather . . .

ETHEL: You and your gardening!

FRANK: Well, it's true—think what a mess there'd be if all the flowers and vegetables and crops came popping up all in a minute—that's what all these social reformers are trying to do, trying to alter the way of things all at once. We've got our own way of settling things, it may be slow and it may be a bit dull, but it suits us all right and it always will.

ETHEL: Oh, do listen to Sylvia, she's off on 'Bird of

Love Divine' now, and you know how it always makes
Reg laugh!

FRANK: Poor old Sylvia!

ETHEL: We ought to go back really, it'll be tea-time
in a minute.

FRANK: It's cosy in here.

ETHEL (*settling herself against him*): Getting quite dark,
isn't it?

> *They sit together in silence as—*

THE LIGHTS FADE

ACT I

SCENE III

TIME: *May,* 1926.

> *It is late in the evening, about ten-thirty. The french
> windows are open as it is very warm.* MRS. FLINT *is
> sitting in an arm-chair by the fireplace.* ETHEL,
> SYLVIA, VI *and* QUEENIE *are at the table having supper
> which consists of cold ham, tomatoes, cheese, pickles and
> tea.*

ETHEL: . . . Run into the kitchen, Queenie, there's
a dear, and see if the soup's all right. Dad ought to be
home soon, it's getting on for eleven.

QUEENIE (*rising reluctantly*): All right, if my legs will
get me that far.

ETHEL: When you've done that you'd better go to
bed—you, too, Vi, you must be dog tired, all that standing about . . .

QUEENIE (*as she goes*): I wonder if they'll open up the

shop again to-morrow—I'll have to go along in the morning and see.

VI: Are you going to wait up for dad, Mum?

ETHEL: Yes, I'm all right—they said in Regent's Park his shift would be back before ten—I wish I hadn't missed him with those sandwiches. Seems silly trailing all that way for nothing . . .

SYLVIA: Feels sort of flat now, doesn't it? It all being over, I mean.

MRS. F.: It's wicked, that's what it is, downright wicked, those strikers upsetting the whole country like that . . .

ETHEL: I wish Reg'd come home; I wish I knew where he was.

VI: I'll give that Sam Leadbitter a piece of my mind when I see him. Encouraging Reg to make a fool of himself—I'll tell him off, you see if I don't.

ETHEL: Telling people off's no good, when they think they're in the right.

SYLVIA: I was talking to Mr. Rogers only a couple of weeks ago, his brother works up North, you know, and he said that conditions were something terrible, he did really.

ETHEL: I'm so afraid something's happened to him.

VI: Don't worry, Mother, worrying never does any good anyhow.

ETHEL: I can't help it.

SYLVIA: Mr. Rogers says this is only just the beginning of a whole lot more trouble—he says the Government may have won this time but next time it won't be so easy . . .

VI: A fat lot he knows about it, he never sets foot outside that shop of his from one year's end to another.

SYLVIA: Mr. Rogers is a very clever man, Vi—he's a great reader, too; why you never see him without he's got a book in his hand.

VI: I shouldn't think he sold much at that rate.

MRS. F.: You and your Mr. Rogers.

SYLVIA: He's been very kind to me and I like him, so there.

MRS. F.: Like him! I should just think you did—we get nothing but Mr. Rogers this and Mr. Rogers that from morning till night. I'd like to know what Mrs. Rogers has to say about it, I must say.

SYLVIA: Now look here, Mrs. Flint, if you're insinuating . . .

MRS. F.: You give me a pain, Sylvia, really you do, the way you keep on about that man—just because he pays you a few shillings every now and again for designing them Christmas cards and calendars, you're doing nothing more nor less than throwing yourself at his head.

SYLVIA (*furious*): Mrs. Flint, how can you!

ETHEL (*wearily*): Oh, do shut up, you two—I've got enough to think about without listening to you snapping at each other. Sylvia can go and live with Mr. Rogers for all I care.

SYLVIA: That's a nice way to talk, Ethel, I must say.

ETHEL: Now look here, Sylvia, I'm tired, see? We're all tired. And what's more, I'm worried to death about Reg. I 'aven't slept properly for three nights wondering what's happened to him. I know Vi had that message from Sam saying he was all right, but I shan't believe he is until I see him. If on top of all that I have to hear you and mother go on nag, nag, nag at each other over nothing at all, I shall lose my temper, and that's a fact. You never stop, either of you, and I'm sick to death of it.

Mrs. F.: I'm sure I haven't said anything.

Ethel: Oh, yes, you have. You're always giving Sylvia sly digs about Mr. Rogers. You know perfectly well Sylvia isn't strong enough to do any steady work, and the odd commissions she gets from that novelty shop come in very handy. If Mr. Rogers has taken a fancy to her, so much the better, she's old enough to look after herself, 'eaven knows, and if he murdered his wife and strangled his children and run off to Australia with her, it still wouldn't be anything to do with you, so shut up!

Mrs. F. (*struggling to get out of her chair*): Help me up—help me up—I'm not going to stay here and be insulted by my own daughter.

Ethel: You're not being insulted by anyone, be quiet.

Sylvia: It's all my fault—I'm in the way in this house and I always have been and you needn't think I don't know it . . .

Ethel: It's a pity you've stayed so long then.

Sylvia (*bursting into tears*): Oh, Ethel, how can you! I'll leave to-morrow, I'll never set foot in the house again . . .

Mrs. F.: And a good job too.

Vi: Oh, don't cry, Auntie Sylvia, mother didn't mean it. She's nervy to-night, we all are . . .

Sylvia (*sobbing*): I don't care how nervy she is, if only I had my health and strength I'm sure I wouldn't have to be beholden to anybody.

Mrs. F.: Health and strength indeed! You're as strong as a cart horse!

ETHEL: Take your grandmother up to bed, Vi, for God's sake.

VI: Come on, Granny—I'll help you upstairs . . .

ETHEL: Stop crying, Sylvia—I didn't mean what I said. I don't know which way to turn to-night what with one thing and another . . .

MRS. F. (*shaking* VI *off*): I can manage by myself, thank you.

SYLVIA: If you wished to hurt me, you've certainly succeeded——

ETHEL: Nobody wished to hurt you—do stop crying, you'll only give yourself one of your headaches . . .

QUEENIE *comes into the room.*

QUEENIE: What in the world's happening? I thought the strikers had got in!

VI: It's only Auntie Sylvia and Granny as usual.

SYLVIA: That's right, blame me! Everything's always my fault.

MRS. F.: I'm an old woman and the sooner I'm dead the better—I know you're all itching to see me in my coffin . . .

VI: Don't talk so silly, Granny, come on upstairs.

MRS. F.: It's coming to something when your own flesh and blood turns on you as if you was a criminal . . .

VI: Never mind, Gran, it'll all be forgiven and forgotten in the morning . . .

VI *leads* MRS. FLINT *still talking, from the room.*

ETHEL *puts her head wearily down on her arms.*

QUEENIE *goes over to her.*

QUEENIE: Have another cup of tea, Mum, it'll buck you up.

ETHEL: I'm all right.

285

QUEENIE: Here—I'll pour it out.

ETHEL: You'd better give your Aunt Sylvia a cup of tea.

SYLVIA (*bridling*): I don't want anyone to put themselves out on my account, I'm sure.

QUEENIE (*pouring out a cup of tea*): Nobody is, Aunt Sylvia, here you are, the sugar's just by you. Here you are, Mum.

ETHEL: Thank you, dear. Now slip along up to bed, there's a good girl.

QUEENIE: I'd rather wait till dad comes, he can't be long now.

ETHEL: Very well.

SYLVIA (*with martyred politeness*): Would you like me to wait up for Frank, Ethel, and you go to bed?

ETHEL: No thanks, Sylvia—I couldn't sleep, anyway.

SYLVIA: I've been sleeping terribly badly lately, what with all the upset and the heat and everything . . .

ETHEL: Go on up now then and take an aspirin.

SYLVIA: I daren't, it always makes my heart go funny. Doctor Morgan says it does do that with some people. He gave me some tablets but I'm afraid they're not much good. I'll take two to-night just to see what happens.

ETHEL: I shouldn't overdo it if I was you.

SYLVIA: They're quite harmless. (*She gets up.*) I'll take my tea up with me.

ETHEL (*relieved*): Nothing like a nice cup of tea in bed.

SYLVIA (*smiling wanly*): Good-night, Ethel—good-night, Queenie.

QUEENIE: Good-night, Aunt Sylvia.

ETHEL: Good-night, Syl, sleep well.

SYLVIA (*going out*): I'm afraid there's not much hope of that!

ETHEL: Poor Sylvia, she's a bit of a trial sometimes.

QUEENIE: I don't know how you stand her, Mum.

ETHEL: She hasn't got anybody but us, you know. I wouldn't like to think of her living all by herself, she couldn't afford it anyhow.

QUEENIE: She could if she did a bit of work.

ETHEL: Well, she's tried once or twice, and it's never been any good. Remember when she answered that advertisement in 1923, and got herself to Bexhill as a companion to Mrs. Phillips? Oh, dear! (*She laughs.*)

QUEENIE (*also laughing*): She was home inside two weeks and in bed for four.

ETHEL: If it hadn't been for poor Bertie getting killed in the war, she'd have been all right, I expect.

QUEENIE: What was he like?

ETHEL: A bit soppy I always thought, but still she liked him.

QUEENIE: How awful to be so dependent on a man living or dying that it could ruin your whole life. I don't think I ever would be.

ETHEL: Well, don't be too sure. If your dad had gone I wouldn't have been the woman I am to-day, far from it.

QUEENIE: You wouldn't have gone on moping about it always though, would you?

ETHEL: I don't rightly know. My heart would have broke and I suppose I should have had to put it together again as best I could.

QUEENIE: Oh, Mum!

ETHEL: What is it?

QUEENIE: You do make me feel awful sometimes.

ETHEL: Good 'eavens, child, why?

QUEENIE: Oh, you just do.

ETHEL (*looking at her out of the corner of her eye*): Heard from Billy since he went?

QUEENIE (*offhand*): Oh yes, just a post-card with a camel on it.

ETHEL: A camel?

QUEENIE: Yes, his ship stopped somewhere where there was camels, and so he sent me a picture of one.

ETHEL: His poor mother misses him something dreadful. We all miss him really, don't we?

QUEENIE (*looking away*): Yes—I suppose we do.

> *There is the sound of the front door bell.*

ETHEL (*sharply*): There's the bell!

QUEENIE (*jumping up*): I'll go!

> *She runs into the hall, but VI has opened the door before her. There is the sound of voices and PHYLLIS BLAKE comes in followed by VI and QUEENIE.*

PHYLLIS: Please forgive me for calling so late, Mrs. Gibbons, but I just popped over on my bike to see if Reg had come back yet.

VI: Well, he hasn't.

ETHEL: That's all right, dear, sit down and have a cup of tea.

PHYLLIS: Thanks very much, Mrs. Gibbons, I must be getting back in a minute.

ETHEL (*at the table*): Time for one cup anyway. (*She pours it out.*)

QUEENIE: Dad's not back either, but he's due at any minute, him and Mr. Mitchell next door have been driving a bus.

PHYLLIS: Both of them?

VI: Mr. Mitchell's the conductor.

PHYLLIS: Have you heard from Reg, Mrs. Gibbons?

ETHEL: No, I'm afraid not, dear. He's off somewhere with Sam Leadbitter and those men at that club they belong to—I don't know what they've been up to, I'm sure.

VI: I went to Sam's bookshop in the Tottenham Court Road two days ago, the day Reg had a row with dad and slammed out and said he wasn't coming back, and Sam said he was all right but he'd promised not to tell where he was until the strike was over.

QUEENIE: Mother's afraid he might have got himself into trouble.

PHYLLIS: He'll be all right, Mrs. Gibbons, don't you worry.

ETHEL: I can't help it, I'm afraid. You read in those nasty bits of newspaper they hand round, about there being riots and people being arrested and houses being burst down and soldiers charging the crowds and all sorts of horrors . . .

QUEENIE: You can't always believe what you read in the papers, even little ones.

VI: If you ask me I shouldn't think he's been doing anything at all but run around the streets hollering, that's all any of 'em seem to do.

ETHEL (*hopelessly*): I wish he'd come back whatever he's been doing. I wish your dad hadn't gone at him like that. I shan't have a moment's peace until I know he's safe.

VI: I'm ₎going to see that Sam Leadbitter again to-morrow morning first thing and if he won't tell me where Reg is I'll stand in the shop and yell until he does.

At this moment there is a great commotion outside in the garden. FRANK *and* BOB's *voices are heard singing 'Rule Britannia' at the top of their lungs. They come in, grimy but gay.*

FRANK (*striking an attitude in front of* ETHEL): . . . Britons never, never, never shall be slaves!

ETHEL: 'Old your noise, Frank Gibbons, you'll wake up the whole street.

FRANK: Who cares! We have come unscathed, my friend and I, through untold perils, and you grumble about a bit of noise.

ETHEL: You've come unscathed through a few public houses, too, or I'm no judge.

BOB: Well, there's no denying, Mrs. G., we had a couple at the Plough with Captain Burchell, who brought us all the way from Baker Street in his car, and then just one more next door with me.

FRANK: That makes three all told, not so bad when you come to think we've saved our country from the 'orrors of bloody revolution.

ETHEL: And don't swear either. You'd better go and wash while I dish up your supper. You'll stay and have a bite, won't you, Bob?

BOB: No, thanks all the same. Nora's got something for me next door.

FRANK: Have a drink?

ETHEL: You've had quite enough drink, Frank, and well you know it.

BOB: Better not, old man. Ethel's right, the women are always right, that's why we cherish them, isn't it? Queenie?

ETHEL: You'd better cherish yourself next door, Bob Mitchell. Nora'll be having one of her upsets if she's got something hot ready for you and you're not there to eat it.

BOB: All right, all right—I thought I'd just deliver your old man safe and sound into your loving arms—good-night, all.

FRANK: That's right, drive my best pal out of the house, that's all the thanks he gets for saving my life.

ETHEL: How d'you mean, saving your life?

FRANK: An old lady at Cricklewood attacked me with an umbrella, and quick as a flash he wrested it from her and hit her on the bottom with it!

VI (*giggling*): Oh, Dad, you are awful!

FRANK: Good-night, cock, see you to-morrow.

BOB: Righto, sweet dreams. Toodle-ooo, everybody!

> *He goes out again, through the french windows.*

ETHEL: Go on, Frank. (*She starts cutting some bread.*) Here, Queenie, this bread's like iron, run into the kitchen and make your dad a bit of toast while I get the soup, the toaster's on the dresser.

QUEENIE (*taking the bread and going out*): All right, Mum.

> *FRANK goes out after her.*

VI: I'll get the soup, Mother, you stay here, you're tired.

PHYLLIS: Can I help?

ETHEL: No, thank you, dear.

> *VI goes out.*

> *ETHEL sits down in the arm-chair by the fireplace.*

PHYLLIS: Mr. Gibbons and Mr. Mitchell were in the war together, weren't they?

ETHEL: Yes, and to hear them talk, you'd think they were the only ones that was.

There is the sound of the front door bell.
There's the bell! (*She jumps up.*)

PHYLLIS: I'll go, Mrs. Gibbons.

> PHYLLIS *runs out of the room.*
>
> ETHEL *stands by the fireplace waiting anxiously. There is the sound of voices in the hall, then* SAM *comes in holding* REG *by the arm.* PHYLLIS *follows them.* REG'S *head is bandaged.* ETHEL *gives a cry.*

ETHEL: Reg! What's happened?

SAM: He's all right, Mrs. Gibbons——

ETHEL: Here, Reg, sit down here, dear.

REG (*sitting down*): Don't fuss, Mother, I'm all right.

SAM: There was some trouble in the Whitechapel Road, and he got hit by a stone. That was yesterday.

ETHEL: What was he doing in the Whitechapel Road yesterday or any other time?

REG (*smiling a little*): Hallo, Phyl, what are you doing here?

PHYLLIS: I came over on me bike to find out where you were.

REG: Oh, I see . . . thanks.

ETHEL: I've been worrying my heart out about you, you ought to be ashamed of yourself.

> FRANK *comes in, followed by* VI.

FRANK: Hallo—what's up?

ETHEL: It's Reg, he's been hurt.

SAM: It's nothing serious, I took him to the hospital last night, the doctor said it was only a graze.

VI (*grimly*): This is all your fault, Sam, you know that, don't you?

FRANK (*going over to* REG): Shut up a minute, Vi . . feel all right, son?

REG (*sullenly*): Of course I feel all right.

ETHEL: He'd better go up to bed, hadn't he?

FRANK: Leave him where he is a minute.

ETHEL: Don't go for him to-night, Frank, he looks worn out.

FRANK: I'm not going for anybody. I want my supper.

He goes to the table and sits down. ETHEL *takes the bowl of soup from* VI *and serves it to him. She is looking at* REG *anxiously out of the corner of her eye as she does so.* QUEENIE *enters with the toast.*

VI: You may not be going for anybody, Dad, but I am.

SAM: I think I'll be getting along now.

VI: Not until you've heard what I've got to say, you're not.

REG: Oh, shut up, Vi, what's it got to do with you?

VI: It's all very fine for you to say that nothing serious has happened, Sam, but I should like to remark here and now that it's small thanks to you that it hasn't. You're nothing but a great silly show-off, anyhow, and you've been filling Reg up with your rotten ideas till he can't see straight. Reg thinks you're wonderful, he's younger than you and easily led, but I don't think you're wonderful. I'd think more of you if you did a bit more and talked a bit less. And the next time you come here on a Sunday evening and start pawing me about and saying that Love's the most glorious thing in the world for rich and poor alike, you'll get such a smack in the face that'll make you wish you'd never been born. . . .

SAM: Look here, Vi . . .

VI: You get out of this house once and for all and don't you show your nose in it again until you've changed your way of thinking. I don't want to have anything to do with a man who listens to a lot of dirty foreigners and goes against his own country. There may be a lot of things wrong but it's not a noisy great gas-bag like you that's going to set them right.

SAM: If that's the way you feel, there isn't anything more to be said.

VI: You're right, dead right, there isn't. Go on, get out! I don't want ever to see you again as long as I live!

In silence SAM *turns and goes out of the room.* VI *waits until she hears the front door slam and then bursts into tears and rushes out into the garden.*

FRANK: Where's the pepper got to?

QUEENIE: In the sideboard—here——— (*She gets it.*)

ETHEL: Oh, dear—I'd better go after her.

FRANK: Much better leave her alone.

REG: Vi hasn't any right to go at Sam like that. What does she know about anything anyway?

FRANK: You keep quiet, son. I'll talk to you presently.

ETHEL: He really ought to go to bed, Frank, he looks that seedy . . . (*To* REG.) Is your head paining you, dear?

REG (*irritably*): No, Mum, it's all right, just aching a bit, that's all.

PHYLLIS: I think I'd better be getting back now, Mrs. Gibbons.

ETHEL: Very well, dear, be careful how you go, there's probably a lot of people about to-night.

PHYLLIS: Good-night, Queenie.

QUEENIE: Good-night, Phyl.

PHYLLIS: Good-night, Mr. Gibbons.

FRANK: Good-night, Phyllis.

PHYLLIS: I hope your head'll be better in the morning, Reg.

REG: Thanks for coming round.

PHYLLIS: Good-night.

REG: See you to-morrow?

PHYLLIS: Oh—all right.

    PHYLLIS goes out.

FRANK (*lighting a cigarette*): Run out into the garden, Queenie, and fetch Vi in, it's time we was all in bed.

QUEENIE: Righto, Dad.

    She goes into the garden.

FRANK: Go on up, Ethel, I'll turn out.

ETHEL: Promise me you won't be hard on him to-night, Frank—look, he's as white as a sheet.

REG (*defiantly*): I feel fine, Mum, don't worry about me.

FRANK: Well, that's good news, anyway.

ETHEL: Come in and say good-night to me on your way to bed.

REG: All right.

    ETHEL stands about helplessly for a moment, and then, one more imploring look at FRANK, she goes out of the room.

    FRANK takes a bottle of whisky, a syphon and two glasses out of the sideboard.

FRANK: Feel like a drink, Reg?

REG (*surprised*): Oh—yes, thanks.

    FRANK pours two drinks out in silence and takes one over to REG.

FRANK: Here you are.

REG (*taking it*): Thanks, Dad.

FRANK: Here goes. (*He drinks.*)

REG (*also drinking*): Here goes.

    QUEENIE and VI come in from the garden. VI is no longer crying.

QUEENIE: Has Mum gone up?

FRANK: Yes, a couple of minutes ago.

QUEENIE: Will you turn out?

FRANK: Yes; you might shut the windows though. Is Percy in all right?

QUEENIE (*shutting the windows*): Yes, he's asleep in the kitchen.

VI: Good-night, Dad.

FRANK (*kissing her*): Good-night, old girl.

QUEENIE (*looking at the table*): I suppose I'd better clear these things.

FRANK: Leave them for Edie in the morning.

QUEENIE: All right. Good-night, Dad.

FRANK (*kissing her*): Good-night, Queenie.

QUEENIE: Good-night, Reg.

VI: Good-night, Reg.

REG: Good-night.

> VI *and* QUEENIE *go out and shut the door after them.*
>
> FRANK *stands leaning against the mantelpiece looking down at* REG.

Well, Dad—let's have it and get it over with.

FRANK: Easier said than done, you and me don't quite see things the same way, do we?

REG: No, I suppose not.

FRANK: That's the trouble really, it's a pity, too, and I don't see what there is to be done about it. Got any ideas?

REG: I'm not a kid any more, you know, Dad. I'm grown-up now.

FRANK: Yes, I realise that all right.

REG: I know you think all the things I believe in are wrong . . .

FRANK: That's where you make a mistake, son, I

don't think any such thing. You've got a right to your opinions the same as I've got a right to mine. The only thing that worries me is that you should get it into your head that everybody's against you and what's more that all these ideas you've picked up, from Sam and Sam's friends, are new. They're not new, they're as old as the hills. Anybody with any sense has always known about the injustice of some people having a lot and other people having nothing at all, but where I think you go wrong is to blame it all on systems and governments. You've got to go deeper than that to find out the cause of most of the troubles of this world, and when you've had a good look, you'll see likely as not that good old human nature's at the bottom of the whole thing.

REG: If everybody had the same chance as everybody else, human nature'd be better, wouldn't it?

FRANK: It doesn't seem as though we were ever going to find that out, does it? It looks like a bit of a deadlock to me.

REG: As long as we go on admitting that, the workers of the world will go on being ground down and the capitalists will go on fattening on their blood and sweat.

FRANK: Oh, don't let's start all that now, let's use our own words, not other people's.

REG: I don't know what you mean.

FRANK: Oh, come off it, Reg, a kid of your age to be talking about blood and sweat and capitalism! When I was rising twenty I had a damn sight more cheerful things to think about than that, I can tell you.

REG: Old people always think that all young people want is to enjoy themselves.

FRANK: Don't you sit there and tell me you 'aven't

been enjoying yourself tip-top these last few days running about the streets and throwing stones and yelling your head off . . .

REG: It's no use talking, Dad, you don't understand, and you never will.

FRANK: No, you're quite right, arguing never got anybody anywhere, I'll just give you one bit of advice, and then we'll call it a day. How does that suit?

REG (*suspiciously*): What is it?

FRANK: It's this son. I belong to a generation of men, most of which aren't here any more, and we all did the same thing for the same reason, no matter what we thought about politics. Now all that's over and we're all going on as best as we can as though nothing had happened. But as a matter of fact several things did happen and one of them was the country suddenly got tired, it's tired now. But the old girl's got stamina and don't you make any mistake about it and it's up to us ordinary people to keep things steady. That's your job, my son, and just you remember it, and the next time you slam out of the house without a word and never let your mother know where you are and worry her to death, I'll lather the living daylight out of you. Now cut along upstairs and get a bit of sleep.

REG (*rising*): All right, Dad.

FRANK: And don't forget to go in and say goodnight to your mum.

REG: All right, Dad—thanks, Dad.

REG *goes out.*

FRANK *looks round the room, finishes his drink, turns out the lights and follows him as—*

THE CURTAIN FALLS

ACT II

SCENE I

TIME: *October, 1931. It is about ten o'clock in the morning. FRANK is alone in the room finishing his breakfast and reading the* Daily Mirror. *He has aged rather during the last six years. His hair is much thinner on the top and his eyes are not what they were which necessitates his wearing glasses for reading. He is dressed in the trousers and waistcoat of a new pepper and salt suit but no coat. He also has a wing collar and a grand grey silk tie and carpet slippers.* QUEENIE, *wrapped in a Japanese silk kimono and with her hair done up in a net, rushes into the room, grabs her handbag off the sideboard and rushes out again.* FRANK *looks up, stirs his tea thoughtfully and goes on reading his paper.* EDIE *comes in with a tray. During the ensuing scenes there are various sounds of commotion going on in the house. Scamperings up and down the stairs; doors slamming; bath water running and occasional signs of altercation between members of the family.*

EDIE: Mrs. Gibbons said I could clear now so as to give me time to go and dress.

FRANK: Righto, Edie, just leave me with tea.

EDIE (*piling plates on to the tray*): That bath takes a terrible time to run out, it's my belief the plug-hole's stopped up.

FRANK: Better pop round to the tobacconist's and telephone Mr. Freeman.

EDIE: I shan't have time this morning.

FRANK: To-morrow'll do.

EDIE: Wasn't it awful about poor Mrs. Flint's dress?

FRANK: What happened to it?

EDIE: Percy's been curled up on it all night, covered it with 'airs he 'as. She nearly 'ad a fit when she found 'im. Wonder you didn't 'ear the noise going on.

FRANK: The whole 'ouse has been in an uproar since eight o'clock.

EDIE: Well, we don't 'ave weddings every day of the week, do we?

FRANK: No, thank God.

EDIE (*going out with the tray*): One thing we've got a lovely day for it.

> FRANK *left alone for a moment goes on with his paper.*
> EDIE *returns.*

D'you mind if I move your tea on to the sideboard a minute, I'll 'ave to change the cloth.

FRANK: All right—I'll give you a hand.

> *He places the teapot, milk jug, sugar basin and his cup on the sideboard and helps* EDIE *to change the tablecloths during the ensuing few lines.*

EDIE: I went with Mrs. Gibbons to the Plough last night to see the upstairs room. They've done it up lovely. We 'ad a look at the cake too, it's ever so pretty. Mrs. Gibbons says I can 'ave a bit to take 'ome to Ernie.

FRANK: Ernie must be getting quite a big boy now.

EDIE: 'E's nearly sixteen but you'd never think it—'e's short like dad, you know.

FRANK: Oh, I see.

EDIE: 'E started trying to shave himself the other day with dad's razor, you'd have died laughing if you'd seen 'im.

FRANK: Did he cut himself?

EDIE: Not badly, just took the top off one or two spots.

> EDIE *goes out.*
>
> FRANK *puts the tea-things back on the table and sits down again. Presently* BOB MITCHELL *taps at the window.* FRANK *gets up and lets him in.*

BOB: Well, we've got a nice day for it.

FRANK: Want a cup of tea?

BOB: No, thanks—I'll have a Goldflake though, if you've got one.

FRANK: There's a packet on the mantelpiece, chuck us one too while you're at it.

> BOB *takes a cigarette himself and throws the packet over to* FRANK, *who misses it.*

FRANK: Missed it! Can't see a thing with these glasses.

BOB: You'll get used to 'em.

FRANK: How's Nora?

BOB: A bit more cheerful, she always is when Billy's home, one thing her legs don't pain her any more, she just hasn't got any feeling in 'em at all. The doctor says she won't get no worse nor no better either—just stay about the same.

FRANK: Well, as long as she's a bit brighter in herself I suppose we mustn't grumble.

BOB: It was that last miscarriage six years ago that did her in, you know, she'd probably have been all right if it hadn't been for that.

FRANK: Poor old Nora.

BOB: Well, this is a nice conversation for us to be having on the festive day, I will say. How's the happy bridegroom?

FRANK: The happy bridegroom locked himself in the bathroom for nearly an hour this morning; you'd think he hadn't washed for a month.

BOB: Natural anxiety, old man—can't blame 'im!

FRANK: Funny to think of starting off on an 'oneymoon, isn't it? Seems a hell of a long time ago since we did.

BOB: Where did you go for yours?

FRANK: Ramsgate, and it pissed with rain without stopping all the time.

BOB: We went to Swanage, Nora had relatives near there; it was awful.

FRANK: Well, Reg and Phyl ought to enjoy themselves all right. It'll be a change anyway going abroad for the first time. I got them special rates all along the line. Even old Baxter himself took a hand.

BOB: Where are they stopping to-night?

FRANK: Dover. Then they get the morning boat and they're in Nice first thing the next day.

BOB: Pretty posh going to the South of France for your honeymoon nest par?

FRANK: Well, we're only young once.

BOB: You've held that job at Tickler's steady ever since the war, haven't you?

FRANK: Yes, but I nearly lost it once.

BOB: How was that?

FRANK: Well, I'm all right on the business side, you know, travellers' cheques and letters of credit and what not, but once one of our young gentlemen downstairs smashed himself up in a car and I had to go behind the counter for a month—oh dear!—Mr. Baxter sent for me to his office. "Listen, Frank," he says, "there have been complaints. You've issued no less than four sets of tickets to the wrong places inside of the last week through not being able to pronounce the foreign names properly! And as we can't afford to have our customers losing themselves all over the Continent you'd better go back to your figures!" After that he engaged a couple of Ladida young chaps with Oxford accents. You should hear them! I thought one of 'em had swallowed a fishbone the other day, but he was only saying Marseilles!

> SYLVIA *comes hurriedly into the room. She is dressed in a very old wrapper and her head is swathed in a towel. She sees* BOB, *gives a scream of horror and runs out again. She speaks the ensuing dialogue through the half open door.*

SYLVIA: Fancy me coming in looking like this in front of Mr. Mitchell! What will he think?

FRANK: Don't worry. He's broadminded.

SYLVIA: I had my hair set yesterday and I didn't dare let the damp get to it while I was having my bath.

FRANK: What d'you want, anyway?

SYLVIA: Mrs. Flint's feather-boa—she says it's in a box on the table by the window—one of its tassels is loose.

FRANK: Hold on a minute. (*He takes a box off the table by the window, brings it to her and hands it round the door.*) Is this it?

SYLVIA: Yes, that's it—thanks.

> *She goes.*

303

FRANK (*shuts the door and comes back into the room*): This house has been a fair circus all the morning, I give you my word.

BOB: Reg is doing all right, isn't he now?

FRANK: Yes, he got his raise. He's assistant clerk to one of the managers.

BOB: No more of that Bolshie nonsense?

FRANK: Oh no, he's got quite a lot of horse sense, you know, underneath. He had a nice look at the Labour Government and saw what a mess they was making of everything. You should have heard him the other night when the election results came through—jumping up and down like a jack-in-the-box he was. He's Britain for ever now all right.

BOB: Well, that's good news.

FRANK: Sam shook him a bit too, you know, giving up that old Bombshell Bookshop of his and marrying Vi and settling down. Oh yes, we've all gone back to being the backbone of the Empire.

> REG *comes in in his shirt-sleeves. He carries two ties in his hand.*

REG: Dad—— (*He sees* BOB.) Oh, hallo, Uncle Bob.

BOB: Hallo, Reg—feeling nervous?

REG (*grinning*): My legs feel a bit funny. Is Billy nearly ready?

BOB: Yes, and he's got the ring all right too. I saw him put it in his pocket myself. He'll be here in a minute.

REG: Which tie d'you think, Dad? The bow, or the long one?

FRANK: Let's have a look. (*He holds them both up.*) Try the bow, it looks more dressy.

REG (*tying the bow in front of the glass on the mantelpiece*): Aunt Sylvia's been having a good cry upstairs.

FRANK: What about?

REG: Oh, first of all, she said she felt seedy and that weddings always upset her anyhow, then Granny flew at her and said if only she'd had the sense to get married herself we should all have been saved a lot of trouble!

FRANK: I don't know how those two would get on without each other and that's a fact.

BOB: I'll be getting along now and get myself spruced up for the happy moment.

FRANK: Righto.

BOB: See you at the church, Reg.

REG: You might tell Billy to get a move on, Uncle Bob.

BOB: I will.

    BOB *goes out.*

    FRANK *sits down in the arm-chair and looks thoughtfully at* REG.

FRANK: Well, son!

REG: Well, Dad!

FRANK: I suppose I ought to be giving you a few bits of fatherly advice by rights.

REG (*blandly*): What about, Dad?

FRANK: Well, there's the facts of life, for instance.

REG: I could probably tell you a few things about them.

FRANK: I bet you could at that. (*There is a pause.*) Reg——

REG (*solemnly*): Yes, Dad?

FRANK: And I'll trouble you to wipe that innocent look off your face before I say what I've got to say.

REG: What have you got to say, Dad?

FRANK: That's right, make the whole thing easy for me.

REG: I don't know what you're talking about.

FRANK: I'm not talking about anything yet.

REG: All right—fire away.

FRANK (*with an effort*): Would you say—taken by and large—that you'd been a good boy on the whole—since you've grown up?

REG: Depends what you mean by good.

FRANK: You know what I mean all right, so don't talk so soft.

REG: Women?

FRANK: Yes.

REG: Oh, I've had my bits of fun every now and again.

FRANK: Never got yourself into any sort of trouble, have you, without telling me?

REG: No, Dad.

FRANK: Marriage is a bit different you know, from just—having a bit of fun.

REG (*fidgeting*): Yes—I expect it is.

FRANK: Women aren't all the same by any manner of means, some of them don't care what happens so long as they have a good time; marriage isn't important to them beyond having the ring and being called Mrs. Whatever it is. But your mother wasn't that sort and I don't think Phyllis is either. She's a nice girl and she loves you a lot.

REG: I know, Dad.

FRANK: And when a woman loves you that much she's liable to be a bit over-sensitive you know. It's as well to remember that.

REG: I'll remember, Dad.

306

FRANK: Just go carefully with her—be gentle. You've got a long time to be together, all your lives, I hope. It's worth while to go easy and get to know each other gradual. And if later on, a long time later on, you ever get yourself caught up with someone else, just see to it that Phyllis doesn't get hurt by it. Put your wife first always. Lots of little things can happen on the side without doing much harm providing you don't make a fool of yourself and keep quiet about it. But anything that's liable to bust up your home and your life with your wife and children's not worth it. Just remember that and you won't go far wrong.

REG: All right, Dad—thanks a lot.

FRANK: I only hope you'll have the luck I've had. I can't say more than that, can I?

REG: No, Dad.

FRANK: Well, I'd better be getting myself dressed up —so long, son.

He rather clumsily puts his arms round REG *for a minute and goes out of the room.*

REG left alone, takes a cigarette out of the packet on the table, lights it and then returns to the glass and scrutinises his face in it. BILLY *enters through the french window. He has grown matured and set with the years. He is now wearing the uniform of a Petty Officer.*

BILLY: Don't worry, old man—you look gorgeous.

REG (*turning*): Oh, it's you, is it?

BILLY: All ready for the ball and chain?

REG: You're too bloody cheerful by half.

BILLY: Of course I am. I'm a sailor, aren't I? All sailors are bright and breezy, it's in the regulations.

REG: You must be the life and soul of your ship.

BILLY (*helping himself to a cigarette*): Oh, I am, I am.

Only the other morning the Admiral sent for me, "Mitchell," he said, "make me laugh." So I told him the one about the parrot. "Mitchell," he said, "the ship's yours." "What'll I do with it?" I said. "Scuttle it," he said, and cut his throat from ear to ear.

REG: Have you got the ring all right?

BILLY: Well, as a matter of fact, I dropped it down the whatsit, but don't worry, we sent for a plumber.

REG: I'd better go and get my coat, we'll have to be starting in a minute.

BILLY: Righto.

On his way out he bangs into QUEENIE *coming in.* QUEENIE *is wearing a blue bridesmaid's dress and hat and is carrying a bunch of flowers.*

QUEENIE: Why can't you look where you're going, you nearly knocked me down.

REG: Sorry, old girl——

He goes out.

QUEENIE *sees* BILLY.

QUEENIE: Oh, it's you.

BILLY: Yes. (*He turns away.*)

QUEENIE: Well, it's a nice day anyhow, isn't it?

BILLY: Fine.

QUEENIE (*puts her flowers on the sideboard and comes over to him*): You haven't said anything to Reg, have you? You haven't said anything to anyone?

BILLY: Of course not.

QUEENIE (*looking down*): I'm awfully sorry about last night, Billy, really I am.

BILLY: No need to be sorry, it's not your fault.

QUEENIE: When you've gone back, they'll all be asking me questions—I don't know what to say.

BILLY (*not looking at her*): Tell 'em the truth. I love

you and asked you to marry me. You don't love me and said No. It's simple enough.

QUEENIE: It sounds horrid when you say it like that.

BILLY: No use pretending, is there?

QUEENIE: No, I suppose there isn't. I am sorry though all the same, you do believe that, don't you?

BILLY: Yes, I believe it all right.

QUEENIE: I never did say I would, did I? I mean I never let you think——

BILLY: I'm not blaming you, I told you that last night. I just can't help feeling a bit low—that's natural enough, isn't it?

QUEENIE: I suppose you won't write to me any more now, will you?

BILLY: You're a funny girl, I must say.

QUEENIE: I don't see anything so very funny about that.

BILLY: You want everything, don't you?

QUEENIE: It's unkind to talk like that.

BILLY: You know, I love you more than anyone else and want to marry you, don't you? You've always known that anyway. You turn me down flat and then want me to go on writing to you. What shall I have to write about to you any more? If you've taken the trouble to read my letters up to date you might remember they was mostly about the future, and what fun we were going to have when we were together. All that's gone now, hasn't it? I'll send you a weather report every so often if you like.

QUEENIE: If you're going to turn nasty about it there's no use saying any more.

BILLY: There's someone else, isn't there?

QUEENIE: I don't know what you mean.

BILLY: I mean what I say. You're in love with someone else, aren't you?

QUEENIE: It's no business of yours if I am.

BILLY: It's true though, isn't it?

QUEENIE: Now look here, Billy——

BILLY: Why couldn't you have told me last night, or a long time ago. Don't you trust me?

QUEENIE: You haven't got any right to ask me things like that.

BILLY: Listen here, Queenie. You've been the only girl I've cared a damn about for getting on seven years now. We haven't seen much of each other on account of me being away at sea, but you've known all the time that I was thinking of you and hoping that as the years went by you'd grow out of some of your highfalutin ideas and think me good enough to be your husband. All that gives me the right to ask you anything I like——

QUEENIE: No, it doesn't.

BILLY: Is there someone else or isn't there?

QUEENIE: Yes, there is, if you must know. So there!

BILLY: Are you going to marry him?

QUEENIE: If you say a word about this to anyone I'll never speak to you again as long as I live.

BILLY: Are you going to marry him?

QUEENIE: No.

BILLY: Why not?

QUEENIE: That's my affair.

BILLY: Is he married already?

QUEENIE: I wish you'd leave me alone.

BILLY: Is he?

QUEENIE: Yes, he is! Now are you satisfied?

BILLY (turning away): Oh, Queenie, you're an awful fool—I do wish you weren't.

QUEENIE: Who are you calling a fool? People can't help their feelings.

BILLY: No, but they can have enough sense not to let their feelings get the better of them. What you're doing's wrong whichever way you look at it. There's your mother and father to start with, it'll break their hearts if ever they find out about it. Then there's the man's wife whoever she is, you're laying up trouble there. But most important of all there's you. You won't get much out of it in the long run and don't you fool yourself. You're not that kind of girl really, whatever you may think. It looks to me as if you're on the way to mucking things up all round for yourself and everyone else——

QUEENIE: Thanks very much for the lecture.

BILLY: You're quite right. It's no good me saying any more. I'll go up and talk to Reg. Good-bye and good luck.

> *He goes quickly out of the room.*
>
> QUEENIE *stands still for a moment looking after him biting her lip. She looks, just for a second, as though she might be going to cry, then she tosses her head and, turning to the glass begins to fiddle about with her hat.*
>
> ETHEL *comes in followed by* FRANK. ETHEL *is elaborately dressed in grey silk.* FRANK *has enhanced the glory of his pepper and salt suit by the addition of a large white buttonhole and some obviously new boots.*

ETHEL: Vi and Sam ought to be here by now—I wonder where they are.

FRANK (*to* QUEENIE): Been talking to Billy?

QUEENIE: Yes. He's upstairs with Reg.

FRANK (*sitting down*): These boots are giving me what for all right. If they're like this now, what are they going to be like by the evening?

QUEENIE: A couple of weddings in one year is a bit too much of a good thing if you ask me.

FRANK: Well, here's hoping you get off soon and make the third.

QUEENIE: I wish you wouldn't say things like that, Dad, it sounds so vulgar.

FRANK: Very sorry, I'm sure.

QUEENIE: When I marry, if I ever do, it will be in a registry office anyway—all this commotion.

FRANK: Your mother wouldn't like that—would you, Ethel?

ETHEL: I certainly would not.

QUEENIE: I shouldn't let you know. I shouldn't let anybody know. I'd do it on the quiet. I don't like to think of everyone staring at me and making remarks.

ETHEL: I never heard such nonsense.

FRANK: Our Queenie has ideas of her own, Ethel, or anyway she thinks they're her own.

QUEENIE: I'll never be a bridesmaid again anyhow as long as I live—look at this dress—and the hat.

ETHEL: You've done something to it, haven't you?

QUEENIE: You bet I have. I wouldn't have worn it as it was.

ETHEL: You'll look different from all the others.

QUEENIE: So I should hope.

ETHEL: Marjorie will be upset. She and Phyl took such a lot of trouble——

QUEENIE: They don't know anything about clothes either of them. Thank heavens none of the girls at the shop can see me looking such a sight.

FRANK: It seems to me they must be a pretty fancy

lot, them girls at your shop! We're always being told what they like and what they don't like.

QUEENIE: All right, Dad, there's no need for you to be sarcastic.

ETHEL: Don't snap at your father, Queenie. I don't know what's come over you lately.

QUEENIE (*with an edge on her voice*): Nothing's come over me—I just don't like looking common.

FRANK: I shouldn't worry about that if I was you—it can't be helped. After all according to some people's standards I suppose you are common.

ETHEL: Frank, how can you say such a thing! She's nothing of the sort.

FRANK: It's your mother's fault really, you know. She caught me on the 'op! I was all set to marry a duchess when along she come and busted up the whole thing with her fatal charm. And what's more the duchess never forgave me. That's why I haven't set foot inside Buckingham Palace these last thirty years.

QUEENIE: You think you're very funny, don't you, Dad?

FRANK: I think you're the one that's funny, if you must know.

QUEENIE: Why, what have I done?

FRANK: It isn't what you've done, my girl, it's what you're trying to do.

QUEENIE: And what's that, may I ask?

FRANK: You're trying to be something you're not. There's nothing funnier than that. To see you flouncing about and putting on airs just because you happen to have polished Lady Kiss-me-quick's nails is enough to make a cat laugh.

QUEENIE (*angrily*): You don't believe in people trying

to better themselves, do you? Just because you're content to stick in the same place all your life and do your bit of gardening on Saturday afternoons in your shirt-sleeves——

ETHEL: Don't you dare speak to your father like that!

QUEENIE: Living in a suburb and doing your own cooking and washing up may be good enough for you, but it isn't good enough for me. I'm sick of this house and everybody in it, and I'm not going to stand it much longer, you see——

ETHEL: You're a wicked ungrateful girl and you ought to be ashamed of yourself.

QUEENIE: Well, I'm not, so there!

ETHEL: If it wasn't for being Reg's wedding day I'd lock you in your room till you came to your senses.

FRANK: Well, a few years ago we had Reg nagging at us because we were living on the fat of the land while the poor workers was starving. Now we have Queenie turning on us because we're not good enough for her. I don't know what's wrong with our children, Ethel, my girl. Seems to me Vi's the only one who's got any real sense.

QUEENIE: Vi! Vi's different from me—can't you see —she always has been! She doesn't like the things I like or want the things I want. She's perfectly happy in that mangy little flat doing her own housework and making her own clothes. She likes bossing Sam too. Why he's a changed man since he married her.

ETHEL: And a good job too.

QUEENIE: It seems to me that all the spirit's gone out of him. He's just like anybody else now—just respectable.

FRANK: Well, what's the matter with that?

QUEENIE: Oh, nothing. What's the use of arguing! You don't understand what I'm talking about.

FRANK: Don't waste your breath on us then, Queenie. We're as we are and that's how we're going to stay, and if you don't like it you can lump it. One of these days when you know a bit more, you'll find out that there are worse things than being ordinary and respectable and living the way you've been brought up to live. In the meantime—as long as you're with us I mean—your mum and me'd be much obliged if you'd keep your tongue between your teeth and behave yourself. Now you'd better go upstairs, slap some more paint on your face, make yourself look as much like a tart as possible and do the girls at the shop credit. Go on—'op it!

QUEENIE: Thanks very much—I will!

She flounces out of the room and slams the door.

ETHEL: There now. She'll be snapping our heads off for the rest of the day.

FRANK: We spoilt her when she was little. We've always spoilt her.

ETHEL: No, Frank, it isn't only that. She's upset about something—sort of strung up, she has been for a long time. I wish I knew what it was.

FRANK: You mean you think she's in some sort of trouble?

ETHEL: I don't know what to think. When Billy came back last year and they went out together nearly every evening, I thought everything was going to be all right, then they had words, I don't know what about, I'm sure, and off he went.

FRANK: Don't worry, old girl, it'll all come out in the wash.

EDIE, *resplendent in a green dress and hat, rushes in.*

EDIE: The car's come. It looks ever so nice all done up with white ribbons.

FRANK: Good! Let's have a look, Ethel. You'd better call Reg, Edie—tell him it's here.

EDIE *runs out.*

FRANK *takes* ETHEL *by the hand and they go out into the hall and apparently open the front door because they can be heard making exclamations of approval of the car.*

REG *and* BILLY *come clattering down the stairs and into the room.* REG *is palpably nervous.*

REG: I suppose we ought to be starting, oughtn't we?

BILLY: Yes, it's about time now, it wouldn't do for the blushing bride to get there before we do.

FRANK *and* ETHEL *return.*

ETHEL: Have you seen the car? Mr. Stevens has done it up lovely!

REG: Yes, we saw it drive up.

FRANK: Feeling nervous, son?

REG: Yes, a bit.

ETHEL (*emotionally*): Oh Reg!

REG: Cheer up, Mother.

ETHEL (*fumbling for her handkerchief*): I can't hardly believe it—it seems only the other day that——

REG (*putting his arm round her*): All right, Mum, we know all about that. I was a little toddler cutting me first teeth and look at me now, a great grown man——

FRANK: Don't start getting weepy now, Ethel, it's a wedding, not a funeral!

ETHEL: Oh, hold your noise, Frank, and be quiet.

REG (*kissing her*): See you at the church, Mum. Cheero, Dad—come on, Billy.

FRANK: Cheero, son—don't forget to send the car straight back.

BILLY: I'll see to that—it'll be back in five minutes.

ETHEL: Have you said good-bye to your Grannie and Auntie Syl?

REG: Yes—I saw them upstairs.

BILLY (*sternly*): Come *on*.

REG: All right. Good-bye all——

He and BILLY *go out.*

ETHEL *sinks into a chair and weeps a little.*

FRANK: Come off it, Ethel, there's nothing to cry about.

ETHEL: I can't help it.

FRANK: You'll make your nose red.

ETHEL: I don't care if I do. He's our only son, isn't he? And he's going away from us, isn't he? That's enough to make any woman cry.

FRANK: Well, they'll be back from the honeymoon in two weeks and living just round the corner——

ETHEL: It's all very fine for you—you didn't bring him into the world and hold him at your breast——

FRANK: I should have looked a proper fool if I had.

ETHEL: You don't know anything about it, you haven't got any feelings.

FRANK (*comforting her*): Come on now—shut up crying and put your hat straight.

SYLVIA *comes in leading* MRS. FLINT *by the arm.* SYLVIA *is wearing an artistic confection of brown and orange, also a necklace of thick amber beads.* MRS. FLINT *is in purple satin and a black flowered hat. She is led to her chair and settles herself in it.*

MRS. F.: If I could lay my hands on that cat I'd kill it.

Half an hour it took me to pick the hairs off and the front of the skirt all creased too.

SYLVIA: It doesn't show.

MRS. F. (*looking balefully at* SYLVIA): Is that the new hat we've heard such a lot about?

SYLVIA: Yes, it is.

MRS. F. (*grunting*): Oh!

SYLVIA: Why, is there anything the matter with it?

ETHEL (*peaceably*): I think it's very nice, don't you, Frank?

FRANK: It looks fine.

MRS. F.: There's something a bit funny about the crown, isn't there?

SYLVIA: I don't know what you mean.

MRS. F.: Well, of course, if you're satisfied.

ETHEL: Do be quiet, Mother, don't take any notice of her, Sylvia.

MRS. F.: That'll be no change. Nobody ever does take any notice of me. But old as I am I can at least get myself to the church on me feet which is more than can be said for Phyllis's aunt who has to be wheeled in.

SYLVIA: She's bed-ridden, poor woman.

MRS. F.: I shouldn't be surprised if she could walk as well as anybody if she liked.

> VI *and* SAM *come in.* QUEENIE *follows them.* SAM *has improved with the years. He is neatly dressed and wears an air of respectability which was lacking before.*
> VI *looks very assured and smart in a pink dress and hat.*

VI: The front door was open so we came straight in.

ETHEL (*kissing her*): Why, Vi, how pretty you look, dear.

VI (*showing off her dress*): I only finished it at eleven o'clock last night.

318

SAM: The whole flat's been covered in paper patterns and bits of stuff and pins for the last ten days. Has Reg gone?

FRANK: Yes, he and Billy went about two minutes ago. They're sending the car straight back.

QUEENIE: I hope they'll get a move on. I've got to be on time to meet Marjorie and Doreen and Amy Weaver.

VI: It does look nice that dress, doesn't it, Sam?

SAM: Very nice indeed.

QUEENIE: I think it's awful.

VI: Oh, you always say that, Queenie, it was exactly the same at my wedding.

BOB MITCHELL *comes in through the french window*.

BOB: Hallo, Vi—hallo, Sam—car come back yet?

ETHEL: Tell Edie to keep an eye out for it, Queenie.

QUEENIE (*going to door and shouting through it*): Edie—keep a look out for the car—you'd better stay by the drawing-room window.

EDIE (*off*): All right.

MRS. F.: On my wedding day there was a thunderstorm and a man got struck by lightning just opposite the church.

FRANK: That must have cheered things up.

MRS. F.: One side of his face was all twisted.

QUEENIE: Why, Grannie, did you stop in the middle of the service and pop out to have a look?

MRS. F.: We did not, and I'll thank you, Miss, not to be saucy.

QUEENIE: Saucy indeed—what a way to talk.

FRANK: I'm surprised at you, Mother, I am really, using such expressions in front of our Queenie. You know she meets all the best people nowadays.

QUEENIE: Oh, shut up, Dad.

FRANK: Better sit down, hadn't we, all of us? No sense in standing about.

ETHEL (*looking at the clock*): It ought to be back by now.

FRANK: Don't fuss, Ethel.

MRS. F. (*reminiscently*): It seems only yesterday.

ETHEL: What does, Mother?

MRS. F.: The day you and Frank married. I can see your poor Aunt Connie now coughing her heart out in the vestry. It was only three months after that she was taken.

FRANK (*cheerfully*): That's right. (*He winks at* BOB.)

MRS. F.: I'll be lucky if I last out another year.

FRANK: Oh, dear, oh, dear!

MRS. F. (*darkly*): I don't suppose anybody'd mind much—there's many as might say it was a blessing in disguise I shouldn't wonder.

FRANK: Now then, Mother—none of that.

MRS. F.: Doctor Spearman said my heart was thoroughly worn out ever since that bronchitis I 'ad in February.

SYLVIA (*contemptuously*): Doctor Spearman!

MRS. F.: He's a better man than your Doctor Lewis any day of the week. If it hadn't been for him having presence of mind Mrs. Spooner would be dead as a door-nail at this very minute.

SYLVIA: That's what you say.

MRS. F.: Eleven o'clock she was doing her shopping and she was putting the joint in the oven at twelve —a nice bit of leg of lamb it was too, and at half-past one she was in the 'ospital lying flat on 'er back on the operating table—and if it hadn't been for Doctor Spearman——

ETHEL: I wonder what's happened to that car—it's getting on you know.

BOB: Shall I go out and have a look?

FRANK: No—Edie's watching out for it.

ETHEL: I suppose Billy remembered to tell the driver all right. He's a new man you know, not the same one we had for Vi's wedding. He might not have understood.

FRANK: Well, if it comes to the pinch we can walk, anyway, can't we? It's only just up the road.

SAM: Vi oughtn't to do much walking.

VI: Don't be silly, Sam. It's weeks away yet.

SAM: All the same, it's silly to go taking risks.

FRANK (*at door, shouting*): Any signs yet, Edie?

EDIE: No—— (*She appears.*) Mrs. Baker and Miss Whitney just come out of number twelve—you should see 'em—got up to kill they are.

SYLVIA: That Miss Whitney—stuck up thing!

ETHEL: Well, she'll have to sit next to Mr. Bolton at the table whether she likes it or not.

FRANK: Go back to the front room, Edie.

QUEENIE: Don't hang out of the window though, it looks silly.

EDIE (*reproachfully*): As if I would! (*She goes.*)

SYLVIA: I had those pains again in the night, Ethel, something terrible they were—started about two o'clock.

MRS. F.: It's all those sweets you eat. There's nothing like sweets for giving you wind.

SYLVIA: It was *not* wind!

QUEENIE: It's nearly ten to—I think I'd better go on in a minute.

FRANK: I wish everybody'd stop fussing. It gives me the pip.

ETHEL: It shouldn't have taken Reg and Billy more than three or four minutes to get there.

MRS. F.: I'm sure I hope nothing dreadful's happened to them.

VI: Oh, Grannie, what could have?

MRS. F.: Accidents will happen.

QUEENIE: Well, they can't have been struck by lightning anyhow.

SYLVIA: I shouldn't think there was the chance of many accidents just between here and St. Michael's.

MRS. F.: Well, you never know.

FRANK (*irritably*): All right, all right, have it your own way. There's been a terrible accident, the wedding's off. Reg 'as got concussion and we're all going to spend the rest of the day yelling our eyes out! How's that?

SYLVIA: Some people seem to think of nothing but horrors, it's morbid, that's what it is.

MRS. F.: I'll thank you not to call me names, Sylvia Gibbons.

SYLVIA: You make me tired.

ETHEL: Don't answer back, Sylvia, it'll only mean a row.

SYLVIA: I'm sure I don't want to say anything to anybody, but really——

MRS. F.: Pity you don't keep quiet then!

SYLVIA (*losing her temper*): Who are you to talk to me like that—I've had about enough of your nagging——

FRANK: Shut UP, Sylvia.

VI: You know, it's no good arguing with her, Auntie Syl.

SYLVIA (*violently*): I don't know any such thing. I tell you I'm sick of it—morning, noon and night it's the same thing—she's at me all the time, and I won't stand it. I've got as much right to be in this house as she has, just because she's old and pretends her heart's weak she thinks she can say what she likes, but I'll tell you one thing here and now, and that is that I've had enough trouble and sorrow and suffering in my life to put up with her eternal nagging and nasty insinuations. She's nothing but a spiteful, mischief-making old cat, and if I have any more of it, old as she is, I'll slap her face till her teeth rattle!

> SYLVIA *bursts into violent hysterical tears.* MRS. FLINT, *with a cry of rage, struggles up from her chair.* FRANK *and* BOB *endeavour to calm her.* ETHEL *and* VI *and* SAM *help* SYLVIA *sobbing into a chair.* QUEENIE *regards the proceedings with obvious contempt. Everybody talks at once.* EDIE *rushes in from the hall.*

EDIE (*excitedly—above the din*): It's here—it's here— the car's here.

> *The general noise dies down into silence.* SYLVIA'S *sobs subside. Everyone straightens themselves.*

FRANK (*quietly*): Come on, Mother—it's time to go to the church.

VI. Come on, Grannie—come with me.

MRS. F.: I'm all right.

VI (*coaxingly*): You'd better, dear, you know what you are and it's quite a long service——

FRANK: Take her to the outside one, Vi, there's no need to trail all the way upstairs.

> VI *leads* MRS. FLINT, *still protesting, out of the room.* BOB *goes out with* SYLVIA *who is making gallant efforts to control herself.* SAM, QUEENIE *and* EDIE *follow them.*

FRANK *looks at* ETHEL *and laughs, then he slips his arm through hers—as they go.*

FRANK: Come on, old girl——

THE LIGHTS FADE

ACT II

SCENE II

TIME: *November, 1931. It is about midnight.*

The room is empty and the door into the hall open.

The stage is dark except for a glow from the dying fire.

Presently QUEENIE *can be seen tip-toeing down the stairs. She is wearing a hat and coat and carrying a small suit-case. She puts this down just inside the door, switches on the light, goes, still on tip-toe, over to the fireplace and props a letter up on the mantelpiece. Then, with a hurried look round, she switches off the light again and goes out into the hall taking her suitcase with her. The front door is heard to open and close softly.*

There is a slight pause. The clock on the mantelpiece strikes twelve. There is a scuffling noise at the window, it opens and the curtains blow out in the draught. BOB's *voice is heard to say 'Oh dear'! He comes in followed by* FRANK. *They are both in ordinary suits but wearing their war medals. They are also both a little bit drunk.*

FRANK: God help poor sailors on a night like this!

BOB: Where's the light?

FRANK (*fastening the window*): Over by the door. Lucky this was open, we'd have woke up Ethel if we'd of come in by the front.

BOB (*switching on the light*): 'Ere we are.

FRANK: Better shut that door while you're at it.

BOB: Righto. (*He shuts it.*)

FRANK: Now then.

BOB: Now then what?

FRANK (*at the sideboard*): One more nightcap.

BOB: You won't half have a thick head in the morning!

FRANK (*producing whisky and glasses*): What about you?

BOB: I'm past caring, old man.

FRANK: That's right—say when—— (*He pours out the whisky.*)

BOB: Here, go easy——

FRANK: 'Old it while I put the soda in.

BOB (*taking the glass*): Your eyes look terrible! All swimmy.

FRANK: Never you mind about my eyes—yours don't look so good from here! (*He squirts the syphon violently, splashing them both.*)

BOB: Look out!

FRANK: Oh dear! Now I've wetted me Victoria Cross.

BOB: Don't you wish you had one?

FRANK: Fat lot of good it'd do me if I 'ad.

The pouring out of the drink having been accomplished he holds up his glass.

FRANK: I would like to take this opportunity of saying that my old regiment's the finest in the world. To-night we have all here present been united in friendship and memory.

BOB: You'll wake up your missus in a minute and she'll unite you with a slap in the chops for coming home tiddley!

FRANK (*ignoring him, swaying slightly*): When I see before me all these well-remembered faces and recall, with a tug of the 'eart-strings, the hardships and perils we endured together——

BOB: Now listen, old man, I've heard all this once already to-night, you know——

FRANK (*sternly*): Don't interrupt! My old regiment's the finest in the world——

BOB: Next to the East Surreys it is.

FRANK: Here's to the Buffs! (*He drinks.*)

BOB: Here's to the East Surreys!

FRANK (*affectionately*): The East Surreys is the finest regiment in the world too——

BOB: That's right.

FRANK (*drinking*): Here's to the East Surreys!

BOB (*drinking*): Here's to the Buffs!

FRANK (*sitting down at the table*): What was that one that chap told us about the couple in the park?

BOB (*also sitting*): You mean the one when the copper comes up and starts arguing and the woman says——

FRANK: No, no, no, not that one—the one when the man says to the girl—what was it now?—You've gone and put it clean out of me head.

BOB: You don't mean the one the little bald bloke with glasses told us?

FRANK: No, no, no—that was the one about the woman in the bath when the 'ouse caught on fire—bloody funny it was too, I will say—— (*He starts to laugh.*)

BOB: Oh, shut up, you'll start me off. (*He laughs.*)

FRANK (*wiping his eyes*): That little bastard can tell 'em all right and no mistake about it——

BOB (*convulsed*): It wasn't what he said so much as

the way he said it—dry, you know, that's what he was—
dry——

FRANK: That reminds me—— (*He rises and goes to
the whisky bottle.*)

BOB: Here, 'old on, old cock—I got to get home——

FRANK: I'll see you home and then, and then we'll
have one more with you.

BOB: I suppose there's nothing to eat, is there?

FRANK (*pouring fresh drinks*): 'Ave a look in the
sideboard.

BOB (*on his knees at the sideboard cupboard*): There's a
cruet and some A.I. Sauce—here we are—biscuits——

     He produces an opened tin of Huntley and Palmer's.

FRANK: There ought to be some fish paste by rights.

BOB (*groping in the cupboard*): Oh, blast! I stuck me
finger in the jam!

FRANK (*crouching down*): Here—let me have a look.
(*After a moment he produces a bottle of bloater paste and the
A.I. Sauce. He puts them on the table.*)

BOB (*admiringly*): That's fine.

FRANK: The butter's in the larder so we'd better do
without it—Sylvia sleeps just over the kitchen and she's
got ears like a hawk. We can spread the paste on the
biscuits and put a bit of A.I. on top to pep it up.

BOB: It ought to sit nicely on that dinner we had!
Where's a knife——

FRANK: In the drawer.

     BOB *finds a knife in the drawer and they both sit down
     again at the table.*

BOB (*holding up his glass*): Huntley and Palmer! (*He
drinks.*)

FRANK (*doing the same*): Crosse and Blackwell—God
bless 'em! (*He drinks.*)

BOB (*giggling*): We shan't half look silly if Ethel catches us.

FRANK: It's me own house, isn't it? I can do what I like in it. An Englishman's home is his castle.

BOB (*proffering the bloater paste*): Here, smell that a minute.

FRANK: What's the matter with it.

BOB: Seems a bit off to me.

FRANK (*smelling it*): No—don't be so fancy—it's only the rubber round the top.

BOB (*accepting the explanation*): All right, all right—I only wondered.

FRANK: Heard from Billy lately?

BOB: Yes—he writes once a week—he's in Malta now.

FRANK: Good old Billy! He's a fine boy.

BOB: So's Reg.

FRANK (*raising his glass*): Here's to 'em both. Our sons!

BOB (*doing the same*): Our sons!
    They both drink.

FRANK: Seems sort of funny, doesn't it?

BOB: What does?

FRANK: Getting old.

BOB: Yes, you're a grandfather! Think of that.

FRANK: I wish it had been a boy instead of a girl, Vi's kid, still there's lots of time yet.

BOB: I suppose Reg and Phyl will be having one soon?

FRANK: Well, he's got a Baby Austin already! (*He laughs delightedly at his own joke.*)

BOB (*also laughing*): He come to the office in it the other day—I saw him out of Mr. Freedman's window. Drove up as if he owned the street he did——

FRANK: Mr. Freedman likes him, doesn't he?

BOB: Of course he does. Everybody likes Reg, he's the most popular chap in the office.

FRANK: Is he really?

BOB: You bet he is.

FRANK (*almost painfully pleased*): That's good, isn't it?

BOB: You know, I've never said much about it, but I always thought that maybe Billy and Queenie might—one day——

FRANK: Oh, Queenie gives me a headache—all her airs and graces—a good hiding is what she needs.

BOB: That wouldn't be any use—some girls get like that—no doing anything with them.

FRANK (*patting BOB's arm affectionately*): Listen, Bob, old man. I want exactly what you want, see? I've wanted Queenie and Billy to get together ever since they were kids. I'd rather have Billy in the family than anyone else in the world, and that's a fact—you know that, don't you?

BOB: Of course I do.

FRANK: But it's no use trying to drive people the way they don't want to go.

BOB: I think Billy'd stand by her always, whatever she did.

FRANK (*almost sharply*): How d'you mean?

BOB: I don't know—I just mean he loves her, that's all.

FRANK: Funny, isn't it, about having children and seeing what they grow up like. There's Vi, for instance. I've never had a moment's worry about her since the day she was born, always behaves nicely, always good to her mother——

BOB: Nothing the matter with Vi.

FRANK: Then there's Queenie—as different from her as chalk from cheese. She's a fine girl too, in some ways; she's got more go than Vi, you know, and smart! Whew! Always was, even when she was little— that's what makes her a bit hard to manage now, you know—she's too quick for us.

BOB: Reg is the one for my money.

FRANK (*smiling*): Now you're talking——

They sit in silence for a moment looking back over the years.

BOB: Well, it's a strange world and no mistake. I was thinking that to-night looking at all those chaps in your regiment—wondering what they were feeling like —some of 'em looked all right, of course, but some looked a bit under the weather.

FRANK: We've been lucky.

BOB: You've said it.

FRANK: I wonder when the next war'll be.

BOB: Not in our time, nor in our sons' time, thank God!

FRANK: I wouldn't bank on that.

BOB: How could there be? Everybody's disarming.

FRANK: We are.

BOB: There's the good old League of Nations.

FRANK: It don't seem able to have stopped Japan turning nasty.

BOB: Japan! Who cares about Japan? It's a nice long way off for one thing.

FRANK: Lots of trouble can start from a long way off.

BOB: Oh, don't you worry your head about Japan.

FRANK (*thoughtfully*): Of course I know if they really start behaving badly, all we got to do is to send a couple of battleships along and scare the little sods out of their wits.

BOB: That's right.

FRANK: All the same——

BOB: We've got the finest Navy in the world and don't you forget it.

FRANK: As long as we treat it right.

BOB: How d'you mean?

FRANK: What about Invergordon?

BOB: That wasn't the Navy's fault.

FRANK: I never said it was.

BOB: Well then!

FRANK: It was the fault of the old men at the top. It always is the fault of the old men at the top. They're the ones that muck things up. We can't afford to have much more of that sort of thing, you know.

BOB: Well, we've got a brand new Government now and everything in the garden's lovely.

FRANK (*raising the glass*): Here's hoping!

BOB: Chuck us another biscuit.

FRANK (*pushing the tin towards him*): Here——

BOB: I'll have to be pushing off home in a minute.

FRANK: Finish up and have one more before you go.

BOB: Now listen, Frankie boy, we're up to the gills already.

FRANK (*at the sideboard*): Just a little one for the road.

BOB: The road? I only got about three yards to go.

FRANK: We don't have a binge like this every day of the week.

BOB (*making a dive at him*): Here, that's enough.

> *He catches* FRANK'S *arm to prevent him pouring out too much, causing him to drop the bottle on the floor with a crash.*

FRANK: Now you've done it.

BOB: Oh, dear!

FRANK (*starting to laugh*): Thank God there wasn't much left.

BOB (*also laughing*): I wish you could have seen your face when it went!

FRANK: Quiet a minute—listen!

> *There is the sound of footsteps on the stairs.*

BOB: Here—I'd better 'op it.

FRANK: That's right, leave your best pal to face the barrage alone.

BOB: Come on, pull yourself together—we're for it.

FRANK: Chest up—chin up!

> *They are standing rigidly to attention when* ETHEL *comes into the room. She is wearing a dressing-gown and her hair is in curlers.*

ETHEL: And what d'you think you're doing if I may make so bold?

FRANK: Bob was just going home.

ETHEL: Oh! Just going home, was he?

BOB: Sorry we woke you up, Ethel.

ETHEL: What was that you broke?

FRANK: Only the poor old Johnny Walker.

ETHEL: I suppose you know what the time is, don't you?

FRANK: Who cares? Time was meant for slaves!

ETHEL: You go up to bed, Frank Gibbons. I'll have something to say to you later.

BOB: It was my fault, Ethel——

ETHEL: You ought to be ashamed of yourselves, both of you—men of your age—coming home drunk and waking up the whole house.

FRANK: You're not a whole house, Ethel, old girl—
you're just—just a little bungalow—for better or for
worse—— (*He giggles.*)

ETHEL: I'll give you bungalow! Go on, Bob, it's
time you went home.

FRANK: Don't be hard on him, Ethel—he's my pal—
he may be looking a bit silly now, I'll admit, but he's my
pal all the same.

BOB: Who's looking silly?

FRANK: You do!

BOB: What about you?

ETHEL: You both look silly—but it's nothing to
what you're going to look in the morning. Go on,
Bob. I'm not going to stand here much longer catching
me death.

BOB: All right—I can take a hint. Good-night, Mrs.
G. Good-night, Sergeant. It's been a pleasure. (*To*
FRANK.) Steady the Buffs!

> BOB *goes cheerfully, if a trifle unsteadily, out of the
> french window.*

> ETHEL *follows him up and locks them after him. She
> turns and regards* FRANK *thoughtfully for a moment.*

FRANK (*holding up his hand*): All right, all right—you
don't have to say nothing! I know.

ETHEL: The next time you go to a regimental dinner
you can go to a hotel afterwards and sleep it off. I won't
have it, d'you hear? This is my dining-room, this is, not
a bar parlour! Go on, get up to bed and don't make a
noise either—— (*She turns and catches sight of* QUEENIE'S
note on the mantelpiece.) What's that?

FRANK: What's what?

ETHEL (*going to it*): This letter.

FRANK: I haven't written no letters.

ETHEL (*taking it*): It's Queenie's writing——— (*She opens it.*)

FRANK: Here—you can't read the girl's private letters.

ETHEL (*grimly*): It's addressed to you and me.

FRANK: Well, I'll be damned!

ETHEL *reads the letter through and then stands quite still.* FRANK *goes over to her. She hands it to him.*

ETHEL: She's gone. Read it. (*Sits down quietly in the chair by the fire and buries her face in her hands.*)

FRANK (*reads the letter carefully*): Who's this man? Have you ever seen him?

ETHEL: No.

FRANK: I'll fetch her back—I'll give her the hiding of her life.

ETHEL: You can't find her. She doesn't say where she's gone.

FRANK (*reading*): —we love each other—his wife won't divorce him—we can't live without each other, so we are going away. (*He crumples the letter in his hand.*) It's our own fault—we might have known something like this would happen—we let her have her own way too much, ever since she was a child—Queenie—— (*His voice breaks.*)

ETHEL *sits quite still without saying anything.* (*Kneeling on the floor by her chair.*) We'll trace her all right —don't you worry. We can find out who the man is through the shop. It must have been there she met him. We'll get her back.

ETHEL (*with sudden violence*): I don't want her back! She's no child of mine. I don't want ever to see her again as long as I live.

FRANK: Don't say that, Ethel.

ETHEL (*controlling herself*): I mean it, I've done my best to bring her up to behave respectable, to be a good girl, but it hasn't been any use.

FRANK: If she loves this man all that much—maybe it was too strong for her—maybe she couldn't help herself——

ETHEL (*looking at him*): You don't see what she's done the same way as I do—do you?

FRANK: I don't know.

ETHEL: You and me never have quite seen eye to eye about what's right and what's wrong. You'd have her back to-morrow if she'd come, wouldn't you? But I wouldn't. You've always encouraged her and told her how clever she was, and let her twist you round her little finger——

FRANK: All I've done is to try laughing at her instead of scolding her.

ETHEL: Well, you've got something to laugh at now, haven't you?

FRANK: Don't go for me, Ethel—she's my girl as well as yours.

ETHEL: I'm not going for anybody. I've done my best. I can't do more.

FRANK: You can't stop loving the girl all at once, even if she has done wrong.

ETHEL: I can try.

FRANK: What's the sense of that?

ETHEL: It isn't anything to do with sense—it's how you feel.

FRANK: I've never seen you like this before—hard as nails you are.

ETHEL: What d'you expect me to be?

FRANK: I don't know—I suppose you never cared

for Queenie as much as you did the other two.

ETHEL: It's not fair to say that.

FRANK: It's true though, isn't it?

ETHEL: No, it is not. She's almost been the most trouble, that's true enough, and she's certainly never put herself out to try and help me like Vi has; that's true too, but I've cared for her just as much as the others, and don't you start saying I haven't. It's no use trying to lay the blame for this at my door. What she's done she's done on her own, and I'll never forgive her for it until the end of my days.

FRANK: If you feel like that it's not much good talking about it, is it?

He gets up and walks away from her.

ETHEL (*after a pause—rising*): Will you turn out or shall I?

FRANK (*turning pleadingly*): Ethel——

ETHEL (*stonily*): I'm going back to bed now. You might put those things back in the sideboard before you come up.

She goes out without looking at him.

When she has gone he puts QUEENIE'S *letter in his pocket, goes wearily over to the table and puts the biscuits, A.I. Sauce and bloater paste into the cupboard. He sits down at the table for a minute and finally buries his head in his arms as—*

THE LIGHTS FADE

336

ACT II

SCENE III

TIME: *May*, 1932. *It is about four-thirty on a fine afternoon. The french windows are wide open. Out of sight in the garden* FRANK *is weeding. From next door comes the sound of* BOB *mowing his lawn.*

MRS. FLINT *is knitting in her chair by the fireplace.* SYLVIA *is at table with a newspaper and a dictionary, doing a crossword puzzle. A brand new shining radio stands on a little table above the fireplace. It is playing softly.* EDIE *comes in and out with the tea-things.*

SYLVIA (*with satisfaction, scribbling*): Got it!

MRS. F.: What?

SYLVIA: A biblical name in five letters with an S in the middle—Moses.

MRS. F.: I could have thought of that.

SYLVIA: Pity you didn't then, I asked you just now.

MRS. F.: Why's tea being laid so early?

SYLVIA: Because Frank's taking us to the Majestic.

MRS. F.: I wish somebody'd turn that wireless off—it's getting on my nerves.

SYLVIA (*rising*): Ethel'd have it playing all day just because Reg gave it to her—— (*She turns the radio off.*)

MRS. F.: Well, the skies'll fall next, I shouldn't wonder, you doing something I asked you without grumbling.

SYLVIA: Now then, Mrs. Flint, don't start.

MRS. F.: I wasn't starting anything, just passing a remark.

337

SYLVIA (*folding up the paper*): Well, I've done that now all except the long one across and the short one down with an X in it.

MRS. F.: I must say, having a steady job at the library's done you a world of good.

SYLVIA: I don't know what you're talking about.

MRS. F.: You're not so touchy as you used to be—flying off at the least thing.

SYLVIA (*primly*): I'm very glad, I'm sure.

MRS. F.: It was a lucky day for all of us when you met that Mrs. Wilmot.

SYLVIA: I don't know to what you're referring.

MRS. F.: Oh yes, you do.

SYLVIA: I wish you'd stop going at me about everything for once.

MRS. F.: I was only saying it was a good thing you meeting that Mrs. Wilmot.

SYLVIA: Well, we won't argue about it, will we?

MRS. F.: You haven't had one of your headaches for weeks, have you?

SYLVIA (*sharply*): No, I have not.

MRS. F.: There you are, then.

SYLVIA: Perhaps you'd rather have me the way I was before—not sleeping a wink at night and suffering and being in error.

MRS. F.: In what?

SYLVIA: Error!

MRS. F.: Oh, so that's what it was.

SYLVIA: And you needn't sneer at Mrs. Wilmot either—she's a wonderful woman.

MRS. F.: She must be, to make you believe there wasn't anything the matter with you. It's what I've been saying for years.

SYLVIA (*brightly*): Well, then, we won't say anything more about it, will we?

MRS. F.: We will if we feel like it.

> FRANK *comes in from the garden. He is in his shirt-sleeves.*

FRANK: How long before tea's ready?

EDIE (*on her way in with the milk and sugar*): About five minutes—the kettle's on.

FRANK: Tell Ethel to start without me, Sylvia—I've got one more bed to do. Where is she?

SYLVIA: Upstairs lying down.

FRANK (*catching sight of a vase on the mantelpiece*): Who put that May in here?

SYLVIA: I did—it's such a pretty colour.

FRANK (*taking it out of the vase*): You ought to know better than to bring May into the house.

SYLVIA: Why ever not?

FRANK: It's unlucky.

SYLVIA (*with a great display of amusement*): Why Frank, really! What a thing to believe——

FRANK: You was born in the country the same as I was, Sylvia—it's a long while ago, I'll admit, but still——

SYLVIA (*tossing her head*): There's no need to be nasty —you and your old May——

FRANK (*going out again*): Well, don't do it again.

SYLVIA: Frank's been a changed man since Queenie went.

MRS. F.: I haven't noticed much difference.

SYLVIA: Do you think she'll ever come back?

MRS. F.: She'll get a piece of my mind if she does. Bringing disgrace on all of us.

SYLVIA: Frank had a letter from her the other day.

MRS. F.: How d'you know?

SYLVIA: It came by the midday post along with that letter I had from Mrs. Wilmot—Edie was upstairs doing the front room and I took it in myself. I recognised the handwriting——

MRS. F.: Think he told Ethel?

SYLVIA: Not very likely—she doesn't let him mention her name if she can help it. It had a French stamp.

MRS. F.: Disgusting!

ETHEL (*coming in*): What's disgusting?

MRS. F.: Gracious, Ethel, what a start you gave me!

ETHEL: What was disgusting?

SYLVIA: A French stamp.

ETHEL: French stamp? What are you talking about?

SYLVIA: We were talking about the letter Frank had from Queenie.

ETHEL (*going over to the table*): Oh, were you?

MRS. F.: Then it *was* from Queenie?

SYLVIA: You knew about it?

ETHEL: It's a pity that Christian Science of yours hasn't taught you to mind your own business among other things, Sylvia.

SYLVIA: Well, I'm sure I don't see what I've done!

ETHEL: You know perfectly well I won't 'ave Queenie's name spoken in this house. She's gone her own way, and that's that. She doesn't belong here any more.

MRS. F. (*with relish*): I always knew that girl would come to no good.

ETHEL: Once and for all, will you hold your tongue, Mother! I'm sick to death of you and Sylvia gabbing and whispering behind my back.

MRS. F.: Well, I like that, I must say——

ETHEL: I don't care whether you like it or not—be quiet. Where's Frank?

SYLVIA (*sullenly*): In the garden—he's started on another bed.

ETHEL: Tea's just ready.

SYLVIA: He said to begin without him.

> EDIE *comes in with the tea-pot.* ETHEL *sits down at the table and begins to pour out. There is a silence.* EDIE *goes out again.*

SYLVIA (*to* MRS. FLINT): Are you coming to the table or shall I bring it over to you?

MRS. F.: I'll stay here—the less I open my mouth the better.

ETHEL: Here, Syl, take it over to her.

SYLVIA (*brings cup of tea over to* MRS. F.): Bread and butter?

MRS. F.: No, thank you. (*As* SYLVIA *turns to go.*) I'll 'ave a petit beurre if there is one.

SYLVIA (*fetching her the plate of biscuits*): All right.

> SYLVIA, *after* MRS. FLINT *has helped herself to biscuits, returns to the table and sits down. There is another silence,* ETHEL *gets up and turns on the radio again.*

ETHEL: Sorry I flew out at you like that, Sylvia.

SYLVIA (*gracefully*): It doesn't matter, I'm sure.

ETHEL: I dropped off to sleep on my bed this afternoon and had a bad dream.

SYLVIA: What was it?

ETHEL: I can't remember—I woke up feeling as if the world had come to an end.

SYLVIA (*cheerfully*): Well, they say dreams go by contraries.

ETHEL: Yes, they do, don't they?

MRS. F.: These teeth of mine are getting worse and worse—I can't bite a thing.

ETHEL: Try soaking 'em.

MRS. F.: I am.

ETHEL: I wish Frank'd come in to his tea—we shall be late next thing we know.

SYLVIA: Why not take a cup out to him, he never eats much anyhow.

ETHEL (*glancing at the clock*): It's nearly half-past now.

SYLVIA: I'll take it if you like.

ETHEL: No, I will. Once he starts weeding he'd go on all night if we let him.

> ETHEL *pours out a cup of tea and goes out into the garden with it.*

SYLVIA: You'd better be going upstairs to put your hat on, hadn't you?

MRS. F.: Lots of time. Frank'll have to wash before he goes.

> *There is a ring at the front door bell.*

SYLVIA: Now I wonder who that is?

MRS. F.: It might be Reg and Phyl.

SYLVIA: Can't be—they've gone to Sevenoaks with them friends of theirs.

MRS. F. (*listening*): Has Edie gone?

SYLVIA: Yes—I heard her come out of the kitchen.

> *The door opens and* VI *comes quickly into the room. She looks pale and is trembling.*

SYLVIA: Why, Vi? Whatever's the matter?

VI: Where are mum and dad?

SYLVIA: In the garden.

VI (*hurriedly*): Take Granny upstairs—there's been an accident—it's Reg and Phyl—I've got to tell mum and dad.

MRS. F.: What's that?

SYLVIA: What sort of an accident? What happened?

VI: They were in Reg's car and a lorry came out of a turning——

SYLVIA: Are they badly hurt?

VI: They're dead.

SYLVIA: Oh, my God!

VI: Mrs. Goulding was with them, she knew I had a telephone and so she rang me up from the hospital. She was in the back and got thrown out—please take Granny upstairs—I must tell them alone.

SYLVIA (*bursting into tears*): Oh, my God! Oh, my God!

VI: Don't cry, Auntie Sylvia—they'll hear you—don't let them hear you.

SYLVIA (*sobbing*): I can't believe it—I can't——

MRS. F.: Help me up.

VI (*doing so*): Auntie Sylvia—please——

SYLVIA, *with a great effort at control but still sobbing, helps* MRS. FLINT *out of the room.*

VI *closes her eyes for a minute, braces herself and goes out into the garden. The room is empty for a minute or two, and there is no sound except the radio playing softly and the mowing machine next door.*

Presently FRANK *and* ETHEL *come in alone. His arm is round her and they neither of them speak. He brings her slowly to the chair by the fireplace and puts her gently down into it. Then he draws up another chair and sits next to her. He reaches out for her hand and they sit there in silence as—*

THE LIGHTS FADE

ACT III

Scene I

TIME: *December the 10th, 1936.*

> *It is just after ten o'clock in the evening. The remains of supper have been pushed aside to make way for the radio, which is standing in the middle of the table.*
>
> *Round it are sitting* FRANK, ETHEL, SYLVIA, VI *and* SAM.
>
> *King Edward the Eight's farewell broadcast after his abdication is just finishing.* SYLVIA *is in tears. Everyone else is silent.*
>
> FRANK *and* ETHEL *have aged a good deal in the four years since* REG'S *death. They are only fifty-two and fifty-one respectively, nevertheless they look older.* SYLVIA, *on the other hand, who is after all the same age as* ETHEL, *looks, if anything, a little younger than before. This is doubtless attributable to the assurance acquired from Christian Science and the brisk example of Mrs. Wilmot.* VI *and* SAM *appear to be the settled, comfortable married couple that they are.* SAM *indeed, having put on weight, seems definitely middle-aged.*
>
> *At the end of the broadcast the radio makes a few discordant wheezes and groans.* FRANK *gets up and turns it off.*

FRANK: Well—that's that. (*He gets himself a cigarette from the mantelpiece.*) There won't be anything more to listen to to-night, all the stations have closed down.

SYLVIA (*sobbing*): It's dreadful—dreadful——

FRANK: Anyway it's no use going on about it now.

344

SYLVIA: It was a wonderful speech—fairly broke your heart to listen to it. (*She blows her nose.*)

FRANK: Well—I suppose he had to make it, but I somehow wish he hadn't.

> *There is silence for a moment, broken only by* SYLVIA'S *sniffs.* ETHEL *gets up and takes a calendar down from the wall by the fireplace.*

SYLVIA: Ethel—what are you doing?

ETHEL (*going out of the room with it*): It's near the end of the year anyhow.

VI (*getting up*): Better put the radio back where it belongs—give me a hand, Sam——

> *They move the radio back on to its little table.*

SAM: We'll have to be going in a minute. Mrs. Burgess said she couldn't stay after half-past ten and we can't leave the children in the house all by themselves.

VI: I'll pop up and get me hat—I left it in mum's room.

> *She goes out.*

SAM: How's the library going, Aunt Sylvia?

SYLVIA (*putting the table straight*): All right—but I'm leaving it next month.

SAM: I thought you liked working there.

SYLVIA: Oh, it's not bad, but I'm going in with Mrs. Wilmot. She wants me to assist her in her reading and rest room in Baker Street.

SAM: Oh, I see.

SYLVIA: How are the children?

SAM: Sheila's all right, but Joan's been a bit seedy the last few days.

SYLVIA (*brightly*): Poor little thing.

SAM: The doctor said she never quite got over that cold she had in November.

SYLVIA (*indulgently*): Did he indeed?

SAM (*slightly nettled*): Yes, he did. She was running a bit of a temperature a couple of nights ago, so we've kept her in bed ever since.

SYLVIA: I suppose if you believe in doctors, it's best to do what they say.

SAM: Well, it stands to reason they know a bit more about it than we do, doesn't it?

SYLVIA: No, I don't think it does! (*She lightly hums a little tune.*)

SAM (*incensed*): What would you do if you broke your leg? I suppose you'd send for a doctor then, wouldn't you?

SYLVIA (*putting some things into the sideboard cupboard*): I wouldn't break my leg.

SAM (*pressing*): But if you *did*? If you were run over through no fault of your own——

SYLVIA: I should certainly send for treatment.

SAM: There you are then!

SYLVIA (*with a pitying smile*): You don't understand, Sam. After all there isn't any reason why you should. You haven't studied the matter, have you?

SAM: No, I haven't.

SYLVIA: It wouldn't be surgical treatment I should send for. It would be spiritual treatment.

SAM: Would that heal a compound fracture?

SYLVIA: Certainly.

SAM: Before I'd believe that I'd have to see it with my own eyes.

SYLVIA: If you believe first, you wouldn't have to worry whether you saw it with your own eyes or not.

SAM: Oh, yes, I should.

SYLVIA (*with sweet, unassailable superiority*): Dear Sam!

FRANK *comes back.*

FRANK: Where's Ethel?

SYLVIA: In the kitchen, I think.

FRANK: We miss Edie and that's a fact. I've tried to make her get someone else, but she won't.

SYLVIA: There's not so much to do since Mrs. Flint passed on.

FRANK: I do wish you wouldn't talk like that, Sylvia, it sounds so soft.

SYLVIA: I don't know what you mean, I'm sure.

FRANK (*firmly*): Mother died, see! First of all she got 'flu and that turned to pneumonia and the strain of that affected her heart, which was none too strong at the best of times and she DIED. Nothing to do with passing on at all.

SYLVIA: How do you know?

FRANK: I admit it's only your new way of talking, but it gets me down, see?

ETHEL *comes in again, followed by* VI *in her hat and coat.*

ETHEL: What are you shouting about?

FRANK: I'm not shouting about anything at all. I'm merely explaining to Sylvia that mother died. She didn't pass on or pass over or pass out—she DIED.

VI (*giggling*): Oh, Dad, you do make me laugh, really you do!

ETHEL: It's not a fit subject to talk about anyhow.

VI: Come on, Sam—we must be going. Good-night, Mother.

ETHEL: Good-night, dear. If you want to go out to-morrow afternoon I'll come and look after the children.

VI: Thanks a lot. Good-night, Dad.

FRANK (*kissing her*): So long, Vi.

VI: Good-night, Auntie Sylvia. Don't pay any attention to dad. He's an old tease.

SAM: Good-night all.

FRANK: I'll come to the door with you—where's Archie—Ethel?

ETHEL: Asleep in the kitchen. He's been out once to-night.

FRANK (*escorting VI and SAM out*): I'll tell you one thing. As a mouser, Archie knocks poor old Percy into a cocked hat!

> *They go out.*

SYLVIA: I think I'll go up to bed now, Ethel.

ETHEL: All right, dear.

SYLVIA: What about the washing up?

ETHEL: I'll do the lot to-morrow morning. I've left everything in the sink for to-night.

SYLVIA (*dutifully kissing her*): Then good-night.

ETHEL: Good-night.

SYLVIA (*sighing as she goes out*): Oh, dear!

> ETHEL *glances at the clock and then, taking some socks out of a work-basket on the table by the fireplace, sits down in the arm-chair and begins to darn.*
>
> FRANK *comes back.*

FRANK: Vi's looking a bit peaky, isn't she?

ETHEL: She's worried about Joan, I think.

FRANK: She'll be all right—remember the trouble we had with Queenie when she was tiny?

ETHEL (*coldly*): Yes, I do.

FRANK: Sorry—I forgot.

ETHEL: You're lucky.

FRANK (*sadly*): You are a funny woman, Ethel, and no mistake.

ETHEL: I expect I am. We're as God made us, I suppose, and there's nothing to be done about it.

FRANK: Well, all I can say is He might have done a better job on some people without straining Himself.

ETHEL: How often have I told you I won't 'ave you talking like that, Frank.

FRANK: I wasn't meaning you.

ETHEL: I don't care who you was meaning. If you don't believe in anything yourself, you can at least have the decency to spare the feelings of them as do.

FRANK: As a matter of fact I believe in a whole lot of things.

ETHEL: Well, that's nice to know.

FRANK: One of 'em is that being bitter about anybody isn't a good thing, let alone if it happens to be your own daughter.

ETHEL: I'm not bitter. I just don't think of her any more, that's all.

FRANK: That's one of the things I don't believe.

ETHEL: Don't let's talk about it, shall we?

FRANK: I wish you'd have another girl in place of Edie.

ETHEL: I don't need one now there's only the three of us. Sylvia helps every now and again and the char does the heavy cleaning once a week.

FRANK: We could afford it quite easily.

ETHEL: Maybe we could—but getting a strange girl used to our ways would be more trouble than it was worth.

FRANK: What anybody ever wanted to marry Edie for beats me.

ETHEL: No reason why they shouldn't. She was a good girl and a good worker.

FRANK: Exactly the reasons I married you.

ETHEL: Don't talk so silly.

FRANK: She may not be much to look at—I said to myself—but there's a worker if ever I saw one!

ETHEL: Haven't you got anything better to do than to sit there making funny remarks?

FRANK: There's nothing much I want to do.

ETHEL: Why don't you have a nice read of the paper?

FRANK: There's nothing in it but the abdication, and I'm fed up with that.

There is a tap on the window.

ETHEL: That'll be Bob. Now I can get on with me darning.

FRANK *goes to the window, opens it and admits* BILLY. BILLY *is now thirty-four and wearing the uniform of a Warrant Officer. He has grown a little more solid with the years, but apart from this there is not much change in him.*

FRANK: Well, here's a surprise!

BILLY: Hallo, Mr. Gibbons.

ETHEL: Why, Billy—I'd no idea you was back.

BILLY (*shaking hands with her*): I've been transferred from a cruiser to a destroyer—I've got a couple of weeks' leave.

FRANK: D'you like that?

BILLY: You bet I do.

FRANK: What's the difference?

BILLY: Oh, lots of little things. To start with I live in the wardroom—then I keep watches when we're at sea —and well, it's sort of more friendly, if you know what I mean.

FRANK: Like a drink?

BILLY: No, thanks. I just had one with dad.

ETHEL: Is he coming in?

BILLY: Yes, I think so—a bit later on.

ETHEL: He must be glad you're back. It must be lonely for him in that house all by himself since your mother was taken.

FRANK: Nora DIED, Ethel! Nobody took her.

ETHEL: You ought to be ashamed talking like that in front of Billy.

BILLY: It was a blessed release really, you know, Mrs. Gibbons, what with one thing and another. She'd been bedridden so long——

FRANK: Hear the speech?

BILLY: Yes.

FRANK: What did you think of it?

BILLY: Oh, I don't know—a bit depressing—taken all round. He was popular in the Service you know.

FRANK: Yes—I expect he was.

BILLY: He came on board a ship I was in once, in the Mediterranean, that was about five years ago when I was still a T.G.M.

ETHEL: What's that?

BILLY: Torpedo Gunner's Mate.

FRANK: All them initials in the Navy. I can't think how you remember 'em.

BILLY: Oh, you get used to it.

ETHEL: Would you like me to go and make you a cup of tea? It won't take a minute.

BILLY: No, thanks, Mrs. Gibbons—there's something I want to talk to you about as a matter of fact—both of you.

FRANK: All right, son—what is it?

BILLY (*nervously*): Got a cigarette on you? I left mine next door.

FRANK (*producing a packet*): Here you are.

BILLY (*taking one*): Thanks.

FRANK: Match?

BILLY (*striking one of his own*): Got one, thanks.

FRANK (*after a slight pause*): Well?

BILLY: I feel a bit awkward really—I wanted dad to come with me and back me up, but he wouldn't.

FRANK: A man of your age hanging on to his father's coat-tails, I never 'eard of such a thing. What have you been up to?

ETHEL (*with sudden premonition, sharply*): What is it, Billy?

BILLY: It's about Queenie.

There is silence for a moment.

ETHEL (*hardening*): What about her?

BILLY: Does it still make you angry—even to hear her name?

ETHEL: I'm not angry.

FRANK: Have you seen her, Billy?

BILLY: Yes—I've seen her.

FRANK (*eagerly*): How is she?

BILLY: Fine.

There is another silence. BILLY mooches about the room a bit.

ETHEL (*with an obvious effort*): What is it that you wanted to say about Queenie, Billy?

BILLY (*in a rush*): I sympathise with how you feel, Mrs. Gibbons—really I do—and what's more she does too. She knows what a wrong she did you in going off like that. It didn't take her long to realise it. She hasn't had any too good a time, you know. In fact she's been

through a good deal. He left her—the man she went
off with—Major Blount—after about a year. He went
back to his wife. He left Queenie stranded in a sort of
boarding-house in Brussels.

ETHEL (*bitterly*): How soon was it before she found
another man to take her on?

FRANK: Ethel!

BILLY: A long time—over three years.

ETHEL (*bending over her darning*): She's all right now
then, isn't she?

BILLY: Yes—she's all right now.

FRANK: What sort of a bad time did she have—how
d'you mean?

BILLY: Trying to earn a living for herself—getting in
and out of different jobs. She showed dresses off in a
dressmaker's shop for over a year, I believe, but the
shop went broke, and then she got herself a place to
look after some English children. It wasn't a very long
job. She just had to take them across France to
Marseilles and put on a ship to go out to their parents
in India. By that time she had a little money saved and
was coming home to England to try and get her old
manicuring job back when she got ill with appendicitis
and was taken to hospital——

FRANK: Where—where was she taken to hospital?
How long ago?

BILLY: Paris—about a year ago. Then, when she was
in the hospital she picked up with an old Scotswoman
who was in the next bed and a little while later the two
of them started an old English tea room in Menton in
the South of France—you know, just for the English
visitors—that's where I ran into her by accident. We
were doing a summer cruise and the ship I was in laid

off a place called Villefranche for a few days. A couple of pals and I hired a taxi to go for a drive and stopped at Menton to have a cup of tea—and there she was!

ETHEL: Is she there now?

BILLY: No, she isn't there now.

FRANK: Where is she then?

BILLY: She's here.

ETHEL: Here!

FRANK: How d'you mean—here?

BILLY: Next door with dad.

ETHEL (*jumping to her feet and dropping her darning on the floor*): Billy!

BILLY: We were married last week in a registry office in Plymouth.

ETHEL: Married!

BILLY (*simply*): I've always loved her, you know—I always said I'd wait for her.

FRANK (*brokenly*): Oh, son—I can't believe it—Oh, son!

> He wrings BILLY's hand wildly and then almost runs
> out through the french windows.

BILLY: You'll forgive her now, won't you, Mrs. Gibbons?

ETHEL (*in a strained voice*): I don't seem to have any choice, do I?

BILLY: I always thought you'd like to have me for a son——

ETHEL: Better late than never—that's what it is, isn't it? (*She starts half laughing and crying at the same time.*) Better late than—never—oh dear!——

> He takes her in his arms and after holding her close for
> a moment, places her gently in the chair.

BILLY: Shall I get you a little nip of something?

ETHEL (*tearfully*): Yes, please——

BILLY: Where is it?

ETHEL: In the sideboard cupboard.

BILLY *goes quickly to the sideboard, opens the cupboard, takes a bottle of whisky out and pours some, neat, into a glass. He brings it to her. He gives her the glass and she sips a little. He takes her left hand and pats it affectionately.*

FRANK *comes back through the window leading* QUEENIE *by the hand. She is soberly dressed and looks pale. There is a strained silence for a moment.*

QUEENIE: Hallo, Mum.

ETHEL: So you've come back, have you—you bad girl.

QUEENIE (*coming slowly across the room to her*): Yes, Mum.

ETHEL (*putting her arms round her*): A nice way to behave, I must say—upsetting me like this——

THE LIGHTS FADE

ACT III

SCENE II

TIME: *September 30th, 1938.*

It is about nine o'clock in the evening.

ETHEL *and* QUEENIE *have finished their supper and gone upstairs to see if* QUEENIE'S *four months' old son is sleeping all right.* SYLVIA *and* VI *are still at the table.*

SYLVIA: Is there any more hot water in the jug?

VI: No—there isn't.

SYLVIA: I thought I'd like another cup.

VI (*jumping up*): I'll run and get some.

SYLVIA (*not moving*): Don't worry, dear—I'll go.

VI: You stay where you are, Auntie Syl—it won't take a minute.

> *She runs out with the jug.*
>
> SYLVIA, *left alone, sits pensively with her chin resting on her hands. In a moment or two* VI *returns with the hot water.*

SYLVIA (*as she comes in*): I always knew it, you know.

VI: Always knew what?

SYLVIA: That there wouldn't be a war.

VI: Well, I thought there would, I must say, otherwise I shouldn't have sent Sheila and Joan down to Mrs. Marsh in Dorset.

SYLVIA: I know you did, dear. Your mother was worried too about Queenie and little Frankie—but I wasn't. Neither was Mrs. Wilmot.

VI: Fancy that now.

SYLVIA: Mrs. Wilmot laughed outright, you know, when the woman came to try on her gas-mask. "Take that stupid thing away," she said. Just like that—quite simply. The woman was furious.

VI: I'm not surprised.

SYLVIA: It's funny how cross people get when you refuse to believe in evil.

VI: It's rather difficult not to believe in evil, Auntie Syl, when you think of what's going on in different parts of the world just now.

SYLVIA: If enough people believed in good, none of it would happen.

VI: Yes, but they don't do they?

SYLVIA: You remind me of your father sometimes Vi, you're material-minded.

Vi: Well, I can't help that, can I?

Sylvia: Well, if you don't mind me saying so—I think you can.

Vi: As far as I can see facts are facts, Auntie Syl, and if looking at it like that means I'm material-minded I'm afraid that's what I shall go on being.

Sylvia: You don't understand what I mean, dear.

Vi: No—I'm afraid I don't.

Sylvia: To begin with, what you call facts may not be facts at all.

Vi: What are they then?

Sylvia: Illusion—and error.

Vi: Isn't error a fact then?

Sylvia (*a little nettled*): Of course it is in a way— that's just the trouble. But still if you admit it's a fact and regard it as a fact, it makes it more of a fact than ever, doesn't it?

Vi: I shouldn't think it made much difference one way or the other.

Sylvia: But it DOES!

Vi: You mean that when Sheila had toothache the other day I ought to have told her that she hadn't.

Sylvia: I don't mean any such thing.

Vi: What do you mean then?

Sylvia: I mean that if she had been brought up to believe that pain is evil and that evil doesn't really exist at all, she wouldn't have had toothache in the first place.

Vi: But she'd broken it on a bit of toffee and the nerve was exposed.

Sylvia: Nonsense.

Vi: It isn't nonsense, Auntie Syl, it's true.

Sylvia: I wish Mrs. Wilmot was here.

Vi: I'm sure I'm glad she isn't.

SYLVIA: It shows a very small mind to talk like that, Vi—you ought to be ashamed. Mrs. Wilmot is a very remarkable woman.

VI: She sounds a bit silly to me.

SYLVIA: We will not discuss the matter any further.

VI: All right.

SYLVIA: Your very life has been saved at this moment by the triumph of right thinking over wrong thinking.

VI (*equably*): Well, that's nice, isn't it?

SYLVIA: I've often thought Mr. Chamberlain must be a Christian Scientist at heart.

VI: Well, let's hope that Hitler and Mussolini are too, and then we shall all be on velvet.

FRANK *comes in, his hat and coat on*.

FRANK: What are you two looking so glum about?

VI: We were talking about Mr. Chamberlain; Auntie Syl says she thinks he must be a Christian Scientist.

FRANK (*going out again*): That might account for a lot.

SYLVIA: What did you want to say that for, Vi— you're a very aggravating girl.

VI: Sorry.

SYLVIA: Just because you haven't any faith in anything yourself, you think it's funny to laugh at people who have.

VI: I wasn't laughing at all.

FRANK (*having taken off his hat and coat*): Where's your mother?

VI: Upstairs with Queenie and his lordship.

FRANK: Nothing wrong with him, is there?

VI: Oh, no—he's fine. Queenie's not feeling any too good, so she went to bed—her leg was hurting her a bit. It's nothing serious, the doctor came this afternoon

to have a look at her, and said it was only brought on by
the strain of the last week——

FRANK: I'll go up in a minute.

SYLVIA: Did you see anything of the crowds?

FRANK (*laconically*): Yes, I did.

VI: We heard him arrive at the airport, on the radio.

FRANK (*sitting down*): So did I.

VI: Sam's meeting me at the Strand Corner House a
little later on. We thought we'd have a look at the West
End. It ought to be exciting.

FRANK: Well, it's exciting all right, if you like to see a
lot of people yelling themselves hoarse without the
faintest idea what they're yelling about.

SYLVIA: How can you, Frank! They're cheering
because we've been saved from war.

FRANK: I'll cheer about that when it's proved to me.

SYLVIA (*hotly*): You wouldn't care if there was
another war. You're one of those people that think it
doesn't matter that millions and millions of innocent
people should be bombed! Just because you enjoyed
yourself in the last one——

FRANK (*firmly*): Now listen here, Sylvia. Don't you
talk to me like that because I won't 'ave it—see? I did
not enjoy myself in the last war—nobody but a bloody
fool without any imagination would ever say that he
did. And I do not think it doesn't matter if millions and
millions of innocent people are bombed! So you can
get them silly ideas out of your head to start with. But
what I would like to say is this. I've seen something
today that I wouldn't 'ave believed could happen in this
country. I've seen thousands of people, English people,
mark you! carrying on like maniacs, shouting and
cheering with relief, for no other reason but that they'd

been thoroughly frightened, and it made me sick and that's a fact! I only hope to God that we shall have guts enough to learn one lesson from this and that we shall never find ourselves in a position again when we have to appease anybody!

SYLVIA: All you men think about is having Guts and being Top Dog and killing each other, but I'm a woman and I don't care how much we appease as long as we don't have a war. War is wicked and evil and vile— They that live by the sword shall die by the sword— It's more blessed to give than to receive——

FRANK: I don't think it's more blessed to give in and receive a nice kick on the bottom for doing it.

ETHEL (*coming in*): Will you two stop shouting— you'll wake up Frankie!

SYLVIA: He's a war-monger, that's all he is—a war-monger.

FRANK: Judging by the 'eavy way you're breathing, Sylvia, I should say you was in error!

SYLVIA (*bursting into tears of rage*): You're no brother of mine—I don't want to speak to you ever again——

She rushes out of the room and slams the door.

ETHEL: What's the use of arguing with her, Frank? You know it never does any good.

VI: She started it, Mother. She was ever so silly. She's getting sillier and sillier every day.

ETHEL: Don't you talk about your Aunt Sylvia like that.

VI (*kissing her*): Dear old Mum, I'm thirty-five you know now, not fifteen.

ETHEL: All the more reason for you to know better.

VI: There you are, you see! Mum'll never learn.

ETHEL: I don't care if you're a hundred and five, I

won't have you being saucy to your Aunt Sylvia, or to me either for that matter.

VI: What about dad? I can be saucy to him, can't I?

ETHEL: Get on with you, Miss Sharp!

VI: I'm just going anyhow—I'm picking up Sam— we're going to see the crowds. (*She laughs at* FRANK.) Sorry, Dad——

FRANK: You can cheer your head off for all I care.

VI: Maybe I will—I'll just pop up and see Queenie for a minute—good-night all——

FRANK: Good-night.

ETHEL: Don't forget to send round that pram.

VI: Sam'll bring it to-morrow.

She goes out.

ETHEL (*sitting down*): What a week! I wouldn't have believed I could be so tired.

FRANK: Yes—you look a bit done up. How's Queenie?

ETHEL: She's all right. You'd think nobody'd ever had a baby before! All the fuss we've had the last month.

FRANK: She got up too soon.

ETHEL: She had a letter from Billy this afternoon. He wants her to go out there.

FRANK: She can't yet, she's not strong enough.

ETHEL: He didn't say yet—he said after Christmas— all being well.

FRANK: The baby won't be old enough to travel.

ETHEL: She'll leave him here.

FRANK: With us?

ETHEL: Of course—don't be so silly—who else would she leave it with——! She won't be gone more than a year anyway.

FRANK: That'll be fine, won't it?

ETHEL: Fine for you maybe—you won't have to look after it.

FRANK: Perhaps you'd rather she left it with Vi! Or in a home of some sort.

ETHEL: Don't be a bigger fool than you can help— go on upstairs and say good-night to her before she drops off.

FRANK: I'm expecting Bob to come in and have a farewell binge—give me a shout when he comes.

ETHEL: Binge indeed! One small one's all you're going to have, my lad, if I have to come down and take the bottle away from you.

FRANK (cheerfully): I'd like to see you try.

> Left alone ETHEL gets up and goes over to the side-board cupboard. She takes out the whisky bottle, a syphon and two glasses. She has just done this when BOB taps at the window. She lets him in.

BOB: Hallo, Ethel.

ETHEL: Frank's just saying good-night to Queenie— he'll be down in a minute.

BOB: What a week! What with the crisis and the sand bags and me having to pack up all the furniture into the bargain.

ETHEL: Has most of it gone?

BOB: Yes—went this afternoon. I'm sleeping on a camp bed to-night.

ETHEL: Frank'll miss you. So shall I.

BOB: I'm not going very far—you'll both come down and see me, won't you?

ETHEL: Of course we will, Bob. I've often wondered why you stayed on so long in that house all by yourself.

BOB: Oh, I don't know. It was near you and Frank—

and it was somewhere for Billy to come home to.

ETHEL: You'll feel a bit lost, I expect—living in the country.

BOB: Well, I shall have me garden—a damn sight nicer one than I've got here—and there's the sea nearby—and the village pub!

ETHEL: We'll come down and see you quite soon— I'll go and tell Frank you're here.

BOB: Righto. (*There is a slight pause.*) Good-bye, Ethel.

ETHEL (*uncertainly*): Good-bye, Bob. (*She goes to him and kisses him.*) Take care of yourself.

> *She goes swiftly out of the room.*
>
> *After a moment* FRANK *comes in.*

FRANK: Well, he's back. Umbrella and all.

BOB: Yes.

FRANK: Let's have a drink. I'm feeling a bit low— what with one thing and another. (*He starts to pour out the drinks.*) Only one good thing's happened.

BOB: What's that?

FRANK: If Queenie goes out to Singapore after Christmas, we're taking charge of the kid.

BOB: I thought you'd get him.

FRANK: Well, you couldn't have had him—all alone by the sad sea waves.

BOB: All right, all right, no hard feelings.

FRANK (*holding up his glass*): Here goes.

BOB (*doing the same*): Happy days!

FRANK: Remember the first night we moved in? When we had Sylvia's Wincarnis?

BOB: That's going back a bit.

FRANK: Nearly twenty years.

BOB: And here we are—just the same.

FRANK: Are we?

BOB (*with a sigh*): No—I suppose we're not.

FRANK: It's a strange world.

BOB: You've said it.

FRANK: All them years—all the things that happened in 'em—I wouldn't go back over them for all the rice in China—would you?

BOB: Not on your life.

FRANK: Remember that picnic we 'ad at Box Hill in 1923 and you got squiffy and fell down and sprained your ankle?

BOB: Whatever made you think of that?

FRANK: I don't know, I was just thinking——

BOB: Remember that summer holiday—the one we all had together—before Nora got ill?

FRANK: The year we went to Bognor?

BOB: That's right.

FRANK: That must have been earlier still—let's see, Reg was fourteen—that would have been 1922——

BOB: I remember you and Ethel having a row about going out in a boat.

FRANK: Yes—— (*He laughs.*) Ethel's always hated going out in a boat.

BOB: I remember the night we went to your regimental dinner too—the night Queenie went off——

FRANK: Reg was still alive then, wasn't he?

BOB: Yes—that was about a year before.

FRANK (*looking round*): I wonder what 'appens to rooms when people give 'em up—go away and leave the house empty.

BOB: How d'you mean?

FRANK: I don't know. I was just thinking about you going away from next door after all that time and me and Ethel going away too pretty soon. I shouldn't think we'd stay on here much longer—and wondering what the next people that live in this room will be like—whether they'll feel any bits of us left about the place——

BOB: 'Ere, shut up! You're giving me the willies!

FRANK: Have another spot?

BOB: Just a small one.

FRANK (*at sideboard*): Funny you going to live just near where I was born.

BOB: It's about eleven miles, isn't it?

FRANK: Less than that if you go by the marsh road, but it takes longer. I'll probably come back there one day, I hope—that is if I can get round Ethel. She hates the country.

BOB: I suppose it's all according to what you're used to.

FRANK (*handing him his drink*): You don't think the Germans will ever get here, do you?

BOB: No—of course I don't.

FRANK: I'm feeling a bit bad about all this business.

BOB: I'm not feeling too good myself.

FRANK: I'm going to miss you a hell of a lot.

BOB: Same here. You'll be coming down though, won't you?

FRANK: You bet.

BOB (*lifting his glass*): Happy days, old pal.

FRANK (*doing the same*): Happy days, old pal!

THE LIGHTS FADE

ACT III

Scene III

Time: *June, 1939.*

> *It is a warm summer evening and the french windows are wide open. It is still daylight and, as in Act I, Scene I, the May tree is in bloom at the end of the garden. Also as in Act I, Scene I, the room is almost empty of furniture. The pictures have been taken down from the walls and curtains from the windows. There is a muddle of packing-cases, luggage, parcels, shavings, paper and string. The mantelpiece is denuded of ornaments, but the arm-chair is still by the fireplace, and the sideboard, looking strangely bare, is still in its accustomed place, although jutting out from the wall a trifle, as if it were afraid of being left behind. From upstairs comes the sound of intermittent hammering.*
>
> *Vi comes in from the garden wheeling a pram. She wheels it carefully through the window and brings it to a standstill just above the arm-chair. She gives a look to see if its occupant is all right, and then goes to the door.*

Vi (*calling*): Mum . . .

Ethel (*off stage*): Yes, dear?

Vi: I'll have to be getting along now.

Ethel: All right, dear.

Vi: I've brought him in.

> Ethel *appears. She looks a little flustered and untidy.*

Ethel: Has he been good?

Vi: Good as gold. I gave him the post-card Queenie sent with the camel on it—he liked it.

Ethel (*looking into the pram*): He's dropped off now.

366

VI: There's nothing more I can do to help, is there?

ETHEL: No, thanks, dear—everything's done now. They're coming for the rest of the stuff in the morning. I'm just getting a bit of supper for your dad and me in the kitchen—we're going to walk round to the flat afterwards.

VI: I do hope you'll like it, Mum.

ETHEL: Well, it's got a nice view of the Common, I will say that for it.

VI: You'll find it easier on one floor, of course.

ETHEL: Yes—I suppose I will.

VI: It looked quite nice to me—a bit modernistic, of course.

ETHEL: Well, that can't be helped.

VI: It'll be a comfort anyway having running hot water instead of having to fuss about with a geyser.

ETHEL: One thing less for your dad to grumble about.

VI (*listening*): He's enjoying himself with that hammer, isn't he?

ETHEL: The more noise the better's his motto.

VI (*calling*): Dad . . .

FRANK (*upstairs*): Hallo . . .

VI: I'm going now.

FRANK: Righto—see you in the morning.

VI: Good-night, Mum.

ETHEL (*kissing her absently*): Good-night, dear.

VI: I'll bring Archie round to-morrow when I come. The children'll miss him.

ETHEL: I don't see why you don't keep him really, you know. After all, you've got a little garden, which is more than we'll have in the new flat.

VI: Oh, Mum—what'll Dad say?

ETHEL: He won't mind much. Poor old Percy was his choice, you know. He never took to Archie in the same way.

VI: Thanks ever so much, Mum—if you feel after a time you want him back all you've got to do is just say.

ETHEL: All right, dear.

VI: Well—so long.

ETHEL: Thank you for coming, dear—give my love to Sam and the children.

VI: I will. Good-night.

ETHEL: Good-night . . .

VI *goes out.*

ETHEL *bustles about the room a little, then gives one more look into the pram and sits down in the arm-chair with a sigh of weariness.*

FRANK *comes downstairs and into the room. He is in his shirt-sleeves and carries a hammer.*

FRANK: Hallo—having a breather?

ETHEL: I am that. My back's breaking.

FRANK (*putting the hammer down on the sideboard*): Not as young as you were.

ETHEL: Who are you to talk?

FRANK: How's his lordship? (*He looks into the pram.*)

ETHEL: Don't wake him up now.

FRANK: He's dribbling—dirty boy.

ETHEL: I expect you dribbled when you were his age.

FRANK: I do still as a matter of fact, if I happen to drop off in the afternoon.

ETHEL: Well, it's nothing to boast about.

FRANK: Bit snappy, aren't we?

ETHEL: Who wouldn't be with all I've had to do to-day!

FRANK (*bending over her and giving her a kiss*): Poor old crock.

ETHEL: Leave off, Frank—we haven't got time for fooling about.

FRANK: That's just where you're wrong. We've got all the time in the world.

ETHEL: All right—have it your own way.

FRANK (*sitting on a packing-case*): I shall miss that garden.

ETHEL: Well, it's your own fault—you're the one that wanted to move.

FRANK: I know.

ETHEL: You'll have the balcony anyhow. You can put window-boxes all round it.

FRANK: One day—a bit later on—when I stop working, we might get a little place in the country, mightn't we?

ETHEL: And when will that be, may I ask?

FRANK: Oh, I don't know. In a few years, I suppose.

ETHEL: Well, we'll think about that when the time comes.

FRANK: I think you'd like the country, you know, Ethel, once you got used to it.

ETHEL: That's as maybe.

FRANK: I know you're frightened of it being a bit too quiet for you, but when people get old they don't mind so much about being quiet.

ETHEL: We're not all that old yet, you know.

FRANK: We ought to go abroad some day, by rights.

ETHEL: Whatever for?

FRANK: Well, I feel a bit silly sometimes, having been over other people's journeys for twenty years and never so much as set foot out of England myself since 1919.

ETHEL: Well, if you want to go gadding about to foreign parts you'll have to do it by yourself.

FRANK: What a chance! You'd be after me like an electric hare.

ETHEL: You flatter yourself.

FRANK (*pensively*): It's a funny thing . . .

ETHEL: What is?

FRANK: You'd think taking all the furniture out of a room would make it look bigger, but this one looks smaller.

ETHEL (*with a touch of vehemence*): I shall be glad when we're out of it.

FRANK: So shall I—sorry, too, though, in a way.

ETHEL (*rising*): Well, I've rested long enough—I must go and get on with the supper . . .

> FRANK *gets up too and quite quietly puts his arms round her. She submits and rests her head on his shoulder. They stand there together in silence for a moment.*

FRANK: It's been a long time all right.

ETHEL: Yes.

FRANK (*gently*): I don't mind how many flats we move into or where we go or what we do, as long as I've got you . . .

ETHEL (*in a low voice*): Don't talk so silly . . .

> *She disentangles herself from his arms and goes quickly out of the room with her head down.*
>
> FRANK *looks after her for a moment, smiling, then he takes a packet of cigarettes from his pocket, lights one and saunters over to the pram. He stands looking down into it for a little.*

FRANK: Hallo, cock! So you've decided to wake up, 'ave you? Feel like a bit of upsie-downsie? (*He sits down on a packing-case and proceeds to rock the pram gently.*) Well,

Frankie boy, I wonder what you're going to turn out like! You're not going to get any wrong ideas, see? That is, not if I have anything to do with it. . . . There's nobody here to interrupt us, so we can talk as man to man, can't we? There's not much to worry about really, so long as you remember one or two things always. The first is that life isn't all jam for anybody, and you've got to have trouble of some kind or another whoever you are. But if you don't let it get you down, however bad it is, you won't go far wrong. . . . Another thing you'd better get into that little bullet head of yours is that you belong to something that nobody can't ever break, however much they try. And they'll try all right—they're trying now. Not only people in other countries who want to do us in because they're sick of us ruling the roost—and you can't blame them at that! but people here, in England. People who have let 'emselves get soft and afraid. People who go on a lot about peace and good will and the ideals they believe in, but somehow don't seem to believe in 'em enough to think they're worth fighting for. . . . The trouble with the world is, Frankie, that there are too many ideals and too little horse sense. We're human beings, we are—all of us—and that's what people are liable to forget. Human beings don't like peace and good will and everybody loving everybody else. However much they may think they do, they don't really because they're not made like that. Human beings like eating and drinking and loving and hating. They also like showing off, grabbing all they can, fighting for their rights and bossing anybody who'll give 'em half a chance. You belong to a race that's been bossy for years and the reason it's held on as long as it has is that nine times out of ten it's behaved decently and treated people right. Just lately, I'll admit, we've been giving at the knees a bit and letting people down who trusted us and allowing noisy little men to bully us with a lot of guns and bombs and aeroplanes. But don't worry—that won't last—the people themselves, the ordinary people like you and me, know something better than all the fussy old politicians put together—we know what we belong to, where we come from, and where we're going. We may not know it with our brains, but we know it with our roots. And we know another thing too, and it's this. We 'aven't lived and died and struggled all these hundreds of years to get decency and justice and freedom for ourselves without being prepared to fight fifty wars if need be—to keep 'em.

    ETHEL *comes in.*

ETHEL: What in the world are you doing? Talking to yourself?

FRANK: I wasn't talking to myself—I was talking to Frankie.

ETHEL: Well, I'm sure I hope he enjoyed it.

FRANK: He's stopped dribbling anyhow!

ETHEL: Come on in—supper's ready—you'd better close the windows, he might get a chill.

    ETHEL *goes out.*

    FRANK *closes the windows and goes back to the pram.*

FRANK: So long, son . . .

    He goes out as the CURTAIN FALLS

WAYS AND MEANS

A Light Comedy in Three Scenes

from

TO-NIGHT AT 8.30

CHARACTERS:
STELLA CARTWRIGHT
TOBY CARTWRIGHT
OLIVE LLOYD-RANSOME
LORD CHAPWORTH (Chaps)
NANNY
MURDOCH
STEVENS
PRINCESS ELÈNA KRASSILOFF
GASTON

The action of the play takes place in a bedroom in the LLOYD-RANSOME's house, Villa Zephyre, on the Côte d'Azur.

The time is the present.

The Scene is a bedroom in the Villa Zephyre on the Côte d'Azur. The Villa Zephyre belongs to MRS. LLOYD-RANSOME, who is excessively rich, comparatively pleasant and entirely idle, the bedroom therefore is luxurious and tastefully appointed. On the right there is a dressing-table with, above it, a door leading to the bathroom. On the left there is a french window leading on to a small verandah, above that, in the back wall, is a door leading to the passage and the rest of the house. There is a slight recess in the back wall containing a very wide and comfortable bed.

This is occupied at the rise of the curtain by STELLA and TOBY CARTWRIGHT. They are an attractive couple in the thirties. Between them there is a breakfast tray. STELLA is opening and reading letters. TOBY is scanning the Continental Daily Mail. A certain amount of pale sunshine is coming through the window, but this fails to banish from either of their faces an expression of gloomy dissatisfaction. After a consider-able silence, STELLA speaks.

STELLA: Here's a letter from Aunt Hester.
TOBY: Is she well and hearty?
STELLA: Apparently.
TOBY: To hell with her!
  There is a further silence.

375

STELLA (*pensively eating a brioche*): Why do other people's breakfasts always taste much nicer than one's own?

TOBY: Probably because they are.

There is another silence.

STELLA: I knew marrying you was a mistake at least seven years ago, but I never realised the thoroughness of the mistake until now——

TOBY (*reading his paper*): You will be interested to hear that Mrs. S. J. Pendleton gave a small dinner party for Mr. and Mrs. Hubert Weir at the Hotel Normandie in Le Touquet last night——

STELLA: How thrilling.

TOBY: Among the guests were Lord and Lady Haven, Mrs. George Durlap, the Countess Pantulucci, Mr. Henry Bird, Mr. and Mrs. Harvey Lincoln, Miss Styles——

STELLA: Shut up!

TOBY: I beg your pardon?

STELLA: I said shut up.

TOBY (*continuing*): —Mr. and Mrs. Sidney Alford have returned from Vichy and are staying at the Crillon——

STELLA: Toby——

TOBY: They are to be joined in a few days by Mrs. Alford's sister, Lady Croker——

STELLA: Toby, please——

TOBY: Prince and Princess Jean Marie de Larichon have left the Hotel George Cinq en route for the Riviera——

STELLA snatches the paper from him.

STELLA (*angrily*): Mr. and Mrs. Toby Cartwright have left the Villa Zephyre under a cloud——

TOBY (*complacently taking some coffee*): Not yet they haven't——

STELLA: Owing to the idiocy of Mr. Toby Cartwright losing his shirt at the Casino——

TOBY: Oh, God, must we go back over that again!

STELLA: Yes, we must—don't you see—we've got to do something——

TOBY: Darling, what's the use——?

STELLA: Give me the pad and pencil—they're just by you——

TOBY (*taking a pencil and pad from the bedside table*): So what?

STELLA: Give it to me.

TOBY (*giving it to her*): Toby lost fifty pounds—Toby lost fifty pounds—Toby lost fifty pounds—write it down quickly, it would be awful if you happened to forget it——

STELLA (*near tears*): Oh, Toby!

TOBY (*relenting*): All right, darling—I am sorry—really I am.

    He leans towards her, nearly upsetting the breakfast-
    tray.

STELLA: Look out!

TOBY: Damn——

STELLA: It isn't that I want to rub in about the fifty pounds—really it isn't—but we are in the most awful jam, and we've got to concentrate.

TOBY: We concentrated up until four-thirty this morning and nothing came of it——

STELLA: Will you promise not to take offence at anything I say for ten minutes?

TOBY: That means you're going to be absolutely bloody.

STELLA: Promise.

TOBY: All right—I promise.

STELLA: We must face facts. Now then. Our combined incomes amount to seven hundred and fifty pounds a year——

TOBY: Until Aunt Hester dies.

STELLA: Aunt Hester will not die—she's outwitted life for seventy years and is now determined to outwit death.

TOBY: It's indecent.

STELLA: Never mind about that now—our combined overdrafts amount to roughly thirteen hundred pounds —in addition to which, you owe about three thousand——

TOBY: What about you?

STELLA (*writing*): Two thousand.

TOBY: I can't understand why you don't get a job of some sort—look at Liza Herrick—she at least made some effort—she opened a hat shop.

STELLA: And shut it again.

TOBY: No talent—that's what's wrong with you— no marketable talent whatsoever.

STELLA: You seem to forget that on a certain bleak day in 1928 I gave my life into your keeping.

TOBY: Marriage is a sacrament, a mystic rite, and you persist in regarding it as a sort of plumber's estimate.

STELLA: Be quiet. Where was I?

TOBY: Wandering along the paths of memory, dear, with a singularly nasty expression.

STELLA: You will admit, I suppose, that we live beyond our income?

TOBY: You have a genius for understatement.

STELLA: Having managed to rake up seventy-two pounds in order to stay—God knows why—in this over-elaborate house——

TOBY: I don't agree. I think Olive, considering her innate vulgarity, has done this house with remarkable restraint.

STELLA: Olive is not vulgar—she's one of my oldest friends. She was at school with me, and——

TOBY: Well, let's just say that she was at school with you.

STELLA: Now look here, Toby——

TOBY: Go on—concentrate.

STELLA: You're maddening.

TOBY: Go on, write—write down the truth—face facts—put down our congenital idiocy in black and white—write down that we were brought up merely to be amiable and pleasant and socially attractive—that we have no ambition and no talent—except for playing games.

STELLA (*sharply*): And not enough of that.

TOBY: Toby lost fifty pounds—Toby lost fifty pounds——

STELLA: I wrote that down first—but what I didn't write down was that you were a silly, selfish, careless, bloody fool to do it——

TOBY (*furiously*): Look here, Stella——

He makes a violent movement.

STELLA: Look out!

TOBY: Damn!

STELLA: It's no use quarrelling. The fifty pounds has gone—we've already stayed over our time here—the Lorings are expecting us in Venice—we have, at the moment, one hundred and fourteen francs—and

we are down two thousand four hundred francs in the
Bridge Book.

TOBY: That's entirely your fault—you play Bridge
too merrily, Stella.

STELLA: My merriment is entirely a social gesture. I
loathe Bridge.

TOBY: That is no excuse for playing it as though it
were lacrosse.

STELLA: I don't know what you mean.

TOBY: Your bids have a certain girlish devil-may-
care abandon—you whoop through every rubber like a
games' mistress.

STELLA: What do you mean, whoop?

TOBY: What I say—whoop—W-H-O-O-P.

STELLA: Oh, do be quiet! What was I saying?

TOBY: You were saying that we were down two
thousand four hundred francs in the Bridge Book. What
you should have said was, that owing to your——

STELLA: Never mind about that now—within the
next week we shall be asked definitely to leave—Olive
was dropping hints all over the dinner-table last night.

TOBY: We can't leave.

STELLA: We'll have to.

TOBY: Chaps owes you some money, doesn't he?

STELLA: Yes. Backgammon—seven thousand francs.

TOBY: Thank God for that!

STELLA: If we travel to Venice second-class and send
Nanny home——

TOBY: I can't think why you had to bring her in the
first place; I don't have to have a valet, why should you
have a maid?

STELLA: Nanny's not a maid—Nanny's saved our
lives a million times.

TOBY: Wrongly.

STELLA: Anyhow——

There is a knock on the door and GASTON *enters. He is a neatly dressed French valet.*

GASTON: Bon jour, monsieur.

TOBY: Bon jour, Gaston.

GASTON: Bon jour, madame.

STELLA: Bon jour.

GASTON: Lord Chapworth wish to speak to you.

TOBY: Is he there?

STELLA: Tell him to come in. (*She calls.*) Come in, Chaps!

GASTON stands aside to let LORD CHAPWORTH *enter.* LORD CHAPWORTH *is an amiable-looking young man.*

GASTON goes out.

CHAPS: Good morning—how d'you feel?

TOBY: Frightful.

CHAPS: So do I.

TOBY: Good!

STELLA: You look very sweet, Chaps, darling, and very dapper—why are you up so early?

CHAPS: It's after eleven. I came to say good-bye——

STELLA: Of course, you're leaving to-day—I'd forgotten. Are you going to May Bainbridge?

CHAPS: Yes—Guy's picking me up.

STELLA: You must find out all about the chauffeur scandal and wire us immediately.

CHAPS: What chauffeur scandal?

STELLA: Don't be silly, darling, the whole coast is buzzing with it.

CHAPS: Oh, that!—I always thought it was a valet.

TOBY: Chauffeur-valet—a   combined   occupation

rife, apparently, with the most delirious opportunities——

CHAPS: Do you think it's true?—I mean, do you
think May really did——?

STELLA: Certainly—you only have to look at her.

TOBY: Don't be catty, Stella.

STELLA: As May Bainbridge has been consistently
odious to me for years I really don't see why I shouldn't
be as catty as I like.

TOBY: After all, Chaps is going to stay with them.

STELLA: Serve him right.

CHAPS: Oh, old May's not bad—she just has an
unfortunate manner.

STELLA: To be not bad with an unfortunate manner
is not enough——

CHAPS: You seem a bit scratchy this morning.

TOBY: Compared with what took place in the night,
this is purring.

CHAPS: Well, it's a nice sunny day, anyhow.

STELLA: It had better be.

CHAPS: I had an awful evening—I got stuck with
Pearl Brandt—she insisted on playing at the big table
and I lost a packet.

TOBY: You what?

CHAPS: Just dropped about four hundred pounds—
cleaned myself out.

STELLA: Oh, Chaps!

CHAPS: She kept on asking me to go in with her,
she never ran a hand more than two coups except once,
then she passed it after the fourth and it ran eleven
times.

TOBY: Did it occur to you to strike her in the face?

CHAPS: So I wondered if you'd mind waiting for

382

that seven thousand francs I owe you, Stella, until I get my allowance?

TOBY: When do you get your allowance?

CHAPS: First of May.

STELLA (*hurriedly*): Of course I don't mind, Chaps—it doesn't matter a bit.

TOBY: God is love, there is no pain.

CHAPS: It's awfully sweet of you.

STELLA: Don't be silly.

OLIVE LLOYD-RANSOME'S *voice is heard, outside.*

OLIVE (*outside*): Can we come in?

STELLA (*calling*): Of course!

TOBY: Send for a Bridge table and the Corinthian Bagatelle—don't let's waste a moment.

OLIVE LLOYD-RANSOME *and* PRINCESS ELÈNA KRASSILOFF *enter.* OLIVE *is smartly dressed and dark.*

ELÈNA *is fair and rather vague.*

OLIVE: Good morning, everybody—I'm suicidal.

STELLA: Why—what's the matter?

OLIVE: Everything's the matter. I went down twenty mille last night, Precious Bane's got distemper and I had to send him off to the vet. at seven o'clock this morning, and on the top of that I've had a telegram from Nicky and Vera to say they're arriving to-morrow.

TOBY: To-morrow!

OLIVE: It's the most awful bore—it means that I shall have to turn you out, which I absolutely loathe —it also means that I shall have to put off Dolly, because she and Vera aren't speaking and——

STELLA: Why don't you put off Nicky and Vera?

OLIVE: Bob would never forgive me—he worships Nicky. They talk about international finance—also I've already put them off once—I feel absolutely dreadful about the whole business.

TOBY: Don't worry about us—we've got to go to the Lorings anyhow.

OLIVE: But I do—I adore you being here—you're the nicest guests I've ever had in my life.

ELÈNA (*scrutinising the breakfast-tray*): Do you mind if I take one of your lumps of sugar?

TOBY: Not at all—take the whole bowl.

ELÈNA: Angel!

> *She sits down quietly with the bowl of sugar and devours several lumps.*

OLIVE: And to-night we've got the Brandt dinner party—nobody wants to go—I tried to hint that we'd all rather stay in, but they're absolutely set on it—it's something to do with being American, I think, that passion for entertaining in restaurants.

TOBY: That means the Casino again.

STELLA: Yes, dear, that's what that means.

CHAPS: Have you got any messages for May, Olive?

OLIVE (*laughing*): None that I could possibly send her.

ELÈNA: He was lovely that chauffeur—he wore his cap bravely as though he wasn't afraid.

OLIVE: Wasn't afraid of what, darling?

TOBY: George Bainbridge.

ELÈNA: Anything—anything in the world. I remember he drove me to the station once, and I knew the back of his neck reminded me of someone, and who do you think it was?

STELLA (*wearily*): Who?

ELÈNA (*triumphantly*): Dimitri.

OLIVE: Everybody reminds you of Dimitri, darling.

ELÈNA: I loved him dreadfully. (*At the dressing-*

table.) Do you mind if I take a little of your scent?

STELLA (*with false enthusiasm*): Do, dear!

ELÈNA *sprays herself lavishly.*

OLIVE: We're going up to Vence to lunch—do you want to come?

STELLA: We shan't be ready in time.

OLIVE: I'll leave the small car for you—Irving and Pearl want to buy some of that awful pottery.

MURDOCH *enters through the open door. He is a very correct English butler.*

MURDOCH: Excuse me, madame.

OLIVE: What is it, Murdoch?

MURDOCH: Mr. Guy Forster has arrived, madame, for Lord Chapworth.

CHAPS: I must go.

OLIVE: Has his lordship's luggage gone down?

MURDOCH: Yes, madame.

ELÈNA: I love Guy, he's an angel. Where is he, Murdoch?

MURDOCH: In the bar, madame.

ELÈNA: I'll come down.

MURDOCH *exits.*

CHAPS: Good-bye, Stella—Good-bye, Toby.

STELLA: Good-bye.

TOBY: Good-bye.

CHAPS: It's awfully sweet of you to hold that over. Good-bye, Olive.

OLIVE: I'll see you off—don't forget to write in the book—give Guy a drink.

CHAPS: He's probably had three already—come on, Elèna.

ELÈNA *and* CHAPS *go out.*

OLIVE: I do feel so horrid about turning you out.

STELLA: Don't be silly, darling—we've overstayed frightfully, but we were having such a lovely time.

OLIVE: If it were anyone else but Vera and Nicky I'd tell them to go to hell, but Bob really has to discuss business with Nicky and—oh, well, I know you understand perfectly.

TOBY: Of course we do—when are they arriving?

OLIVE: To-morrow afternoon—I must pop down and see Chaps off. The car will be waiting for you at twelve-thirty; we'd better meet in the main square.

STELLA: All right.

OLIVE: You *do* understand, don't you?

She kisses her hand to them and goes out.

There is silence for a moment.

STELLA: Dear Olive!

TOBY: She's done everything but throw us into the drive!

STELLA: We must think—we must think.

TOBY: What's the use of thinking—we haven't even enough to tip the servants.

STELLA: Oh, don't!

TOBY: If we asked Olive to lend us five thousand francs, do you think she would?

STELLA: Of course she would, and she'd dine out on it for a week—I'd rather die than ask her. Anyway, five thousand francs wouldn't be enough—not nearly enough. We've got to pay our train fares—Nanny's fare home—our Bridge debts—the servants—— Oh, God!

There is a knock on the door.

Yes, who is it?

MURDOCH: Murdoch, madame.

TOBY: Come in!

MURDOCH *enters.*

MURDOCH: Mrs. Lloyd-Ransome asked me to come and see you, madame, about your reservations.

STELLA: Reservations?

MURDOCH: On the afternoon train to-morrow. I took the liberty of telephoning in to the hall porter of the Majestic about them.

TOBY: How thoughtful of you, Murdoch.

STELLA: Why the hall porter at the Majestic?

MURDOCH: He happens to be a personal friend of mine, madame—he does a lot of odd jobs.

TOBY: This one may be odder than he bargained for.

MURDOCH: I beg your pardon, sir?

STELLA (*hurriedly*): When did you order these reservations, Murdoch?

MURDOCH: Last night, madame, directly Mrs. Lloyd-Ransome told me.

STELLA (*with an attempt at lighthearted naturalness*): What have you got for us?

MURDOCH: Two single sleepers and one for your maid—that is what Mrs. Lloyd-Ransome told me you required.

TOBY: It's a pity they don't have sitting-rooms on Continental trains.

STELLA: I'm afraid you'll have to change them, Murdoch. You see, we're not going back to London— we're going to Venice.

MURDOCH: That's all right, madame, Mrs. Lloyd-Ransome told me that, too.

STELLA: She didn't happen to mention in passing that my sister was going to have a baby in July?

MURDOCH: I'll send the tickets up to you the

moment they arrive; there's a small laundry bill as well
—I've given that to your maid.

TOBY: You think of everything, Murdoch.

MURDOCH: Thank you, sir.

STELLA: Thank *you*, Murdoch.

> MURDOCH *bows and goes out.*

TOBY: Dear Olive!

STELLA: Last night—she had it all arranged last
night.

TOBY (*pensively*): I think I should like something quite
dreadful to happen to Olive, you know—something
really humiliating, like being sick at a Court Ball.

STELLA: How dare she!

TOBY: It's unsufferable.

STELLA: After all, she badgered us to come.

TOBY: Now she's badgering us to go.

STELLA: Isn't there anyone we could cable to?

TOBY: Don't be silly, dear—we've exhausted every
possible telegraphic saviour years ago.

STELLA: Do you think I could do a little light
prostitution in the Casino to-night?

TOBY: You'd have to work hard to raise ten thousand
francs by to-morrow morning.

STELLA: There's no need to be rude.

TOBY: If you'd thought of that at the beginning of
our stay things might have been much easier.

STELLA: You have the moral standards of a wart-
hog.

TOBY: Think—think—there must be some way out.

STELLA: There isn't—it's no use—nothing's any
use.

TOBY: Listen, darling, this is desperate—we've got
to take a chance.

STELLA: What do you mean?

TOBY: Your bracelet.

STELLA: Don't be so absurd—it wouldn't fetch fifteen pounds.

TOBY (*ringing the bell*): We'll send Nanny into Cannes with it this afternoon.

STELLA: But I tell you——

TOBY: Shut up. Listen, at worst we can get a couple of thousand francs on it.

STELLA: I bet we couldn't.

TOBY: With my waistcoat buttons we could.

STELLA: Even then—what's the use?

TOBY: This is the use—listen—I'll gamble to-night.

STELLA: Oh, no, Toby—no!

TOBY: It's our only chance. I'll be careful, I promise. We'll have enough for three goes of the minimum at the big table——

STELLA: Oh, not the big table!

TOBY: The biggest——

> *He springs out of bed and goes over to the dressing-table.*
>
> NANNY *enters. She is a capable-looking, middle-aged woman.*

STELLA: Nanny, we're in the most awful trouble!

NANNY: I don't wonder—lying about in bed on a lovely morning like this.

TOBY (*springing at her with the bracelet and buttons*): Here, Nanny——

NANNY: What's this?

TOBY: Go into Cannes this afternoon and pop them.

NANNY: Oh, I couldn't—I really couldn't!

TOBY: You must.

NANNY: That lovely bracelet your Aunt Agnes left you.

STELLA: Listen, Nanny, we've got to leave to-morrow and we haven't got any money at all—we owe a lot as well—you must do this for us—go in by the twelve o'clock bus—please, Nanny.

NANNY: I could let you have a little, you know.

TOBY: We wouldn't hear of it, Nanny.

STELLA: Anyhow, a little's no good—we've got to have a lot.

NANNY: I shan't get much on these.

STELLA: Get what you can—promise you will, Nanny.

NANNY: That man in the pawnshop will split his sides when he sees me again.

TOBY: Never mind, Nanny—please!

NANNY: Won't you let me advance you a little?—I could go up to seven pounds.

TOBY: I tell you, Nanny, we couldn't possibly dream of such a thing.

NANNY: Oh, very well.

STELLA: How much do we owe you already?

NANNY: Three hundred and forty-two pounds all told.

STELLA: Oh, dear! (*She collapses on to the bed in helpless laughter.*)

TOBY: Go on, Nanny—go like the wind.

> *He pushes her out of the room.* GASTON *enters and crosses over to run the bath—he disappears into the bathroom.* TOBY *gets into bed again.*

STELLA: It's madness—stark, staring madness!

> TOBY *casually starts to read the paper again.*

You'll lose it, I know you will. Oh, God, I wish I could play the damned game——

>   *There is a pause.*

TOBY (*reading*): Mr. and Mrs. Eugene B. Oglander arrived yesterday at the Hotel Maurice with their daughters Margaret and Helen——

STELLA: It's too humiliating—I wish I were dead!

TOBY: I wonder what the B stands for?

STELLA (*bitterly*): I *know*!

THE LIGHTS FADE

SCENE II

The Scene is the same.

>   TOBY *is lying on the bed, smoking. He is in his dressing-gown and pyjamas.* STELLA, *in a negligee, is doing her face at the dressing-table.*
>   *The time is about* 1.30 *a.m.*

TOBY: Is there no justice in the universe? No decency?

STELLA: Absolutely none, dear. I remember remarking that to Nanny only the other day when the stopper came out of my nail varnish and made the inside of my handbag look like Bortsch.

TOBY: There was no reason in what happened—it had nothing to do with the law of logic or the law of compensation or the law of anything—it was just low, senseless bad luck.

STELLA: Never mind, darling.

391

TOBY: Mind! I shall mind to the end of my days. The whole beastly scene is etched on to my brain in blood. (*Reconstructing his despair.*) I went up to the table —seven, my lucky number, was miraculously vacant—I sat down and waited for the shoe to come round—just as it was two away from me that New Jersey hag tapped me on the shoulder. "It's terrible," she said. "I can't find a place anywheres—will you be a dear and let me have yours just for a little while? I'm feeling so lucky to-night."

STELLA: She was right.

TOBY: Right! She ran the bank seventeen times— collected one hundred and seventy thousand francs with all the delicacy of a starving jaguar let loose in a butcher's shop—and graciously gave me back my place.

STELLA: Whereupon you proceeded to lose our two thousand francs in the brief space of four minutes, borrow five hundred francs from Bertie Gifford, who will never let us forget it, lose that too, and join me in the bar wearing what might be moderately described as a 'set look'.

TOBY: Correct. Have you anything more to say?

STELLA: Not for the moment.

TOBY: Good! Then we might talk of something else.

STELLA: I can't see any necessity to talk at all.

TOBY: That is only because you are temporarily exhausted by your own verbosity. Your natural flow will return in a minute.

STELLA: I was fond of Aunt Agnes and she was fond of me.

TOBY: That rather cloying relationship belongs mercifully to the days before I met you.

STELLA: She left me that bracelet in her will.

TOBY: It seems odd that she should symbolise her almost incestuous love for you by such an undistinguished little trinket.

STELLA: You have a disgusting mind, Toby.

TOBY: I said almost.

STELLA: Aunt Agnes was the most generous woman in the world.

TOBY: I suspect that your memory of her has been softened by time. To the impartial observer she appears to have been a mean old bitch.

STELLA: Toby!

TOBY: If it's all the same to you, I would prefer to leave Aunt Agnes where she rightly belongs, warbling through eternity with the Feathered Choir.

STELLA: It seems a pity that you can't turn your devastating wit to a more commercial advantage—you should write a gossip column.

TOBY: I haven't got a title.

STELLA: Oh, shut up!

TOBY: That was merely rude.

STELLA: There's no sense in going on like this— snapping at each other—we've got to face facts——

TOBY (*rolling over*): Oh, God!

STELLA (*turning round*): Toby, don't you see——

TOBY: Your passion for facing facts is rapidly becoming pathological. You'll go mad, that's what you'll do, and spend your declining years being led about some awful institute by a keeper—facing the fact that you're the Empress Eugènie.

STELLA: Don't be so idiotic.

Toby: I'm sick of facing facts; in future I shall cut every fact I meet stone dead—I intend to relax, to live in a lovely dream world of my own where everything is hilariously untrue. After all, at least three-quarters of the civilised world do it, why shouldn't I?

Stella: Why shouldn't you what?

Toby: Delude myself! I'm going to start deluding myself this very minute. I'm going to begin with the Old Testament and believe every word of it—I'm going to believe in Jehovah and Buddha and Krishna and Mahomet and Luther and Mary Baker Eddy and Aimèe Semple Macpherson—I'm even going to believe in Aunt Agnes!

Stella: Will you shut up about Aunt Agnes!

Toby: It is possible, in my present state of splendid detachment, that I might go off into a Yogi trance and stay upside down for several days—in that case all our troubles would be over—even Olive's social conscience would jib at one of her guests being carried out of the house in a sort of sailor's knot.

Stella: Darling, darling Toby!

She rushes to him and flings her arms round his neck.

Toby: Look out—you're strangling me.

Stella: I've been wanting to strangle you for hours and now I'm doing it—it's heaven!

Toby: This might lead to almost anything.

Stella (*in his arms*): Fiddling while Rome's burning —that's what we're doing.

Toby: In the present circumstances fiddling sounds singularly offensive.

Stella: I didn't mean that sort of fiddling.

Toby: Really, Stella——

Stella: Oh, darling, what are we to do?

TOBY: Let's go quietly but firmly along the passage and murder Pearl Brandt.

STELLA: We should be hanged.

TOBY: It would be worth it.

STELLA: She sleeps alone, you know—Irving is separated from her by the bathroom—it would be deliciously easy.

TOBY (*wistfully*): I hate her so. There's a certain austere scientific beauty about my hatred for that shrill harpy—like higher mathematics.

STELLA: I'd like to fasten that wad of thousand-franc notes to her nose with a safety-pin.

TOBY: I had other plans for them.

STELLA: Hush, darling.

TOBY (*jumping up and striking about the room*): I can't bear it—I really can't!

STELLA: Well, now let's talk about something else. I consider this particular topic exhausted and I don't want to get angry again.

TOBY: Angry!—Again! I shall never stop being angry until the end of my days.

STELLA: Being angry is very bad for you—I believe that when you are angry all the red corpuscles in your blood fight with the white ones.

TOBY: If that's so, my circulation at the moment would make the battle of Mons look like a Morris dance.

STELLA: It's dreadfully late, we'd better go to sleep.

TOBY: I shall never sleep again.

STELLA: Nonsense!—go and brush your teeth.

TOBY: We must think of something.

STELLA: No, we mustn't—we're worn out—go on.

TOBY: But, darling——

STELLA: Go on—leave the door open—the noise of your gargling will give me a sense of security, as though everything was all right.

> TOBY *goes into the bathroom, leaving the door open.* STELLA *gives a few final pats to her face and tries to spray herself with scent, but there isn't any left.*

Toby!

TOBY: What?

STELLA: Were Russians always predatory—even before the Revolution, I mean?

TOBY: I expect so. Why?

STELLA: Elèna's splashed herself from head to foot with the last precious drops of my scent this morning.

TOBY: Personally, I'm very glad—I never cared for it.

STELLA: That's beside the point.

TOBY: It smells like bad salad dressing.

STELLA: Smelt, dear—you can use the past tense now.

TOBY: Good—from now onwards I intend to live in the past anyhow—the present is too unbearable. I intend to go back to the happy scenes of my boyhood.

STELLA: I'm sorry I'm not a rocking-horse.

TOBY: You underrate yourself, darling.

STELLA (*getting into bed*): Witty to the last.

TOBY (*after a pause, during which the sound of gargling is heard*): Stella!

STELLA: What?

TOBY: What are we going to do?

STELLA: I told you just now—I refuse to discuss it— I'm too tired.

TOBY: If you broke your leg we should have to stay, shouldn't we?

STELLA: I have no intention of breaking my leg.

TOBY: Modern women have no courage—in olden times women did brave things for their menfolk every day of the week.

STELLA: I don't look upon you as my menfolk.

TOBY: Think of the girl who put her arm through the latches of the door to save Bonnie Prince Charlie.

STELLA: In my opinion a misguided ass.

TOBY: I won't hear a word against Flora Macdonald.

STELLA: It wasn't Flora Macdonald.

TOBY: Don't be so ignorant, of course it was. Flora Macdonald never stopped doing things like that.

STELLA: It was not.

TOBY: Who was it, then?

STELLA: I don't know who it was, but it was *not* Flora Macdonald.

TOBY (*appearing with a toothbrush*): I suppose you'll tell me it was Grace Darling in a minute.

STELLA: I see no reason for you to suppose any such thing.

TOBY: It was Flora Macdonald.

STELLA: It's a matter of supreme indifference to me whether it was Nell Gwynn or Marie Antoinette.

TOBY: Well, we're getting on—by a process of tedious elimination—we might ultimately arrive at who you think it was.

STELLA: I tell you I don't know who it was, I only know who it wasn't, and it wasn't Flora Macdonald.

TOBY: Oh, God!

He slams into the bathroom in a rage. There is a

moment's pause then a crash. Then TOBY *gives a wail of pain.*

STELLA: What's happened?

TOBY: I'm hurt.

STELLA: What sort of hurt?

TOBY: Badly hurt.

STELLA: Oh, darling!

She jumps out of bed and rushes into the bathroom. The following dialogue takes place off stage.

TOBY (*groaning*): It was the door of that blasted little cupboard——

STELLA: My poor sweet!

TOBY: Do something—it's bleeding.

STELLA: Where's the iodine?

TOBY: How do I know?

STELLA: What a minute—no, that's eye-drops— here——

TOBY: It's agony.

STELLA: Stand still.

TOBY: I don't want to stand still—I want to jump out of the window. This is the end——

STELLA: Don't be so silly!

TOBY: Cotton-wool.

STELLA: There isn't any.

TOBY: There ought to be.

STELLA: Wait a minute—I've got some.

She comes running in and goes to the dressing-table. She rummages in the drawers for a moment and produces some cotton-wool. TOBY *comes in carrying a bottle of iodine. There is an enormous bruise on his forehead which is bleeding slightly.*

Here we are.

TOBY: God, what a crack!

STELLA: Stand still.

TOBY: Do stop telling me to stand still.

STELLA: Don't be so irritable.

TOBY (*as she dabs him with iodine*): Ow!—hell!—ow!——

STELLA: Stand still.

TOBY: Shut up!

STELLA: I'm doing my best—don't be so childish. There!

TOBY (*looking in the glass*): For this to happen—on top of everything else—it's too much!

STELLA: Never mind, darling.

TOBY: It's not even bad enough to keep us here.

STELLA: You might pretend it had given you concussion and behave very peculiarly to-morrow morning.

TOBY: I couldn't carry it through—I'm too depressed.

STELLA: Get into bed, darling.

TOBY: The light's on in the bathroom.

STELLA: I'll turn it out.

> *She goes into the bathroom and does so, while he takes off his dressing-gown and gets into bed.* STELLA *returns.*

TOBY: You don't think we ought to bandage it?

STELLA: No—let the air get to it.

TOBY: Open the window.

STELLA: All right—I was just going to.

TOBY: If you're beastly to me I swear to God I'll yell the place down.

> STELLA *opens the window, switches out all lights except one by the bed, and gets into bed.*

STELLA: Does it hurt?

TOBY: Was that question merely rhetorical or do you really care?

STELLA: Of course I care—it's horrid for you.

TOBY: It does hurt, Stella—it hurts dreadfully.

STELLA: Try to forget about it.

TOBY: That remark was just plain silly.

STELLA: Do you want to read?

TOBY: Read! I doubt if I shall ever be able to read again.

STELLA: I'll turn out the light then.

TOBY: It would make no appreciable difference to me if the light of the world went out. My mind is a trackless waste of impenetrable darkness.

STELLA: That's right, dear.

There is a pause. STELLA *switches out the bed light.*

TOBY: Stella—what *are* we to do?

STELLA: We'll deliver ourselves over to Olive bound and gagged in the morning. We'll meet her delighted, patronising contempt with fortitude—we'll humiliate ourselves without flinching—we'll add up how much we need and borrow it from her gaily, as though we enjoyed it—no matter how broken we are we'll never let her see——

TOBY (*drowsily*): Like Flora Macdonald.

STELLA: It was *not* Flora Macdonald!

THE LIGHTS FADE

SCENE III

The scene is the same about two hours later. Moonlight is streaming into the room.

> TOBY *and* STELLA *are fast asleep. There is a slight*

*noise on the verandah, a shadow falls across the moonlight.
A man steps softly into the room. His face is muffled.
He tiptoes across and trips over the stool in front of the
dressing-table.*

TOBY (*switching on the light*): Who's there?

STELLA (*waking*): Oh, dear!

STEVENS (*covering them with a revolver*): Keep quiet.

TOBY: Scream, dear, he wouldn't dare to shoot.

STELLA: Scream yourself.

STEVENS: Oh yes, I would.

TOBY: What do you want?

STEVENS: I want you to keep quiet.

TOBY: Naturally you do—I meant apart from that.

STEVENS: Where's your jewellery?

TOBY: Number 18, Rue Mirabeau, Cannes.

STELLA: We haven't a thing here—you've chosen
probably the worst room to burgle in the whole world.

STEVENS: Come on—tell me where it is.

> STELLA *makes a sudden movement; he switches his gun
> towards her.* TOBY *throws a pillow and knocks it out of
> his hand—he leaps out of bed, there is a scuffle and* TOBY
> *gets the revolver—he covers the man with it.*

TOBY: Now then!

STEVENS: Look out—it's loaded!

TOBY: I should damn well hope it was.

STELLA: Why aren't you French? We're in France—
you ought to be French.

TOBY: Take off his muffler, Stella. (*To* STEVENS.)
Keep your hands up.

STELLA (*approaching*): Excuse me.

TOBY: Keep them up.

> STELLA *undoes the scarf from round his mouth.*

STELLA: There now!

TOBY: Turn on the other lights, Stella.

STELLA (*doing so*): It's a very expensive scarf. (*She looks at the man.*) My God, it's Stevens!

STEVENS: Oh, madame!

STELLA: Stevens, how *could* you!

TOBY: You ought to be ashamed of yourself.

STEVENS: I had no idea, sir—madame—I didn't realise you was staying here.

STELLA: Did you really mean to burgle this house?

STEVENS: Yes, madame.

STELLA: But why? You can't suddenly become a burglar all in a minute—you were a respectable chauffeur last week.

STEVENS: That was before the crash came, madame.

TOBY: You mean it was before George Bainbridge threw you out.

STEVENS: Yes, sir.

STELLA (*reproachfully*): Oh, Stevens!

STEVENS: He sacked me straight away—without even a reference.

STELLA: You should have applied to Mrs. Bainbridge.

TOBY: Stella!

STEVENS: I'm desperate, madame—I haven't got a bob.

STELLA: That's no excuse for becoming a criminal.

STEVENS: It's the usual excuse—begging your pardon, madame.

STELLA: Do you mean to tell me Mrs. Bainbridge didn't give you so much as a——

TOBY: Stella, be quiet—your behaviour is in the worst possible taste.

STELLA: I think it's a dirty shame—you have my sympathy, Stevens.

STEVENS: Thank you, madame.

TOBY: You'd better get out, Stevens—I'll keep the gun, if you don't mind.

STEVENS: It belongs to Meadows, sir—Mr. Bainbridge's butler—I pinched it. If you wouldn't mind returning it to him I should be much obliged.

TOBY: We ought to hand you over to the police.

STEVENS: Oh, please don't do that, sir. I've had an awful time. I've got a wife and child in Walthamstow, I've got to get back somehow.

STELLA: We can't help you—we would if we could, but——

TOBY: Be quiet, Stella.

STEVENS: Thank you, madame—you're very kind.

TOBY: Go on—get out as quickly as you can.

STEVENS: Yes, sir. Thank you, sir.

TOBY: Go on.

STEVENS *goes to the window.*

STELLA: Stop!

TOBY: Stella!

STELLA: Come back a minute.

TOBY: Don't be an idiot, Stella.

STELLA: Leave this to me—I know what I'm doing.

TOBY: What are you talking about?

STELLA: Sit down, Stevens.

TOBY: Have you gone mad?

STELLA: Shut up—sit down, Stevens.

STEVENS (*bewildered*): Yes, madame. (*He sits down.*)

STELLA: Now then——

TOBY: Look here——

403

STELLA: Put that gun down, Toby, and don't keep on waving it about like pampas grass—Stevens may be a potential thief, but he isn't a murderer and even if he were, he wouldn't murder us, he likes us, don't you, Stevens?

STEVENS: Very much, madame.

STELLA: You seem to forget, Toby, that when we were staying with the Bainbridges in Scotland last September, Stevens lent you seven pounds.

TOBY: I paid it back.

STEVENS: You certainly did, sir; within the month.

STELLA: Do you trust us, Stevens?

STEVENS: Trust you, madame?

STELLA: Yes—I mean will you trust us if we trust you?

STEVENS: I don't understand, madame.

STELLA: I'll explain. We're broke—cleaned out.

STEVENS: Yes, madame.

STELLA: You're broke too—in addition to which you've involved yourself in one of the juiciest scandals the Riviera has known for years.

STEVENS: It wasn't my fault, madame—I——

STELLA: I never imagined for one moment that it was.

TOBY: Look here, Stella—what is the use——?

STELLA: Toby, don't be such a fool—don't you see!

TOBY: See what?

STELLA: God sent Stevens to us to-night, Toby—or it may have been Buddha, or Mahomet or Mary Baker Eddy, but whoever it was he's here hale and hearty and ready to help us—you are ready to help us, aren't you, Stevens!

STEVENS: Help you, madame?

STELLA: If you can help yourself at the same time.

STEVENS: Anything you say, madame—you can rely on me.

TOBY (*at last realising what she means*): Stella—we can't!

STELLA: We can—and we will.

TOBY: You're raving.

STELLA: I'd rather face prison than Olive's patronising sneer to-morrow morning.

STEVENS (*noticing* TOBY'S *wound*): Oh, sir, what have you done to your head?

TOBY: Never mind about that now.

STELLA: Mind about it—it's the most important thing in the world. You did it, Stevens—you knocked him out——

STEVENS: Oh, madame, I'd never do such a thing.

STELLA: Yes, you would—if you were an intelligent professional burglar you would—you'd knock him out; then you'd bind and gag us both—then you'd burgle the house and get away with the swag.

STEVENS: Swag, madame?

STELLA: That's what it's called.

STEVENS: What what's called, madame?

STELLA: The money that you're going to take from this house to-night.

STEVENS (*rising*): Oh, madame!

STELLA: Sit down and listen.

STEVENS *sinks back again*.

A few yards away from this room there is wrapped in plebeian slumber a lady from New Jersey called Mrs. Irving Brandt——

TOBY: Go on, darling—I'm with you.

STELLA: In the top right hand drawer of her dressing-table, just to the left of the door, there is a bundle of one hundred and seventy thousand francs——

STEVENS: Oh, dear!

STELLA: Halves, Stevens, halves!

STEVENS: Oh, madame—I don't think I dare.

TOBY: Be a man, Stevens.

STELLA: Go now—it's the last door on the right at the end of the passage.

TOBY: The carpet is ostentatiously soft, so you won't be heard.

STELLA: If by any chance she wakes up and screams, double back here and out of the window—I'll scream, too, and bathe my husband's head. If, on the other hand, you get away with it—come back here, give us half, tie us both up and get out.

STEVENS: All right, madame—I'll do it.

TOBY: Think of Walthamstow.

STELLA: Go on—last door on the right—dressing table on left of the door—top right hand drawer.

TOBY (*holding out his hand*): Good luck.

    STEVENS *shakes it.*

STELLA (*also shaking his hand*): Good luck, Stevens.

TOBY: Turn out the lights.

STELLA (*doing so*): There.

    STEVENS *slips out of the room. They listen anxiously*
    for a moment.

STELLA (*in a whisper*): Quick—get the bedclothes off the bed—and your dressing-gown cord——

TOBY (*also in a whisper*): My feet are cold.

STELLA (*wrestling with the bedclothes*): Put on your slippers.

TOBY (*doing so*): Handkerchiefs for gags.

    He rummages in the dressing-table drawers.

STELLA: Don't make such a row.

TOBY: My God!

STELLA: What is it?

TOBY: Stevens might bind and gag us and then take all the money.

STELLA: Don't be so absurd—he's utterly honest—you only have to look at him. His moral values may wobble a bit on the sex side, but otherwise I'm certain his integrity is beyond question. Why, he was a valet before he was a chauffeur—he's been trained as a gentleman's gentleman—they're always much more reliable than gentlemen.

TOBY: Hush!—did you hear anything?

STELLA: He's coming back.

> *They stand in silence for a moment.* STEVENS *creeps back into the room. He closes the door softly after him.*

Got it?

STEVENS: Yes.

STELLA: Switch on the bed-light, Toby.

TOBY (*doing so*): Was she asleep?

STEVENS: Snoring, sir.

STELLA: I'm *glad*!

STEVENS: Here you are, madame.

> *He flings the wad of notes on to the bed.*

TOBY: Come on—help divide them.

STEVENS: I'd rather not, sir, if you don't mind—I'd rather you had the money. I happened to find these on the dressing-table—they'll do me nicely.

> *He produces several diamond bracelets, some rings and a jewelled cigarette-case.*

STELLA: Stevens, for shame!—take them back at once!

TOBY: They can be traced.

STEVENS: I'll manage all right, sir.

STELLA: You must take half the money.

STEVENS: I'd really rather not.

TOBY: It's extraordinarily generous of you, Stevens.

STEVENS: You and Madame have always been very nice to me, sir—it feels somehow as if we was old friends.

STELLA: Thank you, Stevens.

TOBY (*giving him some bills*): Here, you must take these, for travelling expenses.

STEVENS: Very well, sir—if you insist.

TOBY: Where shall I put the rest?

STELLA: Put eleven thousand in the drawer and the rest in the inside pocket of your dinner-jacket.

STEVENS: Allow me, sir.

TOBY: Thank you, Stevens.

> STEVENS *puts some notes in the dressing-table drawer and stuffs the rest into* TOBY'S *dinner-coat; he then proceeds to fold it neatly and lay it on the chair.*

STELLA: Never mind about that now, Stevens—bind and gag us.

> *The following dialogue takes place while they are being bound and gagged.*

TOBY: Do you intend to go direct to England?

STEVENS: Yes, sir. I thought of going by boat from Marseilles. I've never seen Gibraltar.

TOBY: It's very impressive.

STELLA: The P. & O. boats always stop at Marseilles, don't they? I remember Blanche came home on one.

STEVENS: I think I shall try another Line this time, madame. I once went P. & O. as far as Egypt with Mr. Bainbridge—and I didn't fancy it.

TOBY: Why not, Stevens?

STEVENS: All them bugles got me down, sir—it was like being in the army all over again.

STELLA: You must look us up when you come to London—we might be able to help you to find a job.

STEVENS: Thank you, madame.

TOBY: We're in the book.

STEVENS: As a matter of fact, I've been thinking for a long time of giving up domestic service—I'd rather get a job that was more steady—more respectable, if you know what I mean.

STELLA: I couldn't know better.

STEVENS: I think my brother will be able to help me.

TOBY: Oh—what does he do?

STEVENS: He's got a very nice position in Barclay's Bank, sir.

TOBY: Oh, I see.

By this time they are both successfully tied to two chairs.

STEVENS: Now for the gags.

STELLA: They're on the dressing-table.

STEVENS politely gags them.

STEVENS: Let me know if they're too tight.

TOBY: They ought to be pretty tight.

STEVENS: I think we might allow ourselves a little poetic licence, don't you, sir?

TOBY: Thank you, Stevens.

STEVENS (*regarding them*): Quite comfy?

They both nod.

Light on or off?—One nod for on—two nods for off.

They both nod once.

Well, I'll be getting along now—thank you very much,

sir and madame—it's been a great pleasure meeting you again. Good-night.

He bows politely and goes out of the window.

They are left tied to the chairs. Behind their gags it is apparent that they are convulsed with laughter. STELLA *loosens her gag enough to speak.*

STELLA: If I'd been May Bainbridge, I'd have married him!

CURTAIN

THE ASTONISHED HEART

A Play in Six Scenes

from

TO-NIGHT AT 8.30

CHARACTERS:

CHRISTIAN FABER
BARBARA (his wife)
LEONORA VAIL
TIM VERNEY
SUSAN BIRCH
SIR REGINALD FRENCH
ERNEST

   The action of the entire play takes place in the drawing-room of the FABERS' *flat in London.*

SCENE I

The action of the entire play takes place in the drawing-room of the FABERS' *flat in London. The flat is on the top floor of one of the newly erected apartment buildings in the region of Hyde Park. The furniture is comfortable and good without conceding too much to prevailing fashion. On the left double doors lead to the hall, dining-room and* BARBARA'S *bedroom and bathroom, etc. On the right other double doors lead to* CHRISTIAN'S *part of the flat, his bedroom, consulting-room and office.*

When the curtain rises it is late afternoon in November 1935. The lights are on but the curtains have not been drawn and BARBARA *is standing looking out of the window into the foggy dusk. She is a tranquil, intelligent woman of about thirty-six or seven. Her back is to the room and she is drumming her fingers on the window pane.* SUSAN BIRCH *is seated on the sofa with her hands clasped on her lap. Her age is somewhere between thirty and forty and she is plainly and efficiently dressed as befits a secretary. She is sitting very still although occasionally she bites her lip nervously.* TIM VERNEY, *a nice-looking man in the early thirties, is standing in front of the fireplace on the right smoking a cigarette. There is an air of strain in the room as though any one of them might cry out at any moment. The silence is broken by* BARBARA.

BARBARA: It looks terribly dreary out, but it's like that anyhow, at this time of year, isn't it?

TIM: Yes.

BARBARA: The traffic seems slower than usual——
I expect that's my imagination.

TIM: Don't you think you'd better come away from
the window now?

BARBARA: Yes, I suppose I had.

> *She comes slowly down and sits on the sofa next to*
> SUSAN.

Don't worry, Tim, about the window I mean, it's
something we've got to get used to like everything else
—part of the whole thing.

TIM: Yes, I know.

BARBARA (*to* SUSAN): She answered the telephone
herself, didn't she?

SUSAN (*with an effort*): Yes.

BARBARA: She ought to be here by now.

SUSAN (*looking at her wrist-watch*): Yes—yes, she
ought.

BARBARA: I suppose Ernest would be shocked if we
had a cocktail, wouldn't he?

TIM: That doesn't matter.

BARBARA (*almost irritably*): I know it doesn't matter,
Tim, I was only thinking how funny it is that whether
Ernest should be shocked or not shocked, should come
into my mind at all—will you ring for him?

TIM: All right. (*He rings the bell by the fireplace.*)

BARBARA (*impulsively patting* SUSAN's *hand*): I expect
you think I'm talking too much.

SUSAN (*trying to smile*): No, I don't, dear.

BARBARA: Talking's useful, it makes a little noise but
not too much, just enough to distract the attention——

SUSAN: I know. (*She gets up.*)

BARBARA: What is it?

SUSAN: I thought perhaps I'd better go into the office.

BARBARA: No, don't, sit down again, stay with us.

SUSAN: Very well. (*She sits down again.*)

> ERNEST, *the butler, enters.*

ERNEST: You rang, madame?

BARBARA: Make a cocktail will you, Ernest, a Dry Martini I think, don't you, Tim?

TIM (*absently*): Yes, a Dry Martini.

ERNEST: Very good, madame.

BARBARA: When Mrs. Vail arrives—I'm—I'm expecting her—— (*Her voice breaks slightly.*)

ERNEST: Yes, madame.

> *He goes out.*

BARBARA: That was silly of me, wasn't it?—Unnecessary—he knew perfectly well we were expecting her——

TIM: She's probably held up in the traffic.

BARBARA: Yes, it's bad at this time of day—I'd like a cigarette, Susan, there's a box just by you.

> SUSAN *silently hands her the box and she takes a cigarette and lights it.*

TIM: Poor woman.

BARBARA: Leonora? Yes—it's awful for her.

SUSAN (*bitterly*): She'll get over it.

BARBARA: So shall we I expect—in time.

SUSAN: It doesn't matter to her, not really, not like it matters to us—she'll cry a lot and be beautifully heart-broken——

BARBARA: Don't be unkind.

SUSAN (*violently*): I hate her.

BARBARA (*turning away*): Oh, don't, Susan—what's the use of that——

SUSAN: I don't care whether it's any use or not—I hate her, more than I've ever hated anyone in my whole life——

BARBARA: You might just as well hate a piece of notepaper, because someone's written something cruel on it.

> SIR REGINALD FRENCH *comes through the double doors on the right. He is an authoritative, elderly surgeon.*

SIR REGINALD: She hasn't arrived yet?

TIM: She's on her way.

SIR REGINALD: Good. (*He turns to go again.*)

BARBARA: There isn't much time is there?

SIR REGINALD (*gently*): No, I'm afraid not.

BARBARA: Is he—conscious?

SIR REGINALD: Only for a brief moment, every now and then.

BARBARA: It's then that he asks for her? In those brief moments?

SIR REGINALD: Yes.

BARBARA: I'll send her straight in when she comes.

SIR REGINALD: Do, my dear.

> *He goes out.*

SUSAN: Oh God! (*She breaks down and cries softly.*)

BARBARA (*putting her arm round her*): Don't, dear.

TIM: Shut up, Susan.

SUSAN: I can't help it—it would have been much better if only you'd let me go into the office when I wanted to.

BARBARA: I'd rather you cried here with us than all by yourself in there.

SUSAN (*dabbing her eyes*): I'm all right now.

BARBARA: Don't make too much of an effort, Susan, it's a dreadful strain—I'd cry if I could—tears are fine, a

little relief—they let the grief out for a minute or two—
I envy them——

>ERNEST *enters with a tray on which is a cocktail-
shaker and four glasses.*

Here are the cocktails. Put them on the small table,
Ernest—Tim, you pour them out—thank you, Ernest.

>ERNEST *puts down the tray and goes out.* TIM *gives
the shaker a couple of extra shakes and pours out a
cocktail for each of them. They take them in silence.*

TIM (*drinking*): He's certainly made it dry enough.

BARBARA (*sipping hers and smiling faintly*): Strong
enough too—oh, dear——

>*There is the sound of the front door-bell. They all
jump slightly.*

TIM: Here she is—at last——

BARBARA (*suddenly*): How extraordinary—d'you see
what I mean? It's the same, exactly the same as a year
ago—you were there, Tim, just where you are now,
with a cocktail glass in your hand—you were there,
Susan, only you had your glasses on and a packet of
papers in your lap—don't you remember—the first time
she ever came into this room——?

>ERNEST *opens the door and announces:* MRS. VAIL
as the lights fade.

SCENE II

When the lights come up on the scene BARBARA, TIM, SUSAN
and ERNEST *are all in the same positions as the preceding
scene.* SUSAN *is wearing glasses and has a packet of
papers in her lap, her jumper is blue instead of grey.*

BARBARA *is wearing a tea gown.* TIM *is in the same suit but wearing a different tie.*

ERNEST (*announcing*): Mrs. Vail.

LEONORA VAIL *enters. She is a lovely creature of about thirty, exquisitely dressed and with great charm of manner.*

BARBARA (*greeting her*): My dear—after all these years——

LEONORA: Isn't it lovely?

They kiss affectionately.

BARBARA: Bring some fresh cocktails, Ernest.

ERNEST: Yes, madame.

He goes out.

BARBARA (*introducing her*): This is Susan Birch, Chris's right hand and this is Tim Verney, Chris's left hand—or perhaps it's the other way round—settle it among yourselves—Leonora Vail—Ames that was——

LEONORA: Leonora Ames, terrible at games! Do you remember?

BARBARA: Of course I do.

They both laugh.

LEONORA (*shaking hands with* SUSAN): How do you do?

SUSAN: How do you do?

LEONORA (*shaking hands with* TIM): I think Barbara wrote that beastly little rhyme herself.

TIM (*smiling*): Was it true?

LEONORA: Absolutely.

BARBARA: I can't possibly say you haven't changed a bit, you've changed more thoroughly than anyone I've ever seen——

LEONORA: Having our hair up makes a great difference.

418

BARBARA: Your voice has changed too, but I recognised it on the telephone.

LEONORA: I'd have known yours anywhere.

TIM: Have a cocktail, it's mostly water now—perhaps you'd rather wait for a fresh one.

LEONORA: That'll do beautifully to start with.

He pours out a cocktail and she holds it up towards
BARBARA.

The nastiest girl in the school.

BARBARA (*laughing*): But the best King Lear.

LEONORA (*also laughing*): Oh, of course—I'd forgotten that.

BARBARA: I foresee a flood of reminiscence.

TIM: So do I—come along, Susan, we'd better go.

BARBARA: No, don't go—you can bear it, Tim, you'll probably discover a lot of useful little psychological echoes from my childhood——

SUSAN (*rising*): I must go anyhow—all these have to be dealt with. (*She indicates the papers in her hand.*)

TIM: Is there a patient in there now?

SUSAN (*glancing at her watch*): Yes, but her time's nearly up.

LEONORA (*to* BARBARA): Does he work all day long, your husband?

BARBARA: Yes, most of the night as well sometimes.

LEONORA: What's he like?

BARBARA: Horrible.

LEONORA: I sympathise, mine was an absolute darling, so much so that I divorced him after eighteen months——

SUSAN: Good-bye, Mrs. Vail.

LEONORA: Good-bye.

TIM: We shall probably meet again very soon.

419

LEONORA: I hope so.

BARBARA: Tell Chris to come in for a second if he can when he's got rid of his patient.

TIM: All right.

He and SUSAN *go out.*

LEONORA: What a nice man.

BARBARA: Tim's a dear, he's extremely brilliant, too, Chris thinks the world of him.

LEONORA: He must be wonderful.

BARBARA: Who, Chris?

LEONORA: Yes, a little frightening though I should think.

BARBARA (*smiling*): Oh no, he's not in the least frightening—he gets a bit abstracted every now and then—when he's working too hard.

LEONORA: Dear Barbara, how nice this is—how long ago is it?——

BARBARA: Seventeen—no eighteen years—I'm thirty-five now, I left long before you did——

LEONORA: I remember missing you dreadfully.

BARBARA: It was after the war when you went to America?

LEONORA: Yes, just after. Father left Brazil in 1918 and at the beginning of 1919 we went to Washington.

BARBARA: When were you married?

LEONORA: Oh, a long while after, several years.

BARBARA: Was he really such a—a darling?

LEONORA: Oh, it was all horrid. He was much older than me, very rich—fortunately—that's all there was to it really.

BARBARA: And you never wanted to marry again?

LEONORA: I wanted to once, but it wasn't possible, everything went wrong——

420

ERNEST *comes in with fresh cocktails.*

BARBARA: I'm so sorry.

LEONORA: I minded horribly at the time but I travelled a bit and got over it, it's a long while ago anyhow.

BARBARA: How long have you been in England?

LEONORA: Only two weeks—I've got a darling little house, only rented of course, I moved in on Monday—when will you come and dine?

BARBARA: Whenever you like.

LEONORA: And your husband, Chris?

BARBARA: I'm sure he'd love to but it all depends, you can never count on him——

LEONORA: I'm longing to see him.

ERNEST *having deposited the cocktail shaker on the tray, goes out, taking with him the empty one.*

BARBARA: He'll probably come in soon for a moment.

LEONORA: Is it never more than a moment?

BARBARA: Oh, yes—not quite as bad as that—but being married to eminence requires a little forbearance, especially if the eminence is dear to you.

LEONORA: No holidays?

BARBARA: Yes—last year we got a full month—we went to Italy, Como first and then down to Venice, it was lovely. He got a bit restive during the last week, but I persuaded him to stay the course.

LEONORA: I should be jealous I think.

BARBARA: Jealous?

LEONORA: But you're better balanced than I am—less emotional—you always were——

BARBARA: It would be tiresome to go on being emotional after twelve years of marriage. (*She gives her a cocktail.*)

LEONORA: I don't really want another.

BARBARA: Come on—one more—I will too.

LEONORA: All right.

BARBARA: Old times. (*She drinks.*)

LEONORA: Old times. (*She drinks.*) What does he do exactly?

BARBARA: Chris?

LEONORA: Yes.

BARBARA (*gently*): He's only one of the most celebrated psychiatrists in the world, dear.

LEONORA (*laughing*): I know that—be patient with me—psychiatrist is only a word to me—it's nothing to do with bone-setting, is it?

BARBARA (*laughing too*): No, nothing whatever—you're thinking of osteopathy——

LEONORA: No, I'm not, it's something like psychiatrist—another word.

BARBARA: Chiropracter.

LEONORA: That's it.

BARBARA: You'd better not mention that to Chris, he doesn't approve of chiropracters at all——

LEONORA: What's a psychiatrist then?

BARBARA: Someone who cures diseases of the mind——

LEONORA: Oh, repressions and inhibitions and all that sort of thing.

BARBARA: Yes, all that sort of thing.

LEONORA: How exciting.

BARBARA: Yes, more interesting than exciting.

LEONORA: You have a superior look in your eye, Barbara, and I resent it deeply.

BARBARA: I'm sorry, dear.

LEONORA: I know I'm idiotic really, but it's most tactless of you to remind me of it. How does he start his treatments? Just a series of embarrassing questions?

BARBARA: Frightfully embarrassing.

LEONORA: I've read about it in books. You have to remember sinister little episodes of your childhood—falling in love with the cook—or being frightened by a goat—then you have to determine the cook or sublimate the goat or something, and you go away completely cured and sleep like a top.

BARBARA: I see that your ignorance was only an affectation, you have the whole thing in a nutshell.

LEONORA: It must be fascinating work, unearthing everybody's rattling little skeletons and fitting them together like Meccano. What about himself?

BARBARA: How do you mean?

LEONORA: Does he know all about himself right from the beginning? Is everything cut and dried and accounted for?

BARBARA: I expect so.

LEONORA: And you? Has he a chart of you hanging up over his desk?

BARBARA: He doesn't need a chart of me, Leonora.

LEONORA: Something in your manner tells me that I've gone too far—oh dear—I didn't meant to—don't be cross.

BARBARA (*smiling*): I'm not in the least cross.

LEONORA: I suppose he'd know all about me in a minute, wouldn't he? The very first second he clapped eyes on me.

BARBARA: Certainly.

LEONORA: How terrifying.

BARBARA: Don't pretend, Leonora, I'm perfectly sure you're not terrified of anyone.

LEONORA: Do his patients fall in love with him?

BARBARA: Practically always.

LEONORA: Don't you hate that?

BARBARA: You are funny, Leonora?

LEONORA: Am I? Nicely funny or nastily funny?

BARBARA: Charmingly funny.

LEONORA: Oh dear, I can't wait to see him, do tell someone to hurry him up, I shall have to go in a minute. He hasn't got a moustache, has he?

BARBARA: No.

LEONORA: Beard?

BARBARA: No beard.

LEONORA: Tall or short?

BARBARA: Short.

LEONORA: Fat?

BARBARA: Not exactly fat, let's say a little podgy.

LEONORA: Oh, Barbara!

BARBARA: He has very little chance of getting exercise you see, still he does his best with those things in the bathroom——

LEONORA (*horrified*): What things?

BARBARA: You know, they're attached to the wall and you gasp and strain and they snap back again—he has a rowing machine too.

LEONORA: I know, I've seen them in gymnasiums on ships.

BARBARA: He finds it very effective.

LEONORA: You're lying, aren't you?

BARBARA: Yes, Leonora.

LEONORA: I suppose he's eight feet high and absolutely bewitching.

BARBARA: If you care for long black moustaches, yes.

LEONORA: I've made up my mind to fall in love with him on sight.

424

BARBARA: He's quite used to that.

LEONORA: You're positively smug about him, Barbara—tell me seriously—do you really adore him?

BARBARA: I love him very much.

LEONORA: How marvellous. And does he love you?

BARBARA: Really, Leonora!

LEONORA: I know I'm behaving badly, but it seems so funny——

BARBARA: What seems so funny?

LEONORA: I know what I mean, but it's awfully difficult to explain.

BARBARA (*drily*): Don't try.

LEONORA: Darling, I think I'd like just another little sip if there's any more in the shaker——

BARBARA: It's practically full——

> BARBARA *refills her glass.* CHRISTIAN FABER *comes into the room. He is about forty years old, tall and thin. He moves quickly and decisively as though there was never quite enough time for all he had to do.*

LEONORA: At last!

CHRIS (*surprised*): What?

BARBARA: This is Mrs. Vail, Chris, one of my oldest friends, we were at school together——

CHRIS (*absently*): Oh—how do you do. (*He shakes hands.*)

BARBARA: Cocktail?

CHRIS: No, I've got some more work to do.

LEONORA: I think it only fair that you should know that until Barbara disillusioned me I thought that you were a chiropracter.

CHRIS (*smiling perfunctorily*): Did you really? (*To* BARBARA.) Listen, dear, we are dining with Mary to-night, aren't we?

BARBARA: Yes.

CHRIS: Well, you go without me and tell her I'll come in for coffee——

BARBARA (*laughing*): She knows that already, darling, she told me on the telephone this morning.

CHRIS (*with a smile*): Mary is one of the most sensible women I know.

LEONORA (*with slightly forced impudence*): I also thought you had a long moustache!

CHRIS (*not quite understanding*): What——?

BARBARA (*quickly*): Moustache, dear, Leonora thought you had a moustache.

CHRIS (*with a completely empty smile*): Oh, no—I haven't a moustache.

He bows politely and goes out.

LEONORA: I'd rather he was a chiropracter.

BARBARA: Never mind.

LEONORA: He didn't even see me, I do think it's a shame.

BARBARA: He saw you all right.

LEONORA: You're being superior again, how odious of you.

BARBARA: When do you want us to come and dine?

LEONORA: I shan't even ask him, I like the other young man much better, Tim whatever his name was, bring him instead—next Wednesday?

BARBARA (*going to her book on the desk*): Wait a minute.

LEONORA: Do you want to go to a play or just sit and talk?

BARBARA: I don't mind a bit, whichever you like— but I'd rather make it Thursday.

LEONORA: All right—Thursday—we'll decide whether to go out or not later.

BARBARA: That'll be lovely.

LEONORA: I really must go now——

BARBARA: You're sure you wouldn't like to stay and have your bones set or anything?

LEONORA: No, I've given up the whole idea.

BARBARA: What whole idea?

LEONORA: About falling madly in love with your husband and him falling madly in love with me and then me having a lovely 'old friends together' scene with you and everyone behaving beautifully and making sacrifices all round——

BARBARA: You were always romantic, even at school, do you remember Monsieur Brachet?

LEONORA: I adored him, didn't I? But still he was rather sweet.

BARBARA: His eyes were very close together.

LEONORA: Practically two in one, darling, but charm —that's what counts, darling——

BARBARA: What's your telephone number?

LEONORA: You're not going to put me off, are you?

BARBARA: Don't be so silly, of course not.

LEONORA: Kensington 3382.

BARBARA (*scribbling it down*): Kensington 3382.

LEONORA: I'll expect you on Thursday—about eight.

BARBARA: Do you really want me to ask Tim?

LEONORA: Of course, he's an angel, and bring your old chiropodist too if he'll come——

BARBARA (*laughing, as they go out*): I'll try to persuade him——

427

Their voices are heard talking and laughing in the hall. TIM *comes in and goes over to the desk, he rummages about on it.* BARBARA *returns.*

BARBARA: Oh, Tim, you made me jump. What are you doing?

TIM: Is there a Bible in the house?

BARBARA: I suppose there must be somewhere. Whatever do you want it for?

TIM: Chris wants a quotation to use in his lecture on Friday——

BARBARA: Does he know a special one——?

TIM: Vaguely—something in Deuteronomy——

ERNEST *enters.*

BARBARA: Have you got a Bible, Ernest?

ERNEST: I think the cook has one, madame.

BARBARA: Ask her if she'll lend it to me for a minute, will you?

ERNEST: Very good, madame.

He goes out.

BARBARA: Isn't she lovely?

TIM: Who? The cook?

BARBARA: No, don't be so silly, Leonora.

TIM: Very smooth and shiny.

BARBARA: Didn't you like her?

TIM: Yes, I suppose so, I only saw her for a moment.

BARBARA: She loved you at first sight, she wants you to dine with her on Thursday.

TIM: Good God!

BARBARA: It's all right, I shall be there to protect you.

TIM: I hate dinner parties.

BARBARA: You mustn't be disagreeable.

ERNEST *re-enters with a Bible.*

Ah, thank you, Ernest.

ERNEST: Have you finished with the cocktail things, madame?

BARBARA: Yes, thank you.

ERNEST *takes the cocktail tray away as* SUSAN *enters.*

SUSAN: Did you find one?

TIM: Yes, it's the cook's.

SUSAN: It's Moses, Deuteronomy twenty something—— It starts with "The Lord shall smite thee——"

They look through the Bible together.

SUSAN (*to* BARBARA): It's for his paper on the Development of Psychopathology starting with Hippocrates——

TIM: This must be it—— (*He reads.*) "The Lord shall smite thee with madness, and blindness, and astonishment of the heart."

SUSAN: Yes, that's it.

She takes the Bible and goes off as the lights fade.

SCENE III

When the lights come up on the scene, CHRIS *and* LEONORA *are discovered standing by the fireplace, his arms are round her and he is kissing her. She is wearing a diaphanous evening gown, he, a dinner jacket. About two months have passed since the preceding scene. The time is after midnight. There is a tray of sandwiches and drinks on the small table by the sofa. She detaches herself from his arms and moves away.*

LEONORA (*in a strained voice*): I must go.

CHRIS (*quietly*): Must you?

LEONORA: Of course.

CHRIS: Isn't that rather inconsistent?

LEONORA: Yes—I suppose it is.

CHRIS: What's the matter?

LEONORA: I didn't mean it to be like this——

CHRIS: Don't go away from me yet.

LEONORA: I must.

CHRIS: Do you want to?

LEONORA (*softly*): No.

CHRIS: Come back to my arms, it's cold over here by the fire.

LEONORA (*with her face turned away from him*): I lied just now when I said I didn't mean it to be like this.

CHRIS: Does it matter?

LEONORA: Yes—it matters dreadfully——

CHRIS (*moving towards her*): My dear——

LEONORA (*with panic in her voice*): Please stay there.

CHRIS (*stopping*): Very well.

LEONORA (*with a rush*): I did mean it to be like this but—but not quite like this—I mean—it was all a trick—I planned it—the first day I came, you remember, when you snubbed me—I teased you about it at dinner to-night—I made up my mind then to make you fall in love with me—now I wish I hadn't—I feel cheap—I feel frightened—I wish with all my heart I hadn't.

CHRIS (*with a smile*): I think it was rather a gay trick. Don't be upset. There's nothing to be upset about. Let's sit down quietly and have a drink.

He comes over to the sofa and pours out a drink.

Will you have one?

LEONORA: No, thank you.

CHRIS (*sitting*): Do come and sit down.

LEONORA: Now you're treating me like a patient.

CHRIS: Only because you're behaving like one.

LEONORA: I see. (*She laughs suddenly.*)

CHRIS: That's better.

LEONORA: Give me a cigarette. (*She sits down next to him.*)

CHRIS: Here. (*He lights one for her.*) You're a lovely creature.

LEONORA: I'm all right outside, but I'm not very pleased with myself inside at the moment.

CHRIS: Pangs of conscience are tiresome, Leonora, they're also exceedingly bad for you.

LEONORA: I'm feeling better now.

CHRIS: I gather that the trick is on again.

LEONORA (*sharply*): That was unkind.

CHRIS: You're very touchy.

LEONORA: What about Barbara?

CHRIS: She's very well, thank you—I had a letter from her this morning.

LEONORA: Are you in love with her?

CHRIS: What on earth did you say that for?

LEONORA: Are you in love with her?

CHRIS: You're behaving like a patient again.

LEONORA: Are you?

CHRIS: Barbara has nothing to do with this.

LEONORA: You're certainly not in love with me.

CHRIS: You have lovely eyes, but there's a little sadness in them, a little disappointment, I could tell your fortune by your eyes—shall I?

LEONORA: I'd rather you didn't.

CHRIS: And your nose——

LEONORA: I'd rather you didn't mention my nose at all.

CHRIS: It's the most unwise nose I've ever seen.

LEONORA: Do stop.

CHRIS: Then there's your mouth——

LEONORA: I must go——

CHRIS: You'd be astounded if you knew how desperately I want to kiss your mouth—again——

LEONORA: Please, Chris——

CHRIS: You're so foolish, up on your romantic high horse—how often have you ridden it wildly until it went lame and you had to walk home?

LEONORA: Often enough to teach me never to do it again.

CHRIS: That's what made the sadness in your eyes— you should never have left school, it was a grave mistake.

LEONORA: You win.

CHRIS: Do I?

LEONORA: I knew you would—quite early in the evening I knew.

CHRIS: Has it been a happy evening—for you?

LEONORA: No, not really—rather strained.

CHRIS: Were you really angry—that first time we met?

LEONORA: Yes—I think I was.

CHRIS: I didn't mean to be rude.

LEONORA: You certainly did.

CHRIS: Yes, now I come to think of it, I did.

LEONORA: Why?

CHRIS: You irritated me, you were so conscious of how absolutely beautiful you looked.

LEONORA: I never thought that.

CHRIS: Your manner demanded attention insistently, like a child banging its spoon on the table, making a clamour—yelling for more· ——

LEONORA: How horrid that sounds.

CHRIS: Quite natural though, I expect you've always been spoilt.

LEONORA: No, I haven't.

CHRIS: Have you had many lovers?

LEONORA (*looking down*): No—not many.

CHRIS: And the few—whoever they were—did you love them?

LEONORA: Please don't be quite so—clinical.

CHRIS (*impulsively*): Forgive me—I wanted to know.

LEONORA: I loved somebody once—very much— never so much before—and never so much since.

CHRIS: I see.

LEONORA: I know you think my conscience is tiresome and, considering how obviously I threw myself at you, a trifle ill-timed, but it's there all the same and it's making me uneasy—— Please listen, I'm being really honest now—if you and I had an—an affair—how much would it hurt Barbara?

CHRIS: I don't know. If she knew, I expect it would upset her a good deal, but it would upset her just as much, if not more, if she thought we wanted to and were denying ourselves on her account. Barbara's that sort of person.

LEONORA: You have been married twelve years.

CHRIS: How naïve you are.

LEONORA: Do you love her? You never answered me before.

CHRIS: Yes, I love her deeply and truly and for ever.

LEONORA: I see.

CHRIS: I don't suppose you do, but it doesn't matter.

433

LEONORA: It matters a lot.

CHRIS: What do you want? Truth or lies—reality or pretence?

LEONORA: How clever of you to know, without looking, what you have in your safe.

CHRIS: Don't be unkind to me, Leonora.

LEONORA: It's you who are unkind to me.

CHRIS: Why? In what way?

LEONORA: It's my own fault of course——

CHRIS: Entirely.

LEONORA: If you feel that it would make our—our flirtation any more satisfactory, I have some X-ray plates of my teeth.

CHRIS: Stop being quarrelsome, Leonora.

LEONORA: I can't help it, you make me angry— horribly angry—I want to hit out at you.

CHRIS: Any other impulse at this particular stage of the proceedings would be abnormal.

LEONORA: You're so superbly sure of yourself, aren't you?

CHRIS (*seriously*): No, the basis of everything I've ever learned is not being sure—not being sure of any-one or anything in the world—myself least of all—— (*He turns away.*)

LEONORA: Hand me my bag, it's just behind you.

CHRIS: What for?

LEONORA: I want to powder my—unwise nose.

CHRIS (*handing it to her*): Here.

LEONORA: Thank you.

> *She opens her bag and scrutinises herself in the glass inside it. She puts on some lipstick and powders her nose.* CHRIS *watches her.*

CHRIS: There's a bit of fluff on the left.

LEONORA: I can see it.

CHRIS: You mustn't be ungracious.

LEONORA: I want to go home now. (*She rises.*)

CHRIS (*also rising*): I'll take you—there's always a taxi on the rank.

LEONORA: Please don't, I'd really rather you didn't.

CHRIS: You must be mad as a hatter.

LEONORA: Why—what do you mean?

CHRIS: To imagine—— Oh, what's the use——

> *He suddenly crushes her in his arms and kisses her violently.*

LEONORA: Don't—please, Chris—don't—— (*She struggles.*)

CHRIS (*pressing her to him*): Don't be unkind—I want you dreadfully—you must know that—don't leave me —not just yet—it wasn't all a trick—it may have started as a trick, but it isn't that now, is it? Is it?

LEONORA (*breaking away from him, breathlessly*): Yes— yes it is.

CHRIS: Liar. (*He takes her hand.*) Look at me.

LEONORA (*near tears*): No. (*She turns away.*)

CHRIS: Please.

> *He turns her slowly and looks into her eyes.*

LEONORA (*in a whisper*): Well—what's my fortune?

CHRIS: You're going to love me a little.

LEONORA (*shaking her head*): That's not enough.

CHRIS: Oh, yes—yes—more than enough.

LEONORA: Are you sure?

CHRIS: Oh, my dear—my dear——

> *She slips into his arms again as the lights fade on the scene.*

SCENE IV

It is now April, three months having passed since the preceding scene. The time is about five or six a.m.

There is a greyness in the room because dawn is not far away.

BARBARA *is sitting in a chair by the fire smoking a cigarette. She is wearing a dressing-gown, and there is an ash-tray by her side, almost filled with cigarette ends. She shivers slightly, then gets up and pours herself a brandy and soda; she returns to her chair and then her attention is caught by the sound of the front door opening softly. She closes her eyes for an instant and bites her lip as though she were trying to gather courage.*

CHRIS *comes quietly in from the left; he is wearing a light overcoat and hat. His face is tired and strained.*

BARBARA (*in as ordinary a voice as she can manage*): Hallo, darling!

CHRIS (*startled*): Barbara!

BARBARA: I'm sorry if I made you jump.

CHRIS: What on earth——?

BARBARA: I couldn't sleep.

CHRIS (*switching on the lights*): Oh, I see——

BARBARA: Not all the lights, Chris.

CHRIS: All right. (*He switches on the desk light and turns the others off again.*)

BARBARA: Would you like a drink?

CHRIS: No—no, thanks.

BARBARA: I'm having one—it's—it's a bit chilly.

CHRIS (*in a flat voice*): I'm awfully sorry, darling.

BARBARA: There isn't anything to be sorry for—I

436

mean this isn't a scene—really it isn't, only I do want to talk to you. I've wanted to for a long while.

CHRIS: I know.

BARBARA: It's probably a bad moment, but—but during the day it's difficult—there never seems to be any time——

CHRIS: I meant it when I said I was sorry—I am—desperately sorry.

BARBARA: Of course you are. Don't be silly—I know that—it's all beastly—I'm sorry, too, I'm sorry for you and me and—I'm even sorry for Leonora—— (*She gives a little laugh.*)

CHRIS (*noticing the ash-tray*): Have you smoked all those to-night?

BARBARA: Yes—it looks awfully unattractive, doesn't it—like after a party—— (*She empties the ash-tray into the fireplace.*)

CHRIS (*looking away from her*): You know about me loving you all the same, don't you—more than anybody in the world?

BARBARA: Yes, of course I do, but I'd rather you didn't go on about it just at the moment. I want so very much not to be emotional.

CHRIS: Are you very unhappy?

BARBARA: Not any more than you, I don't suppose. That's the worst of the whole business, nobody's having a good time. How is Leonora?

CHRIS: She's all right, I've just left her.

BARBARA: I didn't imagine you'd been to a Masonic dinner, darling.

CHRIS (*smiling wryly*): No, I didn't think you did.

BARBARA: I hate her quite normally with all my feminine instincts; sometimes I get almost violent, all

437

by myself—it's funny, isn't it, after so many years?—
I've got over wishing to strangle her, though, now; I
just wish she'd never been born.

CHRIS: I think I do, too.

BARBARA: I don't see how we can go on like this
quite, do you? It really is too uncomfortable—that's
why I sat up for you. I'm dreadfully worried, the
personal, loving you part of the affair I could manage, I
think—painful as it is—but it's everything else, too—
we're all in a state, Tim and Susan—I think even
Ernest's getting a bit agitated—— (*She laughs again
nervously.*) You're working under such tremendous
pressure, and you're so terribly strained and tired—
we're all frightened that you'll crack up or something.

CHRIS: Don't worry, I shan't crack up.

BARBARA: Do you want to marry her?

CHRIS: No—it isn't anything to do with marriage.

BARBARA: Does she want you to marry her?

CHRIS: No, I don't think so—no, I'm sure she
doesn't.

BARBARA: I can't see why that should make me feel a
bit better, but it does.

CHRIS: Oh, Baba—— (*He breaks off miserably.*)

BARBARA (*brightly*): And I'll trouble you not to call
me Baba just now, darling—as a psychologist you really
ought to know better.

CHRIS (*trying to smile at her*): All right.

BARBARA: I have a plan, you know, otherwise I
wouldn't have pounced like this, but before I tell you
what it is, I want to know a little more.

CHRIS: Very well, fire away.

BARBARA: First of all, how clearly do you see the
situation in your more detached moments, I mean?

CHRIS: Quite clearly, but the detached moments are getting rarer, I'm afraid.

BARBARA: Can you be detached now?

CHRIS: I'm trying with all my might.

BARBARA: Don't worry about me, please don't! I can tread water indefinitely—it would be different if I were still in love with you, but I'm not, any more than you are with me; that was all settled years ago. We are tremendously necessary to each other, though, and I hope to God we always shall be, and I want to know—I want to know—— (*Her voice breaks.*)

CHRIS: How long?

BARBARA (*with control*): Yes.

CHRIS: I'm submerged now—I can't tell.

BARBARA: Very well then, you must go away.

CHRIS: Go away! How can I?

BARBARA: You must.

CHRIS: I've thought of it. I wanted to but it's quite impossible, also even if I could, even if there wasn't work or anything to prevent me, it wouldn't be any use —running away never is any use.

BARBARA: I didn't mean you to go away alone, it's too late for that now. I meant you to go away with her —take two months, three months if necessary—go to the most lovely, beautiful place you can think of— relax utterly—give yourself up to loving her without any sense of strain or responsibility—don't think about work or me or any of the things that are standing in the way——

CHRIS: I can't, Baba, you know I can't.

BARBARA: I don't know anything of the sort. It's clear, cold sense. I'm not being noble and self-sacrificing and thinking only of your happiness. I'm

439

thinking of my own happiness too, and, more important still, of your job—you can't deal wisely and successfully with twisted nerve-strained people if you're twisted and nerve-strained yourself. You must see that. It isn't your passion for Leonora alone that's undermining you, it's the fight you're putting up, you're being torn in half——

CHRIS: Darling, you're making me so dreadfully ashamed.

BARBARA: That's idiotic, unreasonable and idiotic. You said just now that you were submerged—that's true, you are; you've crushed down your emotions for years, and now you're paying for it. It's nothing to be ashamed of, with your sort of temperament it was inevitable—it had to happen, I've been waiting for it.

CHRIS: Baba!

BARBARA: Let me go on. I'm not submerged, I'm seeing the whole thing clearly—unless you put a stop to this agonising battle between your emotions and your intelligence, you'll break completely.

CHRIS (*tortured*): How can I put a stop to it? It's there—it's there all the time—every moment of the day and night—it started so easily, so gaily—little more than a joke; there were no danger signals whatever. I felt just a few conscience pangs over you, but not seriously, the whole thing was so apart from us and all we mean to each other—my intelligence lied to me—my intelligence insisted that it was nothing, just a little emotional flutter that would probably loosen me up and do me a power of good; then suddenly I felt myself being swept away and I started to struggle, but the tide was stronger than I knew; now I'm far from the land, darling—far from my life and you and safety—I'm struggling still, but the water's terribly deep and I'm frightened—I'm frightened. (*He comes close to her and puts his head down on her shoulder.*)

BARBARA (*gently*): I know—I really do know——

CHRIS: It isn't Leonora, it's nothing to do with Leonora any more; it's the thing itself—her face and her body and her charm make a frame, but the picture's in me, before my eyes constantly, and I can't get it out——

BARBARA: Stop struggling.

CHRIS: I can't! If I stop struggling I shall be lost for ever. If I didn't know all the processes it would be easier, but I do—I watch myself all the time—when I'm talking to patients—in case I make a slip; it's as much as I can do sometimes to prevent myself from suddenly shrieking in their faces—'Why are you here? What do you come to me for? How can I help you when there's a little brooch between us—a little brooch with emeralds and sapphires that someone gave to Leonora years ago —long before I ever knew her—how can I ease your poor mind when a handsome young man is burnt to death in a plane—here in the room—he was the one she really loved, you know, the only one she ever really loved——'

BARBARA: Oh, my dear—oh, my poor dear!

CHRIS (*with a great effort at control*): Tim and Susan are fine--their behaviour's almost too good. There's no reproach in their eyes, just a concentrated determination to bolster me up as much as they can. Nurse Hoskins is not so good—she ushers in the patients warily now—I think she listens outside the door, too, in case of accidents. Then there's Leonora herself—she's having a hell of a time. The ecstasy's still there—just for a few

441

flaming moments—but in between there are bad hours.
You see, I'm finding out things all the time—things
about her and things about myself. We're seldom alone
together—the ghosts of the people she loved before, or
thought she loved, come and join us—they make me
sick with jealousy, Baba—me of all people. We can
laugh about that one day, can't we? I ask her questions,
you see, because I can't stop myself—and out of her
answers the scenes build themselves—and it's those
dead moments that torture me. Can you imagine the
foolishness of that? Things that happened years ago
long before I even knew she existed—then I lose control
and say dreadful cruel things to her. I distort her
memories for her, smear them with mockery, dissect
them in front of her until they're spoilt and broken into
little pieces. Then she cries, not false crying, but real
tears for something that's lost . . . and all the time my
brain's raising its eyebrows at me and sneering, and then
the only thing left is to be sorry—humbly bitterly sorry
—and swear never again to be unkind—never, never,
never again—until the next time——

    *He leaves her and goes over to the window. She
watches him and then takes a cigarette and lights it.*

BARBARA (*quietly*): It's only the strain that makes all
that, darling. I wish I could make you see. If only I
could get it into your head that there is no reason in the
world why you shouldn't love Leonora as much as you
want to—for as long as it lasts—you'd be able to give
yourself up to it and be happy—you'd probably have
quarrels—one always does—but they'd be normal ones,
not these dreadful twisted agonies. You must do as I
say—it's your only chance. Let Tim take over everything for three months; he can manage all right with

Susan. Wipe me from your mind entirely; I shall go away somewhere myself. Laura's in Paris, I can go and stay with her, and Mary's taken the Birrels' house in Kent for six months. It's absolutely lovely and I shall be so much happier than I am now, if only I know you're being sensible and giving yourself space.

CHRIS: Space?

BARBARA: Room to enjoy the best parts of it, without that horrid feeling of hours passing—without the consciousness that there's work to be done the next day and people to see and decisions to make.

CHRIS: It sounds easy, but it wouldn't be.

BARBARA: After a week or so it would, really—I know I'm right—anyhow it's worth trying.

CHRIS: It is running away all the same——

BARBARA: What on earth does that matter? It's being wise that matters. Take the car—don't stop too long in one place, forget everything but just what you're doing at the moment. You really must try it, darling—you see, I've had time to think and you haven't had any time at all.

CHRIS: You don't hate her, do you?

BARBARA (*suddenly angry*): Good God! what does it matter if I do!

CHRIS: I'm sorry.

BARBARA: I'm fighting for you. Leonora's only on the fringe of the business. It's you and me that make my world and the work you've got to do, and the happiness we've had and can have again. My jealousy is not for the desire you have for her, nor for the hours of illusion you buy from her. I'm jealous of the time in between—the waste—those bad hours you told me about just now. I sense futility in all that, and it's that

443

futility that's nagging at you and humiliating you so. Stop trying to balance yourself—come off your tight-rope, it's better to climb down than fall down, isn't it?

CHRIS: It's bitter, isn't it, to be made to put on rompers again at my age?

BARBARA: Whether you intended it or not, that remark was definitely funny.

CHRIS: I miss not being able to laugh.

BARBARA: That'll all come back.

CHRIS: Just at this moment—this now—this immediate moment I'm all right, you know—I expect it's because you're so strong.

BARBARA: Well, make the most of it.

CHRIS: You needn't tell me it won't last, I know that.

BARBARA: Hang on to it anyhow as long as you can, even when you're submerged again, try to remember it.

CHRIS: Have you ever loved anyone else, since me?

BARBARA: No, I've never happened to want to.

CHRIS: Would you have, if you had wanted to, I mean?

BARBARA (*lightly*): I expect so.

CHRIS: I wonder how much I should mind.

BARBARA: Do stop whirling about among fictions, there are enough facts to occupy us, God knows. Go away—offer yourself up—get on with it.

CHRIS: It all seems so unreal!

BARBARA: It's real enough to make us damned uncomfortable!

CHRIS (*turning*): I don't believe I really love her at all.

BARBARA: This is no moment to go into a technical argument about that, my sweet. Love is a very comprehensive term, you're certainly obsessed, by her, or

444

by yourself through her, and that's quite enough.   Oh, dear, it's more than enough—— (*She gives a little laugh.*) Please, Chris——

CHRIS: All right.

BARBARA (*cheerfully*): Well, that's settled—we'll lash Tim into a frenzy of responsibility to-morrow—I mean to-day—you'd better try to get some sleep now.

CHRIS: Yes—I'll try.

BARBARA: Good morning, darling—— (*She puts her arms round him, kisses him lightly and goes quickly out of the room.*)

CHRIS (*as the door closes on her*):   Thank you, Baba.

> He leans against the window with his head in his arms as the lights fade.

SCENE V

Seven months have passed since the preceding scene.   It is midnight on the night before the first scene of the play.

When the lights go up on the scene LEONORA *is lying face downwards on the sofa, sobbing.* CHRIS *is leaning on the mantelpiece gazing into the fire.*

CHRIS: For the love of God stop crying. (*She continues to sob.*)   I'm sorry—I've said I was sorry——

LEONORA: I can't bear any more.

CHRIS (*coming over to her*): Darling, please——

LEONORA: Don't—don't come near me.

CHRIS: You must forgive me—you must!

LEONORA (*slowly sitting up*): It isn't forgiving—it's that I can't bear any more.   I mean it this time—I really can't!

CHRIS (*bitterly*): I should like to know what you propose to do then.

LEONORA: I'm going—I'm going away for good.

CHRIS: I see.

LEONORA (*rising*): I'm going now——

CHRIS (*holding her arms*): No, you're not.

LEONORA: Please, Chris——

CHRIS: You can't possibly go.

LEONORA: You're hurting me.

CHRIS (*coldly*): Why do you struggle then?

LEONORA: Don't be such a fool, what's the use of behaving like this?

CHRIS: I was under the impression that you loved me——

LEONORA: Let go of my arms.

CHRIS: More than anyone or anything in the world. How long ago was that you said that to me—how long ago—answer me . . . (*He shakes her.*)

LEONORA (*crying again*): Oh, for God's sake, Chris——

CHRIS: You love me so much that you have to lie to me—you love me so much that you play small shabby little tricks on me—you twist me and torture me until I'm driven beyond endurance—then you sob and cry and say I'm cruel.

LEONORA (*almost screaming*): Let me go!

CHRIS: Stay still——

LEONORA (*frantically*): You're mad—don't look at me like that—you're mad——

CHRIS (*grimly*): Answer me one question, my darling—my dear darling——

LEONORA: Let me go—let me go!

CHRIS: Why did you say you hadn't been out to dine with him when you had?

LEONORA: Because I knew you'd make a dreadful scene about it.

CHRIS: Why didn't you stay the night with him then —you wanted to, didn't you? What held you back? Your love for me! Or was it fear——?

LEONORA (*wrenching herself free from him*): Oh, what's the use—what's the use——

CHRIS (*brokenly*): Do you think I like this situation? You not loving me any more, and me wanting you so——

LEONORA (*turning*): Why do you say that—you've worked it all up in your imagination. None of it's true —none of it's real.

CHRIS: Don't lie any more.

LEONORA: I'm not—I'm not.

CHRIS: How do I know? You've lied before—I've caught you out, trivial enough they were, I grant you, but they were lies all the same—little lies or big lies— what's the difference? Perhaps you forget that charming little episode in Cairo——

LEONORA: Oh, God!

CHRIS: All right—all right. I know I'm dragging things up from the past—why shouldn't I? After all, the past held portents enough—sign-posts pointing to the present—this present now—this dreary misery.

LEONORA (*with a great effort to be calm*): Listen, Chris, I want to go away for a little. I must— I've told you—I really can't bear any more.

CHRIS: You can't bear any more! What about me?

LEONORA: It's not my fault that you imagine things and torture yourself.

447

CHRIS: Tell me one thing—without lying or evading—tell me one thing honestly——

LEONORA (*wearily*): What is it?

CHRIS: Do you still—love me?

LEONORA: Oh, Chris! (*She turns away hopelessly.*)

CHRIS: Do you?

LEONORA (*tonelessly*): Yes.

CHRIS: As much as you did in the beginning?

LEONORA: Differently, Chris, things have changed—a year has gone by since the beginning.

CHRIS: That's an evasion.

LEONORA: It's the truth—nothing stays the same.

CHRIS: You wanted me in the beginning, didn't you? Whenever I came near you—whenever I touched you—it was more important than anything in the world, wasn't it?

LEONORA: Yes—it was.

CHRIS: And now it isn't any more?

LEONORA: Chris—what's the use of——

CHRIS: Answer me!

LEONORA (*quivering*): What do you want me to say—I'll answer—I'll say whatever you want.

CHRIS: I want the truth.

LEONORA: There isn't any truth anywhere—you've smashed everything into bits——

CHRIS: Do you love me as much as you did in the beginning?

LEONORA (*violently*): No—no—no!

CHRIS: At last!

LEONORA: That's what you wanted, isn't it?—the truth—that's the truth!

CHRIS: Then you have been lying—for weeks—for months probably——

LEONORA: Yes, I have—I have.

CHRIS: When did it die, this poor shabby love of yours?

LEONORA (*wildly*): A long while ago—you strangled it yourself with your insane jealousies and cruelties. You never trusted me—never for a minute—you've spoiled hours that could have been perfect by making scenes out of nothing. You've humiliated me and shamed me—you've dug up things that were once dear to me and made them look cheap and horrible. I can't even go back into my own memory now without finding you there jeering on every threshold—walking with me through the empty rooms—making them tawdry—shutting them off from me for ever. I hate you for that bitterly.

CHRIS: Sentiment for the dead at the expense of the living—very interesting—quite magnificent!

LEONORA: The dead at least have the sense to be quiet.

CHRIS: Long live the dead!

LEONORA (*with bitterness*): You are one of them now.

> *There is a dreadful silence for a moment. They stand quite still looking at each other.*

CHRIS (*quietly*): Did you mean that?

LEONORA (*hesitantly*): Yes—I think I did.

CHRIS: Oh—please—please don't mean that!

LEONORA: Let me go away now.

CHRIS: Couldn't you wait another minute?

LEONORA: It isn't any use—you know it isn't.

CHRIS: Very well.

LEONORA: Good-bye, Chris.

CHRIS: I love you, my darling.

LEONORA: No, it's not love, it hasn't anything to do with love.

CHRIS: I know it's over now—I really do—I won't make any more scenes.

LEONORA: Good-bye.

She goes to him slowly and kisses him—he crushes her in his arms.

CHRIS (*hoarsely*): Is it quite dead—quite dead?

LEONORA (*struggling*): Don't, Chris—please!

CHRIS: All passion spent—everything tidied up and put back in the box.

LEONORA: Let me go.

CHRIS: The last time I shall kiss you—the last time I shall feel you in my arms—the very last time of all——

LEONORA (*trying to twist away from him*): Chris——

CHRIS: Stay still!

LEONORA: Let me go!

CHRIS: God damn you, stay still!

He kisses her again violently and throws her away from him. She staggers and falls.

How does it feel to be so desirable—to be wanted so much—tell me, please—I want to know—I want to know what your heart's doing now, your loving female heart! How enviable to be able to walk away into the future, free of love, free of longing, a new life before you and the dead behind you—not quite the dead, though, let's say the dying—the dying aren't as sensibly quiet as the dead—they can't help crying a little—you must walk swiftly out of earshot and don't—don't, I implore you, look back, it would make too dreary a picture for your neat, sentimental memory book. There's little charm in dying—it's only clinically interesting—the process of defeat, but your viewpoint is far from clinical, my sweet—you're a sane, thrilling animal without complications, and the fact that my life has been broken on your loveliness isn't your fault. I don't believe it's even mine—it's an act of God, darling, like fire and wind and pestilence. You're in on a grand tragedy, the best tragedy of all, and the best joke, the triumphant, inevitable defeat of mind by matter! Just for a minute I'm seeing it all clearly, myself and you and the world around us—but it's only a last flare, like a Verey light shooting through the sky, it'll splutter out in a second leaving everything darker than before, for me too dark to bear. You see, I had a life to live and work to do and people to love, and now I haven't any more. They're eager to help, those people I loved and who love me. I can see them still, gentle and wise and understanding, trying to get to me, straining to clutch my hand, but it's too late—they can't reach me. . . . Get up and go—it doesn't matter any more to me whether you're here or in the moon. Get up and go——

LEONORA *rises to her feet. She is trembling.* CHRIS *goes over to the window and stands there with his back to her.*

She takes her bag from the table, and goes quietly out of the room, closing the door behind her.

CHRIS *turns at the sound of the door closing and stands tense and quivering waiting for the front door to slam. When it does he starts to walk about the room. He goes to the table and pours out a tumbler of neat whisky. He drinks it down in one gulp and chokes a little. He pours himself another and drinks it, then he sits down for a moment, waiting for it to have some effect. Suddenly he stands up, then the tension of his muscles relaxes and with infinite weariness he goes to the window, opens it wide, climbs on to the sill and drops.*

The lights fade on the scene.

451

SCENE VI

This scene is the continuation of Scene I.

BARBARA, Tim *and* SUSAN *are in the same places and* ERNEST *is standing by the door.*

ERNEST (*announcing*): Mrs. Vail.

LEONORA *comes in. Her eyes are red from crying. She is obviously trying with all her will to control herself.*

BARBARA: Leonora—— (*She takes her hand.*) I'm so glad you came——

LEONORA: Is he—is he——?

BARBARA: He asked for you.

TIM (*brusquely*): You'd better go in—at once.

BARBARA: Here, drink this—— (*She hands her her cocktail.*) It's important that you don't break down.

LEONORA: I'll be all right.

BARBARA: Please drink it.

LEONORA: Very well. (*She gulps it down.*)

BARBARA: Tim, will you please take her——

TIM: Come this way, will you?

TIM *goes to the doors on the right and holds one open for* LEONORA. *She says 'Thank you' huskily as she goes through.* TIM *follows her and returns in a moment.*

BARBARA: It wasn't so foggy.

SUSAN: What?

BARBARA: Last year, I mean, when she came for the first time—it wasn't so foggy.

SUSAN: No—I remember—it wasn't.

BARBARA *wanders about the room.*

BARBARA: I wish—I do wish this moment hadn't had to happen too.

TIM (*gently*): Do sit down, my dear.

BARBARA: No—I'm all right—I like wandering——

TIM (*at cocktail shaker*): Do you want some more, Susan?

SUSAN: No, thank you.

BARBARA (*with a tremulous smile*): It's too much of a good thing—it really is—— (*She breaks off and turns her head away.*)

> TIM *and* SUSAN *look at her miserably. She recovers herself quickly and comes back to the sofa again.*

I have a dreadful feeling that I'm making it all much horrider for you——

TIM: Don't be so foolish!

BARBARA: I know what I mean, though—I'm behaving well, almost consciously well; that's always much more agonising for other people.

SUSAN: No, it isn't—it's ever so much better.

BARBARA (*blowing her nose*): I'm not at all sure. If I broke down, collapsed completely, there'd be something to do—something for us all to do—smelling salts and brandy and all that.

TIM: Burnt feathers.

BARBARA: Yes, burnt feathers. (*She gives a polite little laugh.*)

SUSAN (*looking at the door*): I wonder——

TIM (*quickly*): Don't wonder anything—it's better not.

BARBARA: You mustn't snap at Susan, Tim, it's beastly of you.

TIM: Sorry, Susan, I didn't mean to snap.

SUSAN (*trying to smile at him*): I didn't even hear——

BARBARA (*suddenly*): I wish she'd come out now—I wish to God she'd come out now.

TIM: She will—in a minute——

They wait in silence. Presently LEONORA *comes quietly back into the room. She goes to* BARBARA.

BARBARA: Is it all over? Is he——?

LEONORA: Yes.

BARBARA: Oh—oh, dear—— (*She sinks back again on to the sofa.*)

LEONORA: He didn't know me, he thought I was you, he said—'Baba—I'm not submerged any more'—and then he said 'Baba' again—and then—then he died.

LEONORA *goes out of the room very quickly as the Curtain falls.*

"RED PEPPERS"

An Interlude with Music

from

TONIGHT AT 8.30

CHARACTERS:
GEORGE PEPPER
LILY PEPPER
BERT BENTLEY
MR. EDWARDS
MABEL GRACE
ALF

The action of the play takes place on the stage, a dressing-room, and the stage again of the Palace of Varieties in one of the smaller English provincial towns.

The time is Saturday night, present day.

"RED PEPPERS"

AN INTERLUDE WITH MUSIC

The interlude occurs in the Palace Theatre of Varieties in one
of the smaller English provincial towns on a Saturday
night.

GEORGE and LILY PEPPER are a singing and dancing
comedy act. They are both somewhere in the thirties.
They have been married for many years and in the
Profession since they were children. Their act consists of
a 'Man-About-Town' Dude number for which they wear
smooth red wigs, tails, silk hats and canes, and a 'Sailor'
number for which they wear curly red wigs, sailor clothes
with exaggerated bell-bottomed trousers and carry tele-
scopes. They are first discovered performing 'in one' before
a backcloth on which is painted an ordinary street scene.

"HAS ANYBODY SEEN OUR SHIP?"
(Sailor Number)

VERSE I

What shall we do with the drunken sailor?
So the saying goes.
We're not tight but we're none too bright
Great Scott! I don't suppose!
We've lost our way
And we've lost our pay,
And to make the thing complete,
We've been and gone and lost the bloomin' fleet!

REFRAIN I

Has anybody seen our ship?
The H.M.S. Peculiar.
We've been on shore
For a month or more,
And when we see the Captain we shall get 'what for'.
Heave ho, me hearties,
Sing Glory Halleluiah,
A lady bold as she could be
Pinched our whistles at 'The Golden Key'.
Now we're in between the devil and the deep blue sea
Has anybody seen our ship?

    Ad lib. from orchestra.

GEORGE (*singing*): La la la la—la la la la——
LILY: Here, what are you singing about?
GEORGE: What am I singing about?
LILY: Yes, what are you singing about?
GEORGE: What's the matter with my singing?
LILY: What isn't the matter with it!
GEORGE: Don't you think I could ever do anything with my voice?
LILY: Well, it might be useful in case of fire!
GEORGE: Oi! Skip it.
LILY: Who was that lady I saw you walking down the street with the other morning?
GEORGE: That wasn't a lady, that was my wife!
LILY: Keep it clean. Keep it fresh. Keep it fragrant!
GEORGE: Was that your dog I saw you with in the High Street?
LILY: Yes, that was my dog.
GEORGE: What's his name?

LILY: Fruit Salts.

GEORGE: Fruit Salts?

LILY: Yes, Fruit Salts.

GEORGE: Why?

LILY: Ask him—Eno's.

GEORGE: Keep it clean. Keep it fresh. Keep it fragrant!

BOTH: La la la la—la la la la.

GEORGE: Why did you leave school?

LILY: Appendicitis.

GEORGE: Appendicitis?

LILY: Yes, appendicitis.

GEORGE: What do you mean, appendicitis?

LILY: Couldn't spell it!

GEORGE: I heard you had adenoids.

LILY: Adenoids?

GEORGE: Yes, adenoids.

LILY: Don't speak of it.

GEORGE: Why not?

LILY: Adenoids me!

GEORGE: Oi! Skip it! Skip it!

Both: La la la la—la la la la.

GEORGE: I saw a very strange thing the other day.

LILY: What was it?

GEORGE: Twelve men standing under one umbrella and they didn't get wet.

LILY: How's that?

GEORGE: It wasn't raining! (Wait for it—wait for it.)

LILY: Do you know what a skeleton is?

GEORGE: Do I know what a skeleton is?

LILY: Do you know what a skeleton is?

GEORGE: Yes.

LILY: Well, what is it?

GEORGE: A lot of bones with the people scraped off!

LILY: Keep it clean. Keep it fresh. Keep it fragrant.

GEORGE: Why is twelve midnight like the roof of a house?

LILY: Why is twelve midnight like the roof of a house?

GEORGE: Yes, why is twelve midnight like the roof of a house?

LILY: S'late!

BOTH: La la la la—la la la la.

LILY: Where did you go last night?

GEORGE: The cemetery.

LILY: Anyone dead?

GEORGE: All of 'em?

LILY: Are we going fishing?

GEORGE: Yes, we're going fishing.

LILY: We're not taking the dog with us, are we?

GEORGE: Of course we're taking the dog with us.

LILY: Why?

GEORGE: He's got the worms!

REFRAIN 2

Has anybody seen our ship?
The H.M.S. Disgusting,
We've three guns aft
And another one fore
And they've promised us a funnel for the next world
  war.
Heave ho, me hearties,
The quarter-deck needs dusting.
We had a binge last Christmas year,
Nice plum puddings and a round of beer,

But the captain pulled his cracker and we cried 'Oh dear!
Has anybody seen our ship?'

REFRAIN 3

Has anybody seen our ship?
The H.M.S. Suggestive
She sailed away
Across the bay,
And we haven't had a smell of her since New Year's
    Day.
Heave ho, me hearties,
We're getting rather restive,
We pooled our money, spent the lot,
The world forgetting by the world forgot.
Now we haven't got a penny for the you know what!
Has anybody seen our ship?

VERSE 2 (*if necessary*)

What's to be done with the girls on shore
Who lead our Tars astray?
What's to be done with the drinks galore
That make them pass away?
We got wet ears
From our first five beers—
After that we lost control,
And now we find we're up the blinking pole!

*Their exit consists of a neat walk off together, one
behind the other, with their telescopes under their arms.
Unfortunately, in course of this snappy finale, LILY, who
is behind GEORGE, drops her telescope and hurriedly
retrieves it thereby ruining the whole effect. GEORGE*

461

shoots her a look of fury and mutters something to her out of the corner of his mouth. The curtain falls and they take a call before it breathless and smiling, but with a certain quality of foreboding behind their smiles.

The curtain rises on the interior of their dressing-room. It is a fairly squalid room, for although they are comparatively well-known in the provinces, they have never, to date, achieved the dignity of the star dressing-room or the pride of topping the bill. The room is three sides of a square. There is a wooden shelf all the way round with, above it, mirrors and lights at set intervals.

Down stage on the right there is a door leading to the passage. Down stage on the left there is a lavatory basin with a screen round it. In the centre is a wooden hanging arrangement for clothes.

GEORGE'S dressing place is on the right and LILY'S is on the left.

As the curtain rises on the scene they both enter in silence but wearing expressions of set rage. They are still breathless and extremely hot. GEORGE goes to his dressing place and LILY goes to hers. They both take off their wigs and fling them down, then, still in silence, they proceed to rip off their sailor clothes. These are made with zippers in order to facilitate their quick change. LILY is wearing a brassiere and silk knickers, and GEORGE a vest and drawers. They both have black shoes with taps on them and black socks and sock suspenders.

GEORGE: Now then.

LILY: Now then what?

GEORGE (*contemptuously*): Now then what!

LILY: I don't know what you're talking about.

GEORGE: Oh, you don't, don't you?

LILY: No I don't, so shut up.

GEORGE: I suppose you don't know you mucked up the whole exit!

LILY: It wasn't my fault.

GEORGE: Whose fault was it then, Mussolini's?

LILY (*with sarcasm*): Funny, hey?

GEORGE (*witheringly*): I suppose you didn't drop your prop, did you? And having dropped it, you didn't have to go back for it, leaving me to prance off all by meself —who d'you think you are, Rebla?

LILY: The exit was too quick.

GEORGE: It was the same as it's always been.

LILY: It was too quick, I tell you, it's been too quick the whole week, the whole number's too quick——

GEORGE: Bert Bentley takes that number at the same tempo as he's always done.

LILY: You and your Bert Bentley, just because he stands you a Welsh rarebit at the Queen's you think he's God Almighty.

GEORGE: Bert Bentley's the best conductor in the North of England and don't you make any mistake about it.

LILY: Best conductor my foot! I suppose he thinks it's funny to see us leaping up and down the stage like a couple of greyhounds.

GEORGE: If you're a greyhound I'm Fred Astaire.

LILY: Oh, you're Fred Astaire all right, with a bit of Pavlova thrown in—you're wonderful, you are—there's nothing you can't do, except behave like a gentleman.

GEORGE: Oh, so you expect me to behave like a gentleman, do you? That's a good one, coming from you.

LILY: Oh, shut up, you make me tired.

GEORGE: I make *you* tired! I suppose it was me that mucked up the exit—I suppose it was me that dropped me bloody telescope!

LILY (*heated*): Now look here, George Pepper——

GEORGE: Stop George Peppering me—why can't you admit it when you're in the wrong?—— You mucked up the exit—nobody else did—you did!

LILY: Well, what if I did? It was an accident, wasn't it? I didn't do it on purpose.

GEORGE: It doesn't matter how you did it or why you did it, you did it.

LILY (*screaming*): All right, I did it!

GEORGE (*triumphantly*): Well, don't do it again.

> *There is a knock on the door.*

LILY: Who is it?

ALF (*outside*): Me, Alf.

LILY: All right, come in.

> ALF, *the callboy, enters. He is laden with the* PEPPERS' *discarded evening suits, silk hats and canes. He plumps them down.*

ALF: There!

GEORGE: Thanks. (*He gets some money out of his coat pocket.*) Here, tell Fred to pop out and get me twenty Player's and a large Guinness.

LILY: Why can't you wait and have it with your steak?

GEORGE: You mind yours and I'll mind mine.

ALF: You'll have to wait until Mabel Grace is finished.

LILY: She's been finished for years as far as I'm concerned.

GEORGE: What's the matter with Mabel Grace?

LILY: Ask the public, dear, just ask the public.

ALF (*about to leave*): Same as usual, I suppose, between the houses?

GEORGE: Yes, and tell 'em not to forget the salt, like they did last night.

ALF: Righto.

> ALF *goes out.*
>
> LILY *starts to pack various things into a large hamper which has emblazoned on it in large black letters: "The Red Peppers".*

GEORGE: What did you want to say that about Mabel Grace for in front of him?

LILY (*grandly*): It happens to be my opinion.

GEORGE: Well, in future you'd better keep your opinions to yourself in front of strangers.

LILY (*mumbling*): If you're so fond of Mabel Grace I wonder you don't go and ask her for her autograph— she'd drop dead if you did—I bet nobody's asked her for one since Trelawney of the Wells.

GEORGE: Mabel Grace is an artist and don't you forget it—she may be a bit long in the tooth now but she's a bigger star than you'll ever be, so there!

LILY: You make me sick, sucking up to the top-liners.

GEORGE: Who sucks up to the topliners?

LILY: You do—look at Irene Baker!

GEORGE: What's the matter with Irene Baker?

LILY: When last heard from she was falling down drunk at the Empire, Hartlepool.

GEORGE: That's a dirty lie, Irene never touches a drop till after the show and well you know it.

LILY (*contemptuously*): Irene! It was Miss Baker this and Miss Baker that, the last time you saw her.

GEORGE: That's all you know.

LILY: Trying to make me think you got off with her, eh? What a chance!

GEORGE: Oh, shut up nagging!

LILY (*muttering*): Irene——!

GEORGE: If a day ever dawns when you can time your laughs like Irene Baker does, I'll give you a nice red apple!

LILY: Time my laughs! That's funny. Fat lot of laughs I get when you write the gags.

GEORGE (*grandly*): If you're dissatisfied with your material you know what you can do with it.

LILY: I know what I'd like to do with it.

GEORGE: You can't even do a straight walk off without balling it up.

LILY: Oh, we're back at that again, are we?

GEORGE: Yes we are, so there!

LILY (*coming over to him*): Now look here, just you listen to me for a minute. . . .

GEORGE: I've been listening to you for fifteen years, one more minute won't hurt.

LILY: I've had about enough of this. I'm sick of you and the whole act. It's lousy, anyway.

GEORGE: The act was good enough for my Mum and Dad and it's good enough for you.

LILY (*with heavy sarcasm*): Times have changed a bit since your Mum and Dad's day, you know. There's electric light now and telephones and a little invention called Moving Pictures. Nobody wants to see the "Red Peppers" for three bob when they can see Garbo for ninepence!

GEORGE: That's just where you're wrong, see! We're flesh and blood we are—the public would rather see flesh and blood any day than a cheesy photograph.

Put Garbo on on a Saturday night in Devonport, and see what would happen to her!

LILY: Yes, look what happened to us!

GEORGE: That wasn't Devonport, it was Southsea.

LILY: Well, wherever it was, the Fleet was in.

GEORGE: If you think the act's so lousy it's a pity you don't rewrite some of it.

LILY: Ever tried going into St. Paul's and offering to rewrite the Bible?

GEORGE: Very funny! Oh, very funny indeed! You're wasted in the Show Business, you ought to write for *Comic Cuts* you ought.

LILY: At that I could think up better gags than you do—"That wasn't a lady, that was my wife!"— "D'you mind if I smoke?" "I don't care if you burn!"— hoary old chestnuts—they were has-beens when your grandmother fell off the high wire.

GEORGE: What's my grandmother got to do with it?

LILY: She didn't fall soon enough, that's all.

GEORGE (*furiously*): You shut your mouth and stop hurling insults at my family. What were you when I married you, I should like to know! One of the six Moonlight Maids—dainty songs and dances, and no bookings!

LILY (*hotly*): When we did get bookings we got number one towns which is more than your Mum and Dad ever did!

GEORGE: Who wants the number one towns, anyway? You can't get a public all the year round like my Mum and Dad by doing a parasol dance twice a year at the Hippodrome Manchester!

LILY: The Moonlight Maids was just as good an act

467

as the "Red Peppers" any day, and a bloody sight more refined at that!

GEORGE: You've said it. That's just what it was—refined. It was so refined it simpered itself out of the bill——

LILY: A bit of refinement wouldn't do you any harm——

GEORGE: Perhaps you'd like to change the act to "Musical Moments" with me playing a flute and you sitting under a standard lamp with a 'cello?

There is a knock at the door.

LILY: Who is it?

BERT (*outside*): Me—Bert Bentley.

GEORGE: Come in, old man.

LILY (*under her breath*): Old man——

BERT BENTLEY *enters. He is the musical director, a flashy little man wearing a tail suit and a white waistcoat that is none too clean.*

BERT (*cheerfully*): Well, well, well, how's tricks?

GEORGE: Mustn't grumble.

BERT: Anybody got a Gold Flake?

GEORGE: Here's a Player's, that do?

BERT (*taking one*): It's your last?

GEORGE: I've sent Fred out for some more.

BERT: Okay—thanks.

GEORGE: Sketch on?

BERT: Yes, the old cow's tearing herself to shreds.

GEORGE: It's a pretty strong situation she's got in that sketch—I watched it from the side first house on Wednesday——

BERT: She nearly got the bird second house.

LILY: Too refined, I expect. For this date.

BERT: Well, they're liable to get a bit restless, you

468

know, when she stabs herself—she takes such a hell of a time about it—that's legits all over—we had Robert Haversham here a couple of months ago—what a make-up—stuck together with stamp paper he was—Robert Haversham the famous tragedian and company! You should have seen the company: a couple of old tats got up as Elizabethan pages with him doing a death scene in the middle of them—he died all right.

GEORGE: Did he buy it?

BERT: He bought it—three and eightpence in coppers and a bottle of Kola.

LILY: Poor old man, what a shame!

BERT: Well, what did he want to do it for? That sort of stuff's no good. They're all alike—a few seasons in the West End and they think they're set.

LILY: Lot of hooligans birding the poor old man.

BERT (with slight asperity): This is as good a date as you can get, you know!

LILY: I've played better.

GEORGE: Oh, dry up, Lil, for heaven's sake! (To BERT.) Sorry I can't offer you a drink, old man, Fred hasn't brought it yet.

BERT: That's all right, George—I'll have one with you in between the houses. By the way, don't you think that exit of yours is dragging a bit?

LILY (explosively): Dragging?

GEORGE: Lil thinks it was a bit too quick.

BERT: Whatever you say, it's all the same to me.

GEORGE: Maybe you could pep it up a little.

LILY: Maybe it would be better if we did the whole act on skates!

GEORGE (conciliatorily): Bert's quite right, you know, Lil.

469

LILY: I don't know any such thing.

BERT: All right, all right, all right—there's no need to get nasty.

GEORGE: Oh, don't take any notice of her, she don't know what she's talking about.

LILY (*with overpowering sweetness*): My husband's quite right, Mr. Bentley, my husband is always quite right. You don't have to pay any attention to me, I don't count—I'm only a feed.

GEORGE: Oh, dry up.

LILY (*continuing*): But I should just like to say one thing, Mr. Bentley, if you'll forgive me for stepping out of my place for a minute, and that is, that if you take that exit any quicker at the second house, I shall not drop my telescope—— Oh no—I shall sock you in the chops with it!

BERT: Who the hell d'you think you are, talking to me like that!

GEORGE: You ought to be ashamed of yourself

LILY: You and your orchestra—orchestra! More like a hurdy-gurdy and flat at that!

BERT: What's wrong with my orchestra?

LILY: Nothing, apart from the instruments and the men what play 'em.

BERT: My orchestra's played for the best artists in the business——

LILY: Yes, but not until they were too old to care.

BERT: I didn't come up here to be insulted by a cheap little comedy act.

GEORGE (*incensed*): What's that! What's that? What's that?

BERT: You heard. You're damned lucky to get this date at all!

GEORGE: Lucky! My God, it's a fill-in—that's all—a fill-in!

BERT: I suppose Nervo and Knox use it as a fill-in, and Lily Morris and Flanagan and Allen?

LILY: They probably have friends living near.

BERT (*making a movement to go*): Before you start saucing me just take a look at your place on the bill—that's all—just take a look at it.

GEORGE: We're in the second half, anyway.

BERT: Only because the acrobats can't make their change.

LILY: It's in our contract—after the interval's in our contract.

BERT: Well, make the most of it while you've got it.

GEORGE: Get the hell out of here, you twopenny-halfpenny little squirt—lucky for you we've got another show to play.

BERT: Not so damned lucky—I've got to look at it.

LILY: Well, it'll be the first time—maybe we'll get the tempos right for a change!

BERT: You set your tempos Monday morning and they haven't been changed since.

LILY: That's your story, but don't forget you were sober on Monday morning.

BERT: Are you insinuating that I drink during the show?

LILY: Insinuating! That's a laugh. I'm not insinuating, I'm stating a fact. I can smell it a mile off.

BERT: What a lady! And what an artist, too—I don't suppose!

GEORGE: Don't you talk in that tone to my wife.

LILY: Send for the manager, George. Send for Mr. Edwards.

BERT: I'm the one that's going to send for Mr. Edwards——

GEORGE: Get out of here before I crack you one——

ALF *knocks at the door.*

LILY: Come in.

ALF *pushes open the door with his foot and comes in carrying a tray on which are two plates of steak and chips with other plates over them to keep them hot, a bottle of A.I. sauce and three bottles of Guinness.*

ALF: You're wanted, Mr. Bentley, the sketch is nearly over.

BERT (*grimly to the* PEPPERS): I'll be seeing you later.

He goes out, slamming the door after him.

GEORGE (*after him*): Lousy son of a——Lounge Lizard.

LILY (*to* ALF): Here, put it down on the hamper.

ALF (*doing so*): I've got the Player's in me pocket.

LILY (*feeling for them*): All right.

GEORGE: Come back later for the tray.

ALF: Righto.

He goes out.

GEORGE: Mr. Edwards—I'll have something to say to Mr. Edwards.

LILY: Lucky to play this date, are we? We'll see about that.

GEORGE: You were right, old girl.

LILY: What about—him?

GEORGE: Yes—dirty little rat.

LILY (*dragging up two chairs to the hamper*): Well, we all make mistakes sometimes—open the Guinness, there's a dear——

GEORGE: He's a little man, that's his trouble, never

trust a man with short legs—brains too near their bottoms.

LILY: Come and sit down.

GEORGE (*opening a bottle of Guinness*): 'Alf a mo'——

LILY: That exit was too quick, you know!

GEORGE: All right—all right——

They both sit down and begin to eat.

They've forgotten the salt again——

LILY: No, here it is in a bit of paper——

GEORGE: Well, thank God for that anyway——

The lights fade on the scene.

When the lights come up on the scene, GEORGE and LILY are sitting at the dressing places freshening their make-ups. They both have a glass of Guiness within reach, and they are both wearing the rather frowsy dressing-gowns that they had put on during the preceding scene. The tray, with the remains of their dinner on it, is on the floor beside the hamper.

GEORGE gets up, opens the door and listens.

LILY: What's on?

GEORGE: The Five Farthings.

LILY: That's the end of the first half—we'd better get a move on——

GEORGE (*returning to his place*): Fancy putting an act like that on at the end of the first half—you'd think they'd know better, wouldn't you?

LILY: I wouldn't think they'd know better about anything in this hole.

GEORGE: It's a badly run house and it always has been.

He proceeds to put on his dress shirt, collar and tie, which are all in one with a zipper up the back. LILY is doing the same on her side of the room. They stuff wads of

Kleenex paper in between their collars and their necks to prevent the make-up soiling their ties.

There is a knock at the door.

LILY: Who is it?

MR. EDWARDS (*outside*): Mr. Edwards.

LILY (*pulling on her trousers*): Just a minute——

GEORGE (*under his breath*): Go easy—Bert Bentley's been at him.

LILY: I'll have something to say about that.

GEORGE: You leave it to me—I'll do the talking.

LILY: That'll be nice—— Come in!

MR. EDWARDS *enters. He is the house manager and very resplendent. He is smoking a large cigar.*

GEORGE (*rising and offering him a chair*): Good evening, Mr. Edwards.

MR. EDWARDS (*disdaining it*): Good evening.

LILY (*amiably*): How's the house?

MR. EDWARDS: Same as usual—full.

GEORGE: That's fine, isn't it?

MR. EDWARDS (*grimly*): I watched your act to-night, first house.

GEORGE (*gaily*): There you are, Lil, what did I tell you—I had a sort of hunch you was out there —I said to my wife—what's the betting Mr. Edwards is out front?—you know—you have a sort of feeling——

LILY: Went well, didn't it?

MR. EDWARDS: I've seen things go better.

GEORGE: We follow Betley Delavine, you know—a ballad singer—they always take a bit of warming up after a ballad singer.

LILY: I'd defy Billy Bennett to get away with it in our place on the bill—I'd defy him—see?

MR. EDWARDS: There isn't anything wrong with your place on the bill.

GEORGE: Well, I'd be willing to make a little bet with you—put the Five Farthings on before us and change Betley Delavine to the end of the first half and see what happens!

LILY: You'd send them out to the bars and they'd stay there.

MR. EDWARDS: I did not come here to discuss the running of my theatre.

GEORGE: Oh—sorry, I'm sure.

MR. EDWARDS: That exit of yours killed the whole act.

GEORGE: A little mishap that's all—anybody might drop a telescope——

LILY: Even a sailor.

MR. EDWARDS: It looked terrible.

GEORGE: The tempo was all wrong, Mr. Edwards.

MR. EDWARDS: Sounded all right to me.

GEORGE: Maybe it did, but we know our own numbers, you know.

MR. EDWARDS: It didn't look like it from the front.

GEORGE: We're never had any trouble before—that exit's stopped the show in every town we've played.

LILY: A musical director can make or mar an act, you know—make or mar it.

MR. EDWARDS: Mr. Bentley is one of the finest musical directors in the business.

LILY: Then he's wasted here, that's all I can say.

GEORGE (*warningly*): Lily!

LILY: Well, if he's so wonderful, why isn't he at the Albert Hall—doing *Hiawatha*——

MR. EDWARDS: I understand you had words with Mr. Bentley.

GEORGE: We did, and we will again if he starts any of his funny business.

MR. EDWARDS: I understand that you accused him of drinking during the show.

LILY: Getting quite bright, aren't you?

GEORGE: Shut up, Lil, leave this to me.

MR. EDWARDS: Did you or did you not?

GEORGE: Look here, who d'you think you are—coming talking to us like this?

MR. EDWARDS: Did you or did you not accuse Mr. Bentley of drinking during the show?

LILY (*heatedly*): Yes, we did, because he does, so there!

MR. EDWARDS: That's serious, you know—it's slander!

LILY: I don't care if it's arson, it's true!

MR. EWARDS: Now look here, Mrs. Pepper, I think it only fair to warn you——

LILY: And I think it's only fair to warn you that unless you get a better staff in this theatre and a better orchestra and a better musical director, you'll find yourself a cinema inside six months!

MR. EDWARDS: You won't gain anything by losing your temper.

GEORGE: And you won't gain anything by coming round back-stage and throwing your weight about—your place is in the front of the house—my theatre this and my theatre that—it's no more your theatre than what it is ours—you're on a salary same as us, and I'll bet it's a damn sight less, too, and don't you forget it——

MR. EDWARDS (*losing his temper*): I'm not going to stand any more of this——

LILY: Oh, go and play with yourself and shut up——

MR. EDWARDS: I'll guarantee one thing, anyhow, you'll never play this date again as long as I'm in charge——

GEORGE: In charge of what, the Fire Brigade!

LILY: Play this date—anybody'd think it was the Palladium to hear you talk——

GEORGE: You'd better be careful, Mr. Edwards— you don't want a scandal like this to get round the profession——

MR. EDWARDS: What are you talking about?

GEORGE: I'm talking about the way this house is run.

MR. EDWARDS (*working up*): You mind your own business.

LILY: More than one act's been mucked up here, you know, by that orchestra of yours—it's beginning to get a name——

MR. EDWARDS: Oh, it is, is it?

GEORGE: They're all over the shop—no discipline.

LILY: What can you expect with a drunk in charge of it!

MR. EDWARDS (*raising his voice*): Look here—you stop talking like that or it'll be the worse for you.

GEORGE: His tempos are wrong and he hasn't got any authority over his men——

LILY: This date's only a fill-in for us, you know——

GEORGE: You ask our agents.

MR. EDWARDS: I shall report this conversation.

LILY: Do—report it to the Lord Mayor—if you're sober enough to remember the lyrics.

GEORGE: Shut up, Lil.

477

MR. EDWARDS: I will not stay here and argue——

GEORGE: You're dead right, you won't——

MR. EDWARDS: You were a flop last time you played here and you've been a flop this time and that's enough for me——

LILY (*screaming*): Flop! What d'you mean flop! We're a bigger draw than anybody on the bill——

There is a knock on the door.

GEORGE (*loudly*): Come in——

> MISS MABEL GRACE *enters. She is a faded ex-West End actress wearing a towel round her head to keep her hair in place, and an elaborate dressing-gown.*

MABEL GRACE (*acidly*): Good evening—I'm sorry to intrude—but you're making such a dreadful noise I'm quite unable to rest——

MR. EDWARDS: I'm very sorry, Miss Grace——

MABEL GRACE: I find it hard enough to play a big emotional scene twice a night in any case——

LILY: Oh, that's an emotional scene, is it? I wondered what it was——

MABEL GRACE: I am not accustomed to being spoken to in that tone, Mrs. Whatever your name is——

LILY: Pepper's the name—Pepper—P E P P E R—same as what you put in your soup.

MABEL GRACE (*coldly*): Very interesting.

MR. EDWARDS: I apologise, Miss Grace.

MABEL GRACE (*grandly*): Thank you, Mr. Edwards.

GEORGE (*in an affected voice*): What you must think of us, Miss Grace—so common—we're mortified, we are really—and you fresh from His Majesty's.

LILY: Fairly fresh.

MABEL GRACE: Mr. Edwards, I'm really not used to

dressing-room brawls—I'll leave it to you to see that there is no further noise——

LILY: Except for the raspberries at the end of your sketch—even Mr. God Almighty Edwards can't control those——

MABEL GRACE: You're almost as vulgar off the stage as you are on, I congratulate you.

LILY (*very loudly*): Vulgar, are we! I'd like to ask you something. If you're so bloody West End why the hell did you leave it?

GEORGE: There'll be an answer to that in next Sunday's edition.

LILY: Thank you, George.

MR. EDWARDS: Look here, you two, I've had about enough of this——

GEORGE: You've had about enough, have you? What about us?

The conversation becomes simultaneous.

LILY: You and your cigar and your shirt-front and your Woolworth studs! Alfred Butt with knobs on——

GEORGE: You get out of here, you fat fool, before I throw you out!——

MABEL GRACE: Thank you for your courtesy, Mr. Edwards——

MR. EDWARDS: I'll see you don't play this date any more or any other date either——

GEORGE: Oh, put it where the monkey put the nuts——

LILY: —Play this date again—thank you for the rabbit—I'd sooner play Ryde Pier in November——

In the middle of the pandemonium ALF *puts his head round the door.*

479

ALF (*yelling*): Red Peppers—three minutes——
GEORGE: Good God! We're off——
LILY (*wildly*): Get out, all of you—get out——

GEORGE *takes* MR. EDWARDS *by the shoulders, and shoves him out of the room.* MABEL GRACE, *laughing affectedly, follows him.*

LILY *and* GEORGE *put on their wigs, powder their make-up, tweak their ties into place, grab their hats and canes—then, muttering curses under their breaths, They collect their sailor clothes and sailor wigs and telescopes and rush out of the room as the lights fade.*

The lights come up on the curtain as the orchestra is playing their introduction music. The curtain rises on the street scene again. They make their entrance for the 'dude' number, "Men About Town".

ROUTINE

"MEN ABOUT TOWN". (Dude Number)

VERSE

We're two chaps who
Find it thrilling
To do the killing
We're always willing
To give the girls a treat.
Just a drink at the Ritz
Call it double or quits
Then we feel the world is at our feet.
Top hats white spats
Look divine on us,

There's a shine on us
Get a line on us
When we come your way.
Gad! Eleven o'clock!
Let's pop into the Troc:
Ere we start the business of the day.

REFRAIN 1

As we stroll down Picc—Piccadilly
In the bright morning air,
All the girls turn and stare
We're so nonchalant and frightfully debonair.
When we chat to Rose, Maud or Lily
You should see the way their boy friends frown,
For they know without a doubt
That their luck's right out,
Up against a couple of men about town.

REFRAIN 2

As we stroll down Picc—Piccadilly
All the girl say "Who's here?
Put your hat straight, my dear,
For it's Marmaduke and Percy Vere de Vere."
As we doff hats, each pretty filly
Gives a wink at us and then looks down
For they long with all their might
For a red-hot night
When they see a couple of men about town.

They proceed to execute a complicated tap dance, during which BERT BENTLEY *vengefully takes the music faster and faster. They try vainly to keep up with it, finally* GEORGE *slips and falls, whereupon* LILY *loses her temper and flings her hat at* BERT BENTLEY.

LILY (*screaming*): You great drunken fool!

THE CURTAIN FALLS AMID DISCORD